THE ELEMENTS OF NON-EUCLIDEAN GEOMETRY

JULIAN LOWELL COOLIDGE Ph.D.
ASSISTANT PROFESSOR OF MATHEMATICS
IN HARVARD UNIVERSITY

Published by

Hawk Press
4836/24, Ansari Road, Daryaganj
New Delhi - 110 002
Phones: +91-11-23278618, +91-11-43667199
E-mail: thehawkpress@gmail.com
www.thehawkpress.com

ISBN: 978-93-93971-61-6

PREFACE

The heroic age of non-euclidean geometry is passed. It is long since the days when Lobatchewsky timidly referred to his system as an 'imaginary geometry', and the new subject appeared as a dangerous lapse from the orthodox doctrine of Euclid. The attempt to prove the parallel axiom by means of the other usual assumptions is now seldom undertaken, and those who do undertake it, are considered in the class with circle-squarers and searchers for perpetual motion– sad by-products of the creative activity of modern science.

In this, as in all other changes, there is subject both for rejoicing and regret. It is a satisfaction to a writer on non-euclidean geometry that he may proceed at once to his subject, without feeling any need to justify himself, or, at least, any more need than any other who adds to our supply of books. On the other hand, he will miss the stimulus that comes to one who feels that he is bringing out something entirely new and strange. The subject of non-euclidean geometry is, to the mathematician, quite as well established as any other branch of mathematical science; and, in fact, it may lay claim to a decidedly more solid basis than some branches, such as the theory of assemblages, or the analysis situs.

Recent books dealing with non-euclidean geometry fall naturally into two classes. In the one we find the works of Killing, Liebmann, and Manning,[1] who wish to build up certain clearly conceived geometrical systems, and are careless of the details of the foundations on which all is to rest. In the other category are Hilbert, Vablen, Veronese, and the authors of a goodly number of articles on the foundations of geometry. These writers deal at length with the consistency, significance, and logical independence of their assumptions, but do not go very far towards raising a superstructure on any one of the foundations suggested.

The present work is, in a measure, an attempt to unite the two tendencies. The author's own interest, be it stated at the outset, lies mainly in the fruits, rather than in the roots; but the day is past when the matter of axioms may be dismissed with the remark that we 'make all of Euclid's assumptions except the one about parallels'. A subject like ours must be built up from explicitly stated assumptions, and nothing else. The author would have preferred, in the first chapters, to start from some system of axioms already published, had he been familiar with any that seemed to him suitable to establish simultaneously the euclidean and the principal non-euclidean systems in the way that he wished. The system of axioms here used is decidedly more cumbersome than some others, but leads to the desired goal.

There are three natural approaches to non-euclidean geometry. (1) The elementary geometry of point, line, and distance. This method is developed in the opening chapters and is the most obvious. (2) Projective geometry, and the theory of transformation groups. This method is not taken up until Chapter XVIII, not because it is one whit less important than the first, but because it seemed better not to interrupt the natural course of the narrative

[1]Detailed references given later

by interpolating an alternative beginning. (3) Differential geometry, with the concepts of distance-element, extremal, and space constant. This method is explained in the last chapter, XIX.

The author has imposed upon himself one or two very definite limitations. To begin with, he has not gone beyond three dimensions. This is because of his feeling that, at any rate in a first study of the subject, the gain in generality obtained by studying the geometry of n-dimensions is more than offset by the loss of clearness and naturalness. Secondly, he has confined himself, almost exclusively, to what may be called the 'classical' non-euclidean systems. These are much more closely allied to the euclidean system than are any others, and have by far the most historical importance. It is also evident that a system which gives a simple and clear interpretation of ternary and quaternary orthogonal substitutions, has a totally different sort of mathematical significance from, let us say, one whose points are determined by numerical values in a non-archimedian number system. Or again, a non-euclidean plane which may be interpreted as a surface of constant total curvature, has a more lasting geometrical importance than a non-desarguian plane that cannot form part of a three-dimensional space.

The majority of material in the present work is, naturally, old. A reader, new to the subject, may find it wiser at the first reading to omit Chapters X, XV, XVI, XVIII, and XIX. On the other hand, a reader already somewhat familiar with non-euclidean geometry, may find his greatest interest in Chapters X and XVI, which contain the substance of a number of recent papers on the extraordinary line geometry of non-euclidean space. Mention may also be made of Chapter XIV which contains a number of neat formulae relative to areas and volumes published many years ago by Professor d'Ovidio, which are not, perhaps, very familiar to English-speaking readers, and Chapter XIII, where Staude's string construction of the ellipsoid is extended to non-euclidean space. It is hoped that the introduction to non-euclidean differential geometry in Chapter XV may prove to be more comprehensive than that of Darboux, and more comprehensible than that of Bianchi.

The author takes this opportunity to thank his colleague, Assistant-Professor Whittemore, who has read in manuscript Chapters XV and XIX. He would also offer affectionate thanks to his former teachers, Professor Eduard Study of Bonn and Professor Corrado Segre of Turin, and all others who have aided and encouraged (or shall we say abetted?) him in the present work.

TABLE OF CONTENTS

CHAPTER I
FOUNDATION FOR METRICAL GEOMETRY IN A LIMITED REGION

CHAPTER II
CONGRUENT TRANSFORMATIONS

CHAPTER III
THE THREE HYPOTHESES

CHAPTER IV
THE INTRODUCTION OF TRIGONOMETRIC FORMULAE

CHAPTER V
ANALYTIC FORMULAE

CHAPTER VI
CONSISTENCY AND SIGNIFICANCE OF THE AXIOMS

CHAPTER VII
THE GEOMETRIC AND ANALYTIC EXTENSION OF SPACE

CHAPTER VIII
THE GROUPS OF CONGRUENT TRANSFORMATIONS

CHAPTER IX
POINT, LINE, AND PLANE TREATED ANALYTICALLY

CHAPTER X
THE HIGHER LINE GEOMETRY

CHAPTER XI
THE CIRCLE AND THE SPHERE

CHAPTER XII
CONIC SECTIONS

CHAPTER XIII
QUADRIC SURFACES

CHAPTER XIV
AREAS AND VOLUMES

CHAPTER XV
INTRODUCTION TO DIFFERENTIAL GEOMETRY

CHAPTER XVI
DIFFERENTIAL LINE-GEOMETRY

CHAPTER XVII
MULTIPLY CONNECTED SPACES

CHAPTER XVIII
THE PROJECTIVE BASIS OF NON-EUCLIDEAN GEOMETRY

CHAPTER XIX
THE DIFFERENTIAL BASIS FOR EUCLIDEAN AND NON-EUCLIDEAN GEOMETRY

CHAPTER I

FOUNDATION FOR METRICAL GEOMETRY IN A LIMITED REGION

In any system of geometry we must begin by assuming the existence of certain fundamental objects, the raw material with which we are to work. What names we choose to attach to these objects is obviously a question quite apart from the nature of the logical connexions which arise from the various relations assumed to exist among them, and in choosing these names we are guided principally by tradition, and by a desire to make our mathematical edifice as well adapted as possible to the needs of practical life. In the present work we shall assume the existence of two sorts of objects, called respectively *points* and *distances*.[2] Our explicit assumptions shall be as follows:—

AXIOM I. **There exists a class of objects, containing at least two members, called points.**

It will be convenient to indicate points by large Roman letters as A, B, C.

AXIOM II. **The existence of any two points implies the existence of a unique object called their distance.**

If the points be A and B it will be convenient to indicate their distance by $\overline{AB}$ or $\overline{BA}$. We shall speak of this also as the distance *between* the two points, or from one to the other.

We next assume that between two distances there may exist a relation expressed by saying that the one is *congruent* to the other. In place of the words

[2]There is no logical or mathematical reason why the point should be taken as undefined rather than the line or plane. This is, however, the invariable custom in works on the foundations of geometry, and, considering the weight of historical and psychological tradition in its favour, the point will probably continue to stand among the fundamental indefinables. With regard to the others, there is no such unanimity. Veronese, *Fondamenti di geometria*, Padua, 1891, takes the line, segment, and congruence of segments. Schur, 'Ueber die Grundlagen der Geometrie,' *Mathematische Annalen*, vol. lv, 1902, uses segment and motion. Hilbert, *Die Grundlagen der Geometrie*, Leipzig, 1899, uses practically the same indefinables as Veronese. Moore, 'The projective Axioms of Geometry,' *Transactions of the American Mathematical Society*, vol. iii, 1902, and Veblen, 'A System of Axioms for Geometry,' same Journal, vol. v, 1904, use segment and order. Pieri, 'Della geometria elementare come sistema ipotetico deduttivo,' *Memorie della R. Accademia delle Scienze di Torino*, Serie 2, vol. xlix, 1899, introduces motion alone, as does Padoa, 'Un nuovo sistema di definizioni per la geometria euclidea,' *Periodico di matematica*, Serie 3, vol. i, 1903. Vahlen, *Abstrakte Geometrie*, Leipzig, 1905, uses line and separation. Peano, 'La geometria basata sulle idee di punto e di distanza,' *Atti della R. Accademia di Torino*, vol. xxxviii, 1902-3, and Levy, 'I fondamenti della geometria metrica-proiettiva,' *Memorie Accad. Torino*, Serie 2, vol. liv, 1904, use distance. I have made the same choice as the last-named authors, as it seemed to me to give the best approach to the problem in hand. I cannot but feel that the choice of segment or order would be a mistake for our present purpose, in spite of the very condensed system of axioms which Veblen has set up therefor. For to reach congruence and measurement by this means, one is obliged to introduce the six-parameter group of motions (as in Ch. XVIII of this work), i.e. base metrical geometry on projective. It is, on the other hand, an inelegance to base projective geometry on a non-projective conception such as 'between-ness', whereas writers like Vahlen require both projective and 'affine' geometry, before reaching metrical geometry, a very roundabout way to reach what is, after all, the fundamental part of the subject.

'is congruent to' we shall write the symbol $\equiv$. The following assumptions shall be made with regard to the congruent relation:—

Axiom III. $\overline{AB} \equiv \overline{AB}$.

Axiom IV. $\overline{AA} \equiv \overline{BB}$.

Axiom V. **If $\overline{AB} \equiv \overline{CD}$ and $\overline{CD} \equiv \overline{EF}$, then $\overline{AB} \equiv \overline{EF}$.**

These might have been put into purely logical form by saying that we assumed that every distance was congruent to itself, that the distances of any two pairs of identical points are congruent, and that the congruent relation is transitive.

Let us next assume that there may exist a triadic relation connecting three distances which is expressed by a saying that the first $\overline{AB}$ is congruent to the sum of the second $\overline{CD}$ and the third $\overline{PQ}$. This shall be written $\overline{AB} \equiv \overline{CD} + \overline{PQ}$.

Axiom VI. **If $\overline{AB} \equiv \overline{CD} + \overline{PQ}$, then $\overline{AB} \equiv \overline{PQ} + \overline{CD}$.**

Axiom VII. **If $\overline{AB} \equiv \overline{CD} + \overline{PQ}$ and $\overline{PQ} \equiv \overline{RS}$, then $\overline{AB} \equiv \overline{CD} + \overline{RS}$.**

Axiom VIII. **If $\overline{AB} \equiv \overline{CD} + \overline{PQ}$ and $\overline{A'B'} \equiv \overline{AB}$, then $\overline{A'B'} \equiv \overline{CD} + \overline{PQ}$.**

Axiom IX. $\overline{AB} \equiv \overline{AB} + \overline{CC}$.

Definition. The distance of two identical points shall be called a *null* distance.

Definition. If $\overline{AB}$ and $\overline{CD}$ be two such distances that there exists a not null distance $\overline{PQ}$ fulfilling the condition that $\overline{AB}$ is congruent to the sum of $\overline{CD}$ and $\overline{PQ}$, then $\overline{AB}$ shall be said to be *greater than* $\overline{CD}$. This is written $\overline{AB} > \overline{CD}$.

Definition. If $\overline{AB} > \overline{CD}$, then $\overline{CD}$ shall be said to be *less than* $\overline{AB}$. This is written $\overline{CD} < \overline{AB}$.

Axiom X. **Between any two distances $\overline{AB}$ and $\overline{CD}$ there exists one, and only one, of the three relations**

$$\overline{AB} \equiv \overline{CD}, \quad \overline{AB} > \overline{CD}, \quad \overline{AB} < \overline{CD}.$$

Theorem 1. If $\overline{AB} \equiv \overline{CD}$, then $\overline{CD} \equiv \overline{AB}$.

For we could not have $\overline{AB} \equiv \overline{CD} + \overline{PQ}$ where $\overline{PQ}$ was not null. Nor could we have $\overline{CD} \equiv \overline{AB} + \overline{PQ}$ for then, by VIII, $\overline{AB} \equiv \overline{AB} + \overline{PQ}$ contrary to X.

Theorem 2. If $\overline{AB} \equiv \overline{CD} + \overline{PQ}$ and $\overline{C'D'} \equiv \overline{CD}$, then

$$\overline{AB} \equiv \overline{C'D'} + \overline{PQ}.$$

The proof is immediate.

Axiom XI. **If A and C be any two points there exists such a point B distinct from either that**

$$\overline{AB} \equiv \overline{AC} + \overline{CB}.$$

This axiom is highly significant. In the first place it clearly involves the existence of an infinite number of points. In the second it removes the possibility of a maximum distance. In other words, there is no distance which may not be extended in either direction. It is, however, fundamentally important to notice that we have made no assumption as to the magnitude of the amount by which a distance may be so extended; we have merely premised the existence of such extension. We shall make the concept of extension more explicit by the following definitions.

Definition. The assemblage of all points C possessing the property that $\overline{AB} \equiv \overline{AC} + \overline{CB}$ shall be called the *segment* of A and B, or of B and A, and written (AB) or (BA). The points A and B shall be called the *extremities* of the segment, all other points thereof shall be said to be *within* it.

Definition. The assemblage of all points B different from A and C such that $\overline{AB} \equiv \overline{AC} + \overline{CB}$ shall be called the *extension* of (AC) beyond C.

Axiom XII. **If** $\overline{AB} \equiv \overline{AC} + \overline{CB}$ **where** $\overline{AC} \equiv \overline{AD} + \overline{DC}$,
then $\overline{AB} \equiv \overline{AD} + \overline{DB}$ **where** $\overline{DB} \equiv \overline{DC} + \overline{CB}$.

The effect of this axiom is to establish a serial order among the points of a segment and its extensions, as will be seen from the following theorems. We shall also be able to show that our distances are scalar magnitudes, and that addition of distances is associative.

Axiom XIII. **If** $\overline{AB} \equiv \overline{PQ} + \overline{RS}$ **there is a single point** C **of** (AB) **such that** $\overline{AC} \equiv \overline{PQ}$, $\overline{CB} \equiv \overline{RS}$.

Theorem 3. If $\overline{AB} > \overline{CD}$ and $\overline{CD} > \overline{EF}$, then $\overline{AB} > \overline{EF}$.

To begin with $\overline{AB} \equiv \overline{EF}$ is impossible. If then $\overline{EF} > \overline{AB}$, let us put $\overline{EF} \equiv \overline{EG} + \overline{GF}$, where $\overline{EG} \equiv \overline{AB}$.

Then $\qquad \overline{CD} \equiv \overline{CH} + \overline{HD}; \quad \overline{CH} \equiv \overline{EF}.$

Then $\qquad \overline{CD} \equiv \overline{CK} + \overline{KD}; \quad \overline{CK} \equiv \overline{AB}$

which is against our hypothesis.

We see as a corollary, to this, that if C and D be any two points of (AB), one at least being within it, $\overline{AB} > \overline{CD}$.

It will follow from XIII that two distinct points of a segment cannot determine congruent distances from either end thereof. We also see from XII that if C be a point of (AB), and D a point of (AC), it is likewise a point of (AB). Let the reader show further that every point of a segment, whose extremities belong to a given segment, is, itself, a point of that segment.

Theorem 4. If C be a point of (AB), then every point D of (AB) is either a point of (AC) or of (CB).

If $\overline{AC} \equiv \overline{AD}$ we have C and D identical. If $\overline{AC} > \overline{AD}$ we may find a point of (AC) [and so of (AB)] whose distance from A is congruent to $\overline{AD}$, and this will be identical with D. If $\overline{AC} < \overline{AD}$ we find C as a point of (AD), and hence, by XII, D is a point of (CB).

Theorem 5. If $\overline{AB} \equiv \overline{AC} + \overline{CB}$ and $\overline{AB} \equiv \overline{AD} + \overline{DB}$ while $\overline{AC} > \overline{AD}$, then $\overline{CB} < \overline{DB}$.

Theorem 6. If $\overline{AB} \equiv \overline{PQ} + \overline{RS}$ and $\overline{A'B'} \equiv \overline{PQ} + \overline{RS}$, then $\overline{A'B'} \equiv \overline{AB}$.

The proof is left to the reader.

Theorem 7. If $\overline{AB} \equiv \overline{PQ} + \overline{RS}$ and $\overline{AB} \equiv \overline{PQ} + \overline{LM}$, then $\overline{RS} \equiv \overline{LM}$. For if $\overline{AB} \equiv \overline{AC} + \overline{CB}$, and $\overline{AC} \equiv \overline{PQ}$, then $\overline{CB} \equiv \overline{RS} \equiv \overline{LM}$.

If $$\overline{AB} \equiv \overline{PQ} + \overline{RS}$$
it will be convenient to write $$\overline{PQ} \equiv (\overline{AB} - \overline{RS}),$$

and say that $\overline{PQ}$ is the difference of the distances $\overline{AB}$ and $\overline{RS}$. When we are uncertain as to whether $\overline{AB} > \overline{RS}$ or $\overline{RS} > \overline{AB}$, we shall write their difference $|\overline{AB} - \overline{RS}|$.

Theorem 8. If $\overline{AB} \equiv \overline{PQ} + \overline{LM}$ and $\overline{AB} \equiv \overline{P'Q'} + \overline{L'M'}$

while $$\overline{PQ} \equiv \overline{P'Q'},$$
then $$\overline{LM} \equiv \overline{L'M'}.$$

Theorem 9. If $\overline{AB} \equiv \overline{PQ} + \overline{RS}$ and $\overline{AB} \equiv \overline{P'Q'} + \overline{R'S'}$

while $$\overline{PQ} > \overline{P'Q'},$$
then $$\overline{RS} < \overline{R'S'}.$$

Definition. The assemblage of all points of a segment and its extensions shall be called a *line*.

Definition. Two lines having in common a single point are said to *cut* or *intersect* in that point.

Notice that we have not as yet assumed the existence of two such lines. We shall soon, however, make this assumption explicitly.

Axiom XIV. **Two lines having two common distinct points are identical.**

The line determined by two points A and B shall be written AB or BA.

Theorem 10. If C be a point of the extension of (AB) beyond B and D another point of this same extension, then D is a point of (BC) if $\overline{BC} \equiv \overline{BD}$ or $\overline{BC} > \overline{BD}$; otherwise C is a point of (BD).

Axiom XV. **All points do not lie in one line.**

Axiom XVI. **If B be a point of (CD) and E a point of (AB) where A is not a point of the line BC, then the line DE contains a point F of (AC).**

The first of these axioms is clearly nothing but an existence theorem. The second specifies certain conditions under which two lines, not given by means of common points, must, nevertheless, intersect. It is clear that some such assumption is necessary in order to proceed beyond the geometry of a single straight line.

Theorem 11. If two distinct points A and B be given, there is an infinite number of distinct points which belong to their segment.

This theorem is an immediate consequence of the last two axioms. It may be interpreted otherwise by saying that there is no minimum distance, other than the null distance.

Theorem 12. The manifold of all points of a segment is dense.

Theorem 13. If A, B, C, D, E form the configuration of points described in Axiom XVI, the point E is a point of (DF).

Suppose that this were not the case. We should either have F as a point of (DE) or D as a point of (EF). But then, in the first case, C would be a point of (DB) and in the second D would be a point of (BC), both of which are inconsistent with our data.

Definition. Points which belong to the same line shall be said to be *on* it or to be *collinear*. Lines which contain the same point shall be said to pass through it, or to be *concurrent*.

Theorem 14. If A, B, C be three non-collinear points, and D a point within (AB) while E is a point of the extension of (BC) beyond C, then the line DE will contain a point F of (AC).

Take G, a point of (ED), different from E and D. Then AG will contain a point L of (BE), while G belongs to (AL). If L and C be identical, G will be the point required. If L be a point of (CE) then EG goes through F within (AG) as required. If L be within (BC), then BG goes through H of (AC) and K of (AE), so that, by 13, G and H are points of (BK). H must then, by 4, either be a point of (BG) or of (GK). But if H be a point of (BG), C is a point of (BL), which is untrue. Hence H is a point of (GK), and (AH) contains F of (EG). We see also that it is impossible that C should belong to (AF) or A to (FC). Hence F belongs to (AC).

Theorem 15. If A, B, C be three non-collinear points, no three points, one within each of their three segments, are collinear.

The proof is left to the reader.

Definition. If three non-collinear points be given, the locus of all points of all segments determined by each of these, and all points of the segment of the other two, shall be called a *Triangle*. The points originally chosen shall be called the *vertices*, their segments the *sides*. Any point of the triangle, not on one of its sides, shall be said to be *within* it. If the three given points be A, B, C their triangle shall be written $\triangle ABC$. Let the reader show that this triangle is completely determined by all points of all segments having A as one extremity, while the other belongs to (BC).

It is interesting to notice that XVI, and 13 and 14, may be summed up as follows[3]:—

[3]Some writers, as Pasch, *Neuere Geometrie*, Leipzig, 1882, p. 21, give Axiom XVI in this form. I have followed Veblen, loc. cit., p. 351, in weakening the axiom to the form given.

Theorem 16. If a line contain a point of one side of a triangle and one of either extension of a second side, it will contain a point of the third side.

Definition. The assemblage of all points of all lines determined by the vertices of a triangle and all points of the opposite sides shall be called a *plane.*

It should be noticed that in defining a plane in this manner, the vertices of the triangle play a special rôle. It is our next task to show that this specialization of function is only apparent, and that any other three non-collinear points of the plane might equally well have been chosen to define it.[4]

Theorem 17. If a plane be determined by the vertices of a triangle, the following points lie therein:—

(*a*) All points of every line determined by a vertex, and a point of the line of the other two vertices.

(*b*) All points of every line which contains a point of each of two sides of the triangle.

(*c*) All points of every line containing a point of one side of the triangle and a point of the line of another side.

(*d*) All points of every line which contains a point of the line of each of two sides.

The proof will come at once from 16, and from the consideration that if we know two points of a line, every other point thereof is either a point of their segment, or of one of its extensions. The plane determined by three points as A, B, C shall be written the plane ABC. We are thus led to the following theorem.

Theorem 18. The plane determined by three vertices of a triangle is identical with that determined by two of their number and any other point of the line of either of the remaining sides.

Theorem 19. Any one of the three points determining a plane may be replaced by any other point of the plane, not collinear with the two remaining determining points.

Theorem 20. A plane may be determined by any three of its points which are not collinear.

Theorem 21. Two planes having three non-collinear points in common are identical.

Theorem 22. If two points of a line lie in a plane, all points thereof lie in that plane.

AXIOM XVII. **All points do not lie in one plane.**

Definition. Points or lines which lie in the same plane shall be called *coplanar.* Planes which include the same line shall be called *coaxal.* Planes, like lines, which include the same point, shall be called *concurrent.*

Definition. If four non-coplanar points be given, the assemblage of all points of all segments having for one extremity one of these points, and for the other, a point of the triangle of the other three, shall be called a *tetrahedron.* The four

[4]The treatment of the plane and space which constitute the rest of this chapter are taken largely from Schur, loc. cit. He in turn confesses his indebtedness to Peano.

given points shall be called its *vertices*, their six segments its *edges*, and the four triangles its *faces*. Edges having no common vertex shall be called *opposite*. Let the reader show that, as a matter of fact, the tetrahedron will be determined completely by means of segments, all having a common extremity at one vertex, while the other extremity is in the face of the other three vertices. A vertex may also be said to be opposite to a face, if it do not lie in that face.

Definition. The assemblage of all points of all lines which contain either a vertex of a tetrahedron, and a point of the opposite face, or two points of two opposite edges, shall be called a *space*.

It will be seen that a space, as so defined, is made up of fifteen regions, described as follows:—

(*a*) The tetrahedron itself.

(*b*) Four regions composed of the extensions beyond each vertex of segments having one extremity there, and the other extremity in the opposite face.

(*c*) Four regions composed of the other extensions of the segments mentioned in (*b*).

(*d*) Six regions composed of the extensions of segments whose extremities are points of opposite edges.

Theorem 23. All points of each of the following figures will lie in the space defined by the vertices of a given tetrahedron.

(*a*) A plane containing an edge, and a point of the opposite edge.

(*b*) A line containing a vertex, and a point of the plane of the opposite face.

(*c*) A line containing a point of one edge, and a point of the line of the opposite edge.

(*d*) A line containing a point of the line of each of two opposite edges.

(*e*) A line containing a point of one edge, and a point of the plane of a face not containing that edge.

(*f*) A line containing a point of the line of one edge, and a point of the plane of a face not containing that edge.

The proof will come directly if we take the steps in the order indicated, and hold fast to 16, and the definitions of line, plane, and space.

Theorem 24. In determining a space, any vertex of a tetrahedron may be replaced by any other point, not a vertex, on the line of an edge through the given vertex.

Theorem 25. In determining a space, any vertex of a tetrahedron may be replaced by any point of that space, not coplanar with the other three vertices.

Theorem 26. A space may be determined by any four of its points which are not coplanar.

Theorem 27. Two spaces which have four non-coplanar points in common are identical.

Theorem 28. A space contains wholly every line whereof it contains two distinct points.

Theorem 29. A space contains wholly every plane whereof it contains three non-collinear points.

Practical limitation. Points belonging to different spaces shall not be considered simultaneously in the present work.[5]

Suppose that we have a plane containing the point E of the segment (AB) but no point of the segment (BC). Take F and G two other points of the plane, not collinear with E, and construct the including space by means of the tetrahedron whose vertices are A, B, F, G. As C lies in this space, it must lie in one of the fifteen regions individualized by the tetrahedron; or, more specifically, it must lie in a plane containing one edge, and a point of the opposite edge. Every such plane will contain a line of the plane EFG, as may be immediately proved, and 16 will show that in every case this plane must contain either a point of (AC) or one of (BC).

Theorem 30. If a plane contain a point of one side of a triangle, but no point of a second side, it must contain a point of the third.

Theorem 31. If a line in the plane of a triangle contain a point of one side of the triangle and no point of a second side, it must contain a point of the third side.

Definition. If a point within the segment of two given points be in a given plane, those points shall be said to be on *opposite sides* of the plane; otherwise, they shall be said to be on the *same side* of the plane. Similarly, we may define opposite sides of a line.

Theorem 32. If two points be on the same side of a plane, a point opposite to one is on the same side as the other; and if two points be on the same side, a point opposite to one is opposite to both.

The proof comes at once from 30.

Theorem 33. If two planes have a common point they have a common line.

Let P be the common point. In the first plane take a line through P. If this be also a line of the second plane, the theorem is proved. If not, we may take two points of this line on opposite sides of the second plane. Now any other point of the first plane, not collinear with the three already chosen, will be opposite to one of the last two points, and thus determine another line of the first plane which intersects the second one. We hereby reach a second point common to the two planes, and the line connecting the two is common to both.

It is immediately evident that all points common to the two planes lie in this line.

[5]This means, of course, that we shall not consider geometry of more than three dimensions. It would not, however, strictly speaking, be accurate to say that we consider the geometry of a single space only, for we shall make various mutually contradictory hypotheses about space.

CHAPTER II

CONGRUENT TRANSFORMATIONS

In Chapter I we laid the foundation for the present work. We made a number of explicit assumptions, and, building thereon, we constructed that three-dimensional type of space wherewith we shall, from now on, be occupied. An essential point in our system of axioms is this. We have taken as a fundamental indefinable, distance, and this, being subject to the categories greater and less, is a magnitude. In other words, we have laid the basis for a metrical geometry. Yet, the principal use that we have made of these metrical assumptions, has been to prove a number of descriptive theorems. In order to complete our metrical system properly we shall need two more assumptions, the one to give us the concept of continuity, the other to establish the possibility of congruent transformations.

AXIOM XVIII. **If all points of a segment (AB) be divided into two such classes that no point of the first shall be at a greater distance from A than is any point of the second; then there exists such a point C of the segment, that no point of the first class is within (CB) and none of the second within (AC).**

It is manifest that A will belong to the first class, and B to the second, while C may be ascribed to either. It is the presence of this point common to both, that makes it advisable to describe the two classes in a negative, rather than in a positive manner.

Theorem 1. If $\overline{AB}$ and $\overline{PQ}$ be any two distances whereof the second is not null, there will exist in the segment (AB) a finite or null number n of points P_k possessing the following properties:

$$\overline{PQ} \equiv \overline{AP_1} \equiv \overline{P_kP_{k+1}}; \quad \overline{AP_{k+1}} \equiv \overline{AP_k} + \overline{P_kP_{k+1}}; \quad \overline{P_nB} < \overline{PQ}.$$

Suppose, firstly, that $\overline{AB} < \overline{PQ}$ then, clearly, $n = 0$. If, however, $\overline{AB} \equiv \overline{PQ}$ then $n = 1$ and P_1 is identical with B. There remains the third case where $\overline{AB} > \overline{PQ}$. Imagine the theorem to be untrue. We shall arrive at a contradiction as follows. Let us divide all points of the segment into two classes. A point H shall belong to the first class if we may find such a positive integer n that

$$\overline{P_nH} < \overline{PQ}, \quad \overline{AH} \equiv \overline{AP_n} + \overline{P_nH},$$

the succession of points P_k being taken as above. All other points of the segment shall be assigned to the second class. It is clear that neither class will be empty. If H be a point of the first class, and K one of the second, we cannot have K within (AH), for then we should find $\overline{AK} \equiv \overline{AP_n} + \overline{P_nK}$; $\overline{P_nK} < \overline{PQ}$ contrary to the rule of dichotomy. We have therefore a cut of the type demanded by Axiom XVIII, and a point of division C. Let D be such a point of (AC) that $\overline{DC} < \overline{PQ}$. Then, as we may find n, so large that $\overline{P_nD} < \overline{PQ}$, we shall either have $\overline{P_nC} < \overline{PQ}$ or else we shall be able to insert a point P_{n+1} within (AC)

making $\overline{P_{n+1}C} < \overline{PQ}$. If, then, in the first case we construct P_{n+1}, or in the second P_{n+2}, it will be a point within (CB), as $\overline{P_nB} > \overline{PQ}$, and this involves a contradiction, for it would require P_{n+1} or P_{n+2} to belong to both classes at once. The theorem is thus proved.

It will be seen that this theorem is merely a variation of the axiom of Archimedes,[6] which says, in non-technical language, that if a sufficient number of equal lengths be laid off on a line, any point of that line may be surpassed. We are not able to state the principle in exactly this form, however, for we cannot be sure that our space shall include points of the type P_n in the extension of (AB) beyond B.

Theorem 2. In any segment there is a single point whose distances from the extremities are congruent.

The proof is left to the reader.

The point so found shall be called the *middle point* of the segment. It will follow at once that if k be any positive integer, we may find a set of points $P_1P_2\ldots P_{2^k-1}$ of the segment (AB) possessing the following properties

$$\overline{AP_1} \equiv \overline{P_jP_{j+1}} \equiv \overline{P_{2^k-1}B}; \quad \overline{AP_{j+1}} \equiv \overline{AP_j} + \overline{P_jP_{j+1}}.$$

We may express the relation of any one of these congruent distances to $\overline{AB}$ by writing $\overline{P_jP_{j+1}} \equiv \frac{1}{2^k}\overline{AB}$.

Theorem 3. If a not null distance $\overline{AB}$ be given and a positive integer m, it is possible to find m distinct points of the segment (AB) possessing the properties

$$\overline{AP_1} \equiv \overline{P_jP_{j+1}}; \quad \overline{AP_{j+1}} \equiv \overline{AP_j} + \overline{P_jP_{j+1}}.$$

It is merely necessary to take k so that $2^k > m+1$ and find $\overline{AP_1} \equiv \frac{1}{2^k}\overline{AB}$.

Theorem 4. When any segment (AB) and a positive integer n are given, there exist $n-1$ points $D_1D_2\ldots D_{n-1}$ of the segment (AB) such that

$$\overline{AD_1} \equiv \overline{D_jD_{j+1}} \equiv \overline{D_{n-1}B}; \quad \overline{AD_{j+1}} \equiv \overline{AD_j} + \overline{D_jD_{j+1}}.$$

If the distance $\overline{AB}$ be null, the theorem is trivial. Otherwise, suppose it to be untrue. Let us divide the points of (AB) into two classes according to the

[6] A good deal of attention has been given in recent years to this axiom. For an account of the connexion of Archimedes' axiom with the continuity of the scale, see Stolz, 'Ueber das Axiom des Archimedes,' *Mathematische Annalen*, vol. xxxix, 1891. Halsted, *Rational Geometry* (New York, 1904), has shown that a good deal of the subject of elementary geometry can be built up without the Archimedian assumption, which accounts for the otherwise somewhat obscure title of his book. Hilbert, loc. cit., Ch. IV, was the first writer to set up the theory of area independent of continuity, and Vahlen has shown, loc. cit., pp. 297–8, that volumes may be similarly handled. These questions are of primary importance in any work that deals principally with the significance and independence of the axioms. In our present work we shall leave non-archimedian or discontinuous geometries entirely aside, and that for the reason that their analytic treatment involves either a mutilation of the number scale, or an adjunction of transfinite elements thereto. We shall, in fact, make use of our axiom of continuity XVIII wherever, and whenever, it is convenient to do so.

following scheme. A point P_1 shall belong to the first class if we may construct n congruent distances according to the method already illustrated, reaching such a point P_n of (AB) that $\overline{P_nB} > \overline{AP_1}$; all other points of (AB) shall be assigned to the second class. B will clearly be a point of the second class, but every point of (AB) at a lesser distance from A than a point of the first class, will itself be a point of the first class. We have thus once more a cut as demanded by Axiom XVIII, and a point of division D_1; and this point is different from A.

Let us next assume that the number of successive distances congruent to $\overline{AD_1}$ which, by 1, may be marked in (AB), is k, and let D_k be the last extremity of the resulting segments, so that $\overline{D_kB} < \overline{AD_1}$. Let D_{k-1} be the other extremity of this last segment. Suppose, first, that $k < n$. Let $\overline{PQ}$ be such a distance that $\overline{AD_1} > \overline{PQ} > \overline{D_kB}$. Let P_1 be such a point of (AD_1) that $\overline{AP_1} > \overline{PQ}$, $k\overline{P_1D_1} < \overline{PQ} - \overline{D_kB}$. Then, by marking k successive distances by our previous device, we reach P_k such a point of (AD_k) that

$$\overline{P_kB} < \overline{D_kB} + (\overline{PQ} - \overline{D_kB}) < \overline{PQ} < \overline{AP_1}.$$

But this is a contradiction, for k is at most equal to $n - 1$, and as P_1 is a point of the first class, there should be at least one more point of division P_{k+1}. Hence $k \geqq n$. But $k > n$ leads to a similar contradiction. For we might then find Q_I of the second class so that $(k-2)\overline{D_1Q_1} < \frac{1}{2}\overline{AD_1}$. Then mark $k - 2$ successive congruent distances, reaching Q_{k-2} such a point of (AD_{k-1}) that $\overline{Q_{k-2}D_{k-1}} > \frac{1}{2}\overline{AD_1}$. Hence,

$$\overline{Q_{k-2}D_k} > \tfrac{1}{2}\overline{AD_1} + \overline{AD_1} > \overline{AQ_1},$$

and we may find a $(k-1)$th point Q_{k-1}. But $k - 1 \geqq n$ and this leads us to a contradiction with the assumption that Q_1 should be a point of the second class; i.e. $k = n$. Lastly, we shall find that D_k and B are identical. For otherwise we might find Q_1 of the second class so that $n\overline{D_1Q_1} < \overline{D_nB}$ and marking n successive congruent distances reach Q_n within (D_nB), impossible when Q_1 belongs to class two. Our theorem is thus entirely proved, and D_1 is the point sought.

It will be convenient to write $\overline{AD_1} \equiv \dfrac{1}{n}\overline{AB}$.

Theorem 5. If $\overline{AB}$ and $\overline{PQ}$ be given, whereof the latter is not null, we may find n so great that $\dfrac{1}{n}\overline{AB} < \overline{PQ}$.

The proof is left to the reader.

We are at last in a position to introduce the concept of number into our scale of distance magnitudes. Let $\overline{AB}$ and $\overline{PQ}$ be two distances, whereof the latter is not null. It may be possible to find such a distance $\overline{RS}$ that $q\overline{RS} \equiv \overline{PQ}$; $p\overline{RS} \equiv \overline{AB}$. In this case the number $\dfrac{p}{q}$ shall be called the *numerical measure* of $\overline{AB}$ in terms of $\overline{PQ}$, or, more simply the *measure*. It is clear that this measure may be equally well written $\dfrac{p}{q}$ or $\dfrac{np}{nq}$. There may, however, be no such distance as $\overline{RS}$. Then, whatever positive integer q may be, we may find $\overline{LM}$ so that

$q\overline{LM} \equiv \overline{PQ}$, and p so that $\overline{LM} > (\overline{AB} - p\overline{LM})$. By this process we have defined a cut in our number system of such a nature that $\frac{p}{q}$ and $\frac{p+1}{q}$ appear in the lower and upper divisions respectively. If $\frac{p}{q}$ be a number of the lower, and $\frac{p'+1}{q'}$ one of the upper division, we shall see at once by reducing to a lowest common denominator that $\frac{p}{q} < \frac{p'+1}{q'}$. Every rational number will fall into the one or the other division. Lastly there is no largest number in the lower division nor smallest in the upper. For suppose that $\frac{p}{q}$ is the largest number of the lower division. Then if $\overline{LM} > (\overline{AB} - p\overline{LM})$, we may find n so large that $\frac{1}{n}\overline{LM} < (\overline{AB} - p\overline{LM})$. Let us put $\overline{L_1M_1} \equiv \frac{1}{n}\overline{LM}$. At the same time as $\overline{PQ} \equiv nq\overline{L_1M_1}$ we may, by 1, find k so large that $\overline{L_1M_1} > (\overline{AB} - (np+k)\overline{L_1M_1})$. Under these circumstances $\frac{np+k}{nq}$ is a number of the lower division, yet larger than $\frac{p}{q}$. In the same way we may prove that there is no smallest number in the upper. We have therefore defined a unique irrational number, and this may be taken as the measure of $\overline{AB}$ in terms of $\overline{PQ}$.

Suppose, conversely, that $\frac{p}{q}$ is any rational fraction, and there exists such a distance $\overline{AB'}$ that $q\overline{AB'} > p\overline{PQ}$. Then in (AB') we may find such a point B that $\overline{AB} \equiv \frac{p}{q}\overline{PQ}$, i.e. there will exist a distance having the measure $\frac{p}{q}$ in terms of $\overline{PQ}$. Next let r be any irrational number, and let there be such a number $\frac{p+1}{q}$ in the corresponding upper division of the rational number system that a distance $q\overline{AB'} > ((p+1)\overline{PQ})$ may be found. Then the cut in the number system will give us a cut in the segment (AB'), as demanded by XVIII, and a point of division B. The numerical measure of $\overline{AB}$ in terms of $\overline{PQ}$ will clearly be r.

Theorem 6. If two distances, whereof the second is not null, be given, there exists a unique numerical measure for the first in terms of the second, and if a distance be given, and there exist a distance having a given numerical measure in terms thereof, there will exist a distance having any chosen smaller numerical measure.

Theorem 7. If two distances be congruent, their measures in terms of any third distance are equal.

It will occasionally be convenient to write the measure of $\overline{PQ}$ in the form M $\overline{PQ}$.

Theorem 8. If $r > n$ and if distances $r\overline{PQ}$ and $n\overline{PQ}$ exist, then $r\overline{PQ} > n\overline{PQ}$.

When m and n are both rational, this comes immediately by reducing to a common denominator. When one or both of these numbers is irrational, we may find a number in the lower class of the larger which is larger than one in the upper class of the smaller, and then apply I, 3.

Theorem 9. If $\overline{AB} > \overline{CD}$, the measure of $\overline{AB}$ in terms of any chosen not null distance is greater than that of $\overline{CD}$ in terms of the same distance.

This comes at once by reduction ad absurdum.

It will hereafter be convenient to apply the categories, congruent greater and less, to segments, when these apply respectively to the distances of their extremities. We may similarly speak of the measure of a segment in terms of another one. Let us notice that in combining segments or distances, the associative, commutative, and distributive laws of multiplication hold good; e.g.

$$r \cdot n\overline{PQ} \equiv n \cdot r\overline{PQ} \equiv rn\overline{PQ}, \quad n(\overline{AB} + \overline{CD}) \equiv n\overline{AB} + n\overline{CD}.$$

Notice, in particular, that the measure of a sum is the sum of the measures.

Definition. The assemblage of all points of a segment, or of all possible extensions beyond one extremity, shall be called a *half-line*. The other extremity of the segment shall be called the *bound* of the half-line. A half-line bounded by A and including a point B shall be written $|AB$. Notice that every point of a line is the bound of two half-lines thereof.

Definition. A relation between two sets of points (P) and (Q) such that there is a one to one correspondence of distinct points, and the distances of corresponding pairs of points are in every case congruent, while the sum of two distances is carried into a congruent sum, is called a *congruent transformation*. Notice that, by V, the assemblage of all congruent transformations form a group. If, further, a congruent transformation be possible (P) to (Q), and there be two sets of points (P') and (Q') such that a congruent transformation is possible from the set $(P)(P')$ to the set $(Q)(Q')$ then we shall say that the congruent transformation from (P) to (Q) has been *enlarged to include the sets* (P') *and* (Q').

It is evident that a congruent transformation will carry points of a segment, line, or half-line, into points of a segment, line, or half-line respectively. It will also carry coplanar points into coplanar points, and be, in fact, a collineation, or linear transformation as defined geometrically. In the eighteenth chapter of the present work we shall see how the properties of congruent figures may be reached by defining congruent transformations as a certain six-parameter collineation group.

Axiom XIX. **If a congruent transformation exist between two sets of points, to each half-line bounded by a point of one set may be made to correspond a half-line bounded by the corresponding point of the other set, in such wise that the transformation may be enlarged to include all points of these two half-lines at congruent distances from their respective bounds.**[7]

[7]The idea of enlarging a congruent transformation to include additional points is due to Pasch, loc. cit. He merely assumes that if any point be adjoined to the one set, a corresponding point may be adjoined to the other. We have to make a much clumsier assumption, and proceed more circumspectly, for fear of passing out of our limited region.

Theorem 10. If a congruent transformation carry two chosen points into two other chosen points, it may be enlarged to include all points of their segments.

Theorem 11. If a congruent transformation carry three non-collinear points into three other such points, it may be enlarged to include all points of their respective triangles.

Theorem 12. If a congruent transformation carry four non-coplanar points into four other such points, it may be enlarged to include all points of their respective tetrahedra.

Definition. Two figures which correspond in a congruent transformation shall be said to be *congruent.*

We shall assume hereafter that every congruent transformation with which we deal has been enlarged to the greatest possible extent. Under these circumstances:—

Theorem 13. If two distinct points be invariant under a congruent transformation, the same is true of all points of their line.

Theorem 14. If three non-collinear points be invariant under a congruent transformation, the same is true of all points of their plane.

Theorem 15. If four non-coplanar points be invariant under a congruent transformation the same is true of all points of space.

Definition. The assemblage of all points of a plane on one side of a given line, or on that given line, shall be called a *half-plane*. The given line shall be called the *bound* of the half-plane. Each line in a plane is thus the bound of two half-planes thereof.

Suppose that we have two non-collinear half-lines with a common bound A. Let B and C be two other points of one half-line, and B' and C' two points of the other. Then by Ch. I, 16, a half-line bounded by A which contains a point of (BB') will also contain a point of (CC'), and vice versa. We may thus divide all half-lines of this plane, bounded by this point, into two classes. The assemblage of all half-lines which contain points of segments whose extremities lie severally on the two given half-lines shall be called the *interior angle* of, or between, the given half-lines. The half-lines themselves shall be called the *sides* of the angle. If the half-lines be $|AB$, $|AC$, their interior angle may be indicated $\measuredangle BAC$ or $\measuredangle CAB$. The point A shall be called the *vertex* of the angle.

Definition. The assemblage of all half-lines coplanar with two given non-collinear half-lines, and bounded by the common bound of the latter, but not belonging to their interior angle, shall be called the *exterior angle* of the two half-lines. The definitions for sides and vertex shall be as before. If no mention be made of the words *interior* or *exterior* we shall understand by the word *angle*, *interior angle.* Notice that, by our definitions, the sides are a part of the interior, but not of the exterior angle. Let the reader also show that if a half-line of an interior angle be taken, the other half-line, collinear therewith, and having the same bound belongs to the exterior angle.

Definition. The assemblage of all half-lines identical with two identical half-lines, shall be called their *interior angle.* The given bound shall be the vertex, and the given half-lines the sides of the angle. This angle shall also be called a *null angle*. The assemblage of all half-lines with this bound, and lying in any chosen plane through the identical half-lines, shall be called their *exterior angle* in this plane. The definition of sides and vertex shall be as before.

Definition. Two collinear, but not identical, half-lines of common bound shall be said to be *opposite*.

Definition. The assemblage of all half-lines having as bound the common bound of two opposite half-lines, and lying in any half-plane bounded by the line of the latter, shall be called an *angle* of the two half-lines in that plane. The definitions of sides and vertex shall be as usual. We notice that two opposite half-lines determine two angles in every plane through their line.

We have thus defined the angles of any two half-lines of common bound. The exterior angle of any two such half-lines, when there is one, shall be called a *re-entrant* angle. Any angle determined by two opposite half-lines shall be called a *straight* angle. As, by definition, two half-lines form an angle when, and only when, they have a common bound, we shall in future cease to mention this fact. Two angles will be congruent, by our definition of congruent figures, if there exist a congruent transformation of the sides of one into the sides of the other, in so far as corresponding distances actually exist on the corresponding half-lines. Every half-line of the interior or exterior angle will similarly be carried into a corresponding half-line, or as much thereof as actually exists and contains corresponding distances.

Definition. The angles of a triangle shall be those non-re-entrant angles whose vertices are the vertices of the triangle, and whose sides include the sides of the triangle.

Definition. The angle between a half-line including one side of a triangle, and bounded at a chosen vertex, and the opposite of the other half-line which goes to make the angle of the triangle at that vertex, shall be called an *exterior angle* of the triangle. Notice that there are six of these, and that they are not to be confused with the exterior angles of their respective sides.

Theorem 16. If two triangles be so related that the sides of one are congruent to those of the other, the same holds for the angles.

This is an immediate result of 11.

The meanings of the words *opposite* and *adjacent* as applied to sides and angles of a triangle are immediately evident, and need not be defined. There can also be no ambiguity in speaking of sides *including* an angle.

Theorem 17. Two triangles are congruent if two sides and the included angle of one be respectively congruent to two sides and the included angle of the other.

The truth of this is at once evident when we recall the definition of congruent angles, and 12.

Theorem 18. If two sides of a triangle be congruent, the opposite angles are congruent.

Such a triangle shall, naturally, be called *isosceles*.

Theorem 19. If three half-lines lie in the same half-plane and have their common bound on the bound of this half-plane; then one belongs to the interior angle of the other two.

Let the half-lines be $|AB$, $|AC$, $|AD$. Connect B with H and K, points of the opposite half-lines bounding this half-plane. If $|AC$, $|AD$ contain points of the same two sides of the triangle BHK the theorem is at once evident; if one contain a point of (BH) and the other a point of (BK), then B belongs to $\measuredangle CAD$.

Theorem 20. If $|AB$ be a half-line of the interior $\measuredangle CAD$, then $|AC$ does not belong to the interior $\measuredangle BAD$.

Definition. Two non-re-entrant angles of the same plane with a common side, but no other common half-lines, shall be said to be *adjacent.* The angle bounded by their remaining sides, which includes the common side, shall be called their *sum*. It is clear that this is, in fact, their logical sum, containing all common points.

Definition. An angle shall be said to be congruent to the sum of two non-re-entrant angles, when it is congruent to the sum of two adjacent angles, respectively congruent to them.

Definition. Two angles congruent to two adjacent angles whose sum is a straight angle shall be said to be *supplementary*. Each shall be called the *supplement* of the other.

Definition. An angle which is congruent to its supplement shall be called a *right angle*.

Definition. A triangle, one of whose angles is a right angle, shall be called a *right triangle*.

Definition. The interior angle formed by two half-lines, opposite to the half-lines which are the sides of a given interior angle, shall be called the *vertical* of that angle. The vertical of a straight angle will be the other half-plane, coplanar therewith, and having the same bound.

Theorem 21. If two points be at congruent distances from two points coplanar with them, all points of the line of the first two are at congruent distances from the latter two.

For we may find a congruent transformation keeping the former points invariant, while the latter are interchanged.

Theorem 22. If $|AA_1'$ be a half-line of the interior $\measuredangle BAA_1$, then we cannot have a congruent transformation keeping $|AB$ invariant and carrying $|AA_1$ into $|AA_1'$.

We may suppose that A_1 and A_1' are at congruent distances from A. Let H be the point of the segment (A_1A_1') equidistant from A_1 and A_1'. We may find a congruent transformation carrying AA_1HA_1' into $AA_1'HA_1$. Let this take the half-line $|AB$ into $|AC$ (in the same plane). Then if $|\overline{AA_1}$ and $|\overline{AA_1'}$ be taken sufficiently small, A_1A_1' will meet AB or AC as we see by I. 16. This will involve a contradiction, however, for if D be the intersection, it is easy to see that we shall have simultaneously $\overline{DA_1} \equiv \overline{DA_1'}$ and $\overline{DA_1} > \overline{DA_1'}$ or

$\overline{DA_1} < \overline{DA_1'}$ for D is unaltered by the congruent transformation, while A_1 goes into A_1'.

There is one case where this reasoning has to be modified, namely, when $|AC$ and $|AB$ are opposite half-lines, for here I. 16 does not hold. Let us notice, however, that we may enlarge our transformation to include the $\measuredangle BAA_1$ and $\measuredangle BAA_1'$ respectively. If $|AB_1$ and $|AC_1$ be two half-lines of the first angle, $|AC_1$ being in the interior angle of $\measuredangle BAB_1$, to them will correspond $|AB_1'$ and $|AC_1'$, the latter being in the interior angle of $\measuredangle BAB_1'$, while by definition, corresponding half-lines always determine congruent angles with $|AB$. If, then, we choose any half-line $|AL$ of the interior $\measuredangle BAA_1'$, it may be shown that we may find two corresponding half-lines $|AL_1$ $|AL_1'$ so situated that $|AL_1$ belongs to the interior $\measuredangle BAL_1'$ and $\measuredangle L_1'AL$ is congruent to $\measuredangle LAL_1$. The proof is tedious, and depends on showing that as a result of our Axiom XVIII, if in any segment the points be paired in such a way that the extremities correspond, and the greater of two distances from an extremity correspond to the greater of the two corresponding distances from the other extremity, then there is one self-corresponding point.[8] These corresponding half-lines being found, we may apply the first part of our proof without fear of mishap.

Theorem 23. If $|AC$ be a half-line of the interior $\measuredangle BAD$, it is impossible to have $\measuredangle BAC$ and $\measuredangle BAD$ mutually congruent.

Theorem 24. An angle is congruent to its vertical.

We have merely to look at the congruent transformation interchanging a side of one with a side of the other.

We see as a result of 24 that if a half-line $|AB$ make right angles with the opposite half-lines $|AC$, $|AC'$, the verticals obtained by extending (AB) beyond A will be right angles congruent to the other two. We thus have four mutually congruent right angles at the point A. Under these circumstances we shall say that they are *mutually perpendicular* there.

Theorem 25. If two angles of a triangle be congruent, the triangle is isosceles.

This is an immediate result of 18.

Given two non-re-entrant angles. The first shall be said to be *greater than* the second, when it is congruent to the sum of the second, and a not null angle. The second shall under these circumstances, and these alone, be said to be *less than* the first. As the assemblage of all congruent transformations is a group, we see that the relations greater than, less than, and congruent when applied to angles are mutually exclusive. For if we had two angles whereof the first was both greater than and less than the second, then we should have an angle that would be both greater than and less than itself, an absurd result, as we see from 23. We shall write $>$ in place of *greater than*, and $<$ for *less than*, $\equiv$ means *congruence*. Two angles between which there exists one of these three relations shall be said to be *comparable*. We shall later see that any two angles are comparable. The reason why we cannot at once proceed to prove this fact, is that, so far, we are not very clear as to just what can be done with our

[8] Cf. Enriques, *Geometria proiettiva*, Bologna, 1898, p. 80.

congruent transformations. As for the *a priori* question of comparableness, we have perfectly clear definitions of greater than, less than, and equal as applied to infinite assemblages, but are entirely in the dark as to whether when two such assemblages are given, one of these relations must necessarily hold.[9]

Theorem 26. An exterior angle of a triangle is comparable with either of the opposite interior angles.

Let us take the triangle ABC, while D lies on the extension of (BC) beyond C. Let E be the middle point of (AC) and let DE meet (AB) in F. If $\overline{DE} > \overline{EF}$ find G of (DE) so that $\overline{FE} \equiv \overline{EG}$. Then we have $\measuredangle BAC$ congruent to $\measuredangle ECG$ and less than $\measuredangle ECD$. If $\overline{DE} < \overline{EF}$ we have $\measuredangle BAC$ greater than an angle congruent to $\measuredangle ECD$.

Theorem 27. Two angles of a triangle are comparable.

For they are comparable to the same exterior angle.

Theorem 28. If in any triangle one angle be greater than a second, the side opposite the first is greater than that opposite the second.

Evidently these sides cannot be congruent. Let us then have the triangle ABG where $\measuredangle BAG > \measuredangle BGA$. We may, by the definition of congruence, find such a point C_1 of (BG) that $\measuredangle C_1AG$ is congruent to $\measuredangle C_1GA$ and hence $\overline{C_1A} \equiv \overline{C_1G}$. It thus remains to show that $\overline{AB} < (\overline{AC_1} + \overline{C_1B})$. Were such not the case, we might find D_1 of (AB) so that $\overline{AD_1} \equiv \overline{AC_1}$, and the problem reduces to comparing $\overline{BC_1}$ and $\overline{BD_1}$. Now in $\triangle BD_1C_1$ we have $\measuredangle BD_1C_1$ the supplement of $\measuredangle AD_1C_1$ which is congruent to $\measuredangle AC_1D_1$ whose supplement is greater than $\measuredangle BC_1D_1$. We have therefore returned to our original problem, this time, however, with a smaller triangle. Now this reduction process may be continued indefinitely, and if our original assumption be false, the inequalities must always lie the same way. Next notice that, by our axiom of continuity, the points C_i of (BG) must tend to approach a point C of that segment as a limit, and similarly the points D_i of (AB) tend to approach a limiting point, D. If two points of (AB) be taken indefinitely close to D the angle which they determine at any point of (BG) other than B will become indefinitely small. On the other hand as C_i approaches C, $\measuredangle APC_i$ will tend to increase, where P is any point of (AB) other than B, in which case the angle is constant. This shows that C, and by the same reasoning D, cannot be other than B; so that the difference between BC_i and BD_i can be made as small as we please. But, on the other hand

$$\overline{C_1G} \equiv \overline{AC_1} \equiv \overline{AD_1}; \quad (\overline{BA} - \overline{BG}) \equiv (\overline{BD_1} - \overline{BC_1}) \equiv (\overline{BD_i} - \overline{BC_i})$$

Our theorem comes at once from this contradiction.

Theorem 29. If two sides of a triangle be not congruent, the angle opposite the greater side is greater than that opposite the lesser.

Theorem 30. One side of a triangle cannot be greater than the sum of the other two.

[9]Cf. Borel, *Leçons sur la théorie des fonctions*, Paris, 1898, pp. 102–8.

Theorem 31. The difference between two sides of a triangle is less than the third side.

The proofs of these theorems are left to the reader.

Theorem 32. Two distinct lines cannot be coplanar with a third, and perpendicular to it at the same point.

Suppose, in fact, that we have AC and AD perpendicular to BB' at A. We may assume $\overline{AB} \equiv \overline{AB'}$ so that by I. 31 AD will contain a single point E either of (CB) or of (CB'). For definiteness, let E belong to (CB'). Then take F on (BC), which is congruent to $(B'C)$, so that $\overline{BF} \equiv \overline{B'E}$. Hence $\measuredangle BB'F$ is congruent to $\measuredangle B'BE$ and therefore congruent to $\measuredangle BB'E$; which contradicts 23.[10]

Theorem 33. The locus of points in a plane at congruent distances from two points thereof is the line through the middle point of their segment perpendicular to their line.

Theorem 34. Two triangles are congruent if a side and two adjacent angles of one be respectively congruent to a side and two adjacent angles of the other.

Theorem 35. Through any point of a given line will pass one line perpendicular to it lying in any given plane through that line.

Let A be the chosen point, and C a point in the plane, not on the chosen line. Let us take two such points B, B' on the given line, that A is the middle point of (BB') and $\overline{BB'} < \overline{CB}$, $\overline{BB'} < \overline{CB'}$. If then $\overline{CB} \equiv \overline{CB'}$, AC is the line required. If not, let us suppose that $\overline{CB} > \overline{CB'}$. We may make a cut in the points of (CB) according to the following principle. A point P shall belong to the first class if no point of the segment (PB) is at a distance from B greater than its distance from B', all other points of (CB) shall belong to the second class. It is clear that the requirements of Axiom XVIII are fulfilled, and we have a point of division D. We could not have $\overline{DB} < \overline{DB'}$, for then we might, by 31, take E a point of (DC) so very near to D that for all points P of DE $\overline{PB} < \overline{PB'}$, and this would be contrary to the law of the cut. In the same way we could not have $\overline{DB} > \overline{DB'}$. Hence AD is the perpendicular required.

Theorem 36. If a line be perpendicular to two others at their point of intersection, it is perpendicular to every line in their plane through that point.

The proof given in the usual textbooks will hold.

Theorem 37. All lines perpendicular to a given line at a given point are coplanar.

Definition. The plane of all perpendiculars to a line at a point, shall be said to be *perpendicular* to that line at that point.

[10]This is substantially Hilbert's proof, loc. cit., p. 16. It is truly astonishing how much geometers, ancient and modern, have worried over this theorem. Euclid puts it as his eleventh axiom that all right angles are equal. Many modern textbooks prove that all straight angles are equal, hence right angles are equal, as halves of equal things. This is not usually sound, for it is not clear by definition why a right angle is half a straight angle. Others observe the angle of a fixed and a rotating line, and either appeal explicitly to intuition, or to a vague continuity axiom.

Theorem 38. A congruent transformation which keeps all points of a line invariant, will transform into itself every plane perpendicular to that line.

It is also clear that the locus of all points at congruent distances from two points is a plane.

Theorem 39. If P be a point within the triangle ABC and there exist a distance congruent to $\overline{AB} + \overline{AC}$, then

$$\overline{AB} + \overline{AC} > \overline{PB} + \overline{PC}.$$

To prove this let BP pass through D of (AC). Then as $\overline{AC} > \overline{AD}$ a distance exists congruent to $\overline{AB} + \overline{AD}$, and $\overline{AB} + \overline{AD} > \overline{BP} + \overline{PD}$. As $\overline{AB} + \overline{AD} > \overline{PD}$ there exists a distance congruent to $\overline{PD} + \overline{DC}$, and hence $\overline{PD} + \overline{DC} > \overline{PC}$,

$$\overline{DC} > \overline{PC} - \overline{PD}; \quad \overline{AB} + \overline{AC} > \overline{BP} + \overline{PC}.$$

Theorem 40. Any two right angles are congruent.

Let these right angles be $\measuredangle AOC$ and $\measuredangle A'O'C'$. We may assume O to be the middle point of (AB) and O' the middle point of $(A'B')$, where $\overline{OA} \equiv \overline{O'A'}$. We may also suppose that distances exist congruent to $\overline{AC} + \overline{CB}$ and to $\overline{A'C'} + \overline{C'B'}$. Then $\overline{AC} > \overline{AO}$ and $\overline{A'C'} > \overline{A'O'}$. Lastly, we may assume that $\overline{AC} \equiv \overline{A'C'}$. For if we had say, $\overline{AC} > \overline{A'C'}$, we might use our cut proceeding in (OC). A point P shall belong to the first class, if no point of (OP) determines with A a distance greater then $\overline{A'C'}$, otherwise it shall belong to the second class. We find a point of division D, and see at once that $\overline{AD} \equiv \overline{A'C'}$. Replacing the letter D by C, we have $\overline{AC} \equiv \overline{A'C'}$, $\triangle ABC$ congruent to $\triangle A'B'C'$, hence $\measuredangle AOC$ congruent to $\measuredangle A'O'C'$.

Theorem 41. There exists a congruent transformation carrying any segment (AB) into any congruent segment $(A'B')$ and any half-plane bounded by AB into any half-plane bounded by $A'B'$.

We have merely to find O and O' the middle points of (AB) and $(A'B')$ respectively, and C and C' on the perpendiculars to AB and $A'B'$, at O and O' so that $\overline{OC} \equiv \overline{O'C'}$.

Theorem 42. If $|OA$ be a given half-line, there will exist in any chosen half-plane bounded by OA a unique half-line $|OB$ making the $\measuredangle AOB$ congruent to any chosen angle.

The proof of this theorem depends immediately upon the preceding one.

Several results follow from the last four theorems. To begin with, any two angles are comparable, as we see at once from 42. We see also that our Axioms III–XIII and XVIII, may be at once translated into the geometry of the angle if straight and re-entrant angles be excluded. We may then apply to angles system of measurement entirely analogous to that applied to distances. An angle may be represented unequivocally by a single number, in terms of any chosen not null angle. We may extend our system of comparison to include straight and re-entrant angles as follows. A straight angle shall be looked upon as greater than every non-re-entrant angle, and less than every re-entrant one. Of two re-entrant angles, that one shall be considered the less, whose corresponding interior angle is the greater. A re-entrant angle will be the logical sum of two non-re-entrant angles, and shall have as a measure, the sum of their measures.

We have also found out a good deal about the congruent group. The principal facts are as follows:—

(a) A congruent transformation may be found to carry any point into any other point.

(b) A congruent transformation may be found to leave any chosen point invariant, and carry any chosen line through this point, into any other such line.

(c) A congruent transformation may be found to leave invariant any point, and any line through it, but to carry any plane through this line, into any other such plane.

(d) If a point, a line through it, and a plane through the line be invariant, no further infinitesimal congruent transformations are possible.

The last assertion has not been proved in full; let the reader show that if a point and a line through it be invariant, there is only one congruent transformation of the line possible, besides the identical one, and so on. The essential thing is this. We shall demonstrate at length in Ch. XVIII that the congruent group is completely determined by the requirement that it shall be an analytic collineation group, satisfying these four requirements.

Suppose that we have two half-planes on opposite sides of a plane a which contains their common bound l. Every segment whose extremities are one in each of these half-planes will have a point in a, and, in fact, all such points will lie in one half-plane of a bounded by l, as may easily be shown from the special case where two segments have a common extremity.

Definition. Given two non-coplanar half-planes of common bound. The assemblage of all half-planes with this bound, containing points of segments whose extremities lie severally in the two given half-planes, shall be called their *interior dihedral angle*, or, more simply, their *dihedral angle*. The assemblage of all other half-planes with this bound shall be called their *exterior dihedral angle*. The two given half-planes shall be called the *faces*, and their bound the edge of the dihedral angle.

We may, by following the analogy of the plane, define null, straight, and re-entrant dihedral angles. The definition of the dihedral angles of a tetrahedron will also be immediately evident.

A plane perpendicular to the edge of a dihedral angle will cut the faces in two half-lines perpendicular to the edge. The interior (exterior) angle of these two shall be called a *plane angle* of the interior (exterior) dihedral angle.

Theorem 43. Two plane angles of a dihedral angle are congruent.

We have merely to take the congruent transformation which keeps invariant all points of the plane whose points are equidistant from the vertices of the plane angles. Such a transformation may properly be called a *reflection* in that plane.

Theorem 44. If two dihedral angles be congruent, any two of their plane angles will be congruent, and conversely.

The proof is immediate. Let us next notice that we may measure any dihedral angle in terms of any other not null one, and that its measure is the measure of its plane angle in terms of the plane angle of the latter.

Definition. If the plane angle of a dihedral angle be a right angle, the dihedral angle itself shall be called *right*, and the planes shall be said to be *mutually perpendicular.*

Theorem 45. If a plane be perpendicular to each of two other planes, and the three be concurrent, then the first plane is also perpendicular to the line of intersection of the other two.

CHAPTER III

THE THREE HYPOTHESES

In the last chapter we discussed at some length the problem of comparing distances and angles, and of giving them numerical measures in terms of known units. We did not take up the question of the sum of the angles of a triangle, and that shall be our next task. The axioms so far set up are insufficient to determine whether this sum shall, or shall not, be congruent to the sum of two right angles, as we shall amply see by elaborating consistent systems of geometry where this sum is greater than, equal to, or less than two right angles. We must first, however, give one or two theorems concerning the continuous change of distances and angles.

Theorem 1. If a point P of a segment (AB) may be taken at as small a distance from A as desired, and C be any other point, the $\measuredangle ACP$ may be made less than any given angle.

If C be a point of AB the theorem is trivial. If not, we may, by III. 4, find $|CD$ in the half-plane bounded by CA which contains B, so that $\measuredangle ACD$ is congruent to the given angle. If then $|AB$ belong to the internal $\measuredangle ACD$, we have $\measuredangle ACB$ less than $\measuredangle ACD$, and, *a fortiori*, $\measuredangle ACP < \measuredangle ACD$. If $|AD$ belong to the internal $\measuredangle ACB$, $|AD$ must contain a point E of CAB, and if we take P within (AE), once more

$$\measuredangle ACP < \measuredangle ACD.$$

Theorem 2. If, in any triangle, one side and an adjacent angle remain fixed, while the other side including this angle may be diminished at will, then the external angle opposite to the fixed side will take and retain a value differing from that of the fixed angle by less than any assigned value.

Let the fixed side be (AB), while C is the variable vertex within a fixed segment (BD). We wish to show that if $\overline{BC}$ be taken sufficiently small, $\measuredangle ACD$ will necessarily differ from $\measuredangle ABD$ by less than any chosen angle.

Let B_1 be the middle point of (AB), and B_2 the middle point of (B_1B), while B_3 is a point of the extension of (AB) beyond B. Through each of the points B_1, B_2, B_3 construct a half-line bounded thereby, and lying in that half-plane, bounded by AB which contains D, and let the angles so formed at B_1, B_2, B_3 all be congruent to $\measuredangle ABD$. We may certainly take $\overline{BC}$ so small that AC contains a point of each of these half-lines, say C_1, C_2, C_3 respectively. We may moreover take $\overline{BC}$ so tiny that it is possible to extend (B_1C_1) beyond C_1 to D_1 so that $\overline{B_1C_1} \equiv \overline{C_1D_1}$. AD_1 will surely meet B_2C_2 in a point D_2, when $\overline{B_1C_1}$ is very small, and as $\overline{AC_3}$ differs infinitesimally from $\overline{AB_3}$, and hence exceeds $\overline{AB}$ by a finite amount, it is greater than $2\overline{AC_1}$ which differs infinitesimally from $2\overline{AB_1}$, or $\overline{AB}$. We may thus find C' on the extension of (AC_1) beyond C_1 so that $\overline{AC_1} \equiv \overline{C_1C'}$. C' will be at a small distance from C, and hence on the other side of B_2D_2 from A and D_1. Let D_1C' meet B_2D_2 at H_2. We now see that, with regard to the $\triangle AB_1D_1$; the external angle at D_1 (i.e. one of the mutually vertical external angles) is $\measuredangle B_1D_1D_2$ congruent to $(\measuredangle B_1D_1C' +$

$\measuredangle C'D_1D_2$), and $\measuredangle B_1D_1C'$ is congruent to $\measuredangle AB_1D_1$, and, hence congruent to $\measuredangle ABD$. The $\measuredangle C'D_1D_2$ is the difference between $\measuredangle B_1D_1D_2$ and $\measuredangle B_1D_1H_2$, and as H_2 and D_2 approach B_2 as a limiting position, the angles determined by B_2, D_2 and D_2, H_2 at every point in space decrease together towards a null angle as a limit. Hence $\measuredangle C'D_1D_2$ becomes infinitesimal, and the difference between $\measuredangle B_1D_1D_2$ and $\measuredangle ABD$ becomes and remains infinitesimal. But as $\overline{AB_1} \equiv \overline{B_1B}$, and $\measuredangle AB_1D_1$ and $\measuredangle B_1BD$ are congruent, we see similarly that the difference between $\measuredangle B_1CD$ and $\measuredangle ABD$ will become, and remain infinitesimal. Lastly, the difference between $\measuredangle B_1CD$ and $\measuredangle ACD$ is $\measuredangle B_1CA$ which will, by our previous reasoning, become infinitesimal with $\overline{B_1C_1}$. The difference between $\measuredangle ABD$ and $\measuredangle ACD$ will therefore become and remain less than any assigned angle.

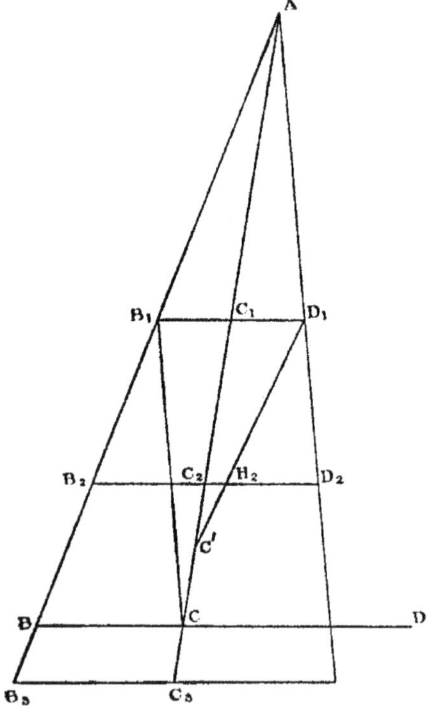

FIG. 1

Several corollaries follow immediately from this theorem.

Theorem 3. If in any triangle one side and an adjacent angle remain fixed, while the other side including this angle becomes infinitesimal, the sum of the angles of this triangle will differ infinitesimally from a straight angle.

Theorem 4. If in any triangle one side and an adjacent angle remain fixed, while the other side including this angle varies, then the measures of the third side, and of the variable angles will be continuous functions of the measure of the variable side first mentioned.

Of course a constant is here included as a special case of a continuous function.

Theorem 5. If two lines AB, AC be perpendicular to BC, then all lines which contain A and points of BC are perpendicular to BC, and all points of BC are at congruent distances from A.

To prove this let us first notice that our $\triangle ABC$ is isosceles, and $\overline{AB}$ will be congruent to every other perpendicular distance from A to BC. Such a distance will be the distance from A to the middle point of (BC) and, in fact, to every point of BC whose distance from B may be expressed in the form $\frac{m}{2^n}\overline{BC}$ where m and n are integers. Now such points will lie as close as we please to every point of BC, hence by II. 31, no distance from A can differ from $\overline{AB}$, and no angle so formed can, by III. 2, differ from a right angle.

Theorem 6. If a set of lines perpendicular to a line l, meet a line m, the distances of these points from a fixed point of m, and the angles so formed with m, will vary continuously with the distances from a fixed point of l to the intersections with these perpendiculars.

The proof comes easily from 2 and 5.

Definition. Given four coplanar points A, B, C, D so situated that no segment may contain points within three of the segments (AB), (BC), (CD), (DA). The assemblage of all points of all segments whose extremities lie on these segments shall be called a *quadrilateral.* The given points shall be called its vertices, and the given segments its sides. The four internal angles $\measuredangle DAB$, $\measuredangle ABC$, $\measuredangle BCD$, $\measuredangle CDA$ shall be called its angles. The definitions of opposite sides and opposite vertices are obvious, as are the definitions for adjacent sides and vertices.

Definition. A quadrilateral with right angles at two adjacent vertices shall be called *birectangular*. If it have three right angles it shall be called *trirectangular*, and four right angles it shall be called a *rectangle.* Let the reader convince himself that, under our hypotheses, birectangular and trirectangular quadrilaterals necessarily exist.

Definition. A birectangular quadrilateral whose opposite sides adjacent to the right angles are congruent, shall be said to be *isosceles*.

Theorem 7. Saccheri's[11]. In an isosceles birectangular quadrilateral a line through the middle point of the side adjacent to both right angles, which is

[11]Saccheri, *Euclides ab omni naevo vindicatus*, Milan, 1732. Accessible in Engel und Staeckel, *Theorie der Parallellinien von Euklid bis auf Gauss*, Leipzig, 1895. The theorem given above covers Saccheri's theorems 1 and 2 on p. 50 of the last-named work. Saccheri's is the first systematic attempt of which we have a record to prove Euclid's parallel postulate, and proceeds according to modern method of assuming the postulate untrue. He builded better than he knew, however, for the system so constructed is self-consistent, and not inconsistent, as he attempted to show.

perpendicular to the line of that side, will be perpendicular to the line of the opposite side and pass through its middle point. The other two angles of the quadrilateral are mutually congruent.

Let the quadrilateral be $ABCD$, the right angles having their vertices at A and B. Then the perpendicular to AB at E the middle point of (AB) will surely contain F point of (CD). It will be easy to pass a plane through this line perpendicular to the plane of the quadrilateral, and by taking a reflection in this latter plane, the quadrilateral will be transformed into itself, the opposite sides being interchanged.

This theorem may be more briefly stated by saying that this line divides the quadrilateral into two mutually congruent trirectangular ones.

Theorem 8. In a rectangle the opposite sides are mutually congruent, and any isosceles birectangular quadrilateral whose opposite sides are mutually congruent is necessarily a rectangle.

Theorem 9. If there exist a single rectangle, every isosceles birectangular quadrilateral is a rectangle.

Let $ABCD$ be the rectangle. The line perpendicular to AB at the middle point of (AB) will divide it into two smaller rectangles. Continuing this process we see that we can construct a rectangle whose adjacent sides may have any measures that can be indicated in the form $\frac{m}{2^n}\overline{AB}$, $\frac{p}{2^q}\overline{AC}$, provided, of course, that the distances so called for exist simultaneously on the sides of a birectangular isosceles quadrilateral. Distances so indicated will be everywhere dense on any line, hence, by 6 we may construct a rectangle having as one of its sides one of the congruent sides of any isosceles birectangular quadrilateral, and hence, by a repetition of the same process, a rectangle which is identical with this quadrilateral. All isosceles birectangular quadrilaterals, and all trirectangular quadrilaterals are under the present circumstances rectangles.

Be it noticed that, under the present hypothesis, Theorem 5 is superfluous.

Theorem 10. If there exist a single right triangle the sum of whose angles is congruent to a straight angle, the same is true of every right triangle.

Let $\triangle ABC$ be the given triangle, the right angle being $\measuredangle ACB$ so that the sum of the other two angles is congruent to a right angle. Let $\triangle A'B'C'$ be any other right triangle, the right angle being $\measuredangle A'C'B'$. We have to prove that the sum of its remaining angles also is congruent to a right angle. We see that both $\measuredangle ABC$ and $\measuredangle BAC$ are less than right angles, hence there will exist such a point E of (AB) that $\measuredangle EAC$ and $\measuredangle ECA$ are congruent. Then $\measuredangle EBC \equiv \measuredangle ECB$ since $\measuredangle ACB$ is congruent to the sum of $\measuredangle EAC$ and $\measuredangle EBC$. If D and F be the middle points of (BC) and (AC) respectively, as $\triangle EAC$ and $\triangle EBC$ are isosceles, we have, in the quadrilateral $EDCF$ right angles at D, C, and F. The angle at E is also a right angle, for it is one half the straight angle, $\measuredangle AEB$, hence $EDCF$ is a rectangle. Passing now to the $\triangle A'C'B'$ we see that the perpendicular to $A'C'$ at F' the middle point of $(A'C')$, will meet $(A'B')$ in E', and the perpendicular to $E'F'$ at E' will meet $(B'C')$ in D'. But, by an easy modification of 9, as there exists one rectangle, the trirectangular quadrilateral $E'F'D'C'$ is also a rectangle. It is clear that $\measuredangle D'E'B' \equiv \measuredangle D'E'C'$ since $\measuredangle F'E'D'$ is a right angle and $\measuredangle F'E'A' \equiv \measuredangle F'E'C'$. Then $\triangle C'E'B'$ is isosceles like $\triangle A'E'C'$. From this comes immediately that the sum of $\measuredangle E'B'C'$ and $\measuredangle E'A'C'$ is congruent to a right angle, as we wished to show.

Theorem 11. If there exist any right triangle where the sum of the angles is less than a straight angle, the same is true of all right triangles.

We see the truth of this by continuity. For we may pass from any right triangle to any other by means of a continuous change of first the one, and then the other of the sides which include the right angle. In this change, by 2, the sum of the angles will either remain constant, or change continuously, but may never become congruent to the sum of two right angles, hence it must always remain less than that sum.

Theorem 12. If there exist a right triangle where the sum of the angles is greater than two right angles, the same is true of every right triangle.

This comes immediately by *reductio ad absurdum.*

Theorem 13. If there exist any triangle where the sum of the angles is less than (congruent to) a straight angle, then in every triangle the sum of the angles is less than (congruent to) a straight angle.

Let us notice, to begin with, that our given $\triangle ABC$ must have at least two angles, say $\measuredangle ABC$ and $\measuredangle BAC$ which are less than right angles. At each point of (AB) there will be a perpendicular to AB (in the plane BC). If two of these perpendiculars intersect, all will, by 5, pass through this point, and a line hence to C will surely be perpendicular to AB. If no two of the perpendiculars intersect, then, clearly, some will meet (AC) and some (BC). A cut will thus be determined among the points of (AB), and, by XVIII, we shall find a point of division D. It is at once evident that the perpendicular to AB at D will pass through C. In every case we may, therefore, divide our triangle into two right triangles. In one of these the sum of the angles must surely be less than (congruent to) a straight angle, and the same will hold for every right triangle. Next observe that there can, under our present circumstances, exist no triangle with two angles congruent to, or greater than right angles. Hence every triangle can be divided into two right triangles as we have just done. In each of these triangles, the sum of the angles is less than (congruent to) a straight angle, hence in the triangle chosen, the sum of the angles is less than (congruent to) a straight angle.

Theorem 14. If there exist any triangle where the sum of the angles is greater than a straight angle, the same will be true of every triangle.

This comes at once by *reductio ad absurdum.*

We have now reached the fundamental fact that the sum of the angles of a single triangle will determine the nature of the sum of the angles of every triangle. Let us set the various possible assumptions in evidence.

The assumption that there exists a single triangle, the sum of whose angles is congruent to a straight angle is called the *Euclidean* or *Parabolic* hypothesis.[12]

[12]There will exist, of course, numerous geometries, other than those which we give in the following pages, where the sum of the angles of a triangle is still congruent to a straight angle,

The assumption that there exists a triangle, the sum of whose angles is less than a straight angle is called the *Lobatchewskian* or *hyperbolic* hypothesis.[13]

The assumption that there exists a triangle, the sum of whose angles is greater than a straight angle, is called the *Riemannian* or *elliptic hypothesis*.[14]

Only under the elliptic hypothesis can two intersecting lines be perpendicular to a third line coplanar with them.

Definition. The difference between the sum of the angles of a triangle, and a straight angle shall be called the *discrepancy* of the triangle.

Theorem 15. If in any triangle a line be drawn from one vertex to a point of the opposite side, the sum of the discrepancies of the resulting triangles is congruent to the discrepancy of the given triangle.

The proof is immediate. Notice, hence, that if in any triangle one angle remain constant, while one or both of the other vertices tend to approach the vertex of the fixed angle, along fixed lines, the discrepancy of the triangle, when not zero, will diminish towards zero as a limit. We shall make this more clear by saying—

Theorem 16. If, in any triangle, one vertex remain fixed, the other vertices lying on fixed lines through it, and if a second vertex may be made to come as near to the fixed vertex as may be desired, while the third vertex does not tend to recede indefinitely, then the discrepancy may be made less than any assigned angle.

Theorem 17. If in any triangle one side may be made less than any assigned segment, while neither of the other sides becomes indefinitely large, the discrepancy may be made less than any assigned angle.

If neither angle adjacent to the diminishing side tend to approach a straight angle as a limit, it will remain less than some non-re-entrant angle, and 16 will apply to all such angles simultaneously. If it do tend to approach a straight angle, let the diminishing side be (AB), while $\measuredangle BAC$ tends to approach a straight angle. Then, as neither $\overline{BC}$ nor $\overline{AC}$ becomes indefinitely great, we see that A must be very close to some point of the extension of (AB) beyond A, or to A itself. If C do not approach A, we may apply 1 to show that $\measuredangle ACB$ becomes infinitesimal. If C do approach A we may take D the middle point of (AC) and extend (BD) to E beyond D so that $\overline{DE} \equiv \overline{EB}$. Then we may apply

e.g. those lacking our strong axiom of continuity. Cf. Dehn, 'Die Legendre'schen Sätze über die Winkelsumme im Dreiecke', *Mathematische Annalen*, vol. liii, 1900, and R. L. Moore, 'Geometry in which the sum of the angles of a triangle is two right angles', *Transactions of the American Mathematical Society*, vol. viii, 1907.

[13]The three hypotheses were certainly familiar to Saccheri (loc. cit.), though the credit for discovering the hyperbolic system is generally given to Gauss, who speaks of it in a letter to Bolyai written in 1799. Lobatchewsky's first work was published in Russian in Kasan, in 1829. This was followed by an article 'Géométrie imaginaire', *Crelle's Journal*, vol. xvii, 1837. All spellings of Lobatchewsky's name in Latin or Germanic languages are phonetic. The author has seen eight or ten different ones.

[14]Riemann, *Ueber die Hypothesen, welche der Geometrie zu Grunde liegen*, first read in 1854; see p. 272 of the second edition of his *Gesammelte Werke*, with explanations in the appendix by Weber.

Euclid's own proof[15] that the exterior angle of a triangle is greater than either opposite interior one, so that the exterior angle at A which is infinitesimal, is yet greater than $\measuredangle ACB$.

Theorem 18. If, in any system of triangles, one side of each may be made less than any assigned segment, all thus diminishing together, while no side becomes indefinitely great, the geometry of these triangles may be made to differ from the geometry of the euclidean hypothesis by as little as may be desired.

A specious, if loose, way of stating this theorem is to say that in the infinitesimal domain, we have euclidean geometry.[16]

[15]Euclid, Book I, Proposition 16.

[16]This theorem, loosely proved, is taken as the basis of a number of works on non-euclidean geometry, which start in the infinitesimal domain, and work to the finite by integration. Cf. e.g. Flye Ste-Marie, *Études analytiques sur la théorie des parallèles*, Paris, 1871.

CHAPTER IV

THE INTRODUCTION OF TRIGONOMETRIC FORMULAE

The first fundamental question with which we shall have to deal in this chapter is the following. Suppose that we have an isosceles, birectangular quadrilateral $ABCD$, whose right angles are at A and B. Suppose, further, that $\overline{AB}$ becomes infinitesimally small, $\overline{AD}$ remaining constant; what will be the limit of the fraction $\frac{\mathrm{M}\,\overline{CD}}{\mathrm{M}\,\overline{AB}}$ where $\mathrm{M}\,\overline{XY}$ means the measure of $\overline{XY}$ in terms of some convenient unit.[17] But, first of all, we must convince ourselves, that, when $\overline{AD}$ is given we may always construct a suitable quadrilateral; secondly, and most important, we must show that a definite limit does necessarily exist for this ratio, as $\overline{AB}$ decreases towards the null distance.

Theorem 1. If AD and AX be two mutually perpendicular lines we may find such a point B on either half of AX bounded by A, that, a line being drawn perpendicular to AB at any point P of (AB) we may find on the half thereof bounded by P, which lies in the same half-plane bounded by AB as does D, a point whose distance from P is greater than $\overline{AD}$.

Let E be a point of the extension of (AD) beyond D. Draw a line there perpendicular to AD. If B be a point of AX very close to A, and if a line perpendicular to AB at P of (AB), meet the perpendicular at E at a point Q, $\overline{PQ}$ differs but little from $\overline{AE}$, and, hence, is greater than $\overline{AD}$.

The net result of theorem 1 is this. If AD be given, and the right $\measuredangle DAX$, any point of AX very near to A may be taken as the vertex of a second right angle of an isosceles birectangular quadrilateral, having A as the vertex of one right angle, and (AD) as one of the congruent sides.

Definition. We shall say that a distance may be made infinitesimal compared with a second distance, if the ratio of the measure of the first to that of the second may be made less than any assigned value.

Theorem 2. If in a triangle whereof one angle is constant, a second angle may be made as *small* as desired, the side opposite this angle will be infinitesimal compared to the other sides of the triangle.

Suppose that we have, in fact, $\triangle PQR$ with $\measuredangle PQR$ fixed, while $\measuredangle PRQ$ becomes infinitesimal. It is clear that one of the angles $\measuredangle PQR$ or $\measuredangle QPR$ must be greater than a right angle. Suppose it be $\measuredangle QPR$. Then, by hypothesis, no matter how large a positive integer n may be, I may find such positions for P and R, that n points Q_i may be found on $|PQ$ so that $\measuredangle PRQ \equiv \measuredangle QRQ_1 \equiv \measuredangle Q_kRQ_{k+1}$, yet $\measuredangle QRQ_n$ is less than any chosen angle. Now if $\overline{RQ}$ remain constantly greater

[17]The general treatment, and several of the actual proofs in this chapter are taken directly from Gérard, *La géométrie non-euclidienne*, Paris, 1892. It has been possible to shorten some of his work by the consideration that we have euclidean geometry in the infinitesimal domain. On the other hand, several important points are omitted by him. There is no proof that the required limit does actually exist, and worse still, he gives no proof that the resulting function of $\mathrm{M}\,\overline{AD}$ is necessarily continuous, thereby rendering valueless his solution of its functional equation.

than a given not null distance, the theorem is perfectly evident. If, on the other hand, $\overline{RQ}$ decrease indefinitely, we may find S on $|PQ$ but not in (PQ), so that $\overline{QR} \equiv \overline{QS}$. Then, as geometry in the infinitesimal domain obeys the euclidean hypothesis, $\measuredangle QRS$ will differ infinitesimally from one half $\measuredangle PQR$. If, then, we require $\measuredangle QRQ_n$ to be less than this last-named amount, Q_n will be within (QS), and $\overline{PQ} < \overline{Q_kQ_{k+1}}$ and $\overline{PQ} < \frac{1}{n}\overline{QR}$. A similar proof holds when $\measuredangle PQR$ is greater than a right angle.

It will follow, as a corollary, that if in any triangle, one angle become infinitesimal, and neither of the other angles approaches a straight angle as a limit, then the side opposite the infinitesimal angle becomes infinitesimal as compared with either of the other sides.

Theorem 3. If in an isosceles birectangular quadrilateral, the congruent sides remain constant in value, while the side adjacent to the two right angles decreases indefinitely, the ratio of the measures of this and the opposite side approaches a definite limit.

It will save circumlocution and involve no serious confusion if, during the rest of this chapter, we speak of the ratio of two distances, instead of the ratio of their measures, and write such a ratio simply $\frac{\overline{PQ}}{\overline{XY}}$. Let us then take the isosceles birectangular quadrilateral $A'ABB'$, the right angles having their vertices at A and B. Let us imagine that A and A' are fixed points, while B is on a fixed line at a very small distance from A. Let C be the middle point of (AB), and let the perpendicular to AB at C meet $(A'B')$ at C', which, by Saccheri's theorem, is the middle point of $(A'B')$. Now, by III. 6, $\measuredangle C'A'A$ differs infinitesimally from a right angle, as $\overline{AC}$ becomes infinitesimal, so that if C_1 be the point of (CC'), or (CC') extended beyond C', for which $\overline{CC_1} \equiv \overline{AA'}$, $\overline{C_1C'} < \frac{1}{n}\overline{A'C'}$. But $\frac{\overline{A'C'}}{\overline{AC}} \equiv \frac{\overline{A'B'}}{\overline{AB}}$. Hence $\frac{\overline{A'C_1}}{\overline{AC}} - \frac{\overline{A'B'}}{\overline{AB}} < \delta$ where δ may be made less than any assigned number. By a repeated use of this process we see that if D be such a point of (AB) that $\overline{AD} = \frac{k}{2^n}\overline{AB}$ and D_1 such a point of the perpendicular at D that $\overline{AA'} \equiv \overline{DD_1}$, then, however small ϵ may be, $\frac{\overline{A'D_1}}{\overline{AD}} - \frac{\overline{A'B'}}{\overline{AB}} < \epsilon$, and what is more, we may take $\overline{AB}$ so small that this inequality shall hold for all such points D at once, for, as $\overline{AB}$ decreases, every ratio $\frac{\overline{A'D_1}}{\overline{AD}}$ gets nearer and nearer to $\frac{\overline{A'B'}}{\overline{AB}}$. Lastly, if P be any point of (AB), and P_1 lie on the perpendicular at P so that $\overline{AA'} \equiv \overline{PP_1}$, we may find one of our points recently called D of such a nature that $\overline{DP_1}$ and $\overline{D_1P_1}$ are infinitesimal as compared with $\overline{AB}$. Hence $\frac{\overline{A'P_1}}{\overline{AP}} - \frac{\overline{A'B'}}{\overline{AB}} < \epsilon$ where ϵ is infinitesimal with $\overline{AB}$. This shows that $\frac{\overline{A'B'}}{\overline{AB}}$ approaches a definite limit, as $\overline{AB}$ approaches the null distance.

This limit is constantly equal to 1 in the euclidean case. In the other cases it is a variable depending on the measure of $\overline{AA'}$. If this measure be x, we may call our limit $\phi(x)$.

Let us next show that the function ϕ is continuous. Take $A'ABB'$ as before, while A_1 and B_1 are respectively on the extensions of (AA'), beyond A', and of (BB') beyond B'. Let the measure of $\overline{AA'}$ be x, while that of $\overline{A'A_1}$ is Δx,

$$\frac{\overline{A'B'}}{\overline{AB}} = \phi(x) + \epsilon, \quad \frac{\overline{A_1B_1}}{\overline{AB}} = \phi(x + \Delta x) + \eta,$$

$$\left| \frac{\overline{A_1B_1} - \overline{A'B'}}{\overline{AB}} \right| = \Delta\phi(x) + \eta - \epsilon.$$

Now $\quad \overline{A_1B_1} < (\overline{A_1A'} + \overline{A'B'}) + \overline{B'B_1}, \quad 2\overline{A_1A'} > |\overline{A_1B_1} - \overline{A'B'}|,$

and, however great m may be, we may take $\overline{A_1A'}$ so small that

$$\overline{A_1A'} < \frac{1}{2m}\overline{AB},$$

then

$$\Delta\phi(x) < \frac{1}{m} + \delta,$$

and, hence, ϕ is a continuous function.

We shall find the actual form of ϕ from its functional equation. Let x be the measure of $\overline{AC}$, $(x - y)$ that of $\overline{AC_1}$, and $(x + y)$ that of $\overline{AC_2}$; where C and C_1 are points within (AC_2). Take a corresponding set of distances upon a line near by, $\overline{BD} \equiv \overline{AC}$; $\overline{BD_1} \equiv \overline{AC_1}$; $\overline{BD_2} \equiv \overline{AC_2}$ while $|AC$ and $|BD$ are in the same half-plane bounded by AB and perpendicular thereto. We know, by 1, that this construction is possible. We shall presently suppose $\overline{AB}$ to be infinitesimal. The perpendicular to CD at C will meet C_2D_2 and C_1D_1 in P and R respectively, while the perpendicular to CD at D will meet these lines at Q and S; the four last-named points will surely exist, if $\overline{AB}$ be very tiny. $\measuredangle CC_2P$ and $\measuredangle CC_1R$ will differ infinitesimally from right angles, so that by 2

$$\left| \frac{\overline{C_2P} - \overline{C_1R}}{\overline{CC_2}} \right| = \epsilon.$$

This infinitesimal ϵ is, in fact, of the second order. For, let us compare ΔCC_2P and ΔCC_1R. $\measuredangle C_1CR \equiv \measuredangle C_2CP$; $\overline{CC_1} \equiv \overline{CC_2}$. Also $\measuredangle CC_2P$ and $\measuredangle CC_1R$ differ infinitesimally. Hence, if, on (CP) or (CP) extended beyond P, we take $\overline{CP'} \equiv \overline{CR}$ we have $\overline{C_2P'} \equiv \overline{C_1R}$; $\overline{C_2P} - \overline{C_1R} < \overline{PP'}$. But $\frac{\overline{PP'}}{\overline{C_2P}} < \delta$ as the angle opposite (PP') is infinitesimal. $\frac{2}{y}\overline{C_2P} = \frac{2}{y}\overline{C_1R} + 2\epsilon$ where ϵ is infinitesimal, as compared with $\text{M}\,\overline{C_2P}$ meaning thereby the measure of $\overline{C_2P}$. Lastly, let us use letters of the type δ, ϵ, η to indicate infinitesimals, and remember that $\overline{AB}$ is an infinitesimal distance.

$$\overline{C_2P} \equiv \overline{D_2Q}, \quad \overline{C_1R} \equiv \overline{D_1S},$$
$$2\overline{C_2P} \equiv |\overline{C_2D_2} - \overline{PQ}|, \quad 2\overline{C_1R} \equiv |\overline{C_1D_1} - \overline{RS}|,$$
$$\overline{CD} \equiv \phi(x)\overline{AB} + \epsilon_1\overline{AB},$$
$$\overline{C_1D_1} \equiv \phi(x-y)\overline{AB} + \epsilon_2\overline{AB},$$
$$\overline{C_2D_2} \equiv \phi(x+y)\overline{AB} + \epsilon_3\overline{AB},$$
$$\overline{PQ} \equiv \phi(\textsc{m}\,\overline{CP})\overline{CD} + \delta_1\overline{CD},$$
$$\overline{RS} \equiv \phi(\textsc{m}\,\overline{CR})\overline{CD} + \delta_2\overline{CD},$$

But $\overline{C_2P} > \overline{CC_2} - \overline{CP}$ and $\overline{C_2P}$ is infinitesimal.

$$\overline{PQ} \equiv \phi(y)\overline{CD} + \delta_3\overline{CD},$$
$$\overline{RS} \equiv \phi(y)\overline{CD} + \delta_4\overline{CD}.$$

Substitute in the first equation connecting $\overline{C_2P}$ and $\overline{C_1R}$

$$[\phi(x+y) + \epsilon_3 - \phi(x)\phi(y) - \phi(x)\delta_3 - \phi(y)\epsilon_1 + \delta_3\epsilon_1]\ \textsc{m}\,\overline{AB} =$$
$$= [\phi(x)\phi(y) + \phi(x)\delta_4 + \phi(y)\epsilon_1 + \delta_4\epsilon_1 - \phi(x-y) - \epsilon_2]\ \textsc{m}\,\overline{AB} + 2y\epsilon.$$

Hence $\phi(x+y) + \phi(x-y) - 2\phi(x)\phi(y) < \eta$ where η may be made less than any assigned value

$$\phi(x+y) + \phi(x-y) = 2\phi(x)\phi(y) \tag{1}$$

This well-known equation may be easily solved. Let us assume that the unit of measure of distance is well fixed

$$\phi(0) = 1, \quad \phi(2x) = 2[\phi(x)]^2 - 1.$$

Let x_1 be a value for x in the interval to which the equation applies, i.e. the measure of an actual distance. We may find k so that $\phi(x_1) = \cos\frac{x_1}{k}$. We have immediately

$$\phi(2x_1) = \cos\frac{2x_1}{k}, \quad \phi\left(\frac{nx_1}{2^m}\right) = \cos\left(\frac{nx_1}{2^m k}\right).$$

We also know that $\phi(x) - \cos\frac{x}{k}$ is a continuous function. If, then, x be any value of the argument, we may find n and m such large integers that $x - \frac{nx_1}{2^m}$ is infinitesimal. Hence $\phi(x) - \cos\frac{x}{k}$ will be less than any assigned quantity, or

$$\phi(x) = \cos\frac{x}{k}. \tag{2}$$

The function cosine has, of course, a purely analytical meaning, i.e. we write

$$\phi(x) = 1 - \frac{x^2}{k^2\,.\,2!} + \frac{x^4}{k^4\,.\,4!} \cdots.$$

Of fundamental importance is the constant k. We shall find that it gives the radius of a sphere (in our usual euclidean geometry) upon which the non-euclidean plane may be developed. We shall, therefore, define the constant $\frac{1}{k^2}$ as the *Measure of Curvature of Space*.[18] To find the nature of the value of k, we see immediately that in the parabolic case $\frac{1}{k^2} = 0$; in the elliptic ϕ is, at most, equal to 1, hence $\frac{1}{k^2}$ is positive. In the hyperbolic case, 1 constitutes a minimum value for ϕ and $\frac{1}{k^2}$ is negative, or k a pure imaginary. Under these circumstances, we may, if we choose, remove all signs of imaginary values from (2) by writing $k' = ik$,

$$\phi(x) = \cosh\left(\frac{x}{k'}\right).$$

As a matter of fact, however, there is little or no gain in doing this.

It is now necessary to calculate another limit, that of the ratio of two simultaneously diminishing sides of a right triangle. Let us, then, suppose that we have a right $\triangle ABC$ whose right angle is $\measuredangle ABC$. We shall imagine that $\overline{AB}$ becomes infinitesimal while $\measuredangle BAC$ is constant. We seek the limit of $\dfrac{\overline{AB}}{\overline{AC}}$.[19] That such a limit will actually exist may be proved by considerations similar to those which established the existence of $\phi(x)$. We leave the details to the reader. The limit is a function of the angle $\measuredangle BAC$, and if θ be the measure of the latter, we may write our function $f(\theta)$; including therein, of course, the possibility that this function should be a constant.

First of all it is incumbent upon us to show that this function is continuous. Take C' on the extension of (BC) beyond C, and let $\Delta\theta$ be the measure of $\measuredangle CAC'$. If $\Delta\theta$ be infinitesimal, then, by 2 $\overline{CC'}$ is infinitesimal as compared with $\overline{AC}$. Hence $\dfrac{\overline{AC'}}{\overline{AB}} - \dfrac{\overline{AC}}{\overline{AB}}$ will become and remain less than any assigned number, and $f(\theta)$ is continuous.

Suppose, now, that we have two half-lines $|OY$, $|OZ$ lying in a half-plane bounded by $|OX$. Let $\measuredangle XOY$ and $\measuredangle XOZ$ be each less than a right angle, and have the measures θ, $\theta + \phi; \phi < \theta$. Take F on $|OZ$, and find B, so that

$$\overline{OF} \equiv \overline{OB}; \quad \measuredangle YOF \equiv \measuredangle YOB,$$

$|OB$ is within the interior angle $\measuredangle XOY$; these points will certainly exist if $\overline{OF}$ be very small. Connect F and B by a line meeting $|OY$ in D, and through F, D, B draw three lines perpendicular to $|OX$, and meeting it in E, C, A respectively, which points also are sure to exist, if $\overline{OF}$ be small enough. C will be separated from the middle point of (EA) by a distance infinitesimal compared with $\overline{EA}$, for the perpendicular to OX at such a point would meet (BF) at a point whose distance from D was infinitesimal as compared with $\overline{OF}$.

[18] This fundamental concept is due to Riemann, loc. cit. We shall consider it more fully in subsequent chapters, notably XIX.

[19] It is strange that Gérard, loc. cit., assumes this ratio from the euclidean case.

$$\frac{\overline{OA}}{\overline{OB}} = f(\theta - \phi) + \epsilon_1,$$
$$\frac{\overline{OC}}{\overline{OB}} = \frac{\overline{OC}}{\overline{OD}} \cdot \frac{\overline{OD}}{\overline{OB}} = f(\theta)f(\phi) + \epsilon_2,$$
$$\frac{\overline{CA}}{\overline{OB}} = f(\theta - \phi) - f(\theta)f(\phi) + \epsilon_3,$$
$$\frac{\overline{OE}}{\overline{OB}} = \frac{\overline{OE}}{\overline{OF}} = f(\theta + \phi) + \epsilon_4$$
$$\frac{\overline{EC}}{\overline{OB}} = f(\theta)f(\phi) - f(\theta + \phi) + \epsilon_5 \cdot \frac{\overline{CA}}{\overline{OB}} - \frac{\overline{EC}}{\overline{OB}} = \delta, \text{infinitesimal.}$$
$$f(\theta + \phi) + f(\theta - \phi) = 2f(\theta)f(\phi).$$

This is the functional equation that we had before, so that $f = \cos\frac{\theta}{l}$ and l must be real. If, then we so choose it that the measure of a right angle shall be $\frac{\pi}{2}$,

$$f(\theta) = \cos\theta.$$

Let us not fail to notice that since $\measuredangle ABC$ is a right angle we have, by III. 17,

$$\lim. \frac{\overline{BC}}{\overline{AC}} = \cos(\frac{\pi}{2} - \theta) = \sin\theta. \tag{3}$$

The extension of these functions to angles whose measures are greater than $\frac{\pi}{2}$ will afford no difficulty, for, on the one hand, the defining series remains convergent, and, on the other, the geometric extension may be effected as in the elementary books.

Our next task is a most serious and fundamental one, to find the relations which connect the measures and sides and angles of a right triangle. Let this be the $\triangle ABC$ with $\measuredangle ABC$ as its right angle. Let the measure of $\measuredangle BAC$ be ψ while that of $\measuredangle BCA$ is θ. We shall assume that both ψ and θ are less than $\frac{\pi}{2}$, an obvious necessity under the euclidean or hyperbolic hypothesis, while under the elliptic, such will still be the case if the sides of the triangle be not large, and the case where the inequalities do not hold may be easily treated from the cases where they do. Let us also call a, b, c the measures of $\overline{BC}$, $\overline{CA}$, $\overline{AB}$ respectively.

We now make rather an elaborate construction.[20] Take B_1 in (AB) as near to B as desired, and A_1 on the extension of (AB) beyond A, so that $\overline{A_1A} \equiv \overline{B_1B}$, and construct $\triangle A_1B_1C_1 \equiv \triangle ABC$, C_1 lying not far from C; a construction which, by 1, is surely possible if BB_1 be small enough. Let B_1C_1 meet (AC) at C_2. $\measuredangle C_1C_2C$ will differ but little from $\measuredangle BCA$, and we may draw C_1C_3

[20]See figure on next page.

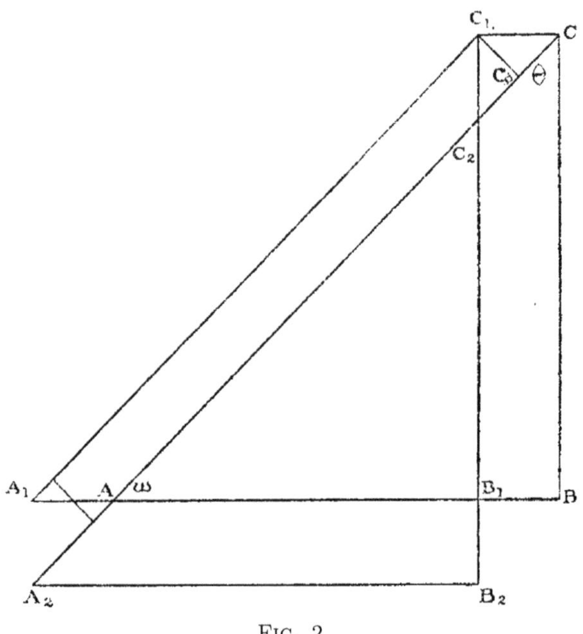

FIG. 2

perpendicular to CC_2, where C_3 is a point of (CC_2). Let us next find A_2 on the extension of (AC) beyond A so that $\overline{A_2A} \equiv \overline{C_2C}$ and B_2 on the extension of (C_1B_1) beyond B_1 so that $\overline{B_1B_2} \equiv \overline{C_1C_2}$, which is certainly possible as $\overline{C_1C_2}$ is very small. Draw A_2B_2. We saw that $\measuredangle C_1C_2C$ will differ from $\measuredangle BCA$ by an infinitesimal (as $\overline{B_1B}$ decreases) and $\angle CC_1B_1$ will approach a right angle as a limit. We thus get two approximate expressions for $\sin\theta$ whose comparison yields

$$\frac{\overline{C_1C_3}}{\overline{C_1C_2}} = \frac{\overline{CC_1}}{\overline{CC_2}} + \epsilon_1 = \frac{\cos\frac{a}{k}\overline{BB_1}}{\overline{CC_2}} + \epsilon_2,$$

for $\overline{CC_1} - \cos\frac{a}{k}\overline{BB_1}$ is infinitesimal in comparison to $\overline{BB_1}$ or $\overline{CC_1}$. Again, we see that a line through the middle point, of (AA_1) perpendicular to AA_2 will also be perpendicular to A_1C_1, and the distance of the intersections will differ infinitesimally from $\sin\psi\overline{AA_1}$. We see that $\overline{C_1C_3}$ differs by a higher infinitesimal from $\sin\psi\cos\frac{b}{k}\overline{AA_1}$, so that

$$\cos\frac{b}{k}\sin\psi\frac{\overline{AA_1}}{\overline{CC_1}} + \epsilon_3 = \frac{\cos\frac{a}{k}\overline{BB_1}}{\overline{CC_2}} + \epsilon_2.$$

Next we see that $\overline{AA_1} \equiv \overline{BB_1}$, and hence

$$\cos\frac{b}{k} = \frac{1}{\sin\psi}\cos\frac{a}{k}\cdot\frac{\overline{C_1C_2}}{\overline{CC_2}} + \epsilon_4.$$

Moreover, by construction $\overline{C_1C_2} \equiv \overline{B_1B_2}$, $\overline{CC_2} \equiv \overline{AA_2}$. A perpendicular to AA_1 from the middle point of (AA_2) will be perpendicular to A_2B_2, and the distance of the intersections will differ infinitesimally from each of these expressions

$$\sin\psi\overline{AA_2}, \qquad \frac{1}{\cos\frac{c}{k}}\overline{B_1B_2}.$$

Hence
$$\cos\frac{b}{k} - \cos\frac{a}{k}\cos\frac{c}{k} < \epsilon,$$

$$\cos\frac{b}{k} = \cos\frac{a}{k}\cos\frac{c}{k}. \tag{4}$$

To get the special formula for the euclidean case, we should develop all cosines in power series, multiply through by k^2, and then put $\frac{1}{k^2} = 0$, getting

$$b^2 = a^2 + c^2$$

the usual Pythagorean formula.

We have now a sufficient basis for trigonometry, the development whereof merely requires a little analytic skill. It may not perhaps be entirely a waste of time to work out some of the fundamental formulae. Let A, B, C be the vertices of a triangle, and let us use these same letters, as is usual in elementary work, to indicate the measures of the corresponding angles, while the measures of the sides shall be a, b, c respectively. Begin by assuming that $\measuredangle ABC$ is a right angle so that $B = \frac{\pi}{2}$. Let D be such a point of (AC) that BD is perpendicular to AC; the measures of $\overline{AD}$ and $\overline{CD}$ being b_1 and b_2, while the measure of $\overline{BD}$ is a_1.

$$\cos\frac{b_1}{k} = \frac{\cos\frac{a}{k}}{\cos\frac{a_1}{k}}, \qquad \cos\frac{b_2}{k} = \frac{\cos\frac{c}{k}}{\cos\frac{a_1}{k}},$$

$$\cos\left(\frac{b_1+b_2}{k}\right) = \cos\frac{b}{k} = \cos\frac{a}{k}\cos\frac{c}{k},$$

$$\cos\frac{a}{k}\cos\frac{c}{k}\left(1-\cos^2\frac{a_1}{k}\right) = \sqrt{\cos^2\frac{a_1}{k} - \cos^2\frac{a}{k}}\sqrt{\cos^2\frac{a_1}{k} - \cos^2\frac{c}{k}},$$

$$\cos^2\frac{a}{k} - \cos^2\frac{c}{k}\left(\cos^2\frac{a_1}{k} - 2\right) = \cos^2\frac{a_1}{k} - \cos^2\frac{a}{k} - \cos^2\frac{c}{k},$$

$$\left(1-\cos^2\frac{a_1}{k}\right)\left(1-\cos^2\frac{a}{k}\cos^2\frac{c}{k}\right) = \left(1-\cos^2\frac{a}{k}\right)\left(1-\cos^2\frac{c}{k}\right),$$

$$\sin\frac{a_1}{k}\sin\frac{b}{k} = \sin\frac{a}{k}\sin\frac{c}{k},$$

$$\frac{\sin\frac{a}{k}}{\sin\frac{b}{k}} = \frac{\sin\frac{a_1}{k}}{\sin\frac{c}{k}}.$$

Now proceeding with the $\triangle ADB$ as we did with the $\triangle ABC$ we shall reach two more sines whose ratio is

$$\frac{\sin\frac{a}{k}}{\sin\frac{b}{k}},$$

and so forth. Continuing thus we have in (AB) and (AC) two infinite series of points. Let the reader show that the limit for each series cannot be other than the point A itself. Now we have just seen in (3) that the limit of this ratio is $\sin A$, hence

$$\sin\frac{a}{k} = \sin\frac{b}{k}\sin A. \tag{5}$$

Let the reader deduce from (4) and (5) that

$$\tan\frac{c}{k} = \tan\frac{b}{k}\cos A. \tag{6}$$

$$\cos B = \cos\frac{b}{k}\sin A. \tag{7}$$

Let us next suppose that $\triangle ABC$ is any triangle. If none of the angles be greater than a right angle, we may connect any vertex with a point of the opposite side by a line perpendicular to the line of that side, and we see at once that

$$\sin\frac{a}{k} : \sin\frac{b}{k} : \sin\frac{c}{k} = \sin A : \sin B : \sin C.$$

Let us show that this formula holds universally, even when this construction is not possible. Let us assume that $B > \frac{\pi}{2}$. We may legitimately assume that A and C are less than $\frac{\pi}{2}$, for the extreme case under the elliptic hypothesis where such is not the fact may easily be treated after the simpler case has been taken up. We shall still have

$$\sin\frac{a}{k} : \sin\frac{c}{k} = \sin A : \sin C.$$

Let E be that point of (AC) which makes BE perpendicular to AC. Let the measures of $\overline{AE}$, $\overline{BE}$, and $\overline{CE}$ be a', b', c', while the measure of $\measuredangle ABE$ is A' and that of $\measuredangle CBE$ is C'.

$$\cos A' = \frac{\tan\frac{b'}{k}}{\tan\frac{c}{k}}, \quad \cos C' = \frac{\tan\frac{b'}{k}}{\tan\frac{a}{k}},$$

$$\sin A' = \frac{\sin\dfrac{a'}{k}}{\sin\dfrac{c}{k}}, \quad \sin C' = \frac{\sin\dfrac{c'}{k}}{\sin\dfrac{a}{k}},$$

$$\sin B = \sin(A' + C') = \frac{\tan\dfrac{b'}{k}}{\sin\dfrac{a}{k}\sin\dfrac{c}{k}}\left(\cos\frac{c}{k}\sin\frac{c'}{k} + \cos\frac{a}{k}\sin\frac{a'}{k}\right),$$

$$\cos\frac{c}{k} = \cos\frac{a'}{k}\cos\frac{b'}{k}, \quad \cos\frac{a}{k} = \cos\frac{c'}{k}\cos\frac{b'}{k},$$

$$\sin B = \frac{\sin\dfrac{b'}{k}}{\sin\dfrac{a}{k}\sin\dfrac{c}{k}}\sin\left(\frac{a'}{k} + \frac{c'}{k}\right),$$

$$a' + c' = b; \quad \sin\frac{b'}{k} = \sin\frac{a}{k}\sin C = \sin\frac{c}{k}\sin A,$$

$$\frac{\sin\dfrac{a}{k}}{\sin A} = \frac{\sin\dfrac{b}{k}}{\sin B} = \frac{\sin\dfrac{c}{k}}{\sin C}. \tag{8}$$

Once more let us suppose that no angle of our triangle is greater than a right angle, and let D be such a point of (BC) that AD is perpendicular to BC:

$$\begin{aligned}
\cos\frac{b}{k} &= \frac{\cos\dfrac{\mathrm{M}\,\overline{DC}}{k}\cos\dfrac{c}{k}}{\cos\dfrac{\mathrm{M}\,\overline{BD}}{k}} \\
&= \frac{\cos\dfrac{c}{k}}{\cos\dfrac{\mathrm{M}\,\overline{BD}}{k}}\left[\cos\frac{a}{k}\cos\frac{\mathrm{M}\,\overline{BD}}{k} + \sin\frac{a}{k}\sin\frac{\mathrm{M}\,\overline{BD}}{k}\right] \\
&= \cos\frac{a}{k}\cos\frac{c}{k} + \sin\frac{a}{k}\sin\frac{c}{k}\cos B.
\end{aligned}$$

If $B > \dfrac{\pi}{2}$ this proof is invalid. Here, however, following our previous notation

$$\cos B = \cos(A' + C') = \frac{\tan^2\dfrac{b'}{k}\cos\dfrac{a}{k}\cos\dfrac{c}{k} - \sin\dfrac{a'}{k}\sin\dfrac{c'}{k}}{\sin\dfrac{a}{k}\sin\dfrac{c}{k}},$$

$$\cos\frac{a}{k} = \cos\frac{b'}{k}\cos\frac{c'}{k}, \quad \cos\frac{c}{k} = \cos\frac{b'}{k}\cos\frac{a'}{k}, \quad b = a' + c',$$

$$\cos B = \frac{\sin^2\dfrac{b'}{k}\cos\dfrac{a'}{k}\cos\dfrac{c'}{k} - \sin\dfrac{a'}{k}\sin\dfrac{c'}{k}}{\sin\dfrac{a}{k}\sin\dfrac{c}{k}}$$

$$= \frac{\cos\frac{b}{k} - \cos\frac{a}{k}\cos\frac{c}{k}}{\sin\frac{a}{k}\sin\frac{c}{k}},$$

$$\cos\frac{b}{k} = \cos\frac{a}{k}\cos\frac{c}{k} + \sin\frac{a}{k}\sin\frac{c}{k}\cos B. \tag{9}$$

A correlative formula may be deduced as follows:[21]

Let
$$\frac{\sin\frac{a}{k}}{\sin A} = \frac{\sin\frac{b}{k}}{\sin B} = \frac{\sin\frac{c}{k}}{\sin C} = \lambda \neq 0,$$

$$\cos^2\frac{b}{k} + \lambda^4\sin^2 A\sin^2 C\cos^2 B - 2\lambda^2\sin A\sin C\cos B\cos\frac{b}{k} = \\ = \cos^2\frac{a}{k}\cos^2\frac{c}{k},$$

$$1 - \lambda^2\sin^2 B + \lambda^4\sin^2 A\sin^2 C\cos^2 B - 2\lambda^2\sin A\sin C\cos B\cos\frac{b}{k} = \\ = 1 - \lambda^2\sin^2 A - \lambda^2\sin^2 C + \lambda^4\sin^2 A\sin^2 C,$$

$$\sin^2 A + \sin^2 C - \sin^2 B \quad = \sin^2 A\sin^2 C\sin^2\frac{b}{k} + 2\sin A\sin C\cos B\cos\frac{b}{k},$$

$$1 - \sin^2 A - \sin^2 C + \sin^2 A\sin^2 C \\ = \sin^2 A\sin^2 C\cos^2\frac{b}{k} - 2\sin A\sin C\cos\frac{b}{k}\cos B + \cos^2 B,$$

$$\cos A\cos C = \cos\frac{b}{k}\sin A\sin C - \cos B,$$

$$\cos B = -\cos A\cos C + \sin A\sin C\cos\frac{b}{k}.\text{[22]} \tag{10}$$

If $ABCD$ be an isosceles birectangular quadrilateral, the right angles being at A and B,

$$\cos\frac{\text{M}\,\overline{CD}}{k} = \cos\frac{\text{M}\,\overline{AC}}{k}\cos\frac{\text{M}\,\overline{BD}}{k}\cos\frac{\text{M}\,\overline{AB}}{k} + \sin\frac{\text{M}\,\overline{AC}}{k}\sin\frac{\text{M}\,\overline{BD}}{k}. \tag{11}$$

The proof of this is left to the reader, as well as the task of showing that the formulae which we have here established are identical with those for a euclidean sphere of radius k. Let him also show that when $\frac{1}{k^2} = 0$, our formulae pass over into those for the euclidean plane.

[21] I owe this ingenious trigonometric analysis to my former pupil Dr. Otto Dunkel.

[22] In finding this formula we have extracted a square root. To be sure that we have taken the right sign, we have but to consider the limiting case $A = 0, B = \pi - C$.

CHAPTER V

ANALYTIC FORMULAE

At the beginning of Chapter I we posited the existence of two undefined objects, points and distances. Between the two existed the relation that the existence of two points implied the existence of a single object, their distance. In this relation the two points entered symmetrically.

These concepts may be further sharpened as follows. Leaving aside the trivial case of the null distance, let us imagine that a distinction is made between the two points, the one being called the *initial* and the other the *terminal* point. The concept distance, where this distinction is made between the two points shall be called a *directed distance*, or, more specifically, the directed distance from the initial to the terminal point. Any not null distance will, thus, determine two directed distances. The directed distance from A to B shall be written $\overrightarrow{AB}$. The relations congruent to, greater than, and less than, when applied to directed distances, shall mean that the corresponding distances have these relations.

Suppose that we have two congruent segments (AB) and $(A'B')$ of the same line. It may be that a congruent transformation which carries the line into itself, and transforms A and B into A' and B', also transforms A' into A. In this case the middle point of (AA') will remain invariant, the extremities of every segment having this middle point will be interchanged. Such a transformation shall be called a *reflection* in this middle point. Conversely, we easily see that a congruent transformation whereby A goes into A', and one other point of (AA') also goes into a point of that segment, is a reflection in the middle point of the segment.

There are, however, other congruent transformations of the line into itself besides reflections. For if A go into A', and any point of (AA') go into a point not of (AA'), then A will be the only point of (AA') which goes into a point thereof, there will be no invariant point on the line, and we have a different form of congruent transformation called a *translation*. It is at once evident that every congruent transformation of the line into itself is either a reflection or a translation. The inverse of a translation is another translation; the inverse of a reflection is the reflection itself.

Theorem 1. The product of two translations is a translation. The assemblage of all translations is a group.

We see, to begin with, that every congruent transformation has an inverse. This premised, suppose that we have a translation whereby A goes into A', and a second whereby A' goes into A''. We wish to show that the product of these two is not a reflection. Suppose, in fact, that it were. A point P_1 of (AA'') close to A must then go into another point P_3 of (AA'') close to A''. If A' be a point of (AA''), the first translation will carry P_1 into P_2 a point of $(A'A'')$, and as P_3 is also a point of $(A'A'')$ the second transformation would be a reflection, and not a translation. If A were a point of $(A'A'')$, P_2 would be a point of (AA'), and hence of $(A'A'')$, leading to the same fallacy. If A'' were a point of (AA'),

P_2 would belong to the extension of $(A'A'')$ beyond A', and P_3 would belong to $(A'A'')$ and not to (AA'').

Let the reader show that the product of a reflection and a translation is a reflection, and that the product of two reflections is a translation.

Definition. Two congruent directed distances of the same line shall be said to have the same *sense*, if the congruent transformation which carries the initial and terminal points of the one into the initial and terminal points of the other be a translation. They shall be said to have *opposite senses* if this transformation be a reflection. The following theorem is obvious—

Theorem 2. The two directed distances determined by a given distance have opposite senses.

Suppose, next, that we have two non-congruent directed distances $\overrightarrow{AB}$, $\overrightarrow{A'C'}$ upon the same line, so that $\overline{A'C'} > \overline{AB}$. There will then (XIII) be a single such point B' of $(A'C')$ that $\overline{AB} \equiv \overline{A'B'}$. If then, $\overrightarrow{AB}$ and $\overrightarrow{A'B'}$ have the same sense, we shall also say that $\overrightarrow{AB}$ and $\overrightarrow{A'C'}$ have the *same sense*, or *like senses*. Otherwise, they shall be said to have *opposite senses*. The group theorem for translations gives at once—

Theorem 3. Two directed distances which have like or opposite senses to a third, have like senses to one another, and if two directed distances have like senses, a sense like (opposite) to that of one is like (opposite) to that of the other, while if they have opposite senses, a sense like (opposite) to that of one is opposite (like) to that of the other.

Let us now make suitable conventions for the measurement of directed distances. We shall take for the absolute value of the measure of a directed distance, the measure of the corresponding distance. Opposite directed distances of the same line shall have measures with opposite algebraic signs. If, then, we assign the measure for a single directed distance of a line, that of every other directed distance thereof is uniquely determined. If, further, we choose a fixed origin D upon a line and a fixed unit for directed distances, every point P of the line will be completely determined by a single coordinate

$$x = \sin \frac{\mathrm{M}\,\overrightarrow{OP}}{k}.$$

In an entirely similar spirit we may enlarge our concepts of angle, and dihedral angle, to directed angle. We choose an initial and a terminal side or face, and define as rotations a certain one parameter, group of congruent transformation which keep the vertex or edge invariant. We thus arrive at the concept for sense of an angle, and set up a coordinate system for half-lines or half-planes of common bound. If in the $\measuredangle ABC$, $|AB$ be taken as initial side, the resulting directed angle shall be written $\measuredangle\overrightarrow{ABC}$.

We have at last elaborated all of the machinery necessary to set up a coordinate system in the plane, and nearly all that is necessary to set up coordinates in space. Let us begin with the plane, and choose two half-lines $|OX$, $|OY$ making a right angle. Their lines shall naturally be called the *coordinate axes*, while O is the *origin*. Let P be any point of the plane, the measure of $\overrightarrow{OP}$ being ρ, while those of $\measuredangle \overrightarrow{XOP}$ and $\measuredangle \overrightarrow{YOP}$ are α and β respectively. We may then put

$$\begin{aligned} \xi &= k \sin \frac{\rho}{k} \cos \alpha, \\ \eta &= k \sin \frac{\rho}{k} \cos \beta, \\ \omega &= \cos \frac{\rho}{k}, \end{aligned} \tag{1}$$

with the further equation

$$\xi^2 + \eta^2 + k^2\omega^2 = k^2.$$

In practice it is better to use in place of ξ, η, ω homogeneous coordinates defined as follows:—

$$\begin{aligned} \omega &= \frac{x_0}{\sqrt{{x_0}^2 + {x_1}^2 + {x_2}^2}}, \\ \xi &= \frac{kx_1}{\sqrt{{x_0}^2 + {x_1}^2 + {x_2}^2}}, \\ \eta &= \frac{kx_2}{\sqrt{{x_0}^2 + {x_1}^2 + {x_2}^2}}. \end{aligned} \tag{2}$$

What shall we say as to the signs to be attached to the radicals appearing in these denominators? In the hyperbolic case ω is essentially positive, so that the radical must have the same sign as x_0. In the elliptic case it is not possible to have two points, one with the coordinates ξ, η, ω and the other with the coordinates $-\xi$, $-\eta$, $-\omega$, for their distance would be $k\pi$, and the opposite angle of every triangle containing them both would be straight, i.e. they might be connected by many straight lines. On the other hand, it is not possible that ξ, η, ω and $-\xi$, $-\eta$, $-\omega$ should refer to the same point, for then that point would determine with itself two distinct distances, which is contrary to Axiom II. Hence, in every case, the radical must have a well-defined sign in order that equations should give a point of our space.

In the limiting parabolic case

$$\xi = \rho \cos \alpha, \quad \eta = \rho \cos \beta, \quad \omega = 1.$$

The formula for the distance of two points P and P' with coordinates (x), (x') is

$$\begin{aligned} \cos \frac{{}_{\mathrm{M}}\overline{PP'}}{k} &= \cos \frac{\rho}{k} \cos \frac{\rho'}{k} + \sin \frac{\rho}{k} \sin \frac{\rho'}{k} \cos (\alpha' - \alpha) \\ &= \omega\omega' + \frac{\xi\xi' + \eta\eta'}{k^2}. \\ \cos \frac{{}_{\mathrm{M}}\overline{PP'}}{k} &= \frac{x_0{x_0}' + x_1{x_1}' + x_2{x_2}'}{\sqrt{{x_0}^2 + {x_1}^2 + {x_2}^2}\,\sqrt{{x_0}'^2 + {x_1}'^2 + {x_2}'^2}} \end{aligned} \tag{3}$$

$$\sin\frac{{}_{\mathrm{M}}\overline{PP'}}{k} = \frac{\sqrt{\left\|\begin{matrix} x_0 & x_1 & x_2 \\ x_0' & x_1' & x_2' \end{matrix}\right\|^2}}{\sqrt{{x_0}^2+{x_1}^2+{x_2}^2}\sqrt{{x_0'}^2+{x_1'}^2+{x_2'}^2}} \tag{4}$$

The signs of the radicals in the denominators are, as we have seen, well determined. The sign of the radical in the numerator of (4), should be so taken as to give a positive value to the whole. Should we seek the measures of directed distances on the line PP', then, after the adjunction of the value of the sign of a single directed distance, that of every other is completely determined. In the euclidean case

$${}_{\mathrm{M}}\overline{PP'} = \frac{1}{x_0x_0'}\sqrt{(x_1x_0'-x_0x_1')^2+(x_2x_0'-x_0x_1')^2}.$$

Returning to (4) and putting $x_i' = x_i + dx_i$ we get for the infinitesimal element of arc

$$\frac{ds^2}{k^2} = \frac{\left\|\begin{matrix} x_0 & x_1 & x_2 \\ dx_0 & dx_1 & dx_2 \end{matrix}\right\|^2}{({x_0}^2+{x_1}^2+{x_2}^2)^2}.$$

Put $\qquad x = \dfrac{kx_1}{x_0}, \quad y = \dfrac{kx_2}{x_0}, \quad x' = x+dx, \quad y' = y+dy,$

$$ds^2 = \frac{dx^2+dy^2+\dfrac{(ydx-xdy)^2}{k^2}}{\left[1+\dfrac{x^2+y^2}{k^2}\right]^2}. \tag{5}$$

In the limiting euclidean case $\dfrac{1}{k^2}=0$,

$$ds^2 = dx^2+dy^2.$$

Returning to the general case, we may improve our formula (5) as follows:—

let $\qquad z = \sqrt{k^2+x^2+y^2}, \quad dz = \dfrac{xdx+ydy}{\sqrt{k^2+x^2+y^2}}.$

If $\qquad dx^2+dy^2-dz^2 = d\sigma^2, \quad ds = \dfrac{kd\sigma}{z}.$

Put $\qquad u = \dfrac{2kx}{k-z}, \quad v = \dfrac{2ky}{k-z}.$

$$1+\frac{u^2+v^2}{4k^2} = \frac{-2z}{k-z},$$

$$\begin{aligned} du^2+dv^2 = {} & \frac{4k^2}{(k-z)^4}[(k-z)^2[dx^2+dy^2] \\ & +2(k-z)(xdx+ydy)dz+(x^2+y^2)dz^2], \end{aligned}$$

$$\frac{(k-z)^2}{4k^2}(du^2+dv)^2 = \left[dx^2+dy^2+\frac{2z dz^2}{k-z}-\frac{k^2-z^2}{(k-z)^2}dz^2\right]$$
$$= d\sigma^2.$$
$$du^2+dv^2 = ds^2\frac{4z^2}{(k-z)^2},$$
$$ds^2 = \left[1+\frac{u^2+v^2}{4k^2}\right]^{-2}(du^2+dv^2)\,. \qquad (6)$$

Comparing this with the usual distance formula

$$ds^2 = Edu^2+2F du\, dv+Gdv^2,$$
$$F=0, \quad E=G=\left[1+\frac{u^2+v^2}{4k^2}\right]^{-2}.$$

Now if K be the measure of curvature of the surface having this distance formula

$$K = -\frac{1}{2E}\Big(\frac{\partial^2\log E}{\partial u^2}+\frac{\partial^2\log E}{\partial v^2}\Big),$$
$$K = \left[1+\frac{u^2+v^2}{4k^2}\right]^2\left[\frac{\left[1+\frac{u^2+v^2}{4k^2}\right]\Big(\frac{1}{2k^2}+\frac{1}{2k^2}\Big)-\frac{u^2}{4k^4}-\frac{v^2}{4k^4}}{\left[1+\frac{u^2+v^2}{4k^2}\right]^2}\right],$$
$$K = \frac{1}{k^2}.$$

Theorem 4. The non-euclidean plane may be developed upon a surface of constant curvature $\frac{1}{k^2}$ in euclidean space.

We shall return to questions of this sort in Chapters XV and XIX[23] of this work.

Let us now take up coordinates in three dimensions. We must make some preliminary remarks about the direction cosines of a half-line. Suppose, in fact, that we have three mutually perpendicular half-lines, $|OX$, $|OY$, $|OZ$, and a fourth half-line $|OP$. The angles $\measuredangle XOP$, $\measuredangle YOP$, $\measuredangle ZOP$ whose measures shall be α, β, γ respectively, shall be called the *direction angles* of the half-line $|OP$. These angles are not directed, but this will cause no inconvenience, as we shall introduce them merely through the expressions $\cos\alpha$, $\cos\beta$. $\cos\gamma$. These shall be called the *direction cosines* of the half-line, O shall be the origin, and OX, OY, OZ the coordinate axes, while the planes determined by them are the

[23]The idea of interpreting the non-euclidean plane as a surface of constant curvature in euclidean space must certainly have been present to Riemann's mind, loc. cit. The credit for first setting the matter in a clear light is, however, due to Beltrami. See his 'Teoria fondamentale degli spazii di curvatura constante', *Annali di Matematica*, Serie 2, vol. ii, 1868, and 'Saggio d'interpretazione della geometria non-euclidea', *Giornale di Matematiche*,vol. vi, 1868.

coordinate planes. Take a second half-line $|OP'$, with direction cosines $\cos\alpha'$, $\cos\beta'$, $\cos\gamma'$. We shall imagine that $\overline{OP}$ and $\overline{OP'}$ are infinitesimal. Under these circumstances, we may find A, B, C where perpendiculars to the axes through P meet them, and A', B', C' bearing the same relation to P'. Let Q' be that point of $|OP'$ which makes $\measuredangle PQ'O$ a right angle, and let $\measuredangle POP'$ have a measure θ. Now we know that geometry in the infinitesimal domain obeys the euclidean hypothesis, hence we have

$$\text{M}\,\overline{OQ'} = \text{M}\,\overline{OP}\cos\theta + \epsilon,$$

the ϵ is infinitesimal as compared with $\text{M}\,\overline{OP}$. In the same spirit

$$\text{M}\,\overline{OQ'} = \text{M}\,\overline{OA}\cos\alpha' + \text{M}\,\overline{OB}\cos\beta' + \text{M}\,\overline{OC}\cos\gamma' + \delta.$$

But clearly
$$\text{M}\,\overline{OA} = \text{M}\,\overline{OP}\cos\alpha + \epsilon, \text{ \&c.}$$

Hence

$$\text{M}\,\overline{OP}\cos\theta = \text{M}\,\overline{OP}[\cos\alpha\cos\alpha' + \cos\beta\cos\beta' + \cos\gamma\cos\gamma'] + \eta,$$

or dividing out $\text{M}\,\overline{OP}$,

$$\cos\theta = \cos\alpha\cos\alpha' + \cos\beta\cos\beta' + \cos\gamma\cos\gamma'. \tag{7}$$

In particular we shall have

$$1 = \cos^2\alpha + \cos^2\beta + \cos^2\gamma. \tag{8}$$

We now set up our coordinate system as follows:—

$$\begin{aligned} \omega &= \cos\frac{\text{M}\,\overline{OP}}{k}, \\ \xi &= k\sin\frac{\text{M}\,\overline{OP}}{k}\cos\alpha, \\ \eta &= k\sin\frac{\text{M}\,\overline{OP}}{k}\cos\beta, \\ \zeta &= k\sin\frac{\text{M}\,\overline{OP}}{k}\cos\gamma, \\ k^2 &= \xi^2 + \eta^2 + \zeta^2 + k^2\omega^2. \end{aligned} \tag{9}$$

From these we pass, as before, to homogeneous coordinates $x_0 : x_1 : x_2 : x_3$. But first we shall introduce a new symbol:

$$(xy) \equiv x_0y_0 + x_1y_1 + x_2y_2 + x_3y_3. \tag{10}$$

We then write

$$\omega = \frac{x_0}{\sqrt{(xx)}}, \quad \eta = \frac{kx_2}{\sqrt{(xx)}},$$

$$\xi = \frac{kx_1}{\sqrt{(xx)}}, \quad \zeta = \frac{kx_3}{\sqrt{(xx)}}. \tag{11}$$

Here, as in the case of the plane, there is no ambiguity arising from the double sign of the radical. There is, however, one modification which we shall occasionally make. We see, in fact, that in the hyperbolic case, since $k^2 < 0$; ξ, η, ζ, ω are real, we must have $(xx) < 0$, and x_0 is a pure imaginary. To remedy this let us write

$$k\dot{x}_0 = x_0, \ \dot{x}_1 = x_1, \ \dot{x}_2 = x_2, \ \dot{x}_3 = x_3.$$

A point will now have real coordinates. This distinction between coordinates (x) and coordinates $(\dot{x})$ shall be consistently maintained in the hyperbolic case.

The cosine of the measure of distance of two points (x) and (y) is easily found. We see at once that we shall have

$$\cos \frac{{}_{\mathrm{M}}\overline{PP'}}{k} = \frac{(xy)}{\sqrt{(xx)}\sqrt{(yy)}}. \tag{12}$$

Let us now see what effect a congruent transformation will have upon our coordinates. First take a congruent transformation keeping the origin invariant. We see at once that the new direction cosines, and so the new coordinates (x'), will be linear functions of the old ones; for a plane through the origin will be characterized by a linear relation connecting the direction cosines of the half-lines with that bound. The variables ξ, η, ζ are thus linearly transformed in such a way that $\xi^2 + \eta^2 + \zeta^2$ has a constant value, while ω is unaltered. Hence x_0, x_1, x_2, x_3 are linearly transformed so that (xx) is an invariant (relative), i.e. they are subjected to an orthogonal substitution.

Let us next suppose that we have a congruent transformation which carries the planes $\xi = 0$ and $\eta = 0$ into themselves, and every half-plane with this axis as bound into itself. The assemblage of all such transformations will form a one-parameter group, and this group may be represented by

$$\begin{aligned}
\omega' &= \omega \cos \frac{d}{k} + \zeta \sin \frac{d}{k}, \\
\xi' &= \xi, \\
\eta' &= \eta, \\
\zeta' &= -\omega \sin \frac{d}{k} + \zeta \cos \frac{d}{k}.
\end{aligned}$$

We see, in fact, that by this transformation every point receives just the coordinates that it would obtain by a translation of the axis OZ into itself through a distance d, so enlarged as to carry into itself every half-plane through that axis. Once more we find that, in the coordinates (x), this will be an orthogonal substitution. Now, lastly, every congruent transformation of space may be compounded out of transformations of these two types. Hence:

Theorem 5. Every congruent transformation of space is represented by an orthogonal substitution in the homogeneous variables $x_0 : x_l : x_2 : x_3$.

In Chapter VIII we shall make a detailed study of these congruent transformations. For the present, let us begin by noticing that the coordinate planes have linear equations, and as we may pass from one of these to any other plane by linear transformations, so the equation of any plane may be written

$$(ux) \equiv u_0x_0 + u_1x_1 + u_2x_2 + u_3x_3 = 0.$$

We see that (xy), (ux), (uv) are concomitants of every congruent transformation, and we shall use them to find expressions for the distance from a point to a plane and the angle between two planes. The existence of the former of these quantities is contingent upon the existence of a point in the plane determining with the given point a line perpendicular to the plane.

Let the plane (u) be that which connects the axis $x_1 = x_2 = 0$ with the point (y). Its equation is $y_2x_1 - y_1x_2 = 0$. The cosines of the angles which this makes with the plane $v_1x_1 = 0$ are the x_2 direction cosines of the two half-lines of OP. If then, the measure of the angle be θ, we have

$$\cos\theta = \frac{y_2}{\sqrt{{y_1}^2 + {y_2}^2}} = \frac{v_1y_2}{\sqrt{{y_1}^2 + {y_2}^2}\,\sqrt{{v_1}^2}} = \frac{(uv)}{\sqrt{(uu)}\,\sqrt{(vv)}}.$$

But both sides of this equation are absolute invariants for all congruent transformations. Hence, we may write, in general:

$$\cos\theta = \frac{(uv)}{\sqrt{(uu)}\,\sqrt{(vv)}}. \tag{13}$$

We find the distance from a point to a plane in the same way. Let the point be (x) and d the distance thence to the point where a perpendicular to the plane $u_1x_1 = 0$ meets it, this being, by definition, the distance from the point to the plane.

$$\sin\frac{d}{k} = \frac{\xi}{k} = \pm\frac{x_1}{\sqrt{(xx)}} = \frac{u_1x_1}{\sqrt{(xx)}\,\sqrt{(uu)}}.$$

Once more we have an invariant form, so that, in general:

$$\sin\frac{d}{k} = \frac{(ux)}{\sqrt{(uu)}\,\sqrt{(xx)}}. \tag{14}$$

The sign of $\sqrt{(xx)}$ is determined. As for that of $\sqrt{(uu)}$, by reversing it, we get opposite directed distances of the same line.

We have now reached the end of the first stage of our journey. Our system of axioms has given us a large body of elementary doctrine, a system of trigonometry, and a system of analytic geometry wherein the fundamental metrical invariants are easily expressed. All of these things will be of use later. At present our task is different. We must show that the system of axioms which has carried us safely so far, will not break down later; i.e. that these axioms are essentially compatible. We must also grapple with a disadvantage which has weighed heavily upon us from the start, rendering trebly difficult many a proof and definition. In Axiom XI we assumed that any segment might be extended beyond either extremity. Yes, but how far may it be so extended? This question we have not attempted to answer, but have dealt with the geometry of such a region as the inside of a sphere, not including the surface. In fact, had we assumed that every segment might be extended a given amount, we should have run into a difficulty, for in elliptic space no distance may have a measure $k\pi$ under our axioms.

The matter may be otherwise stated. Every point will have a set of coordinates in our system. What is the extreme limit of possibility for making points correspond to coordinate sets, and what meaning shall we attach to coordinates to which no point corresponds? We must also adjoin the complex domain for coordinates, and give a new interpretation to our fundamental formulae (12), (13), (14) covering the most general case. Then only shall we be able to continue our subject in the broadest and most scientific spirit.

CHAPTER VI

CONSISTENCY AND SIGNIFICANCE OF THE AXIOMS

The first fundamental question suggested at the close of the last chapter was this. How shall we show that those assumptions which we made at the outset are, in truth, mutually consistent? We need not here go into that elusive question which bothers the modern student of pure logic, namely, whether any set of assumptions can ever be shown to be consistent. All that we shall undertake to do is to point to familiar sets of objects which do actually fulfil our fundamental laws.

Let us begin with the geometry of the euclidean hypothesis, and take as points any class of objects which may be put into one to one correspondence with all triads of values of three real independent variables x, y, z. By the distance of two points we shall mean the positive value of the expression

$$\sqrt{(x'-x)^2+(y'-y)^2+(z'-z)^2}.$$

The sum of two distances shall be defined in the arithmetical sense. It is a perfectly straightforward piece of algebra to show that such a system of objects will obey all of our axioms and the euclidean hypothesis; hence the consistency of our axioms rests upon the consistency of the number system, and that we may take as indubitable. Be it noticed that we have another system of objects which obey all of our axioms if we make the further assumption that

$$x^2+y^2+z^2<1.$$

The net result, so far, is this. If we take our fundamental assumptions and the euclidean hypothesis, points and distances may be put into one to one correspondence with expressions of the above types; and, conversely, any system of geometry corresponding to these formulae will be of the euclidean type. The elementary geometry of Euclid fulfils these conditions. In what immediately follows we shall assume this geometry as known, and employ its terminology.

Let us now exhibit the existence of a system of geometry obeying the hyperbolic hypothesis. We shall take as our class of points the assemblage of all points in euclidean space which lie within, but not upon, a sphere of radius unity. We shall mean by the distance of two points one half the real logarithm of the numerically larger of the two cross ratios which they make with the intersections of their line with the sphere. The reader familiar with projective geometry will see that the segment of two points in the non-euclidean sense will be coextensive with their segment in the euclidean sense, and the congruent group will be the group of collineations which carry this sphere into itself. Lastly, we see that we must be under the hyperbolic hypothesis, for a line is infinitely long, yet there is an infinite number of lines through a given point, coplanar with a given line, which yet do not meet it.

The elliptic case is treated similarly. We take as points the assemblage of all points within a euclidean sphere of small radius, and as the distance of two points $\frac{1}{2i}$ times, the natural logarithm of a cross ratio which they determine with the intersection of their line with the imaginary surface

$$x_0^2 + x_1^2 + x_2^2 + x_3^2 = 0.$$

By a proper choice of the cross ratio and logarithm, this expression may be made positive, as before. The congruent group will be so much of the orthogonal group as carries at least one point within our sphere into another such point. The elliptic hypothesis will prevail, for two coplanar lines perpendicular to a third will tend to approach one another.

We may obtain a simultaneous bird's-eye view of our three systems in two dimensions as follows. Let us take for our class of points the assemblage of all points of a euclidean sphere which are south of the equatorial circle. We shall define the distance of two points in three successive different ways:—

(*a*) The distance of two points shall be defined as the distance which the lines connecting them with the north pole cut on the equatorial plane. A line will be a circle which passes through the north pole. If we interpret the equatorial plane as the Gauss plane, we see that the congruent group will be

$$z' = \alpha z + \beta, \quad \alpha\overline{\alpha} = 1,$$

or rather so much of this group as will carry at least one point of the southern hemisphere into another such point. It is evident from the conformal nature of the transformation from sphere to equatorial plane, that we are under the euclidean hypothesis.

(*b*) The distance of two points shall be defined as one half the logarithm of the cross ratio on the circle through them in a vertical plane which they determine with the two intersections of this circle and the equator. A line here will be the arc of such a circle. The congruent group will be that group of (euclidean) collineations which carries into itself the southern hemisphere. A line will be infinitely long, yet there will be an infinite number of others through any chosen point failing to meet it; i.e. we are under the hyperbolic hypothesis.

(*c*) The distance of two points shall be defined as the length of the arc of their great circle. Non-euclidean lines will be arcs of great circles. Congruent transformations will be rotations of the sphere, and it is easy to see that the sum of the angles of a triangle is greater than a straight angle; we are under the elliptic hypothesis.

We have now shown that our system of axioms is sufficient, for we have been able to introduce coordinates for our points, and analytic expressions for distances and angles. The axioms are also compatible, for we have found actual systems of objects obeying them. Compared with these virtues, all other qualities of a system of axioms are of small import. It will, however, throw considerable light upon the significance of these our axioms, if we examine in part, their mutual independence, by examining the nature of those geometrical systems where first one, and then another of our assumptions is supposed not to hold.

Axiom XIX is popularly known as the axiom of free mobility, or rather, it is the residue of that axiom when we are confined to a limited space. It puts into precise shape the statement that figures may be moved about freely without suffering an alteration either in size or form. We have defined congruent transformations by means of the relation *congruent* which is itself defined in the logical sense, but not descriptively. We might, of course, have proceeded in the reverse order.[24] The ordinary conception in the elementary textbooks seems to be that two figures are congruent if they may be superposed; superposed means that they may be carried from place to place without losing size or shape, and this in turn implies that throughout the transference, each remains congruent to itself.[25]

With regard to the independence of this axiom, we have but to look at any system where the measure of distance in one plane is double that of all the rest of space. A triangle having two vertices in this plane, and one elsewhere, could not be congruently transformed into a triangle of a different sort.

Axiom XVIII is the axiom of continuity. We have laid special stress on it in the course of our work, although the subject of elementary geometry may be pushed very far without its aid.[26] We are not here concerned with the question of the wisdom of such attempts, considered from the didactic point of view. Systems of geometry where this axiom does not hold will occur to every reader; e.g. the Cartesian euclidean system where all points whose coordinates are non-algebraic are omitted. It is interesting to note that whereas the omission of XIX runs directly counter to our sense experience, no amount of observation could tell us whether or no our geometry were continuous.[27]

Axiom XVII is an existence theorem, not holding where the geometry of the plane is alone considered. It is a very curious fact that the projective geometry of the plane is not entirely independent of that of space, for Desargues' theorem that copolar triangles are also coaxal cannot be proved without the aid either of a third dimension, or of the congruent group.[28]

Axiom XVI gives a criterion for circumstances under which two lines must necessarily intersect. It is evident that without some such criterion we should have difficulty in proceeding any distance at all among the descriptive properties of a plane. It is difficult to show the independence of this axiom. The only dense system of geometry known to the writer where it is untrue is the following.[29]

Let us denote by R the class of all rational numbers whose denominators are of the form

$$({a_1}^2+{b_1}^2)({a_2}^2+{b_2}^2)\dots({a_n}^2+{b_n}^2)$$

where a_i and b_i are integers or one may be zero. Let us take as points the

[24]Cf. Pieri, loc. cit.

[25]Cf. Veronese, loc. cit., p. 259, note 1, and Russell, *The Principles of Mathematics*, vol. i, Cambridge, 1903, p. 405.

[26]Cf. Halsted, loc. cit.

[27]Cf. R. L. Moore, loc. cit.

[28]Cf. Hilbert, loc. cit., p. 70; Moulton, 'A simple non-desarguesian plane geometry,' *Transactions of the American Mathematical Society*, vol. iii, 1902; Vahlen, loc. cit., p. 67.

[29]Cf. Levy, loc. cit., p. 32.

assemblage of all points of the euclidean plane whose Cartesian coordinates are rational numbers of the class R. The whole field will be transported into itself by a parallel translation from any one point to any other. Moreover, let x, y and x', y' be the coordinates of two points of the class, where $x^2 + y^2 = x'^2 + y'^2$. We may imagine in fact that

$$x = \frac{p}{s}, \quad y = \frac{q}{s}, \quad x' = \frac{p'}{s}, \quad y' = \frac{q'}{s}, \quad \frac{p^2 + q^2}{s^2} = \frac{p'^2 + q'^2}{s^2}.$$

Then the cosine and sine of the angle which the two points subtend at the origin will be respectively

$$\frac{pp' + qq'}{p^2 + q^2}, \quad \frac{pq' - p'q}{p^2 + q^2},$$

and these are numbers of the class R. The whole field will go into itself by a rotation about the origin. Our system will, therefore, obey XIX. It is of course two-dimensional and not continuous. Moreover XVI will not hold, as the reader will see by easily devised numerical experiments.

There are, also, plenty of geometries of a finite number of points where this axiom does not hold.[30]

Axiom XV is, of course, an existence theorem, untrue in the geometry of a single line.

Axiom XIV gives the fundamental property of straight lines. As an example of a geometry where it does not hold, let us consider the assemblage of all points within a sphere of radius one, and define as the distance of two points the length of an arc of a circle of radius two which connects them. The segment of two points is thus a cigar-shaped region connecting them. We see that the extensions of such a segment and the segment itself do not comprise the segment of two points within the original, and the extensions of the latter. Axioms XII and XIII are also in abeyance, and it seems possible that these three axioms are not mutually independent. The present writer is unable to answer this question.

Axiom XI implies that space has no boundary, and will be untrue of the geometry within and on a sphere.

The first ten axioms amount to saying that distances are magnitudes among which subtraction is always possible, but addition only under restriction.

[30]Veblen, loc. cit., pp. 350-51.

CHAPTER VII

THE GEOMETRIC AND ANALYTIC EXTENSION OF SPACE

We are now in a position to take up the second of those fundamental questions which we proposed at the close of Chapter V, namely, to determine what degree of precision may be given to Axiom XI. This axiom tells us that, popularly speaking, any segment may be extended beyond either end. How far may it be so extended? Are we able to state that there exists a system of geometry, consistent with our axioms, where any segment may be extended by any chosen amount? Or, in more precise language, if $\overline{AB}$ and $\overline{PQ}$ be given, can we always find C so that

$$\overline{AC} \equiv \overline{AB} + \overline{BC}, \quad \overline{BC} \equiv \overline{PQ}.$$

We are already able to answer this question in the euclidean case, and answer it affirmatively. We have seen that there is no inconsistency in that system of geometry, where points are in one to one correspondence with all triads of (real and finite) values of three coordinates x, y, z, and where distances are given by the positive values of expressions of the form

$$\sqrt{(x'-x)^2+(y'-y)^2+(z'-z)^2}.$$

Here, if, as we have said, we restrict the values of x, y, z merely to be real and finite, we have a space under the euclidean hypothesis, where any segment may be extended beyond either extremity by any desired amount. Such a space shall be called *euclidean space*.

The same result will hold in the hyperbolic case. We shall have a consistent geometrical system if we assume that our points are in one to one correspondence with values

$$\dot{x}_0 : \dot{x}_1 : \dot{x}_2 : \dot{x}_3, \quad k^2 < 0,$$
$$k^2\dot{x}_0^2 + \dot{x}_1^2 + \dot{x}_2^2 + \dot{x}_3^2 < 0.$$

Here, also, there will exist on every line distances whose measures will be as large as we please. The space under the hyperbolic hypothesis, where any segment may be extended by any chosen amount shall be called *hyperbolic space*. To put the matter otherwise, we shall have euclidean or hyperbolic geometry if we replace Axiom XII by:—

AXIOM XII$'$. **If the parabolic or hyperbolic hypothesis be true, and if $\overline{AB}$ and $\overline{PQ}$ be any two distances, then there will exist a single point C, such that**

$$\overline{AC} \equiv \overline{AB} + \overline{BC}, \quad \overline{BC} \equiv \overline{PQ}.$$

When we turn to the elliptic case, we find a decidedly different state of affairs. Suppose, in fact, that there is a one to one correspondence between the assemblage of all points, and all sets of real values $x_0 : x_1 : x_2 : x_3$. The distance of two points will depend upon the periodic function

$$\cos^{-1}\frac{(xy)}{\sqrt{(xx)}\sqrt{(yy)}}.$$

If, to avoid ambiguity, we assume that the minimum positive value should be taken for this expression, we should easily find two not null distances, whose sum was a null distance, which would be in disagreement with Axiom X.

The desideratum is this. To find a system of geometry where each point belongs to a sub-class subject to Axioms I–XIX, and the elliptic hypothesis, and where each segment may still be extended by any chosen amount, beyond either end.

AXIOM I. **There exists a class of objects, containing at least two members, called points.**

AXIOM II′. **Every point belongs to a sub-class obeying Axioms I–XIX.**

Definition. Any such sub-class shall be called a *consistent region.*

AXIOM III′. **Any two consistent regions which have a common point, have a common consistent region including this point and all others determining therewith a sufficiently small, not null, distance.**

AXIOM IV′. **If P_0 and P_{n+1} be any two points there may be found a finite number n of points $P_1, P_2, P_3, \ldots P_n$ possessing the property that each set of three successive ones belong to a consistent region, and P_k is within the segment $(P_{k-1}P_{k+1})$.**

Definition. The assemblage of all points of such segments, and all possible successive extensions thereof shall be called a *line.*

An important implication of the last axiom is that any two points may be connected (conceivably in many ways) by a chain of consistent regions, where each successive pair have a consistent sub-region in common. This shows that if we set up a coordinate system like that of Chapter V in any consistent region, we may, by a process of analytic extension, reach a set of coordinates for every point in space. We may also compare any two distances. We have merely to take as unit of measure for one, a distance so small, that a distance congruent therewith shall exist in the first three overlapping consistent regions; a distance congruent with this in the second three and so on to the last region, and then compare the measures of the two distances in terms of the first unit of measure, and the unit obtained from this by the series of congruent transformations. Let the reader show that if once we find $\overline{AB} \overset{>}{\underset{<}{\equiv}} \overline{PQ}$ the same relation will hold if we proceed by any other string of overlapping regions. Having thus defined the congruence of any two distances, we may state our axiom for the extension of a segment, as follows:—

AXIOM V′. **If $\overline{AB}$ and $\overline{PQ}$ be any two distances, there exists a single point C such that $\overline{BC} \equiv \overline{PQ}$, while B is within a segment whose extremities are C and a point of (AB).**

An important corollary from this axiom is that there must exist in the elliptic case a point having any chosen set of homogeneous coordinates (x) not all zero.

For, let (y) be the coordinates of any known point. Consider the line through it whose points have coordinates of the form $\lambda(y) + \mu(x)$. As we proceed along this line, the ratio $\frac{\lambda}{\mu}$ will always change in the same sense, for such will be the case in any particular consistent region. Moreover we may, by our last axiom, find a number of successive points such that the sum of the measures of their distances shall be $k\pi$. Between the first and last of these points the value of $\frac{\lambda}{\mu}$ will have run continuously through all values from $-\infty$ to ∞, and hence have passed through the value 0, giving a point with the required coordinates.

The preceding paragraph suggests two interesting questions. Is it possible that, by varying the method of analytic extension, we might give to any point two different sets of homogeneous coordinates in the same system? Is it possible that two different points should have the same homogeneous coordinates? With regard to the first of these questions, it is a fact that under our hypotheses a point may have several different sets of coordinates, as we shall see at more length in Chapter XVII. For the present it is, however, wiser to limit ourselves to the classical non-euclidean systems, where a point has a unique set of coordinates. We reach the desired limitation by means of the following considerations.

A sufficiently small congruent transformation of any consistent region will effect a congruent transformation of any chosen sub-region, and so of any consistent region including this latter. It thus appears that if two consistent regions have a common sub-region, a sufficiently small congruent transformation of the one may be enlarged to be a congruent transformation of the other. Proceeding thus, if we take any two consistent regions of space, and connect them by a series of overlapping consistent regions, then a small congruent transformation of the one may be analytically extended to operate a congruent transformation in the other. Will the original transformation give rise to the same transformation in the second space, if the connexion be made by means of a different succession of overlapping consistent regions? It is impossible to answer this question *a priori*; we therefore make the following explicit assumption:—

AXIOM VI′. **A congruent transformation of any consistent region may be enlarged in a single way to be a congruent transformation of every point.**

Evidently, as a result of this, a congruent transformation of one consistent region can be enlarged in only one way to be a congruent transformation of any other. Let us next observe that it is impossible that two points of the same consistent region should have the same coordinates in any system. Suppose, on the contrary, that P and Q of a consistent region have the coordinates (x). There will be no limitation involved in assuming that the coordinate axes were set up in this consistent region, and the coordinates of P found directly as in Chapter V, while those of Q are found by an analytic extension through a chain of overlapping consistent regions. Now it is not possible that every infinitesimal congruent transformation which keeps P invariant shall also keep Q invariant, so that a transformation of this sort may be found transforming each overlapping consistent region infinitesimally, and carrying Q to an infinitesimally near point Q'. But in the analytic expression of this transformation, in the form of an orthogonal substitution (in the non-euclidean cases) the values (x) will be invariant, so that Q'' will also have the coordinates (x), and by the same chain of extensions as gave these coordinates to Q. Hence, reversing the order of extensions, when we set up a coordinate system in the last consistent region, that which includes Q and Q', these two points will have the same coordinates. But this is impossible for the coordinate system explained in Chapter V, for a consistent region gives distinct coordinates to distinct points. This proof is independent of Axiom VI$'$.

Our desired uniqueness of coordinate sets will follow at once from the foregoing. For, suppose that a point P have two sets of coordinate values (x) and (x'), not proportional to one another. Every infinitesimal transformation which keeps the values (x) invariant, will either keep (x') invariant, or transform them infinitesimally, let us say, to a set of values (x''). But there is a point distinct from P and close to it which has the coordinates (x''), and this gives two points of a consistent region with these coordinates, which we have just seen to be impossible. Hence, the ratios of the coordinates $(x_0{}')$ must be unaltered by every infinitesimal orthogonal substitution which leaves (x) invariant, i.e. $x_0{}' = \rho x_i$. It is evident, conversely, that if each point have but one set of coordinates, Axiom VI$'$ must surely hold.

It is time to attack the other question proposed above, by supposing that two distinct points shall have the same homogeneous coordinates. They may not lie in the same consistent region, and every congruent transformation which leaves one invariant, will leave the other unmoved also. Let us call two such points *equivalent*. Every line through one of these points will pass through the other. For let a point Q on a line through one of the points have coordinates (y). We may connect it with the other by a line, and the two lines through (Q) lie in part in a consistent region, the coordinates of points on each being represented in the form $\lambda y_i + \mu x_i$. The two lines are identical.

Let us consider the assemblage of all points whose coordinates are linearly dependent on those of three non-collinear points. This assemblage of points may properly be called a *plane*, for those points thereof which lie in any consistent region will lie in a plane as defined in Chapter II. It is clearly a connex assemblage, and will contain every line whereof it contains two non-equivalent points. Let (y), (z), (t) be the coordinates of three points, no two of which are equivalent. Let us consider the point (x) whose coordinates are

$$(ux) = |uyzt|.$$

In the elliptic case, as we have seen, such a point surely exists. In the hyperbolic or parabolic cases, there might not be any such point. It is clear, however, that in these cases there can be no equivalent points. Suppose, in fact, P_0 and P_{n+1} were equivalent. Connect them by a line whereon are P_1, $P_2 \ldots P_n$. Move this line slightly so that the connecting string of points are $P_1{}'$, $P_2{}' \ldots P_n{}'$ very near to the former points. We have constructed two triangles, and $(n-1)$

quadrilaterals, and as we are under the hyperbolic or euclidean hypothesis, the sum of the measures of the angles of all the triangles and quadrilaterals will be less than, or equal to $\pi + (n-1)2\pi + \pi$. But clearly the sum of the measures of the angles at points P_i and P_i' is $2n\pi$, so that the sum of the two angles which the two lines make at P_0 and P_{n+1} is null or negative; an absurd result. Equivalent points can then occur only under the elliptic hypothesis, and there will surely be a point P with the coordinates (x) above.

Let us next make a congruent transformation whereby P goes into an equivalent point P', the plane of $(y)(z)(t)$ goes into itself congruently, for it constitutes the assemblage of all points satisfying the condition $(xX) = 0$, and (xX) is an invariant under every orthogonal substitution. After P has been carried to P', each point of the plane may be returned to its original position by means of a series of congruent transformations, each too small to change P' to an equivalent point, yet keeping the values (x) invariant, coupled, at the end, with a reflection in a plane perpendicular to the given one, in case the determinant of the original orthogonal substitution is negative, and this too will leave P' unchanged. We may therefore pass from P to any equivalent point by a transformation which leaves in place every point of a plane. But there is only one congruent transformation of space which leaves every point of a plane invariant, besides, of course, the identical one. Hence every point in space can have but one equivalent at most.

Our results are, then, as follows. Under the euclidean and hyperbolic hypotheses, there is but one point for each set of coordinates, and our new Axioms I–VI′ will yield us nothing more than euclidean or hyperbolic space. Under the elliptic hypothesis there are two possibilities:—

Elliptic space. This is a space obeying Axioms I–VI′, and the elliptic hypothesis. If n successive segments whose measures are $\frac{k\pi}{n}$ be taken upon a line as indicated in V′, the last extremity of the last segment will be identical with the first extremity of the first. Two lines of the same plane will have one and only one common point, so that no point has an equivalent. We may take as a consistent region the assemblage of all points whose distances from a given point are of measure less than $\frac{k\pi}{4}$. If two points be of such a nature that the expression for the cosine of the measure of the kth part of their distance vanishes, we shall say that the measure of their distance is $\frac{k\pi}{2}$. Two points will always have a determinate distance and a single segment, unless the measure of their distance is $\frac{k\pi}{2}$, in which case they determine two segments with the same extremities. These last two segments may also, with propriety, be called half-lines. The definition of an interior angle given in Chapter II may be retained, but the concept of half-plane is illusory, for a line will not divide the plane. It may, however, be modified much as we have modified the definition of a half-line, and from it a definition built up for a dihedral angle. We leave the details to the reader. An example of elliptic geometry will be furnished by any set of points in one to one correspondence with all sets of homogeneous values

$x_0 : x_1 : x_2 : x_3$ where also $\cos\frac{d}{k} = \frac{(xy)}{\sqrt{(xx)}\sqrt{(yy)}}$. For instance, let us take as points concurrent lines of a four dimensional space (euclidean, for example) and mean by distance the measure of the angle $\leqq \frac{\pi}{2}$ formed by two lines.

Spherical space. This is also a space obeying Axioms I–VI′ and the elliptic hypothesis. Each point will have one equivalent. If n successive congruent distances be taken upon a line whose measures are $\frac{k\pi}{n}$, the last extremity of the last will be equivalent to the first extremity of the first. We may take as a consistent region the assemblage of all points the measures of whose distances from a given point are less than $\frac{k\pi}{2}$. The measure of the distance of two equivalent points shall be defined as the number $k\pi$. Any two nonequivalent points will have a well-defined segment. We may find a definition for a half-line analogous to that given in the elliptic case, and so for half-plane, internal angle, and dihedral angle.

An example of spherical geometry will be furnished by the geometry of a hypersphere in four dimensional euclidean space, meaning by the distance of two points, the length of the shorter arc of a great circle connecting them.

A simple example of a two dimensional elliptic geometry is offered by the euclidean hemisphere, where opposite points of the limiting great circle are considered as identical. A two dimensional spherical geometry is clearly offered by the euclidean sphere.

The elliptic and spherical spaces which we have thus built up are, in one respect, more complete than euclidean or hyperbolic space, in that there is in the first two cases always a point to correspond with every set of real values, not all zero, that may be attached to our four homogeneous coordinates x, while in the latter cases this is not so. We bring our euclidean and hyperbolic geometries up to an equality with the others by extending our concept *point*. Let us begin with the euclidean case where there is a point corresponding to every real set of homogeneous values $x_0 : x_1 : x_2 : x_3$, provided that $x_0 \neq 0$. Now a set of values $0 : y_1 : y_2 : y_3$ will determine at each real point (x) a line, the coordinates of whose points are of the form $\lambda y_i + \mu x_i$, and if (x) be varied off of this line, we get a second line coplanar with the first. Our coordinates $0 : y_1 : y_2 : y_3$ will thus serve to determine a bundle of lines, and this will have exactly the same descriptive properties as a bundle of concurrent lines. We may therefore call the bundle an *ideal point*, and assign to it the coordinates (y). Two ideal points will determine a pencil of planes having the same descriptive properties as a pencil of planes through a common line. We shall therefore say that they determine, or have in common, an *ideal line.* Two lines whose intersection is ideal shall be said to be *parallel*, as also, two planes which meet in an ideal line. These definitions of parallel are for euclidean space only. The assemblage of all ideal points will be characterized by the equation

$$x_0 = 0.$$

This we shall call the equation of the *ideal plane* which is supposed to consist of the assemblage of all ideal points. Ideal points and lines shall also be called *infinitely distant*, while the ideal plane is called the *plane at infinity*. We shall in future use the words *point*, *line*, and *plane* to cover both ideal elements and those previously defined, which latter may be called, in distinction, *actual*. Actual and ideal elements stand on exactly the same footing with regard to purely descriptive properties. No congruent transformation can interchange actual and ideal elements. We shall later return to the meaning of such words as *distance* where ideal elements enter.

In the hyperbolic case we may apply the same principles with slight modification. There will be a real point corresponding to each set of real homogeneous coordinates $(\dot{x})$ for which

$$k^2\dot{x}_0{}^2 + \dot{x}_1{}^2 + \dot{x}_2{}^2 + \dot{x}_3{}^2 < 0.$$

A set of real homogeneous values for $(\dot{x})$, for which this inequality does not hold, will determine a bundle of lines, one through every actual point, any two of which are coplanar; a bundle with the same descriptive properties as a bundle of concurrent lines. We shall therefore say that this bundle determines an ideal point having the coordinates $(\dot{x})$. If

$$k^2\dot{x}_0{}^2 + \dot{x}_1{}^2 + \dot{x}_2{}^2 + \dot{x}_3{}^2 = 0,$$

the ideal point shall be said to be *infinitely distant*. If

$$k^2\dot{x}_0{}^2 + \dot{x}_1{}^2 + \dot{x}_2{}^2 + \dot{x}_3{}^2 > 0,$$

the ideal point shall be said to be *ultra-infinite*. Two lines having an infinitely distant point in common shall be called *parallel*. Through each actual point will pass two lines parallel to a given line. An equation of the type

$$(\dot{u}\dot{x}) = 0, \quad \frac{1}{k^2}\dot{u}_0{}^2 + \dot{u}_1{}^2 + \dot{u}_2{}^2 + \dot{u}_3{}^2 > 0,$$

will give a plane. If the inequality be not fulfilled, the assemblage of all ideal points whose coordinates fulfil the equation (and there can be no actual points which meet the requirement) shall be called an *ideal plane*, the coefficients $(\dot{u})$ being its coordinates. There will thus be a plane corresponding to each set of real homogeneous coordinates $(\dot{u})$ not all zero. An ideal line shall be defined as in the euclidean case, and the distinction between actual and ideal shall be the same as there given. No congruent transformation, as defined so far, can interchange actual and ideal elements.

Let us take account of stock. By the introduction of ideal elements we have made each of our spaces a real analytic continuum. In all but the spherical case there is a one to one correspondence between points and sets of real homogeneous values not all zero, in spherical space there is a one to one correspondence of coordinate set and pair of equivalent points. Each of our spaces will fulfil the fundamental postulates of projective geometry, as we shall develop them in Chapter XVIII, or as they have already been developed elsewhere.[31] Let us show hurriedly, how to find figures to correspond to imaginary coordinate values. Four distinct points will determine six numbers called their *cross ratios*, which have a geometrical significance quite apart from all concepts of distance or measurement.[32] An involution will arise when the points of a line are paired in such a reciprocal manner that the cross ratios of any four are equal to the corresponding cross ratios of their four mates. If there be no self-corresponding points, the involution is said to be *elliptic*. If the points of a line be located by means of homogeneous coordinates $\lambda : \mu$, it may be shown that every involution may be expressed in the form

$$A\lambda\lambda' + B(\lambda\mu' + \lambda'\mu) + C\mu\mu' = 0.$$

In particular if (y) and (z) be the coordinates of two points, there will exist an involution on their line determined by the equations

$$(x) = \lambda(y) + \mu(z), \quad (x)' = \mu(y) - \lambda(z),$$

and by a proper choice of running coordinates any elliptic involution may be put into this form. Did we seek the coordinates of self-corresponding points in this involution, we should get

$$(x) = (y) \pm i(z).$$

Conversely, every set of homogeneous complex values $(y) + i(z)$ will lead us in this way to a definite elliptic involution. The involution may be taken to represent the two sets of conjugate imaginary homogeneous values. We may separate the conjugate values by the following device. It is not difficult to show that if a directed distance be determined by two points, it will have the same sense as the corresponding directed distance determined by their mates in an elliptic involution. To an elliptic involution may thus be assigned either one of two *senses of description*, and we shall define as an imaginary point an elliptic involution to which such a sense has been attached. Had we taken the other sense, we should have said that we had the conjugate imaginary point. An imaginary plane may similarly be defined as an elliptic involution among the planes of a pencil, with a particular sense of description; an imaginary line as the intersection of two imaginary planes. It may be shown geometrically that by introducing imaginary elements under these definitions we have a system of points, lines, and planes, obeying the same descriptive laws of combination as do the real points of lines and planes of projective geometry, or the assemblage of all real homogeneous coordinate sets, which do not vanish simultaneously.[33]

[31]Cf. Pieri, 'I principi della geometria di posizione.' *Memorie della R. Accademia delle Scienze di Torino*, vol. xlviii, 1899.

[32]Cf. Pasch, loc. cit., p. 164, and Chapter XVIII of the present work. The idea of assigning to four collinear points a projectively invariant number originated with Von Staudt, *Beiträge zur Geometrie der Lage,* Part 2, §§ 19–22, Erlangen, 1858–66.

[33]Cf. Von Staudt, loc. cit., § 7, and Lüroth, 'Das Imaginäre in der Geometrie und das Rechnen mit Wurfen,' *Mathematische Annalen*, vol. ix.

Introducing these imaginary expressions, and the corresponding complex values for their homogeneous coordinates, we extend our space to be a perfect analytic continuum.

We must now see what extension must be given to the concept distance, in order to fit the extended space with which we are, henceforth, to deal. To begin with, we shall from this time forth identify the two concepts *distance* and *measure of distance*. In other words, as the concept distance comes into our work effectively only in terms of its measure, i.e. as a number, so we shall save circumlocution by replacing the words *measure of distance* by *distance* throughout. The distance of two points is thus dependent upon the two points, and on the unit. In any particular investigation, however, we assume that the unit is well known from the start, and disregard its existence. We therefore give as the definition of the distance of two points under the euclidean hypothesis

$$d = \frac{1}{x_0 y_0}\sqrt{(x_1 - y_1)^2 + (x_2 - y_2)^2 + (x_3 - y_3)^2}. \tag{1}$$

This is, at worst, a two valued function. When it takes a real value, we give the positive root as the distance, when it is imaginary we may make any one of several simple conventions as to which root to take. If one or both of the points considered be ideal, the expression for distance becomes infinite, unless also the radical vanishes when no distance is determined. Under these circumstances we shall leave the concept of distance undefined, thus getting pairs of points disobeying Axiom II$'$. Notice also that whenever the radical vanishes for non-ideal points we have points which are distinct, yet have a null distance, and when such points are included, Axiom XIII may fail.

We shall in like manner identify the concepts *angle* and *measure of angle* in terms of the unit which gives to a right angle the measure $\frac{\pi}{2}$.

We may proceed in a similar manner in the non-euclidean cases. If (x) and (y) be the coordinates of two points, we shall define as their distance d, the solution of

$$\cos\frac{d}{k} = \frac{(xy)}{\sqrt{(xx)}\,\sqrt{(yy)}}. \tag{2}$$

This equation in d has, of course, an infinite number of solutions. Before taking up the question of which shall be called the distance of the two points, let us approach the matter in a different, and highly interesting fashion due to Cayley.[34] This theory is of absolutely fundamental importance in all that follows.

The assemblage of points whose coordinates satisfy the equation

$$(xx) = 0, \tag{3}$$

shall be called the *Absolute*. This is a quadric surface, real in the hyperbolic case, surrounding, so to speak, the actual domain; imaginary in the elliptic and

[34] Cayley, 'A sixth memoir on Qualities,' *Philosophical Transactions of the Royal Society of London*, 1859.

spherical cases; in the last-named, it is the locus of points which coincide with their equivalents. Every congruent transformation is an orthogonal substitution, i.e. a linear transformation carrying the Absolute into itself. Let us, by definition, enlarge our congruent group so that every such transformation shall be called congruent; certainly it carries a point into a point, and leaves distances unaltered. In the euclidean case we take as *Absolute* the conic

$$x_0 = 0, \quad {x_1}^2 + {x_2}^2 + {x_3}^2 = 0, \tag{4}$$

and define as congruent transformations a certain six-parameter sub-group of the seven-parameter collineation group which carries it into itself. We shall return to the study of the congruent group in the next chapter.

Returning to the non-euclidean cases, let us take two points P_1, P_2 with coordinates (x) and (y), and let the line connecting them meet the Absolute in two points Q_1, Q_2. We obtain the coordinates of these by putting $\lambda(x) + \mu(y)$ into the equation of the Absolute. The ratio of the roots of this equation will give one of the two cross ratios formed by the pair of points P_1P_2 and the pair Q_1Q_2; interchanging the roots we get the other cross ratio of the two pairs of points.[35] The value of such a cross ratio will thus be

$$\frac{(xy) + \sqrt{(xy)^2 - (xx)(yy)}}{(xy) - \sqrt{(xy)^2 - (xx)(yy)}}.$$

By interchanging the signs of the radicals we change this cross ratio into its reciprocal, and this amounts to interchanging the members of one of the two point pairs. Let us denote this expression by $e^{\frac{2id}{k}}$.

$$e^{\frac{id}{k}} = \frac{(xy) + \sqrt{(xx)(yy) - (xy)^2}}{\sqrt{(xx)}\,\sqrt{(yy)}},$$

$$\cos\frac{d}{k} = \frac{(xy)}{\sqrt{(xx)}\,\sqrt{(yy)}}. \tag{5}$$

If we write the cross ratios of the pair of points P_1P_2 and the pair Q_1Q_2 as (P_1P_2, Q_1Q_2), we may re-define our noneuclidean distance by the following theorem:—

Theorem. If d be the distance of two points P_1 and P_2 whose line meets the Absolute in Q_1 and Q_2,

$$d = \frac{k}{2i}\log_e(P_1P_2, Q_1Q_2). \tag{6}$$

The great beauty of this definition is that it brings into clear relief the connexion between distance and the congruent group, for the cross ratio in

[35] For the geometrical interpretation of a cross ratio when some of the elements are imaginary, see Von Staudt, loc. cit., §28, and Lüroth, loc. cit.

question is, of course, invariant under all linear transformation which carry the Absolute into itself, i.e. under all congruent transformations. Let the reader show that a corresponding projective definition may be given for an angle.

Our distances, as so far defined, are infinitely multiple valued functions. There is no great practical utility in rendering them single valued by definition. It is, however, perhaps worth while to carry it through in one case.

If we have two real points of the actual domain, the expression (P_1P_2, Q_1Q_2) will have two values, real in the hyperbolic, pure imaginary in the elliptic and spherical case, and these two are reciprocals, so that the resulting expressions for d will differ only in sign, for each determination of the logarithm. We may therefore take the distance as positive. Did we seek, not for a distance, but a directed distance, then it would be necessary to distinguish once for all between Q_1 and Q_2 and in each particular case between the pair P_1P_2, and the pair P_2P_1, the directed distance will have a definite value sometimes positive, sometimes negative.

Let us specialize by confining ourselves to the hyperbolic case. We have defined the distance of two actual points. Still restricting ourselves to the real domain, suppose that we have an actual and an ultra-infinite point. Let us choose such a unit of measure that $k^2 = -1$. Our cross ratio is here negative, with an absolute value r let us say, so that the distance expression takes the form $\frac{1}{2}[\log r \pm (2m+1)\pi i]$. Let us choose in particular

$$d = \tfrac{1}{2}\log r + \frac{\pi i}{2}.$$

Next consider two ultra-infinite points. If the line connecting them meet the Absolute in real points, we shall have a real cross ratio as before, and hence a real positive distance. If, however, this real line meet the Absolute in conjugate imaginary points, the expression for the cross ratio becomes imaginary, and the simplest expression for their distance is pure imaginary. The absolute value of this expression will run between 0 and $\frac{\pi}{2}$, for the roots of $\frac{1}{2}\log A = X$ differ by πi. We may, hence, represent all of these cross ratios in the Gauss plane by points of the axis of pure imaginaries between 0 and $\frac{\pi}{2}$.

If the line connecting two ultra-infinite points be tangent to the Absolute, the cross ratio is unity, and we may take the distance as zero. The distance from a point of the Absolute to a point not on its tangent will be infinite; the distance to a point on the tangent is absolutely indeterminate, for the cross ratio is indeterminate. We may, in fact, consider the cross ratios of three coincident points and a fourth, as the limiting case of any cross ratio which we please.

Leaving aside the indeterminate case, we are thus able to represent the distance of any two real points of hyperbolic space in the Gauss plane by a point on the positive half of the axis of reals, by a point of the segment of the origin and $\frac{\pi}{2}i$, or by a point of the horizontal half-line $\left|\frac{\pi}{2}i\,\infty\right.$, and as two points move continuously in the real domain of the hyperbolic plane, the points which represent their distance will move continuously on the lines described.

Let us now take two points of the hyperbolic plane, real or imaginary. We see that the roots of $\frac{1}{2}\log A = X$ differ by multiples of πi, so that we may assign to d an imaginary part whose Absolute value $\leqq \dfrac{\pi}{2}$. Moreover, by choosing properly between the two reciprocal values of the cross ratio, we may ensure that the real part of d shall not be negative. If two points be conjugate imaginaries, while their line cuts the Absolute in real points, the cross ratio is imaginary, and the expression for distance is pure imaginary, which we may represent by a point of the segment of the origin and $-\dfrac{\pi}{2}i$. If both pairs of points be conjugate imaginaries, the cross ratio is real and negative, so that the distance may be represented in the form $X-\dfrac{\pi}{2}i$. We shall define as the distance of two points that value of the logarithm of a cross ratio which they form with the intersection of their line and the Absolute, which in the Gauss plane is represented by a point of the infinite triangle whose vertices are ∞, $0+\dfrac{\pi}{2}i$, $0-\dfrac{\pi}{2}i$. The possible ambiguities for points on the sides of this triangle have already been removed by definition.

We have already seen that when euclidean space has been enlarged to be a perfect analytic continuum, imaginary points and distances come in which do not obey all of our axioms. In the hyperbolic case we shall find real, though ultra-infinite, points which do not at all obey the principles laid down for a consistent region.[36] Let us take three points of the ultra-infinite region of the actual hyperbolic plane $x_3 = 0$, say (x), (y), (z). As these points are supposed to be real we may assume that x_1, x_2 are real, while x_0 is a pure imaginary, and that a like state of affairs exists for (y) and (z). We shall further assume that the lines connecting them shall intersect the Absolute in real, distinct points. We have then

$$\begin{aligned} &(yz)^2-(yy)(zz)>0, \quad (xx)>0,\\ &(zx)^2-(zz)(xx)>0, \quad (yy)>0,\\ &(xy)^2-(xx)(yy)>0, \quad (zz)>0. \end{aligned} \tag{7}$$

Let us, for the moment, indicate the distance from (x) to (y) by $\overline{xy}$, and assume

$$\overline{yz} \geqq \overline{zx} \geqq \overline{xy}.$$

We shall also take

$$h=i, \quad \cos\frac{d}{k}=\cosh d.$$

Under what circumstances shall we have?

$$\overline{yz} \geqq \overline{zx}+\overline{xy},$$

$$\cosh(\overline{yz}-\overline{zx}) \geqq \cosh\overline{xy},$$

[36]The developments which follow are taken from Study, 'Beiträge zur nicht-euklidischen Geometrie.' *American Journal of Mathematics*, vol. xxix, 1907.

$$\sqrt{\frac{(yz)^2}{(yy)(zz)}}\sqrt{\frac{(zx)^2}{(zz)(xx)}} - \sqrt{\frac{(xy)^2}{(xx)(yy)}}$$
$$\geqq \sqrt{\frac{(yz)^2 - (yy)(zz)}{(yy)(zz)}}\sqrt{\frac{(zx)^2 - (zz)(xx)}{(zz)(xx)}}.$$

The terms on the left are essentially positive as they represent hyperbolic cosines, those on the right are positive, being hyperbolic sines; we may therefore square the inequality

$$(xx)(yy)(zz) + 2|(yz)(zx)(xy)| - (xx)(yz)^2 - (yy)(zx)^2 - (zz)(xy)^2 \leqq 0. \quad (8)$$

We see that if

$$(yz)(zx)(xy) > 0, \quad (9)$$

we are at liberty to drop the absolute value signs in the second term, and the whole expression is the square of the determinant $|xyz|$ which is zero or negative. We see, therefore, that under these circumstances,

$$|yz| \geqq |zx| + |xy|.$$

To see what region of the ultra-infinite domain is determined by (9), let us sketch the Absolute as a conic, and draw tangents thereunto from (y) and (z). X must lie within the quadrilateral of these tangents or the vertical angle at (y) or (z). The conic and tangents determine four quasi-triangles with two rectilinear and one curvilinear side each. Since $(yy) > 0$ our inequality (9) will hold within the quasi-triangles whose vertices are (y) and (z) and within the verticals of these two angles.

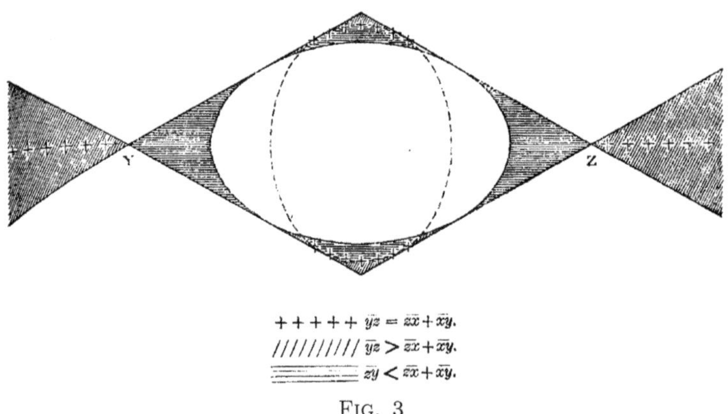

FIG. 3

Let us now assume, on the contrary, that we are in the other quasi-triangles

$$(yz)(zx)(xy) < 0.$$

Our original inequality (8) will still hold if

$$|xyz|^2 - 4(yz)(zx)(xy) < 0, \tag{10}$$

and, conversely, this inequality certainly holds if (7) does. If we look on (y) and (z) as fixed, and (x) as variable, the curve

$$|xyz|^2 - 4(yz)(zx)(xy) = 0,$$

in so far as it lies in the two quasi-triangles we are now considering, will play the part of the segment of (y) and (z).[37] In a region where (8) holds, a rectilinear path is the longest from (y) to (z).

[37]For a complete discussion, see Study, loc. cit., pp. 103–8. Fig. 3 is taken direct.

CHAPTER VIII

THE GROUPS OF CONGRUENT TRANSFORMATIONS

The most significant idea introduced in the last chapter was that of the Absolute, and its connexion with the concept of distance. Every collineation of non-euclidean space which keeps the Absolute in place was defined as a congruent transformation; we had already seen in Chapter V that every congruent transformation was such a collineation. We may go one step further, and say that every analytic transformation which carries the Absolute into itself alone is a congruent transformation. Suppose that we have

$$x_0{}' = f_0(x_0x_1x_2x_3), \quad x_1{}' = f_1(x_0x_1x_2x_3), \quad x_2{}' = f_2(x_0x_1x_2x_3), \quad x_3{}' = f_3(x_0x_1x_2x_3),$$

$$(x'x') = P(xx).$$

P must be a constant, for were it a function of (x) the Absolute would be carried into itself, and into some other surface $P = 0$, which is contrary to hypothesis. Replacing (x) by $\lambda(x) + \mu(y)$ we see that we shall also have

$$(x'y') = P(xy),$$

whence we may easily show that the transformation is a collineation.

It is, of course, evident, that in the complex domain, the congruent groups of elliptic and hyperbolic space are identical, as they are merely the quaternary orthogonal group. In the real domain, however, the structure of the two is quite different, and our present task shall be the actual formation of those groups, pointing out besides certain interesting subgroups. We shall incidentally treat the euclidean group as a limiting case where $\frac{1}{k^2} \equiv 0$.

The group of translations of the hyperbolic line will depend on one parameter, and may be written, if $k^2 = -1$,

$$\begin{aligned} \dot{x}_0' &= \dot{x}_0 \cosh d + \dot{x}_1 \sinh d. \\ \dot{x}_1' &= \dot{x}_0 \sinh d + \dot{x}_1 \cosh d. \end{aligned} \tag{1}$$

We get a reflection by reversing the signs in the second equation. In the elliptic or spherical case we shall have similarly

$$\begin{aligned} x_0{}' &= x_0 \cos d + x_1 \sin d, \\ x_1{}' &= -x_0 \sin d + x_1 \cos d. \end{aligned} \tag{2}$$

To pass to the euclidean case, replace x_0, $x_0{}'$ by kx_0, $kx_0{}'$ and d by $\frac{d}{k}$, divide out k, and then put $\frac{1}{k^2} = 0$.

$$\frac{x_1{}'}{x_0{}'} = x' = x - d. \tag{3}$$

The ternary domain is more interesting. Let us express the Absolute in the hyperbolic plane in the following parametric form

$$\dot{x}_0 = {t_1}^2 + {t_2}^2, \quad \dot{x}_1 = {t_1}^2 - {t_2}^2, \dot{x}_2 = 2t_1t_2.$$

As the Absolute must be projectively transformed into itself, we may put

$$\begin{aligned} \sigma {t_1}' &= \alpha_{11}t_1 + \alpha_{12}t_2, \\ \sigma {t_2}' &= \alpha_{21}t_1 + \alpha_{22}t_2, \end{aligned} \quad |\alpha_{ij}| = \Delta \neq 0,$$

and this will lead to the general ternary transformation

$$\begin{aligned} \rho\dot{x}'_0 &= ({\alpha_{11}}^2 + {\alpha_{12}}^2 + {\alpha_{21}}^2 + {\alpha_{22}}^2)\dot{x}_0 + ({\alpha_{11}}^2 + {\alpha_{21}}^2 - {\alpha_{12}}^2 - {\alpha_{22}}^2)\dot{x}_1 \\ &\qquad + 2(\alpha_{11}\alpha_{12} + \alpha_{21}\alpha_{22})\dot{x}_2, \\ \rho\dot{x}'_1 &= ({\alpha_{11}}^2 - {\alpha_{21}}^2 + {\alpha_{12}}^2 - {\alpha_{22}}^2)\dot{x}_0 + ({\alpha_{11}}^2 - {\alpha_{21}}^2 - {\alpha_{12}}^2 + {\alpha_{22}}^2)\dot{x}_1 \\ &\qquad + 2(\alpha_{11}\alpha_{12} - \alpha_{21}\alpha_{22})\dot{x}_2, \\ \rho\dot{x}'_2 &= 2(\alpha_{11}\alpha_{21} + \alpha_{12}\alpha_{22})\dot{x}_0 + 2(\alpha_{11}\alpha_{21} - \alpha_{12}\alpha_{22})\dot{x}_1 \\ &\qquad + 2(\alpha_{11}\alpha_{22} + \alpha_{21}\alpha_{12})\dot{x}_2. \end{aligned} \tag{4}$$

If we view the matter geometrically, we see that there are three distinct possibilities. First the two fixed points of the Absolute conic are conjugate imaginaries. The real line connecting them is ultra-infinite, and has an actual pole with regard to the Absolute. This will give a rotation about this point, and we shall have

$$(\alpha_{11} + \alpha_{22})^2 - 4\Delta = (\alpha_{11} - \alpha_{22})^2 + 4\alpha_{12}\alpha_{21} < 0.$$

If the fixed points of the Absolute conic be real, the transformation, in the actual domain, will appear as a sliding along a real line, if $\Delta > 0$, or a sliding combined with a reflection in a perpendicular plane through this line if $\Delta < 0$. In the third case the two fixed points of the Absolute conic fall together, and the third fixed point of the plane falls there too. The transformation carries a pencil of parallel lines into itself.

The elliptic case is treated similarly, by a judicious introduction of imaginaries. We may write the Absolute

$$\begin{aligned} x_0 &= i({t_1}^2 + {t_2}^2), \\ x_1 &= {t_1}^2 - {t_2}^2, \\ x_2 &= 2t_1t_2. \end{aligned}$$

Let us now take the binary substitution

$$\begin{aligned} \sigma {t_1}' &= (\alpha + \beta i)t_1 - (\gamma + \delta i)t_2, \\ \sigma {t_2}' &= (\gamma - \delta i)t_1 + (\alpha - \beta i)t_2. \end{aligned}$$

We come thus to the general group of congruent transformations

$$\begin{aligned}\rho x_0' &= (\alpha^2-\beta^2+\gamma^2-\delta^2)x_0 + 2(\gamma\delta-\beta\alpha)x_1 + 2(\beta\gamma+\delta\alpha)x_2,\\ \rho x_1' &= 2(\gamma\delta+\beta\alpha)x_0 + (\alpha^2-\beta^2-\gamma^2+\delta^2)x_1 + 2(\beta\delta-\gamma\alpha)x_2,\\ \rho x_2' &= 2(\beta\gamma-\delta\alpha)x_0 + 2(\beta\delta+\gamma\alpha)x_1 + (\alpha^2+\beta^2-\gamma^2-\delta^2)x_2.\\ \Delta &= (\alpha^2+\beta^2+\gamma^2+\delta^2)^3.\end{aligned} \tag{5}$$

These forms remind us at once of like forms occurring in the theory of functions. Suppose, in fact, that we have the euclidean sphere

$$X^2+Y^2+Z^2=1.$$

The geometry thereof will be exactly our spherical geometry, and we wish for the group of congruent transformations of this sphere into itself. Let us project the sphere stereographically from the north pole upon the equatorial plane, and, considering this as the Gauss plane, take the linear transformation

$$z' = \frac{(\alpha+\beta i)z-(\gamma+\delta i)}{(\gamma-\delta i)z+(\alpha-\beta i)}, \quad \overline{z'} = \frac{(\alpha-\beta i)\overline{z}-(\gamma-\delta i)}{(\gamma+\delta i)\overline{z}+(\alpha+\beta i)}.$$

These equations are seen at once to be transformable into the others by a simple change of variables.

To pass over to the euclidean case, put

$$\begin{aligned} x = \frac{x_1}{x_0}, \quad y = \frac{y_1}{y_0},\\ x' = C_1 + A_1x + B_1y,\\ y' = C_2 + A_2x + B_2y,\\ A_1B_2 - A_2B_1 = {A_1}^2 + {B_1}^2 = {A_2}^2 + {B_2}^2 = 1.\end{aligned} \tag{6}$$

Notice that here the group

$$x' = c_1 + x, \quad y' = c_2 + y,$$

is an invariant sub-group.

The congruent groups in three dimensions are of the same general form as those in two, albeit the structure is a trifle more complicated. We wish for the six-parameter groups leaving invariant respectively a real, non-ruled quadric, an imaginary quadric of real equation, and an imaginary conic with two real equations. The solution has of course, long been known.[38]

The Absolute of hyperbolic space may be interpreted as a euclidean sphere of radius one, and the problem of finding all congruent transformations of hyperbolic space, is the same as that of finding all collineations carrying such a

[38]The literature of this subject is large. The first writer to express the general orthogonal substitution in terms of independent parameters was Cayley, 'Sur quelques propriétés des déterminants gauches,' *Crelle's Journal*, vol. xxxii, 1846. The treatment here given follows broadly Chapters VI and VII of Klein's 'Nicht-euklidische Geometric', lithographed notes, Göttingen, 1893.

sphere into itself. Let us represent this sphere parametrically in terms of its rectilinear generators

$$\begin{aligned}\dot{x}_0 &= z\bar{z} + 1,\\ \dot{x}_1 &= z\bar{z} - 1,\\ \dot{x}_2 &= z + \bar{z},\\ \dot{x}_3 &= -i(z - \bar{z}).\end{aligned}$$

Let us now take the linear transformation

$$z' = \frac{\alpha z + \beta}{\gamma z + \delta}, \qquad \bar{z}' = \frac{\bar{\alpha}\bar{z} + \bar{\beta}}{\bar{\gamma}\bar{z} + \bar{\delta}}.$$

The six-parameter group of congruent transformations of positive modulus will be

$$\begin{aligned}\rho\dot{x}_0' &= (\alpha\bar{\alpha} + \beta\bar{\beta} + \gamma\bar{\gamma} + \delta\bar{\delta})\dot{x}_0 + (\alpha\bar{\alpha} - \beta\bar{\beta} + \gamma\bar{\gamma} - \delta\bar{\delta})\dot{x}_1\\ &\qquad + (\alpha\bar{\beta} + \bar{\alpha}\beta + \gamma\bar{\delta} + \bar{\gamma}\delta)\dot{x}_2 + i(\alpha\bar{\beta} - \bar{\alpha}\beta + \gamma\bar{\delta} - \bar{\gamma}\delta)\dot{x}_3,\\ \rho\dot{x}_1' &= (\alpha\bar{\alpha} + \beta\bar{\beta} + \gamma\bar{\gamma} - \delta\bar{\delta})\dot{x}_0 + (\alpha\bar{\alpha} - \beta\bar{\beta} - \gamma\bar{\gamma} + \delta\bar{\delta})\dot{x}_1\\ &\qquad + (\alpha\bar{\beta} + \bar{\alpha}\beta - \gamma\bar{\delta} - \bar{\gamma}\delta)\dot{x}_2 + i(\alpha\bar{\beta} - \bar{\alpha}\beta - \gamma\bar{\delta} + \bar{\gamma}\delta)\dot{x}_3, \qquad (7)\\ \rho\dot{x}_2' &= (\alpha\bar{\gamma} + \bar{\alpha}\gamma + \beta\bar{\delta} + \bar{\beta}\delta)\dot{x}_0 + (\alpha\bar{\gamma} + \bar{\alpha}\gamma - \beta\bar{\delta} - \bar{\beta}\delta)\dot{x}_1\\ &\qquad + (\alpha\bar{\delta} + \bar{\alpha}\delta + \beta\bar{\gamma} + \bar{\beta}\gamma)\dot{x}_2 + i(\alpha\bar{\delta} - \bar{\alpha}\delta - \beta\bar{\gamma} + \bar{\beta}\gamma)\dot{x}_3,\\ -\rho\dot{x}_3' &= i(\alpha\bar{\gamma} - \bar{\alpha}\gamma + \beta\bar{\delta} - \bar{\beta}\delta)\dot{x}_0 + i(\alpha\bar{\gamma} - \bar{\alpha}\gamma - \beta\bar{\delta} + \bar{\beta}\delta)\dot{x}_1\\ &\qquad + i(\alpha\bar{\delta} - \bar{\alpha}\delta + \beta\bar{\gamma} - \bar{\beta}\gamma)\dot{x}_2 - (\alpha\bar{\delta} + \bar{\alpha}\delta - \beta\bar{\gamma} - \bar{\beta}\gamma)\dot{x}_3.\end{aligned}$$

$$\Delta = [(\alpha\delta - \beta\gamma)(\bar{\alpha}\bar{\delta} - \bar{\beta}\bar{\gamma})]^2.$$

This sub-group might properly be called the group of motions. The total group is made up of these and the six-parameter assemblage of transformations of negative discriminant called *symmetry transformations*. We reach these latter by writing

$$z' = \frac{\alpha'\bar{z} + \beta'}{\gamma'\bar{z} + \delta'}, \qquad \bar{z}' = \frac{\bar{\alpha}'z + \bar{\beta}'}{\bar{\gamma}'z + \bar{\delta}'}.$$

The distinction between motions and symmetry transformations stands out in clear relief when we consider the effect upon the Absolute. The sub-group of motions includes the identical transformation, and any motion may be reached by a continuous change in the six essential parameters from the values which give the identical transformation, without ever causing the modulus to vanish. This shows that as, under the identical transformation, each generator of the Absolute stays in place, so, under the most general motion, the generators of each set are permuted among one another. On the contrary, the most general symmetry transformation will arise from the combination of the most general motion with a reflection, and it is easy to see that a reflection will interchange the two sets of generators.

In the elliptic case we shall have the group of all real quaternary orthogonal substitutions. An extremely elegant way of expressing these is offered by the calculus of quaternions.

Let us, following the Hamiltonian notation, assume three new symbols i, j, k:

$$i^2 = j^2 = k^2 = ijk = -1.$$

We assume that they obey the associative and commutative laws of addition, the associative and distributive laws of multiplication. An expression of the type

$$p_0 + p_1 i + p_2 j + p_3 k$$

is called a *quaternion*, whereof

$$\sqrt{(pp)}$$

is called the *Tensor*. It is easy to show that the tensor of the product of two quaternions is the product of their tensors.

Let us next write

$$x_0{}' + x_1{}'i + x_2{}'j + x_3{}'k = P(x_0 + x_1 i + x_2 j + x_3 k)Q, \tag{8}$$

where P and Q are quaternions. Multiplying out the right-hand side, and identifying the real parts and the coefficients of i, j, k, we have $x_0{}'x_1{}'x_2{}'x_3{}'$ expressed as linear homogeneous functions of $x_0x_1x_2x_3$. The modulus of the transformation will be different from zero, and we shall have

$$(x'x') = (xx) \cdot |P|^2 \cdot |Q|^2.$$

These equations will give the six-parameter group of motions, the group of symmetry transformations will arise from

$$x_0{}' + x_1{}'i + x_2{}'j + x_3{}'k = P'(x_0 - x_1 i - x_2 j - x_3 k)Q',$$

the distinction between motions and symmetry transformations being as in the hyperbolic case.

Our group of motions is half-simple, being made up of two invariant sub-groups $G_3G_3{}'$ obtained severally by assuming that Q or P reduces to a real number. We obtain their geometrical significance as follows:—

The group of motions G_6 can be divided into two invariant three-parameter sub-groups $g_3g_3{}'$ by resolving it into the two groups which keep invariant all generators of the one or the other set on the Absolute. Now were it possible to divide G_6 into invariant three-parameter sub-groups in two different ways, the highest common factor of g_3 or $g_3{}'$ with G_3, would be an invariant sub-group, not only of G_6 but of g_3. This may not be, for g_3 is nothing but the binary projective group which has no invariant sub-groups. Hence the groups $g_3g_3{}'$ are identical with $G_3G_3{}'$, and the latter keep the one or the other set of generators all in place.

It is well worth our while to look more deeply into the properties of these sub-groups. Let us distinguish the two sets of generators of the Absolute by calling the one *left*, and the other *right*. This may be done analytically by adjoining a number i to our domain of rationals. Two lines which cut the same left (right) generators of the Absolute shall be called *left (right) paratactic*.[39] As the conjugate imaginary to each generator of the Absolute belongs to the same set as itself, we see that through each real point will pass a real left and real right paratactic to each real line; and the same will hold for each real plane. Of course there are possible complications in the imaginary domain, but these need not concern us here.

Let us now look at a real congruent transformation which keeps all right generators invariant. Two conjugate imaginary left generators will also be invariant, and every line meeting these two will be carried into itself, every other line will be carried into a line right paratactic to itself. Such a transformation shall be called a *left translation*, since the path curves of all points will be a congruence of left paratactic lines. In fact this congruence will give the path curves for a whole one-parameter family of left translations. Let the reader show that under a translation, any two points will be transported through congruent distances.

Before leaving the elliptic case, let us notice that in the elliptic plane a reflection in a line is identical with a reflection in a point, or a rotation through an angle π, in a spherical plane they are different, and a reflection in a line is the same as a rotation through an angle π coupled with an interchange of each point with its equivalent. In three dimensions, there is never any identity between a rotation and a reflection, on the other hand nothing new is brought in by interchanging each point with its equivalent, for as each plane is hereby transformed into self, we may split up the transformation into a reflection in a plane, a reflection in a second plane perpendicular to the first, and a rotation through an angle π about a line perpendicular to both planes.

To pass to the limiting euclidean case

$$\begin{aligned} x' &= A_0 + A_1x + A_2y + A_3z, \\ y' &= B_0 + B_1x + B_2y + B_3z, \\ z' &= C_0 + C_1x + C_2y + C_3z, \end{aligned} \tag{9}$$

where $\|A_1B_2C_3\|$ is the matrix of a ternary orthogonal substitution.

There will be a three-parameter invariant sub-group; that of all translations

$$\begin{aligned} x' &= A_0 + x, \\ y' &= B_0 + y, \end{aligned}$$

[39]The more common name for such lines is 'Clifford parallels'. The word paratactic is taken from Study, 'Zur Nicht-euklidischen und Liniengeometrie,' *Jahresbericht der deutschen Mathematikervereinigung*, xi, 1902. We have already defined parallels as lines intersecting on the Absolute, and although in the present case such lines cannot both be real, yet it is better to be consistent in our terminology, especially since we shall find in Chapter XVI a transformation carrying parallelism into parataxy. Clifford's discussion is in his 'Preliminary Sketch of Biquaternions', *Proceedings of the London Mathematical Society*, vol. iv, 1873

$$z' = C_0 + z.$$

In like manner we may find the six-parameter assemblage of symmetry transformations.

CHAPTER IX

POINT, LINE, AND PLANE TREATED ANALYTICALLY

The object of the present chapter is to return, as promised in Chapter VI, to the problems of elementary non-euclidean geometry, from the higher point of view gained by extending space to be a perfect analytic continuum. We shall find in the Absolute a *Deus ex Machina* to relieve us from many an embarrassment. We shall leave aside the euclidean case, and, for the most part, handle all of our non-euclidean cases together, leaving to the reader the simple task of making the distinction between the elliptic and the spherical cases. Otherwise stated, our present task is to express the fundamental metrical theorems of point, line, and plane, in terms of the invariants of the congruent group.

Let us notice, at the outset, that the principle of duality plays a fundamental rôle. The distance of two points is $\frac{k}{2i}\times$ logarithm of the cross ratio that they form with the points where their line meets the Absolute, the angle of two planes is $\frac{1}{2i}\times$ logarithm of the cross ratio which they form with two planes through their intersection, tangent to the Absolute; the distance from a point to a plane is $\frac{\pi k}{2}$ minus its distance to the pole of that plane with regard to the Absolute. Two intersecting lines or planes which are conjugate with regard to the Absolute are mutually perpendicular. Two points which are conjugate with regard to the Absolute shall be said to be mutually *orthogonal*. In the real domain of hyperbolic space, if one of two such points be actual, the other must be ideal; the converse is not necessarily true.

Let us begin in the non-euclidean plane, say $x_3 = 0$. Let us take two points A, B with coordinates (x) and (y) respectively, and find the two points of their line which are at congruent distances from them. These shall be called the *centres of gravity* of the two points, and are, in fact, the two points which divide harmonically the given points, and the intersections of their line with the Absolute. We purposely exclude the spherical case, where the centres of gravity will be equivalent points.

The necessary and sufficient condition that the point $\lambda(x) + \mu(y)$ should be at congruent distances from (x) and (y) that

$$\lambda : \mu = \sqrt{(yy)} : \pm\sqrt{(xx)}.$$

The coordinates of the centres of gravity will thus be

$$\left(\frac{x}{\sqrt{(xx)}} \pm \frac{y}{\sqrt{(yy)}}\right). \tag{1}$$

Let the reader discover what complications may arise in the ideal domain.

Let us next take three non-collinear points A, B, C with the coordinates (x), (y), (z). A line connecting (x) with a centre of gravity of (y) and (z) will be

$$\sqrt{(yy)}\,|Xxz| + \sqrt{(zz)}\,|Xxy| = 0.$$

It is clear that such lines are concurrent by threes, in four points which may be called the *centres of gravity* of the three given points. On the other hand the centres of gravity of our pairs of points are collinear in threes. Lastly, notice that a dual theorem might be reached by interchanging the objects, point and line, distance and angle; by taking, in fact, a polar reciprocation in the Absolute:—

Theorem 1. The centres of gravity of the pairs formed from three given points are collinear by threes on four lines. The lines from the given points to the centres of gravity of their pairs are concurrent by threes in four points.

Theorem 1′. The bisectors of the angles formed by three coplanar but not concurrent lines are concurrent by threes in four points. The points where these bisectors meet the given lines are collinear by threes on four lines.

The centres of gravity of the points (x), (y), (z) are easily seen to be

$$\left(\frac{x}{\sqrt{(xx)}} \pm \frac{y}{\sqrt{(yy)}} \pm \frac{z}{\sqrt{(zz)}}\right). \tag{2}$$

Returning to the line BC we see that the coordinates of its pole with regard to the Absolute will have the coordinates (s), where for every value of (r)

$$(rs) \equiv |ryz|.$$

The equation of the line connecting this point with A, i.e. the line through A perpendicular to BC, will be

$$(Xy)(zx) - (Xz)(xy) = 0.$$

If we permute the letters x, y, z cyclically twice, we get two other equations of the same type, and the sum of the three is identically zero, so that

Theorem 2. The lines through each of three given non-collinear points, perpendicular to the line of the other two, are concurrent.

Theorem 2′. The points on each of three coplanar but not concurrent lines, orthogonal to the intersection of the other two, are collinear.

Returning to a centre of gravity of the two points BC, we see that a line through it perpendicular to the line BC will have the equation

$$\begin{vmatrix} \dfrac{(xy)}{\dfrac{(yy)}{\sqrt{(yy)}} + \dfrac{(yz)}{\sqrt{(zz)}}} & \dfrac{(xz)}{\dfrac{(yz)}{\sqrt{(yy)}} + \dfrac{(zz)}{\sqrt{(zz)}}} \end{vmatrix} = 0,$$

$$\left[\frac{(yz)}{\sqrt{(yy)}\sqrt{(zz)}} - 1\right]\left[\frac{(xy)}{\sqrt{(yy)}} - \frac{(xz)}{\sqrt{(zz)}}\right] = 0.$$

The first factor will vanish (in the real domain) only when (y) and (z) are identical, the equation will then be

$$\frac{(xy)}{\sqrt{(yy)}} - \frac{(xz)}{\sqrt{(zz)}} = 0.$$

We see immediately from the form of this equation, that all points of this line are at congruent distances from (y) and (z), thus confirming II. 33.

Theorem 3. If three non-collinear points be given, the perpendiculars to the lines of their pairs at the centres of gravity of these pairs are concurrent by threes in four points, each at congruent distances from all three of the given points.

Theorem 3′. If three coplanar but not concurrent lines be given, the points orthogonal to their intersections on the bisectors of the corresponding angles are collinear by threes on four lines, making congruent angles with all three of the given lines.

Let us now suppose that besides our three original points, we have three others lying one on each of the lines of the first set as follows

$$A' = (ly + mz),$$
$$B' = (pz + qx),$$
$$C' = (rx + sy).$$

Let us, for the moment, suppose that we are restricted to a consistent region of the plane. Then we shall easily see from Axiom XVI that if AA', BB', CC' be concurrent

$$\frac{\sin\frac{\overrightarrow{BA'}}{k}}{\sin\frac{\overrightarrow{CA'}}{k}} \cdot \frac{\sin\frac{\overrightarrow{CB'}}{k}}{\sin\frac{\overrightarrow{AB'}}{k}} \cdot \frac{\sin\frac{\overrightarrow{AC'}}{k}}{\sin\frac{\overrightarrow{BC'}}{k}} < 0.$$

On the other hand, if A', B', C' be collinear,

$$\frac{\sin\frac{\overrightarrow{BA'}}{k}}{\sin\frac{\overrightarrow{CA'}}{k}} \cdot \frac{\sin\frac{\overrightarrow{CB'}}{k}}{\sin\frac{\overrightarrow{AB'}}{k}} \cdot \frac{\sin\frac{\overrightarrow{AC'}}{k}}{\sin\frac{\overrightarrow{BC'}}{k}} > 0.$$

Now, more specifically, we see that

$$\sin^2\frac{\overline{BA'}}{k} = \frac{m^2\left[(yy)(zz) - (yz)^2\right]}{(yy)\left[l^2(yy) + 2lm(yz) + m^2(zz)\right]},$$

whence

$$\left[\frac{\sin\frac{\overrightarrow{BA'}}{k}}{\sin\frac{\overrightarrow{CA'}}{k}} \cdot \frac{\sin\frac{\overrightarrow{CB'}}{k}}{\sin\frac{\overrightarrow{AB'}}{k}} \cdot \frac{\sin\frac{\overrightarrow{AC'}}{k}}{\sin\frac{\overrightarrow{BC'}}{k}}\right] = \left(\frac{mqs}{lpr}\right)^2.$$

The equation of the line AA' will be

$$l|Xxy| + m|Xzx| = 0.$$

And the condition for concurrence for the three lines

$$(lpr + mqs) \cdot |xyz|^2 = 0,$$

and this will give

$$\frac{mqs}{lpr} = -1.$$

On the other hand, we easily see that if A', B', C' be collinear

$$lpr - mqs = 0.$$

Theorem 4. If A', B', C' be three points lying respectively on the lines BC, CA, AB, all six points being in a consistent region, then the expression

$$\frac{\sin \frac{\overrightarrow{BA'}}{k}}{\sin \frac{\overrightarrow{CA'}}{k}} \cdot \frac{\sin \frac{\overrightarrow{CB'}}{k}}{\sin \frac{\overrightarrow{AB'}}{k}} \cdot \frac{\sin \frac{\overrightarrow{BC'}}{k}}{\sin \frac{\overrightarrow{AC'}}{k}},$$

will be equal to -1 when, and only when, AA', BB', CC' are concurrent, while it will be equal to 1, when, and only when, A', B', C' are collinear.

These are, of course, merely the analogs of the theorems of Menelaus and Ceva. It is worth noticing also, that they will afford a sufficient ground for a metrical theory of cross ratios.

Let us next suppose that A' is a point where a bisector of an angle formed by the lines BA, CA, meets BC. We find l and m easily in this case, by noticing that A' must be at congruent distances from AB and AC, thus getting

$$(y\sqrt{(zz)(xx) - (xz)^2} + z\sqrt{(xx)(yy) - (xy)^2}),$$

$$\sin \frac{\overline{BA'}}{k} : \sin \frac{\overline{CA'}}{k} = \sin \frac{\overline{BA}}{k} : \sin \frac{\overline{CA}}{k}.$$

Theorem 5. If three noncollinear points be given, each bisector of an angle formed by the lines connecting two of the points with the third will meet the line of the two points in such a point that the ratio of the sines of the kth parts of its distances from the two points is equal to the corresponding ratio for these two with the third point.

Theorem 5$'$. If three coplanar but non-concurrent lines be given, each centre of gravity of a pair of points where two of the lines meet a third determines with the intersection of this pair of lines such a line, that the ratio of the sines of the angles which it makes with these two lines, is equal to the corresponding ratio for the two lines with the third.

Theorem 6. The locus of a point which moves in a plane, in such a way that the ratio of the sines of the kth parts of its distances from two points is constant, is a curve of the second order.

Theorem 6$'$. The envelope of a line which moves in such a way in a plane, that the ratio of the sines of its angles with two fixed lines is constant, is an envelope of the second class.

It would be quite erroneous to suppose that either of these curves would be, in general, a circle. Let the reader show that if an angle inscribed in a semicircle be a right angle, the euclidean hypothesis holds.

Our next investigation shall be connected with parallel lines. We suppose, for the moment, that we are in the hyperbolic plane, and that $k = i$. We shall hunt for the expression for the angle which a parallel to a given line l passing through a point P makes with the perpendicular to l through P. This shall be called the *parallel angle* of the distance from the point to the line, and if the latter be d the parallel angle shall be written[40]

$$\Pi(d).$$

Let us give to the point P the coordinates (y), while the given line has the coordinates (u). Let (v) be the coordinates of a parallel to (u) through (y). Let D be the point where the perpendicular to (u) through (y) meets (u). We seek $\cos\Pi(d)$.

Since (u) and (v) intersect on the Absolute

$$(uu)(vv) - (uv)^2 = 0.$$

The equation of the line PD will be

$$|xyu| = 0.$$

The cosine of the angle formed by u and PD will be

$$\cos\Pi(d) = \frac{|yuv|}{\sqrt{vv}\,\sqrt{(uu)(yy) - (yu)^2}}$$

squaring, and remembering that

$$(vy) = 0,$$

$$\cos^2\Pi(d) = \frac{\begin{vmatrix} (yy) & (uy) & 0 \\ (uy) & (uu) & (uv) \\ 0 & (uv) & (vv) \end{vmatrix}}{(vv)[(uu)(yy) - (uy)^2]},$$

$$\cos\Pi(d) = \frac{i(uy)}{\sqrt{(uu)(yy) - (uy)^2}},$$

$$\cos\Pi(d) = \tanh d. \tag{3}$$

From these we easily see

$$\sin\Pi(d) = \mathrm{sech}(d); \quad \tan\Pi(d) = \mathrm{csch}(d). \tag{4}$$

[40]The concept *parallel angle* and the notation $\Pi(d)$ are due to Lobatchewsky.

Furthermore, if $\measuredangle ACB$ be a right angle

$$\cos\measuredangle ABC = \frac{\cos\Pi(\overline{BC})}{\cos\Pi(\overline{AB})} \qquad \sin\measuredangle ABC = \frac{\operatorname{ctn}\Pi(\overline{CA})}{\operatorname{ctn}\Pi(\overline{AB})}. \tag{5}$$

$$\cos\measuredangle ABC = \frac{\sin\measuredangle CAB}{\sin\Pi(AC)}. \tag{6}$$

$$\sin\Pi(\overline{AB}) = \sin\Pi(\overline{BC})\sin\Pi(\overline{CA}) = \tan\measuredangle CAB\tan\measuredangle ABC. \tag{7}$$

Let the reader prove the correctness of the following construction for the parallels to P through l:

Drop a perpendicular from P on l meeting it in Q. Take S a convenient point on the perpendicular to PQ at P, and let the perpendicular to PS at S meet l at R. Then with P as a centre, and a radius equal to (QR), construct an arc meeting RS in T. PT will be the parallel required.[41]

Be it noticed that, as we should expect,

$$\underset{d \doteq 0}{\text{limit}} \frac{\cos\Pi(d)}{d} = 1.$$

Let us now find the equations of the two parallels to the line (u) which pass through the point (y). These two cannot, naturally, be rationally separated one from the other, so that we shall find the equations of both at once. Let the coordinates of the line which connects the other intersections of the parallels and the Absolute be (w). The general form for an equation of a curve of the second order through the intersections of (u) and (w) with the Absolute will be

$$l(ux)(wx) - m(xx) - 0,$$

and this will pass through (y) if

$$l : m = (yy) : (uy)(wy).$$

Since this curve is a pair of lines meeting in (y) the polar of (y) with regard to it will be illusory, i.e. the coefficients of (x) will vanish in

$$(yy)(uy)(wx) + (yy)(wy)(ux) - 2(uy)(wy)(xy) = 0.$$

This last equation may be written

$$(uy)\begin{vmatrix}(wx) & (wy)\\ (yx) & (yy)\end{vmatrix} + (wy)\begin{vmatrix}(ux) & (uy)\\ (yx) & (yy)\end{vmatrix} = 0.$$

[41]The formulae given may be used as the basis for the whole trigonometric structure. Cf. Manning, *Non-euclidean Geometry*, Boston, 1901. Manning's reasoning is open to very grave question on the score of rigour.

Now, by the harmonic theory of a quadrangle inscribed in a curve of the second order, w will pass through the intersection of (u) with the polar of y with regard to the Absolute, so that we may write

$$w_i = \lambda u_i + \mu y_i.$$

Substituting

$$[2\lambda(uy) + \mu(yy)] \begin{vmatrix} (ux) & (uy) \\ (yx) & (yy) \end{vmatrix} = 0.$$

The coefficients of $x_0 x_1 x_2$ will vanish if

$$\lambda = -(yy), \quad \mu = 2(uy).$$

Under these circumstances

$$\begin{aligned} (wx) &= -(yy)(ux) + 2(uy)(xy), \\ (wy) &= (yy)(uy). \end{aligned}$$

Which leads to the required equation

$$(uy)^2(xx) + (ux)^2(yy) - 2(ux)(uy)(xy) = 0. \tag{8}$$

To get the euclidean formula, replace x_0 by $k_0 x_0$ and divide by k. We get the square of the usual expression

$$[(uy)x_0 - (ux)y_0]^2 = 0. \tag{9}$$

The principles which we have followed in studying the metrical invariants of the plane may be extended with ease to three dimensions. We have merely to adjoin the fourth homogeneous point or line coordinate.

Let us have four points, not in one plane, with the coordinates (x), (y), (z), (t) respectively. We easily see that the eight points

$$\left(\frac{x}{\sqrt{(xx)}} \pm \frac{y}{\sqrt{(yy)}} \pm \frac{z}{\sqrt{(zz)}} \pm \frac{t}{\sqrt{(tt)}}\right), \tag{10}$$

will be points of concurrence, four by four, of lines from each of the given points to the centres of gravity of the other three. These eight may, in fact, be called the *centres of gravity* of the four points. The centres of gravity will form with the given points a *desmic configuration*.[42] The meaning of this phrase is as follows. Let us indicate the centres of gravity by the signs prefixed to their radicals, giving always to the first radical a positive sign. We may then divide our twelve points into three lots as follows:—

$$\begin{array}{cccc} (x) & (y) & (z) & (t) \\ (++++) & (++--) & (+-+-) & (+--+) \\ (+++-) & (++-+) & (+-++) & (+---) \end{array} \tag{11}$$

[42]The desmic configuration was first studied by Stephanos, 'Sur la configuration desmique de trois tétraèdres,' *Bulletin des Sciences mathématiques*, série 2, vol. iii, 1878.

We see that a line connecting a point of one lot, with any point of a second, will pass through a point of the third. The twelve points will thus lie by threes on sixteen lines, four passing through each. In like manner we shall find that if we take the twelve planes obtained by omitting in turn one point of each lot, two planes of different lots are always coaxal with one of the third. Let the reader who is unfamiliar with the desmic configuration, study the particular case (in euclidean space) of the vertices of a cube, its centre, and the ideal points of concurrence of its parallel edges.

Theorem 7. If four non-coplanar points be given, the lines from each to the four centres of gravity of the other three will pass by fours through eight points which form, with the original ones, a desmic configuration.

Theorem 7′. If four non-concurrent planes be given, the lines where each meets the planes which severally are coaxal with each of the three remaining planes and a plane bisecting a dihedral angle of the two still left, lie by fours in eight planes which, with the original ones, form a desmic configuration.

Let the reader show that the centres of gravity of the six pairs formed from the given points will determine a second desmic configuration, and dually for the planes bisecting the dihedral angles.

Let us seek for a point which is at congruent distances from our four given points. It is easy to see that there cannot be more than eight such points. Their coordinates are found to be (s) where, for all values of r,

$$(rs) \equiv \sqrt{(xx)}\,|ryzt| \pm \sqrt{(yy)}\,|rztx| \pm \sqrt{(zz)}\,|rtxy| \pm \sqrt{(tt)}\,|rxyz|. \qquad (12)$$

Theorem 8. If four non-coplanar points be given, the eight points which are severally at congruent distances from them form, with the original four, a desmic configuration.

Theorem 8′. If four non-concurrent planes be given, the eight planes which severally meet them in congruent dihedral angles, form, with the original four, a desmic configuration.

As there are eight points at congruent distances from the four given points, so there will be eight planes at congruent distances from them, we have but to take the polars of the eight points with regard to the Absolute. In like manner, if we consider not the points (x), (y), (z), (t) but their four planes, there will be eight points at congruent distances from them. The coordinates of these latter eight will be

$$\left| x\sqrt{\left\| \begin{matrix} y_0 & y_1 & y_2 & y_3 \\ z_0 & z_1 & z_2 & z_3 \\ t_0 & t_1 & t_2 & t_3 \end{matrix} \right\|^2} \pm y\sqrt{\left\| \begin{matrix} z_0 & z_1 & z_2 & z_3 \\ t_0 & t_1 & t_2 & t_3 \\ x_0 & x_1 & x_2 & x_3 \end{matrix} \right\|^2} \right.$$

$$\pm z\sqrt{\left\|\begin{matrix} t_0 & t_1 & t_2 & t_3 \\ x_0 & x_1 & x_2 & x_3 \\ y_0 & y_1 & y_2 & y_3 \end{matrix}\right\|^2} \pm t\sqrt{\left\|\begin{matrix} x_0 & x_1 & x_2 & x_3 \\ y_0 & y_1 & y_2 & y_3 \\ z_0 & z_1 & z_2 & z_3 \end{matrix}\right\|^2}.$$

Theorem 9. If four non-coplanar points be given, the eight points which, severally, are at congruent distances from the planes of the first four, form, with the first four points, a desmic configuration.

Theorem 9′. If four non-concurrent planes be given, the eight planes which, severally, are at congruent distances from the points of concurrence of the first four, form, with the first four planes, a desmic configuration.

The parallel angle of a point with regard to a plane can be defined as its parallel angle with regard to any line of the plane through the foot of the perpendicular. If the distance from the point to the plane be x, we shall have for the parallel angle

$$\cos \Pi(x) = k \tan \frac{x}{k}. \tag{13}$$

Definition. A line shall be said to be parallel to a plane, if the point common to the two be on the Absolute. The cone of parallels to a plane (u) through a point (y) will have the equation

$$(uy)^2(xx) + (ux)^2(yy) - 2(ux)(uy)(xy) = 0. \tag{14}$$

We now pass to certain metrical invariants of non-euclidean space expressed in line coordinates. We take as coordinates for the line joining (x) and (y) the usual Plueckerian form

$$p_{ij} = x_i y_j - x_j y_i.$$

The coordinates of the polar of this line with regard to the Absolute, the Absolute polar let us say, will be

$$q_{ij} = p_{kl}.$$

The condition for the intersection of two lines (p) and (p') will be, naturally

$$(p \mid p') \equiv \Sigma\, p_{ij} p'_{kl} = 0. \tag{15}$$

Each will meet the Absolute of polar of the other if

$$\Sigma\, p_{ij} {p'}_{ij} = 0. \tag{16}$$

Notice that $(p \mid p')$ is an invariant under the general group of collineations, while $\Sigma\, p_{ij} {p'}_{ij}$ is invariant under the congruent group only.

We shall mean by the distance of two lines the distance of their intersections with a third line perpendicular to them both. It is easy to see that if two lines be not paratactic, there will be two lines meeting both at right angles, and these are indistinguishable in the rational domain, that is, in the general case.

If, thus, d be taken to indicate the distance of two lines, $\sin^2 \frac{d}{k}$ will be a root of an irreducible quadratic equation, whose coefficients are rational invariants under the congruent group. Let us seek for this equation.

Let one of our lines be p given by the points (x), (y), while the other is (p') given by (x') and (y'). For the sake of simplifying our calculations we shall make the obviously legitimate assumptions

$$(xy) = (xy') = (x'y) = (x'y') = 0.$$

The distances which we wish to find are

$$\sin \frac{d_1}{k} = \frac{\sqrt{(xx)(x'x') - (xx')^2}}{\sqrt{(xx)}\,\sqrt{(x'x')}} \qquad \sin \frac{d_2}{k} = \frac{\sqrt{(yy)(y'y') - (yy')^2}}{\sqrt{(yy)}\,\sqrt{(y'y')}}.$$

We have

$$(xx)(yy) - (xy)^2 = \Sigma\, {p_{ij}}^2,$$

and this will vanish only when (p) is tangent to the Absolute, a possibility which we now explicitly exclude both for (p) and (p').

$$(xx)(yy) = \Sigma\, {p_{ij}}^2, \quad (x'x')(y'y') = \Sigma\, {p'_{ij}}^2,$$

$$\begin{aligned}
(p \mid p')^2 &= |xyx'y'|^2 \\
&= \begin{vmatrix} (xx) & 0 & (xx') & 0 \\ 0 & (yy) & 0 & (yy') \\ (xx') & 0 & (x'x') & 0 \\ 0 & (yy') & 0 & (y'y') \end{vmatrix} \\
&= [(xx)(x'x') - (xx')^2][(yy)(y'y') - (yy')^2],
\end{aligned}$$

$$\sin^2 \frac{d_1}{k} \sin^2 \frac{d_2}{k} = \frac{[(xx)(x'x') - (xx')^2]}{(xx)(x'x')} \frac{[(yy)(y'y') - (yy')^2]}{(yy)(y'y')}. \tag{17}$$

$$\sin^2 \frac{d_1}{k} \sin^2 \frac{d_2}{k} = \frac{(p \mid p')^2}{\Sigma\, {p_{ij}}^2\, \Sigma\, {p_{ij}}'^2}. \tag{18}$$

$$\sin^2 \frac{d_1}{k} \sin^2 \frac{d_2}{k} = 1 - \cos^2 \frac{d_1}{k} - \cos^2 \frac{d_2}{k} + \frac{(xx')^2(yy')^2}{\Sigma\, {p_{ij}}^2\, \Sigma\, {p_{ij}}'^2};$$

$$\Sigma\, p_{ij}{p_{ij}}' = \begin{vmatrix} (xx') & (xy') \\ (yx') & (yy') \end{vmatrix} = (xx')(yy'),$$

$$\cos^2 \frac{d_1}{k} + \cos^2 \frac{d_2}{k} = 1 + \frac{(\Sigma\, p_{ij}{p_{ij}}')^2 - (p \mid p')^2}{\Sigma\, p_{ij}\, \Sigma\, {p_{ij}}'^2},$$

$$\sin^2 \frac{d_1}{k} + \sin^2 \frac{d_2}{k} = 1 - \frac{(\Sigma\, p_{ij}{p_{ij}}')^2 - (p \mid p')^2}{\Sigma\, {p_{ij}}^2\, \Sigma\, {p_{ij}}'^2},$$

$$\Sigma {p_{ij}}^2\, \Sigma {p_{ij}}'^2 \sin^4 \frac{d}{k} + \left[(\Sigma p_{ij}p_{ij}')^2 - (p \mid p')^2 - \Sigma {p_{ij}}^2\, \Sigma {p_{ij}}'^2\right] \sin^2 \frac{d}{k} + (p \mid p')^2 = 0. \quad (19)$$

$$\Sigma {p_{ij}}^2\, \Sigma {p_{ij}}'^2 \cos^4 \frac{d}{k} + \left[(p \mid p')^2 - (\Sigma p_{ij}p_{ij}')^2 - \Sigma {p_{ij}}^2 {p_{ij}}'^2\right] \cos^2 \frac{d}{k} + (\Sigma p_{ij}p_{ij}')^2 = 0. \quad (20)$$

The square roots of the products of the roots of these two equations are well-known metrical invariants, and have been studied under the names of *moment* and *commoment* of the two lines.[43] We shall return to the moment presently, attaching a particular value to the signs of the radicals in the denominator. If two lines intersect the moment must be zero, and if each intersect the absolute polar of the other, the commoment must vanish, thus bringing us back to equations (15), (16).

To reach the limiting euclidean case we replace, as usual, x_0 by kx_0, divide out k^2, and put $\frac{1}{k^2} = 0$. Then, since

$$\lim_{k \doteq \infty} k \sin \frac{d}{k} = d.$$

We have $d^2 =$

$$\frac{(p \mid p')^2}{({p_{01}}^2 + {p_{02}}^2 + {p_{03}}^2)({p_{01}}'^2 + {p_{02}}'^2 + {p_{03}}'^2) - (p_{01}p_{01}' + p_{02}p_{02}' + p_{03}p_{03}')^2}, \quad (21)$$

the usual formula.

With regard to the signs of the roots in (19) we see that in the hyperbolic case, where the two lines are actual, one of the points chosen to determine each line will be actual and the other ideal, so that

$$\Sigma {p_{ij}}^2 < 0, \quad \Sigma {p_{ij}}'^2 < 0,$$

$$(p \mid p')^2 < 0,$$

$$\sin^2 \frac{d_1}{k} \sin^2 \frac{d_2}{k} < 0.$$

The square of the moment of the two lines is negative, so that one distance will be real and the other pure imaginary. In the elliptic case the two distances will be real.

We shall mean by the angle of two non-intersecting lines the angles of the plane, one through each, which contain the same common perpendicular. This

[43]See D'Ovidio, 'Studio sulla geometria proiettiva,' *Annali di Matematica*, vi, 1873, and 'Le funzioni metriche fondamentali negli spazii di quantesivogliono dimensioni', *Memorie dei Lincei*, i, 1877.

will be k times the corresponding distance of the absolute polars of the lines. We thus get for the angles θ of the two lines (p), (p')

$$\Sigma\, p_{ij}{}^2\, \Sigma\, p_{ij}'^2 \sin^4\theta + [(\Sigma\, p_{ij}p_{ij}')^2 - (p \mid p')^2 - \Sigma\, p_{ij}{}^2\, \Sigma\, p_{ij}'^2] \sin^2\theta + (p \mid p')^2 = 0.$$

To get the euclidean formula we make the usual substitutions and divisions, and put $\frac{1}{k} = 0$, thus getting the well-known formula

$$\sin^2\theta = \frac{(x_1{}^2 + x_2{}^2 + x_3{}^2)(x_1'^2 + x_2'^2 + x_3'^2) - (x_1x_1' + x_2x_2' + x_3x_3')^2}{(x_1{}^2 + x_2{}^2 + x_3{}^2)(x_1'^2 + x_2'^2 + x_3'^2)}. \tag{22}$$

The coordinates of the line q cutting p and p' at right angles will be given by

$$(p \mid q) = (p' \mid q) = \Sigma\, p_{ij}q_{ij} = \Sigma\, p_{ij}'q_{ij} = (q \mid q) = 0.$$

We have defined as a parallel, two lines whose intersection is on the Absolute; let us now give the name *pseudoparallel* to two coplanar lines whose plane touches the Absolute. The necessary and sufficient condition that two lines should be either parallel or pseudoparallel is that they should intersect, and that there should be but a single line of their pencil tangent to the Absolute. These conditions will be expressed by the equations

$$(p \mid p') = [\Sigma\, p_{ij}{}^2\, \Sigma\, p_{ij}'^2 - (\Sigma\, p_{ij}p_{ij}')^2] = 0 \tag{23}$$

Let the reader notice that when we pass to the limit in the usual way for the euclidean case, our equations (23) become

$$(p \mid p') = \sin\theta = 0. \tag{24}$$

Let us now look at paratactic lines, i.e. lines which meet the same two generators of one set of the Absolute. Of course it is in the elliptic case only that two such lines can be real. It is immediately evident that two paratactic lines have an infinite number of common perpendiculars whereon they always determine congruent distances, we have, in fact, merely to look at the one-parameter group of translations of space which carry these two lines into themselves. Conversely, suppose that the distances of two lines be congruent. Besides our previous equations connecting (x) (y) (x') (y'), we have

$$\frac{(xx')^2}{(xx)(x'x')} = \frac{(yy')^2}{(yy)(y'y')}.$$

The lines p, p' meet the Absolute respectively in the points

$$\left(x\sqrt{(yy)} \pm iy\sqrt{(xx)}\right) \left(x'\sqrt{(y'y')} \pm iy'\sqrt{(x'x')}\right).$$

It is clear, however, that every point of the line

$$\left(x\sqrt{(yy)} + iy\sqrt{(xx)}\right) \left(x'\sqrt{(y'y')} + iy'\sqrt{(x'x')}\right),$$

and of the line

$$\left(x\sqrt{(yy)} - iy\sqrt{(xx)}\right)\left(x'\sqrt{(y'y')} - iy'\sqrt{(x'x')}\right),$$

belongs to the Absolute; the lines are paratactic. Lastly, the absolute polars of paratactic lines are, themselves, paratactic. Hence

Theorem 10. The necessary and sufficient condition that two lines should be paratactic is that their distances or angles should be congruent.

This condition may be expressed analytically by equating to zero the discriminant of either of our equations (19), (20).

$$\{[(p \mid p') + (\Sigma\, p_{ij}p_{ij}')]^2 - \Sigma\, p_{ij}{}^2\, \Sigma\, p_{ij}{}'^2\}\{[(p \mid p') + (\Sigma\, p_{ij}p_{ij}')]^2 \\ - \Sigma\, p_{ij}{}^2\, \Sigma\, p_{ij}{}'^2\} = 0. \quad (25)$$

This puts in evidence that intersecting lines cannot be paratactic unless they be parallel, or pseudoparallel.

In conclusion, let us return for an instant to the moment of two real lines.

$$\sin\frac{d_1}{k}\sin\frac{d_2}{k} = \frac{(p \mid p')}{\sqrt{\Sigma\, p_{ij}{}^2}\,\sqrt{\Sigma\, p_{ij}{}'^2}}.$$

We shall assume that the radicals in the denominator are taken positively, so that the sign of the moment is that of $(p \mid p')$. We now proceed to replace our concept of a line by the sharper concept of a *ray* as follows. Let us, in the hyperbolic case assume always $\dot{x}_0 > 0$, and in the elliptic case $x_0 > 0$. The coordinates

$$p_{ij'} = \begin{vmatrix} y_i' & y_j' \\ z_i' & z_j' \end{vmatrix}, \quad p_{ij} = \begin{vmatrix} y_i & y_j \\ z_i & z_j \end{vmatrix},$$

shall be called the coordinates of the ray from (y) to (z), and this shall be considered equivalent to any other ray whose coordinates differ therefrom by a positive factor. Interchanging (y) and (z) will give a second ray, said to be *opposite* to this. The relative moment of two rays is thus determined, both in magnitude and sign. We shall later see various applications of this concept.

CHAPTER X

THE HIGHER LINE GEOMETRY

In Chapter IX we took some first steps in non-euclidean line-geometry. The object of the present chapter is to continue the subject in the special direction where the fundamental element is not, in general, a line, but a pair of lines invariantly connected.[44]

Let us start in the real domain of hyperbolic space and consider a linear complex whose equation is

$$(\dot{a} \mid \dot{p}) = 0.$$

The dots indicate that the coordinates of a point are $\dot{x}_0, \dot{x}_1, \dot{x}_2, \dot{x}_3$, and choosing such a unit of measure that $k^2 = -1$, we have for the Absolute

$$-\dot{x}_0{}^2 + \dot{x}_1{}^2 + \dot{x}_2{}^2 + \dot{x}_3{}^2 = 0.$$

The polar of the given complex will have the coordinates

$$\dot{a}_{0i} = r\dot{b}_{jk}, \quad \dot{a}_{jk} = -r\dot{b}_{0i}, \quad i, j, k = 1, 2, 3,$$

and the congruence, whose equations are

$$(\dot{a} \mid \dot{p}) = \Sigma\, \dot{a}_{0i}\dot{p}_{0i} - \Sigma\, \dot{a}_{jk}\dot{p}_{jk} = 0,$$

will be composed of all lines of our complex and its absolute polar, or common to all complexes of the pencil

$$(l\dot{a}_{01} - m\dot{a}_{23}) \ldots (l\dot{a}_{23} + m\dot{a}_{01}).$$

These complexes shall be said to form a *coaxal pencil*, and the two mutually absolute polar lines, which are the directrices of the congruence, shall be called *axes* of the pencil. We get their plückerian coordinates by giving to $l : m$ such values that the complex shall be special. Let us now write

$$\begin{aligned} \dot{a}_{01} + i\dot{a}_{23} &= \rho X_1, \\ \dot{a}_{02} + i\dot{a}_{31} &= \rho X_2, \\ \dot{a}_{03} + i\dot{a}_{12} &= \rho X_3. \end{aligned} \tag{1}$$

A complex coaxal with the given line will be obtained by multiplying the numbers (X) by $(l + mi)$.

A pair of real lines which are mutually absolute polar, neither of which is tangent to the Absolute, shall be called a *proper cross*. They will determine a pencil of coaxal complexes. If either of the lines have the plückerian coordinates

[44]Practically the whole of this chapter is sketched, without proofs, by Study in his article, 'Zur nicht-euklidischen etc.,' loc. cit. The elliptic case is developed at length in the author's dissertation, 'The dual projective geometry of elliptic and spherical space,' Greifswald, 1904. For the hyperbolic case, see the dissertation of Beck, 'Die Strahlenketten im hyperbolischen Raume,' Hannover, 1905.

(a), then the three numbers (X) given by equations (1) may be taken to represent the cross. These coordinates (X) are homogeneous in the complex (i.e. imaginary) domain, for the result of multiplying them through by $(l+mi)$ is to replace the complex $(\dot{a})$ by a coaxal complex, and therefore to leave the axes of the pencil unaltered.

Conversely, suppose that we have a triad of coordinates (X) which are homogeneous in the imaginary domain. The coordinates of the lines of the corresponding cross will be found from (1) by assigning to ρ such a value that the coordinates $(\dot{a})$ shall satisfy the fundamental plückerian identity. For this it is necessary and sufficient that the imaginary part of $\rho^2(XX)$ should vanish, i.e.

$$\begin{aligned} \sigma\dot{a}_{0\,1} &= \Big(\frac{X_i}{\sqrt{(XX)}} + \frac{\overline{X_i}}{\sqrt{(\bar{X}\bar{X})}}\Big), \\ \sigma\dot{a}_{j\,k} &= -i\Big(\frac{X_i}{\sqrt{(XX)}} - \frac{\overline{X_i}}{\sqrt{(\bar{X}\bar{X})}}\Big). \end{aligned} \tag{2}$$

To get the other line of the cross, i.e. the Absolute polar of the line $(\dot{a})$, we merely have to reverse the sign of one of our radicals.

There is one, and only one case, where our equations (2) become illusory, namely where

$$(XX) = 0.$$

This will arise when

$$(\dot{a} \mid \dot{a}) = \Sigma\,\dot{a}_{0i}{}^2 - \Sigma\,\dot{a}_{ik}{}^2 = 0,$$

i.e. when the directrices of the congruence are tangent to the Absolute. All complexes of the pencil will here be special, and will be determined severally by lines intersecting the various tangents to the Absolute at this point. Any mutually polar lines of the pencil of tangents, will, conversely, serve to determine the coaxal system. We may then represent such a pencil of tangent lines by a set of homogeneous values (X) where $(XX) = 0$, and, conversely, every such set of homogeneous values will determine a pencil of tangents to the Absolute. We shall therefore define such a pencil of tangents as an *improper cross*.

Theorem 1. There exists a perfect one to one correspondence between the assemblage of all crosses in hyperbolic space, and the assemblage of all points of the complex plane of elliptic space. Improper crosses will correspond to points of the elliptic Absolute.

We shall say that two crosses intersect if their lines intersect. The N. S. condition for this in the case of two proper crosses will be

$$\frac{(XY)}{\sqrt{(XX)}\,\sqrt{(YY)}} = \frac{\pm(\bar{X}\bar{Y})}{\sqrt{(\bar{X}\bar{X})}\,\sqrt{(\bar{Y}\bar{Y})}}.$$

Geometrically a line may intersect either member of a cross. This ambiguity disappears in the case of perpendicular intersection.

Theorem 2. Two intersecting crosses will correspond to points, the cosine of whose distance is real, or pure imaginary; crosses intersecting orthogonally will correspond to orthogonal points of the elliptic plane.

The assemblage of crosses which intersect a given cross orthogonally will be given by means of a linear equation. A linear equation will be transformed linearly into another linear equation, if the variables and coefficients be treated contragrediently. Geometrically we shall imagine that our assemblage of crosses, *cross space* let us say, is doubly overlaid, the crosses of one layer being represented by points and those of the other by lines in the complex plane, we have then

Theorem 3. The necessary and sufficient condition that two crosses of different layers should intersect orthogonally is that the corresponding line and point of the complex plane should be in united position.

If a cross be improper, the assemblage of all crosses cutting it orthogonally will be made up of all lines through the point of contact, and all lines in the plane of contact. This assemblage, reducible in point space, is irreducible in cross space.

The collineation group of cross space, is the general group depending on eight complex, or sixteen real parameters

$$\rho X_i{}' = \sum_{j}^{1..3} a_{ij} X_i, \quad |a_{ij}| \neq 0. \tag{3}$$

When will this indicate a transformation of point space? It is certainly necessary that improper crosses should go into improper crosses, hence the substitution must be of the orthogonal type. Moreover, the Absolute of hyperbolic space will be transformed into itself, so that our transformation of point space must be a congruent one. Conversely, it is immediately evident that a congruent transformation will transform cross space linearly into itself. Also, an orthogonal substitution in cross coordinates will carry an improper cross into an improper cross, and will carry intersecting crosses into other intersecting crosses. The corresponding transformation in point space is not completely determined, for a polar reciprocation in the Absolute of point space appears as the identical transformation of cross space. A transformation which carries intersecting crosses into intersecting crosses may thus be interpreted either as a collineation, or a correlation of point space.

Theorem 4. Every collineation or correlation of hyperbolic space which leaves the Absolute invariant will be equivalent to an orthogonal substitution in cross space, and every such orthogonal substitution may be interpreted either as a congruent transformation of hyperbolic space, or a congruent transformation coupled with a polar reciprocation in the Absolute.

Let us now inquire as to what are the simplest figures of cross space. The simplest one dimensional figure is the *chain* composed of all crosses whose coordinates are linearly dependent, by means of real coefficients, on those of two given crosses,

$$\rho X_i = aY_i + bZ_i, \quad i = 1,\ 2,\ 3. \tag{4}$$

Interpreting these equations in the complex plane we see that we have ∞^1 points of a line so related that the cross ratio of any four is real. If this line be represented in the Gauss plane, the chain will be represented by a circle. If the line be imaginary, the real lines, one through each point of the chain, will generate a linear pencil or a regulus.[45]

The crosses of the chain will cut orthogonally another cross (of the other layer) called the *axis* of the chain. The axis being proper, the chain will contain two improper crosses, namely, the pencils of tangents to the Absolute where it meets the actual line of the chain.

There is a theorem of very great generality connected with chains, which we shall now give. Suppose that we have a congruence of lines of such a nature that the corresponding cross coordinates (U) are analytic functions of two real parameters u, v. The cross of common perpendiculars to the cross (U) and the adjacent cross $(U + dU)$ will be given by

$$X_i = \begin{vmatrix} U_j & U_k \\ \dfrac{\partial U_j}{\partial u} & \dfrac{\partial U_k}{\partial u} \end{vmatrix} du + \begin{vmatrix} U_j & U_k \\ \dfrac{\partial U_j}{\partial v} & \dfrac{\partial U_k}{\partial v} \end{vmatrix} dv. \tag{5}$$

There are two sharply distinct sub-cases, (a)

$$\left| U \frac{\partial U}{\partial u} \frac{\partial U}{\partial v} \right| \equiv 0. \tag{6}$$

Here there is but one common perpendicular to (U) and all adjacent crosses. Such a congruence shall be called *synectic*. Let us exclude this case for the moment and pass to the other, where, (b)

$$\left| U \frac{\partial U}{\partial u} \frac{\partial U}{\partial v} \right| \not\equiv 0. \tag{7}$$

We shall mean by the *general position* of a line in such a congruence, one where this determinant does not vanish. We have then the theorem:[46]

Theorem 5. The common perpendiculars to a line, in the general position, of a non-synectic congruence, and each adjacent line will generate a chain.

Let us find, in point coordinates, the equation of the surface obtained by splitting off from a chain its improper crosses. We easily see that there will be two crosses of the chain which intersect orthogonally; taking these and the axes to determine the coordinate system, we may express our chain in the simple form

$$X_1 = a(p + qi), \quad X_2 = b(r + si), \quad X_3 = 0.$$

[45]The concept 'chain of imaginary points' is due to Von Staudt. See his 'Beiträge', loc. cit., pp. 137–42. For an extension, see Segre, 'Su un nuovo campo di ricerche geometriche,' *Atti della R. Accademia delle Scienze di Torino*, vol. xxv, 1890.

[46]The analogous theorem for euclidean space is due to Hamilton, see his paper on 'Systems of Rays', *Transactions of the Royal Irish Academy*, vol. xv, 1829.

Eliminating a/b we get

$$(p\dot{a}_{31} + q\dot{a}_{02})(r\dot{a}_{10} - s\dot{a}_{23}) = (p\dot{a}_{02} - q\dot{a}_{31})(r\dot{a}_{23} + s\dot{a}_{01}).$$

This gives the equation of the chain surface in point coordinates

$$(ps - qr)(-\dot{x}_0{}^2 + \dot{x}_3{}^2)\dot{x}_1\dot{x}_2 + (pr + qs)(\dot{x}_1{}^2 + \dot{x}_2{}^2)\dot{x}_0\dot{x}_3 = 0. \tag{8}$$

If
$$(ps - qr) = 0 \quad \text{or} \quad (pr + qs) = 0,$$

we have two real and two imaginary linear pencils; the conditions for this in cross coordinates will be invariant under the orthogonal, but not under the general group. The general form of our surface is a ruled quartic, having a strong similarity to the euclidean cylindroid.

The simplest two dimensional system of crosses is the *chain congruence*. This is made up of all crosses which have coordinates linearly dependent with real coefficients on those of three given crosses which do not cut a fourth orthogonally

$$X_i = aY_i + bZ_i + cT_0,$$

$$|XYZ| \neq 0, \quad i = 1,\ 2,\ 3. \tag{9}$$

Theorem 6. The crosses which correspond to the assemblage of all points of the real domain of a plane will generate a chain congruence.

Theorem 7. The common perpendiculars to pairs of crosses of a chain congruence will generate a second chain congruence in the other layer. Each congruence is the locus of the axes of the ∞^2 chains of the other; the two are said to be reciprocal to one another.

The reciprocal to the chain congruence (9) will have equations

$$U_i = p\begin{vmatrix} Y_i & Y_k \\ Z_j & Z_k \end{vmatrix} + q\begin{vmatrix} Z_j & Z_k \\ T_j & T_k \end{vmatrix} + r\begin{vmatrix} T_j & T_k \\ Y_i & Y_k \end{vmatrix}. \tag{10}$$

Let the reader show that the chain congruence may be reduced to the canonical form

$$X_1 = a(p + qi), \quad X_2 = b(r + si), \quad X_3 = c(t + ri),$$

where a, b, c are real homogeneous variables.

There are various sub-cases under the congruent group. If

$$(ps - qr) = 0,$$

the congruence will be transformed into itself by a one-parameter group of rotations.

Again, let

$$(ps - qr) = 0, \quad (pr - qt) = 0.$$

Here we see that

$$\frac{(XX')}{\sqrt{(XX)}\,\sqrt{(X'X')}}$$

is real for any two crosses of the congruence, i.e. the congruence consists in all crosses through the point (1, 0, 0, 0).

Leaving aside the special cases the following theorems may be proved for the general case.

Theorem 8. The chain congruence, considered as an assemblage of lines in point space, is of the third order and class. It is generated by common perpendiculars to the pairs of lines of a regulus. Those lines of the congruence which meet a line of the reciprocal congruence, orthogonally generate a quartic surface, those which meet such a line obliquely generate a regulus whose conjugate belongs to the reciprocal congruence. The two congruences have the same focal surface of order and class eight.

Another simple two-parameter system of crosses is the following

$$\rho X_i = aY_i + bZ_i + cT_i,$$

$$pY_i + qZ_i + sT_i \neq 0, \quad |YZT| = 0, \ (a\,b\,c\,p\,q\,r) \text{ real.}$$

All these crosses cut orthogonally the cross

$$U_i = \begin{vmatrix} Y_j & Y_k \\ Z_j & Z_k \end{vmatrix}.$$

Conversely, let us show that every cross orthogonally intersecting (U) may be expressed in this form. As such a form as this is invariant for all linear transformations, we may suppose

$$Y_3 = Z_3 = T_3 = 0.$$

We have then the equations

$$\begin{aligned} aY_1 + bZ_1 + cT_1 &= (r + ir')X_1, \\ aY_2 + bZ_2 + cT_2 &= (r + ir')X_2, \end{aligned}$$

which amount to four linear homogeneous equations in five unknowns a, b, c, r, r' and these may always be solved. There will be found to be one singular case where the same cross has ∞^1 determinations.

The assemblage of crosses cutting a cross orthogonally is but a special case of what we have already defined as a synectic congruence. If

$$X = X(uv), \quad \left| X \frac{\partial X}{\partial u} \frac{\partial X}{\partial v} \right| \equiv 0,$$

there will be but one common perpendicular to a cross and its adjacent crosses. This corresponds to the fact that there will exist an equation

$$f(X_1, X_2, X_3) = 0,$$

so that our congruence is represented by a curve, the tangent at any point representing the common perpendicular just mentioned (in the other layer), and, conversely, every curve will be represented by a synectic congruence. The points and tangents will be represented by two synectic congruences so related that each cross of one is a cross of striction of a cross of the other, and all its adjacent crosses. We may reach a still clearer idea of these congruences by anticipating some of the results of differential geometry to be proved in later chapters. For, if we look upon the congruence of lines generated by our crosses, we see that the two focal points on each are orthogonal and the two focal planes mutually perpendicular. From this we shall conclude that our line-congruence is one of normals, and the characteristics of the developable surfaces of the congruence will be geodesics of the focal surface, to which the lines of the other congruence are binormals. We shall, moreover, show in a later chapter that if r_1 and r_2 be the radii of curvature of normal sections of a surface in planes of curvature, then the Gaussian expression for the curvature of the surface at that point will be

$$\frac{1}{k\tan\frac{r_1}{k}}\cdot\frac{1}{k\tan\frac{r_2}{k}}+\frac{1}{k^2}.$$

In the present instance as the two focal points are orthogonal

$$\frac{r_2}{k}=\frac{\pi}{2}+\frac{r_1}{k},\qquad \frac{1}{k\tan\frac{r_1}{k}}\cdot\frac{1}{k\tan\frac{r_2}{k}}+\frac{1}{k^2}=0.$$

Our congruence is made up of normals to surfaces of Gaussian curvature zero, i.e. to surfaces whose distance element may be written

$$ds^2=du^2+dv^2.$$

Theorem 9.[47] A synectic congruence will represent the points of a curve of the complex plane. It will be made up of crosses whose lines are normals to a series of surfaces of Gaussian curvature zero. The characteristics of the developable surfaces are geodesics of the focal surfaces. Their orthogonal trajectories are a second set of geodesics whose tangents will generate a like congruence.

In conclusion, let us emphasize the distinction between these congruences and the non-synectic ones, where the common perpendiculars to a cross and its adjacent ones generate a chain.

Did we wish to represent the imaginary as well as the real members of a synectic or non-synectic congruence, we should be obliged to introduce into our representing plane, points with hypercomplex coordinates. We shall not enter into this extension, for, after all, the real point of interest of the subject lies merely in this, namely, to give a real interpretation for the geometry of the complex plane.

As we identify the geometry of the cross in hyperbolic space with that of a point of the complex plane, so we may relate a cross of elliptic (or spherical) space to a pair of real points of two plane. The modus operandi is as follows:—

We start, as before, with a pencil of coaxal linear complexes defined by

[47]Cf. Study, 'Zur nicht-euklidischen etc.,' cit., p. 328.

$$\begin{aligned} a_{01}+a_{23} &= \rho\, {}_lX_1, \quad a_{01}-a_{23}=\sigma\, {}_rX_1,\\ a_{02}+a_{31} &= \rho\, {}_lX_2, \quad a_{02}-a_{31}=\sigma\, {}_rX_2,\\ a_{03}+a_{12} &= \rho\, {}_lX_3, \quad a_{03}-a_{12}=\sigma\, {}_rX_3, \end{aligned} \tag{11}$$

If we replace our complex by another coaxal therewith, we shall merely multiply $({}_lX)({}_rX)$ by two different constants. Conversely, when we wish to move back from the independently homogeneous sets of coordinates $({}_lX)({}_rX)$ to the degenerate complexes of the pencil, i.e. to the lines of the cross defined thereby, we have to take for ρ and σ such values that the fundamental plückerian identity is satisfied,

$$\begin{aligned} \tau a_{0i} &= {}_lX_i\sqrt{({}_rX_r X)} + {}_rX_i\sqrt{({}_lX_l X)},\\ \tau a_{jk} &= {}_lX_i\sqrt{({}_rX_r X)} - {}_rX_i\sqrt{({}_lX_l X)}. \end{aligned} \tag{12}$$

The two separately homogeneous coordinate triads $({}_lX)({}_rX)$ may be taken to represent this proper cross, and, conversely, as all quantities involved so far are supposed to be real, every real pair of triads will correspond to a single cross.

Theorem 10. The assemblage of all real crosses of elliptic or spherical space may be put into one to one correspondence with the assemblage of all pairs of points one in each of two real planes.

Our doubly homogeneous coordinates have a second interpretation which is of the highest interest. Let us write the coordinates of a point of the Absolute in terms of two independent parameters, i.e. of the parameters determining the one and the other set of linear generators

$$x_0 : ix_1 : x_2 : ix_3 = (\lambda_1\mu_1 - \lambda_2\mu_2) : (\lambda_1\mu_1 + \lambda_2\mu_2) : (\lambda_1\mu_2 + \lambda_2\mu_1) : (\lambda_1\mu_2 - \lambda_2\mu_1).$$

The plückerian coordinates of a generator of the left or right system will thus be

$$\begin{aligned} p_{01} &= p_{23} = 2\lambda_1\lambda_2, & q_{01} &= -q_{23} = 2\mu_1\mu_2,\\ p_{02} &= p_{31} = i({\lambda_1}^2 + {\lambda_2}^2), & q_{02} &= -q_{31} = i({\mu_1}^2 + {\mu_2}^2),\\ p_{03} &= p_{12} = ({\lambda_1}^2 - {\lambda_2}^2), & q_{03} &= -q_{12} = -({\mu_1}^2 + {\mu_2}^2). \end{aligned}$$

The parameter (λ) of a left generator which meets a given line (a) will satisfy

$$2\lambda_1\lambda_2(a_{01}+a_{23}) + i({\lambda_1}^2 + {\lambda_2}^2)(a_{02}+a_{31}) + ({\lambda_1}^2 - {\lambda_2}^2)(a_{03}+a_{12}) = 0.$$

Similarly, for a right generator we have

$$2\mu_1\mu_2(a_{01}-a_{23}) + i({\mu_1}^2 + {\mu_2}^2)(a_{02}-a_{31}) - ({\mu_1}^2 - {\mu_2}^2)(a_{03}-a_{12}) = 0.$$

We thus get as a necessary and sufficient condition that two lines should be right (left) paratactic, that the differences (sums) of complementary pairs of plückerian coordinates in the one shall be proportional to the corresponding differences (sums) in the other. If the lines be (p) and (p'), the first of these conditions will be

$$[(p \mid p') + \Sigma p_{ij} pij']^2 - \Sigma {p_{ij}}^2 \Sigma {p_{ij}}'^2 = 0,$$

while the second is

$$[(p \mid p') - \Sigma p_{ij} pij']^2 - \Sigma {p_{ij}}^2 \Sigma {p_{ij}}'^2 = 0.$$

If these equations be multiplied together, we get (25) of Chapter IX.

If a line pass through the point $(1, 0, 0, 0)$ its last three plückerian coordinates will vanish, while the first three are proportional to those of its intersections with $x_0 = 0$. It thus appears that in (11) the coordinates $({}_lX)$ and $({}_rX)$ are nothing more nor less than the coordinates of the points, where the plane $x_0 = 0$ is met respectively by the left and the right paratactic through the point $(1, 0, 0, 0)$ to the two lines of the cross, for a line paratactic to the one is also paratactic to the other. It will, however, be more convenient to consider $({}_lX)$ and $({}_rX)$ as standing for points in two different planes, called, respectively, *the left and right representing planes.* We shall speak of two crosses as being paratactic, when their lines are so, and the necessary and sufficient condition therefore, invariant under the group of cross space, is that they should be represented by identical points in the one or the other plane.[48]

As in the hyperbolic case, so here, we shall look upon cross space as doubly overlaid, and assign a cross to the upper layer if it be determined by two points in the representing planes, while it shall be assigned to the lower layer if it be determined by two lines. Under these circumstances we may say:—

Theorem 11. In order that two crosses of different layers should intersect orthogonally, it is necessary and sufficient that they should be represented by line elements in the two planes.

We may go still further in this same direction. We shall mean by the right and left *Clifford angles* of two crosses, the angles of right and left paratactics to them through any chosen point. Let the reader show that the magnitude of these angles is independent of the choice of the last-named point. If, thus, we choose the point $(1, 0, 0, 0)$, the cosines of the Clifford angles will be

$$\frac{({}_lX_lY)}{\sqrt{({}_lX_lX)}\sqrt{({}_lY_lY)}}, \quad \frac{({}_rX_rY)}{\sqrt{({}_rX_rX)}\sqrt{({}_rY_rY)}}.$$

Now, from equations (19) and (20) of Chapter IX, we see that

$$\sin\frac{d}{k}\sin\frac{d'}{k} = \sin\theta\sin\theta' = \frac{(p \mid p')}{\sqrt{\Sigma {p_{ij}}^2}\sqrt{\Sigma {p_{ij}}'^2}},$$

[48]The whole question of left and right is considered most carefully in Study's 'Beiträge', cit., pp. 126, 156.

$$\cos\frac{d}{k}\cos\frac{d'}{k} = \cos\theta\cos\theta' = \frac{\Sigma\, p_{ij}p_{ij}'}{\sqrt{\Sigma\, p_{ij}^2}\,\sqrt{\Sigma\, p_{ij}'^2}};$$

hence, we easily find

$$(1)\quad \cos\left(\frac{d}{k}+\frac{d'}{k}\right) = \frac{({}_rX{}_rY)}{\sqrt{({}_rX{}_rX)}\,\sqrt{({}_rY{}_rY)}},$$

$$\cos\left(\frac{d}{k}-\frac{d'}{k}\right) = \frac{({}_lX{}_lY)}{\sqrt{({}_lX{}_lX)}\,\sqrt{({}_lY{}_lY)}}, \qquad (13)$$

or else

$$(2)\quad \cos\left(\frac{d}{k}-\frac{d'}{k}\right) = \frac{({}_rX{}_rY)}{\sqrt{({}_rX{}_rX)}\,\sqrt{({}_rY{}_rY)}},$$

$$\cos\left(\frac{d}{k}+\frac{d'}{k}\right) = \frac{({}_lX{}_lY)}{\sqrt{({}_lX{}_lX)}\,\sqrt{({}_lY{}_lY)}}.$$

The ambiguity can be removed by establishing certain conventions with regard to the signs of the radicals, into which we shall not enter.[49] We may, however, state the following theorem:—

Theorem 12. The Clifford angles of two lines have the same measures as the sums and differences of the kth parts of their distances, or the sums and differences of their angles. The necessary and sufficient condition that two lines should intersect is that their Clifford angles should be equal or supplementary.

When we adjoin the imaginary domain to the real one, serious complications will arise which can only be removed by careful definition. Without going into a complete discussion, we merely give the facts.[50]

If $({}_lX{}_lX) = 0$, $({}_rX{}_rX) \neq 0$, we shall say that we have a *left improper cross*, and denote thereby a left generator of the Absolute, conjoined to a non-parabolic involution among the right generators. There will be ∞^3 such improper crosses, and ∞^3 right improper crosses, whose definition is obvious. Left and right improper crosses together will constitute what shall be called *improper crosses of the first sort*. Improper crosses of the second sort shall be defined, as in hyperbolic space, as pencils of tangents to the Absolute, corresponding to sets of values for which $({}_lX{}_lX) = ({}_rX{}_rX) = 0$. The definitions of parataxy and orthogonal intersection may be extended to all cases, their analytic expression being as in the real domain.

The general group of linear transformations of cross space will depend upon sixteen essential parameters. It will be made up of the sixteen-parameter subgroup G_{16} of all transformations of the type

$$\rho\, {}_lX_i' = \sum_j a_{ij}\, {}_lX_j, \quad \sigma\, {}_rX_i' = \sum_j b_{ij}\, {}_rX_j, \quad |a_{ij}| \times |b_{ij}| \neq 0, \qquad (14)$$

[49]For an elaborate discussion, see Study, 'Beiträge,' cit., especially p. 130.

[50]Cf. the author's 'Dual projective Geometry', loc. cit., § 3.

and the sixteen-parameter assemblage H_{16} of all transformations of the type

$$\rho\,{}_lX_i' = \sum_j a_{ij}\,{}_rX_j, \quad \sigma\,{}_rX_i' = \sum_j b_{ij}\,{}_lX_j, \quad |a_{ij}| \times |b_{ij}| \neq 0. \tag{15}$$

Notice that under G_{16} left and right parataxy of crosses of the same layer are invariant, while under H_{16} the two sorts of parataxy are interchanged.

The group G_{16} will contain, as a sub-group, the group of all motions, while H_{16} includes the assemblage of all symmetry transformations. Let the reader show that there can be no collineations of point space under G_{16}, except congruent transformations, and that the necessary and sufficient condition that (14) should represent a motion of point space is that the transformations of the two representing planes should be of the orthogonal type.

The group G_{16} is half-simple, being composed entirely of two invariant subgroups ${}_lG_8$, ${}_rG_8$, of which the former is made up of the general linear transformation for $({}_lX)$ with the identical transformation for $({}_rX)$, while in the latter, the rôles of $({}_lX)$ and $({}_rX)$ are interchanged. The highest common factors of the group of motions with ${}_lG_8$ and ${}_rG_8$ respectively, will be the groups of left and right translations (cf. Chapter IX).

The simplest assemblages of crosses in elliptic space bear a close analogy to those of hyperbolic space, although possessing more variety in the real domain. Let

$${}_lX_i = a\,{}_lY_i + b\,{}_lZ_i, \quad {}_rX_i = a\,{}_rY_i + b\,{}_rZ_i,$$
$$|{}_lX\,{}_lY\,{}_lS| \times |{}_rX\,{}_rY\,{}_rT| \not\equiv 0.$$

The assemblage of crosses so defined shall be called a *chain*. The properties of these chains are entirely analogous to those in the hyperbolic case. For instance, take a congruence of crosses whose coordinates are analytic functions of two essential parameters (u), (v). Let us further assume that $({}_lY)$ $({}_rY)$ being crosses of the system

$$\left|{}_lY \frac{\partial}{\partial u}{}_lY \frac{\partial}{\partial v}{}_lY\right| \times \left|{}_rY \frac{\partial}{\partial u}{}_rY \frac{\partial}{\partial v}{}_rY\right| \not\equiv 0.$$

The meaning of this restriction is that neither $({}_lY)$ nor $({}_rY)$ can be expressed as functions of a single parameter, so that the crosses of the congruence cannot be assembled into the generators of ∞^1 surfaces, those of each surface being paratactic. Let the reader then show that for every such congruence, the common perpendiculars to a line in the general position, and its immediate neighbours, will generate a chain.

The chains of elliptic cross space will have the same subclassifications under the congruent group, as in the hyperbolic plane. Let the reader show that the general chain may be represented by means of a homographic relation between the points of two linear ranges in the representing planes, and that the special chain, composed of two pencils, arises, when the relation is a congruent one.

Suppose, next, that we have

$$\rho\,{}_lX_i = a\,{}_lY_i + b\,{}_lZ_i, \quad \sigma\,{}_rX_i = a\,{}_rY_i + b\,{}_rZ_i,$$

$${}_lY_i = r\,{}_lZ_i, \quad |{}_rY\,{}_rZ\,{}_rT| \neq 0.$$

This is a new one-parameter family of crosses called a *strip*, or, more exactly, a *left strip*. The common perpendiculars to pairs of crosses of the left strip will generate a right strip (whereof the definition is obvious), and each strip shall be said to be reciprocal to the other. A left strip of the upper layer will be represented by a point of the left plane, and a linear range of the right plane. The reciprocal strip in the lower layer will be represented by the pencil through the point in the left plane, and the line of the range in the right.

In point space, the lines of a strip are generators of a quadric, whose other generators belong to the reciprocal strip. Owing to the parataxy of the generators of such a quadric, it will intersect the Absolute in two generators of each set. We shall call our quadric a *Clifford surface*, when we wish to refer to it as a figure of point space. We shall show in Chapter XV, that these surfaces have Gaussian curvature zero, since they are generated by paratactic lines, and are minimal surfaces, since their asymptotic lines form an orthogonal system.[51]

The simplest two dimensional system of crosses will be, as before, the chain congruence

$${}_lX_i = a\,{}_lY_i + b\,{}_lZ_i + c\,{}_lT_i, \quad {}_rX_i = a\,{}_lX_i + b\,{}_lY_i + c\,{}_lZ_i$$

$$|{}_lY\,{}_lZ_lT| \times |{}_rY\,{}_rZ\,{}_rT| \neq 0.$$

We may solve the first three equations for a, b, c, and substitute in the last

$${}_rX_i = \sum_j a_{ij}\,{}_lX_j, \quad |a_{ij}| \neq 0.$$

This, again, may easily be reduced to the canonical form

$${}_rX_i = a_i\,{}_lX_i \tag{16}$$

The reciprocal congruence will be given by

$${}_lU_i = a_i\,{}_rU_i.$$

There are various sub-classes under the congruent group. If the squares of no two of our quantities a_i in (16) be equal, we have the general congruence, if we have one such equality, the congruence will be transformed into itself by a one-parameter group of rotations. If all three squares be equal, we have a bundle of crosses through a point. The general congruence will have all of the properties mentioned in (8).

A different sort of congruence will arise in the case where

$$|{}_lY\,{}_lZ_lT| = 0, \quad |{}_rY\,{}_rZ\,{}_rT| \neq 0. \tag{17}$$

This congruence will contain ∞^1 strips, whose reciprocals generate the reciprocal congruence. The common perpendiculars to all non-paratactic crosses of the

[51] Cf. Klein, 'Zur nicht-euklidischen Geometrie,' *Mathematische Annalen*, vol. xxxvii, 1890.

congruence will generate a bundle, those to paratactic crosses, the reciprocal congruence. Such a congruence will be generated by the common perpendiculars to the paratactic lines of two pencils which have different centres and planes, but a common line and paratactic axes. In point space the line congruence will be of order and class two. The canonical form will be[52]

$$
\begin{aligned}
{}_lX_1 &= a_1\,{}_rX_1,\\
{}_lX_2 &= a_2\,{}_rX_2,\\
{}_lX_3 &= 0.
\end{aligned}
$$

If, in addition to (17), we require the first minors of $|{}_lY\,{}_lZ\,{}_lT|$ all to vanish, we shall have a bundle of paratactic crosses. If, on the other hand, we have

$$|{}_lY{}_lZ{}_lT| = |{}_rY{}_rZ{}_rT| = 0,$$

without the vanishing of the first minors of either determinant, we have ∞^2 crosses cutting a given cross orthogonally. The equations of the congruence may be reduced to the canonical form

$$
\begin{aligned}
\rho\,{}_lX_1 &= a, & \sigma\,{}_rX_1 &= b,\\
\rho\,{}_lX_2 &= b, & \sigma\,{}_rX_2 &= c,\\
\rho\,{}_lX_3 &= 0, & \sigma\,{}_rX_3 &= 0.
\end{aligned}
\tag{18}
$$

The cross $(1,0,0)$ $(0,1,0)$ will be singular, having ∞^1 determinations.

In general, if we have

$$F({}_lX_1\,{}_lX_2\,{}_lX_3) = 0, \quad \phi({}_rX_1\,{}_rX_2\,{}_rX_3) = 0,$$

the line-congruence can be assembled into ∞^1 surfaces with left, and ∞^1 surfaces with right paratactic generators. Such surfaces will have Gaussian curvature zero. We shall show also in Chapter XVI that the lines of such a congruence are normals to a series of surfaces of Gaussian curvature zero.

---

[52]Apparently nothing has ever been published concerning this type of congruence. The theorems here given are taken from an unpublished section of the author's dissertation, cit.

CHAPTER XI

THE CIRCLE AND THE SPHERE

The simplest curvilinear figures in non-euclidean geometry are circles, and it is now time to study their properties.[53]

Definition. The locus of all points of a plane at a constant distance from a given point which is not on the Absolute is called a *circle.* The given point shall be called the *centre* of the circle, its absolute polar, which will also turn out to be its polar with regard to the circle, shall be called the *axis* of the circle. A line through the centre of the circle shall be called a *diameter.* Let the reader show that all points of a circle are at constant distances from the axis, a distance whose measure becomes infinite in the limiting euclidean case.

To get the equation of the circle whose centre is (a) and whose radius is r, i.e. this shall be the measure of the distance of all points from the centre, we have

$$\frac{(ax)}{\sqrt{(aa)}\,\sqrt{(xx)}} = \cos\frac{r}{k},$$

$$\cos^2\frac{r}{k}(aa)(xx) - (ax)^2 = 0. \tag{1}$$

It is evident that when $\cos^2\dfrac{r}{k} \neq 0$, this curve has double contact with the Absolute, the secant of contact being the axis, and, conversely, every such curve of the second order will be a circle. The absolute polar of a circle will, hence, be another circle, so that the circle is self-dual:—

Theorem 1. *Definition.* The locus of all points of a plane at a constant distance from a given point thereof is a circle whose centre is the given point.

Theorem 1′. The envelope of all lines of a plane which make a constant angle with a given line is a circle having the given line as axis.

Note that a circle of radius $\dfrac{\pi k}{2}$ is a line, and that circle of radius 0 is two lines.

Restricting ourselves, for the moment, to the real domain of the hyperbolic plane, we see that if the centre be ideal, the axis will be actual, and the curve will appear in the actual domain as the locus of points at a constant distance from the axis, an actual line. In this case the circle is sometimes called an *equidistant curve*. If the centre be actual we shall have what may be more properly called a *proper* circle. Notice that to a dweller in a small region of the hyperbolic space, a proper circle would appear much as does a euclidean circle to a euclidean dweller, while an equidistant curve would appear like two parallel lines. These

[53]For a very simple treatment of this subject by means of pure Geometry, see Riccordi, 'I cercoli nella geometria non-euclidea,' *Giornale di Matematica*, xviii, 1880. Riccordi's results had previously been reached analytically by Battaglini, 'Sul rapporto anarmonico sezionale e tangenziale delle coniche,' ibid., xii, 1874.

distinctions will, naturally, disappear in the elliptic case; in the spherical, the circle will have two centres, which are equivalent points.

If the point (a) tend to approach the Absolute (analytically speaking) the equation (1) will tend to approach an indeterminate form. The limiting form for the curve will be a conic having four-point contact with the Absolute. Such a curve shall be called a *horocycle*, the point of contact being called the centre, and the common tangent the axis. If (u) be the coordinates of the axis, we have

$$(uu) = 0,$$

and the equation of the horocycle takes the form

$$({u_1}^2 + {u_2}^2)(xx) + C(ux)^2 = 0.$$

Theorem 2. A tangent to a circle is perpendicular to the diameter through the point of contact.

Theorem 2′. A point on a circle is orthogonal to the point where the tangent thereat meets the axis.

These simple theorems may be proved in a variety of ways. For instance every circle will be transformed into itself by a reflection in any diameter, hence the tangent where the diameter meets the curve must be perpendicular to the diameter. Or, again, if $\overline{AB} \equiv \overline{AC}$, a line from A to one centre of gravity of B, C will be perpendicular to BC; then let B and C close up on this centre of gravity. Or, lastly, the equation of the tangent to the circle (1) at a point (y) will be

$$(xy)(aa) - N(ax)(ay) = 0.$$

The diameter through (y) will have the equation

$$|xya| = 0.$$

If we indicate these two lines by (u) and (v), then

$$(uv) = (aa)\,|yay| - N(ay)\,|aya|.$$

Let the reader show that these theorems hold also in the case of the horocycle.

Theorem 3. The locus of the centres of gravity of pairs of points of a circle whose lines are concurrent on the axis, is the point of concurrence, and the diameter perpendicular to these lines.

Theorem 3′. The envelope of the bisectors of the angles of tangents to a circle from points of a diameter, is this diameter, and its absolute pole.

Theorem 4. If two tangents to a circle (horocycle) make a constant angle, the locus of their point of intersection is a concentric circle (horocycle).

Theorem 4′. If two points of a circle (horocycle) are at a constant distance, the envelope of their line is a coaxal circle (horocycle).

The element of arc of a circle of radius (r) will be, by Chapter IV (5),

$$ds = k\sin\frac{r}{k}d\theta.$$

The circumference of the circle is thus

$$k\sin\frac{r}{k}\int_0^{2\pi} d\theta = 2\pi k\sin\frac{r}{k}.$$

Let the tangents at P and P' meet at Q, the centre of the circle being A. Let $\Delta\phi$ be the angle between the tangents, and let P'' be the point on the tangent at P whose distance from P equals PP', or, in the infinitesimal, equals ds. The $\Delta PAP'$ and $\Delta P'PP''$ are isosceles, hence

$$\Delta\phi = 2\measuredangle P'PP'',$$

$$\tan\frac{\overline{P'P''}}{2k} = \sin\frac{\overline{PP'}}{k}\tan\frac{\Delta\phi}{4}$$

$$\text{limit}\frac{\Delta\phi}{ds} = \text{limit}\frac{4\tan\dfrac{\overline{P'P''}}{2k}}{\overline{PP'}\sin\dfrac{\overline{PP'}}{k}} = \text{limit}\frac{\overline{2P'P''}}{\overline{PP'^2}}.$$

But
$$\tan\frac{\overline{PQ}}{k} = \sin\frac{r}{k}\tan\tfrac{1}{2}d\theta = \frac{ds}{2k},$$

$$\tan\frac{\overline{PQ}}{k} = \tan\frac{\overline{AQ}}{k}\cos\tfrac{1}{2}(\pi - \Delta\phi) \text{ by IV (6)},$$

$$\text{limit}\tan\frac{\overline{PQ}}{k} = \tfrac{1}{2}\tan\frac{r}{k}\Delta\phi.$$

Hence
$$\text{limit}\frac{\Delta\phi}{ds} = \text{limit}\frac{\overline{2P'P''}}{\overline{PP'^2}} = \frac{1}{k\tan\dfrac{r}{k}}. \qquad (2)$$

We shall subsequently define this expression as the curvature of the circle at the point (P). We see that, as we should expect, it is constant.

We shall next take up simple systems of circles. We leave to the reader the task of making the slight modifications in what follows necessary to adapt it to the case of spherical geometry. In the general case two circles, neither of which is a line, will intersect in four points, real, or imaginary, in pairs. If two circles lie completely without one another they will have four real common tangents, the absolute polars of such circles will intersect in four real points. The difficulty of visualization disappears in the hyperbolic case where we take one at least of the circles as an equidistant curve. If we identify the euclidean hemisphere, where opposite points of the equator are considered identical, with the elliptic plane, we see how two circles there also can intersect in four real points. In the spherical case, by Chapter VIII, the Absolute is the locus of all points which are identical with their equivalents. A point will have one absolute polar, a line two equivalent absolute poles. The absolute polar of a circle is two equivalent circles, which are also the absolute polars of the equivalent circle. Two real circles cannot intersect in more than two real points.

Two circles which intersect in four points will have three pairs of common secants. The problem of finding the common secants of two conics will, in general, lead to an irreducible equation of the third degree. When, however, the two conics have double contact with a third, the equation is reducible, and one pair of secants appears which intersect on the chords of contact, and are harmonically separated by them.[54] In the case of two circles these secants shall be called the *radical axes*.

Theorem 5. If two circles intersect in four points, two common secants called radical axes are concurrent with the axes of the circles and harmonically separated by them, They are perpendicular to one another and to the line of centres. The centres of gravity of the intersections of the circles with a radical axis are the intersections with the other radical axis and with the line of centres.

Theorem 5$'$. If two circles have four common tangents, two intersections of these, called centres of similitude, lie on the line of centres, are harmonically separated by the centres and are mutually orthogonal. The bisectors of angles of the tangents at a centre of similitude are the line of centres and the line to the other centre of similitude.

If the equations of the two circles be

$$\cos^2\frac{r_1}{k}(aa)(xx)-(ax)^2=0,\quad \cos^2\frac{r_2}{k}(bb)(xx)-(bx)^2=0,$$

the equations of the radical axes will be

$$\left(\cos\frac{r_2}{k}\sqrt{(bb)}(ax)+\cos\frac{r_1}{k}\sqrt{(aa)}(bx)\right)\left(\cos\frac{r_2}{k}\sqrt{(bb)}(ax)-\cos\frac{r_1}{k}\sqrt{(aa)}(bx)\right)=0. \qquad (3)$$

The last factor equated to zero will give

$$\frac{\dfrac{(ax)}{\sqrt{(aa)}\sqrt{(xx)}}}{\cos\dfrac{r_1}{k}}=\frac{\dfrac{(bx)}{\sqrt{(bb)}\sqrt{(xx)}}}{\cos\dfrac{r_2}{k}},$$

and the two sides of this equation will, by Ch. IV (4), be the cosines of the kth parts of the distances from (x) to the points of contact of tangents, thence to the two circles.

[54]This theorem is, of course, well known. Cf. Salmon, *Conic Sections*, sixth edition. London, 1879, p. 242.

Theorem 6. If a set of circles through two points have the line of these points as a radical axis, the points of contact of tangents to all of them from a point of the line lie on a circle whose centre is this point.

Theorem 6′. If a set of circles tangent to two given lines have the intersection of the lines as a centre of similitude, the envelope of tangents to them at the points where they meet a line through this centre of similitude will be a circle with this line as axis.

Consider the assemblage of all circles through two given points. If the line connecting the two points be a radical axis for two of these circles it will be perpendicular to their line of centres at one centre of gravity of the two points, and in every case a perpendicular from the centre of a circle on a secant will meet it at a centre of gravity of the two points of the circle on that line. We thus see—

Theorem 7. The assemblage of all circles through two common points will fall into two families according as the perpendicular from the centre on the line of these points passes through the one or the other of their centres of gravity. Two circles of the same family, and they only, will have the line as a radical axis.

Theorem 7′. The assemblage of all circles tangent to two lines will fall into two families according as the centres lie on the one or the other bisector of the angles of the lines. Two circles of the same family, and they only, will have the intersection of the lines as a centre of similitude.

Let us now take a third point, and consider the circles that pass through all three.

Theorem 8. Four circles will pass through three given points. Each line connecting two of the given points will be a radical axis for two pairs of circles.

Theorem 8′. Four circles will touch three given lines. Each intersection of two lines will be a centre of similitude for two pairs of circles.

Theorem 9. The radical axes of three circles pass by threes through four points.

Theorem 9′. The centres of similitude of three circles lie by threes on four lines.

Of course when two circles touch one another, their common tangent replaces one radical axis, and the point of contact one centre of similitude. Two circles will have double contact when, and only when, they are concentric. We get at once from (6) and (9)

Theorem 10. Four circles may be constructed to cut each of three circles at right angles twice.

Theorem 10′. Four circles may be constructed so that the points of contact of tangents common to them and to each of three given circles form two pairs of orthogonal points.

It is here assumed that no two of the given circles are concentric. There is no reason to expect that because two circles intersect at right angles in two points they will in the other two. Let the circles be

$$\cos^2\frac{r_1}{k}(aa)(xx)-(ax)^2=0,\quad \cos^2\frac{r_2}{k}(bb)(xx)-(bx)^2=0.$$

Let (y) be a point of intersection; the lines thence to the centres are

$$|xya|=0,\quad |xyb|=0.$$

The cosine of the angle formed by them will be

$$\begin{aligned}\cos\theta &= \frac{\begin{vmatrix}(yy) & (ay)\\ (by) & (ab)\end{vmatrix}}{\sqrt{(yy)(aa)-(ay)^2}\,\sqrt{(yy)(bb)-(by)^2}}\\ &= \frac{(ab)-\cos\frac{r_1}{k}\cos\frac{r_2}{k}\sqrt{(aa)}\,\sqrt{(bb)}}{\sin\frac{r_1}{k}\sin\frac{r_2}{k}\sqrt{(aa)}\,\sqrt{(bb)}}.\end{aligned} \tag{4}$$

This gives two values for the angle which will be equal when, and only when

$$(ab)=0.$$

The condition of contact will be

$$\cos\theta=\pm 1,\quad \cos\left(\frac{r_1}{k}\pm\frac{r_2}{k}\right)=\frac{(ab)}{\sqrt{(aa)}\,\sqrt{(bb)}}; \tag{5}$$

and of orthogonal intersection

$$\cos\frac{r_1}{k}\cos\frac{r_2}{k}=\frac{(ab)}{\sqrt{(aa)}\,\sqrt{(bb)}}, \tag{6}$$

these last two facts being, also, geometrically evident. We see that two circles cannot have four rectangular intersections, for if

$$(ab)=0,\quad \cos\frac{r_2}{k}=0, \tag{7}$$

the circle is a line.

Theorem 11. The necessary and sufficient condition that two circles should cut at the same angle at all points is that their centres should be mutually orthogonal.

Theorem 11′. The necessary and sufficient condition that two circles should determine by their points of contact, congruent distances on all four common tangents, is that their axes should be mutually perpendicular.

Notice that these two conditions are really identical.

We shall define as a sphere that surface which is the locus of all points of space at congruent distances from a point not on the Absolute.

Theorem 12. A sphere is the locus of all points at a constant distance from a given point not on the Absolute. It is, when not a plane, a quadric with conical contact with the Absolute.

Theorem 12′. A sphere is the envelope of planes meeting at a constant angle a plane which is not tangent to the Absolute. It is, when not a point, a quadric with conical contact with the Absolute.

Note that a plane and point are special cases of the sphere.

The fixed point shall be called the centre, the plane of conical contact the *axial plane* of the sphere. A line connecting any point with the centre of a sphere is perpendicular to the polar plane of the point, a tangent plane is perpendicular to the line from the point of contact to the centre, to the diameter through the point of contact let us say.

Theorem 13. Two spheres will intersect in two circles whose planes are perpendicular to the line of centres and to one another, and are harmonically separated by the axial planes.

Theorem 13′. The common tangent planes to two spheres envelop two cones of revolution whose vertices are mutually orthogonal and harmonically separated by the centres.

Theorem 14. Three spheres not containing a common circle will meet in three pairs of circles whose planes are collinear by threes in four lines.

Theorem 14′. Three spheres not tangent to a cone of revolution have three such pairs of common tangent cones whose vertices are collinear in threes on four lines.

Theorem 15. Four spheres whose centres are not coplanar intersect in twelve circles whose planes pass by sixes through eight points which, with the centres of the spheres, form a desmic configuration.

Theorem 15′. Four spheres whose axial planes are not concurrent are enveloped in pairs by twelve cones of revolution whose vertices lie by sixes in eight planes which, with the axial planes, determine a desmic configuration.

Theorem 16. The necessary and sufficient condition that two spheres should cut at the same angle along their two circles is that their centres should be mutually orthogonal.

Theorem 16′. The necessary and sufficient condition that two spheres should, by their contact, determine congruent distances on the generators of the two circumscribed cones, is that their axial planes should be mutually perpendicular.

We shall terminate this chapter by giving an unusually elegant transformation from euclidean to non-euclidean space.[55] Let us assume that we have a euclidean space where a point has the homogeneous coordinates x, y, z, t and a hyperbolic space for which $k^2 = -1$, a point being given by our usual $(\dot{x})$ coordinates. Let us then write

$$\rho x = \dot{x}_1, \quad \rho y = \dot{x}_2, \quad \rho z = \sqrt{\dot{x}_0{}^2 - \dot{x}_1{}^2 - \dot{x}_2{}^2 - \dot{x}_3{}^2}, \quad \rho t = \dot{x}_0 - \dot{x}_3. \tag{8}$$

To each point of hyperbolic space will correspond two points of euclidean space. Let us choose that for which the real part of $\sqrt{\dot{x}_0{}^2 - \dot{x}_1{}^2 - \dot{x}_2{}^2 - \dot{x}_3{}^2}$ is greater than zero. When the real part vanishes, we may, by adjoining to our domain of rationality a square root of minus one, distinguish between the imaginary roots, and so choose one in particular. We may thus say that to every point of hyperbolic space, not on the Absolute, will correspond a point of euclidean space above the plane $z = 0$, and to each points of the Absolute will correspond points of this plane. The transformation is real, so that real and actual points will correspond to real ones. Conversely, we get from (8)

$$\sigma\dot{x}_0 = x^2 + y^2 + z^2 + t^2, \quad \sigma\dot{x}_1 = 2xt, \quad \sigma\dot{x}_2 = 2yt, \quad \sigma\dot{x}_3 = x^2 + y^2 + z^2 - t^2, \tag{9}$$

and to each point of euclidean space, above, or on the z plane, will correspond a point of hyperbolic space, not on, or on the Absolute.

Suppose that we have a euclidean sphere of centre (a, b, c, d) and radius r. If we write for short

$$(a^2 + b^2 + c^2 - d^2r^2) = p^2,$$

the equation of this sphere may be written

$$(dx - at)^2 + (dy - bt)^2 + (dz - ct)^2 = d^2r^2t^2,$$
$$d^2(x^2 + y^2 + z^2) - 2dt(ax + by + cz) + p^2t^2 = 0. \tag{10}$$

Transforming we get, after splitting off a factor $\dot{x}_3 - \dot{x}_0$ which corresponds to the euclidean plane at infinity,

$$d^2(\dot{x}_0 + \dot{x}_3) - 2d(a\dot{x}_1 + b\dot{x}_2 + c\sqrt{\dot{x}_0{}^2 - \dot{x}_1{}^2 - \dot{x}_2{}^2 - \dot{x}_3{}^2}) + p^2(\dot{x}_0 - \dot{x}_3) = 0,$$

[55] This transformation seems to have been first given in the second edition of *Wissenschaft und Hypothese*, by Poincaré, translated by F. and L. Lindemann, Leipzig, 1906, p. 258. This is fruitfully used in the dissertation of Münich, 'Nicht-euklidische Cykliden,' Munich, 1906. We have adapted the notation to conform to our own usage.

$$[(d^2+p^2)\dot{x}_0 - 2ad\dot{x}_1 - 2bd\dot{x}_2 + (d^2-p^2)\dot{x}_3]^2$$
$$= 4c^2d^2({\dot{x}_0}^2 - {\dot{x}_1}^2 - {\dot{x}_2}^2 - {\dot{x}_3}^2). \quad (11)$$

This is a sphere of hyperbolic space whose centre is

$$(d^2+p^2,\ 2ad,\ 2bd,\ p^2-d^2),$$

and whose radius r_1 is given by

$$\cosh r_1 = \frac{c}{\sqrt{p^2-a^2-b^2}}.$$

Conversely, if we have the hyperbolic sphere

$$(\dot{a}_0\dot{x}_0 - \dot{a}_1\dot{x}_1 - \dot{a}_2\dot{x}_2 - \dot{a}_3\dot{x}_3)^2$$
$$= \cosh^2 r_1({\dot{a}_0}^2 - {\dot{a}_1}^2 - {\dot{a}_2}^2 - {\dot{a}_3}^2)({\dot{x}_0}^2 - {\dot{x}_1}^2 - {\dot{x}_2}^2 - {\dot{x}_3}^2), \quad (12)$$

we get from (9)

$$[(\dot{a}_0 - \dot{a}_3)(x^2+y^2+z^2) - 2\dot{a}_1xt - 2\dot{a}_2yt + (\dot{a}_0+\dot{a}_3)t^2]$$
$$= \pm 2\cosh r_1\sqrt{{\dot{a}_0}^2 - {\dot{a}_1}^2 - {\dot{a}_2}^2 - {\dot{a}_3}^2}\,zt. \quad (13)$$

We have here two spheres which differ merely in the z coordinate of their centre, i.e. two spheres which are reflections of one another in the z plane. If the hyperbolic sphere were real and actual, one of the euclidean spheres would lie wholly above the z plane, and the other wholly below it. We may say that (leaving aside special cases) a hyperbolic sphere will correspond to so much of a euclidean sphere as is above or in the z plane, and to the reflection in the z plane of so much of the sphere as is below it.

A euclidean sphere for which $c = 0$, that is, one whose centre is in the z plane will correspond to a plane in hyperbolic space, a hyperbolic sphere for which

$$\dot{a}_0 - \dot{a}_3 = 0,$$

that is, one whose centre is in the plane which corresponds to the euclidean plane at infinity, will correspond to a plane in euclidean space. A euclidean circle perpendicular to the z plane will correspond to a hyperbolic line, a hyperbolic circle which is perpendicular to the plane $\dot{a}_0 - \dot{a}_3 = 0$, will correspond to a euclidean line.

We may go a step further in this direction. Suppose that we have two euclidean spheres given by an equation of the type (13), and the condition that they shall be mutually orthogonal is that

$$-\dot{a}_0\dot{a}_0' + \dot{a}_1\dot{a}_1' + \dot{a}_2\dot{a}_2'$$
$$\pm\cosh r_1\cosh r_1'\sqrt{{\dot{a}_0}^2 - {\dot{a}_1}^2 - {\dot{a}_2}^2 - {\dot{a}_3}^2}\,\sqrt{{\dot{a}_0}'^2 - {\dot{a}_1}'^2 - {\dot{a}_2}'^2 - {\dot{a}_3}'^2}$$
$$+\dot{a}_3\dot{a}_3' = 0,$$

$$\cosh r_1 \cosh r_1{}' = \pm \frac{-\dot{a}_0\dot{a}_0{}' + \dot{a}_1\dot{a}_1{}' + \dot{a}_2\dot{a}_2{}' + \dot{a}_3\dot{a}_3'}{\sqrt{-\dot{a}_0{}^2 + \dot{a}_1{}^2 + \dot{a}_2{}^2 + \dot{a}_3{}^2}\ \sqrt{-\dot{a}_0{}'^2 + \dot{a}_1{}'^2 + \dot{a}_2{}'^2 + \dot{a}_3{}'^2}}.$$

But this gives immediately that the corresponding hyperbolic spheres are also mutually orthogonal, and conversely. We thus have a correspondence of orthogonal spheres to orthogonal spheres. We see next that the lines of curvature of any surface will go into any lines of curvature of the corresponding surface, and hence the Darboux-Dupin theorem must hold in hyperbolic space, namely, in any triply orthogonal system of surfaces, the intersections are lines of curvature.

Were we willing to sacrifice the real domain, we might in a similar manner establish a correspondence between spheres of euclidean and of elliptic space.

CHAPTER XII

CONIC SECTIONS

The study of the metrical properties of conics in the non-euclidean plane, is, in the last analysis, nothing more nor less than a study of the invariants and covariants of two conics. We shall not, however, go into general questions of invariant theory here, but rather try to pick out those metrical properties of non-euclidean conics which bear the closest analogy to the corresponding euclidean properties.[56]

First of all, let us classify our conics under the real congruent group; that is, in relation to their intersections with the Absolute. This may be done analytically by means of Weierstrass's elementary divisors, but the geometric question is so easy that we give the results merely. We shall begin with the real conics in the actual domain of hyperbolic space.

(1) Convex hyperbolas. Four real absolute points, no real absolute tangents.

(2) Concave hyperbolas. Four real absolute points, four real absolute tangents.

(3) Semi-hyperbolas. Two real and two imaginary absolute points and tangents.

(4) Ellipses. Four imaginary absolute points and tangents.

(5) Concave hyperbolic parabolas. Two coincident, and two real and distinct absolute points and tangents.

(6) Convex hyperbolic parabolas. Two coincident, and two real and distinct absolute points. Two coincident, and two conjugate imaginary absolute tangents.

(7) Elliptic parabolas. Two coincident, and two conjugate imaginary absolute points and tangents.

(8) Osculating parabolas. Three real coincident, and one real distinct absolute point, and the same for absolute tangents.

(9) Equidistant curves.

(10) Proper circles.

(11) Horocycles.

In the real elliptic, or spherical, plane, we shall have merely—

(1) Ellipses;

(2) Circles.

In what follows we shall limit ourselves to *central conics*, i.e. to those which cut the Absolute in four distinct points. A real central conic in the actual domain of the hyperbolic plane will have a common self-conjugate triangle with

[56]The treatment of conics in the present chapter is in close accord with three articles by D'Ovidio, 'Le proprietà focali delle coniche,' 'Sulle coniche confocali,' and 'Teoremi sulle coniche', all in the *Atti della R. Accademia delle Scienze di Torino*, vol. xxvi, 1891. These articles suffer from the curious blemish, not uncommon in Italian mathematical publications, that the theorems are not given in distinctive type. See also Story, 'On the non-euclidean Properties of Conics,' *American Journal of Mathematics*, vol. v, 1882; Killing, 'Die nicht-euklidische Geometrie in analytischer Behandlung,' Leipzig, 1885, and Liebmann, 'Nicht-euklidische Geometrie,' in the *Sammlung Schubert*, xlix, Leipzig, 1904.

the Absolute which is real, except in the case of the semi-hyperbola. In the elliptic case it will surely be real. Taking this as the coordinate triangle we may write the equation of the Absolute in typical form, while that of the conic is

$$\sum_{i}^{0..2} c_i x_i^2 = 0. \tag{1}$$

We assume that no two of our c's are equal, and that none of them are equal to zero.

Our plane being $x_3 = 0$, we shall use the letters h, k, l as a circular permutation of the numbers 0, 1, 2, and define the vertices of the common self-conjugate triangles as *centres* of the conic, while its sides are called the *axes*. Be it noticed that in speaking of *triangle* in this sense we are using the terminology of projective geometry where a triangle is a figure of three coplanar, but not concurrent lines, and not the exact definition of Chapter I, which is meaningless except in a restricted domain. There will, however, arise no confusion from this.

Theorem 1. Each centre of a central conic is a centre of gravity for every pair of points of the conic collinear therewith.

Theorem 1′. Each axis of a central conic is a bisector of an angle of each pair of tangents to the conic concurrent thereon.

The three pairs of lines which connect the pairs of intersections of a central conic with the Absolute shall be called its pairs of *focal lines*. The three pairs of intersections of its absolute tangents shall be called its pairs of *foci*.

Theorem 2. Conjugate points of a focal line of a conic are mutually orthogonal.

Theorem 2′. Conjugate lines through a focus of a conic are mutually perpendicular.

Theorem 3. Two focal lines of a central conic pass through each vertex, and are perpendicular to the opposite axis.

Theorem 3′. Two foci of a central quadric lie on each axis, and are orthogonal to the opposite centre.

The coordinates of the focal lines f_h, f_h', through the centre $u_h = 0$, will be

$$u_h : u_k : u_l = 0 : \sqrt{c_h - c_k} : \pm\sqrt{c_l - c_h}. \tag{2}$$

The coordinates of the foci F_h, F_h' on the opposite axis will be

$$x_h : x_k : x_l = 0 : \sqrt{c_l(c_h - c_k)} : \pm\sqrt{c_k(c_l - c_h)}. \tag{3}$$

The polars of the foci with regard to the conic shall be called *directrices*, the poles of the focal lines its *director points*. A directrix d_h perpendicular to the axis x_h will have the equation

$$\sqrt{c_k(c_h - c_k)}x_k + \sqrt{c_l(c_l - c_h)}x_l = 0. \tag{4}$$

Let (x) be a point of the conic. Eliminating x_h by means of (1) we get

$$(xx) = \frac{(c_h - c_k)}{c_h} x_k{}^2 - \frac{(c_l - c_h)}{c_h} x_l{}^2.$$

We then have

$$\cos \frac{\overline{PF_h}}{k} = \frac{\sqrt{c_l(c_h - c_k)}x_k + \sqrt{c_k(c_l - c_h)}x_l}{\sqrt{(c_h - c_k)x_k{}^2 - (c_l - c_h)x_l{}^2}\,\sqrt{(c_l - c_k)}}. \tag{5}$$

$$\sin \frac{\overline{PF_h}}{k} = \frac{\sqrt{c_k(c_h - c_k)}x_k + \sqrt{c_l(c_l - c_h)}x_l}{\sqrt{(c_h - c_k)x_k{}^2 - (c_l - c_h)x_l{}^2}\,\sqrt{(c_k - c_l)}}. \tag{6}$$

If d_h be the corresponding directrix

$$\sin \frac{\overline{Pd_h}}{k} = \frac{\sqrt{c_k(c_h - c_k)}x_k + \sqrt{c_l(c_l - c_h)}x_l}{\sqrt{(c_h - c_k)x_k{}^2 - (c_l - c_h)x_l{}^2}\,\sqrt{\frac{c_k}{c_h}(c_h - c_k) + \frac{c_l}{c_h}(c_l - c_h)}}, \tag{7}$$

the signs of the radicals in the numerators of the two expressions being the same

$$\frac{\sin \frac{\overline{PF_h}}{k}}{\sin \frac{\overline{Pd_h}}{k}} = \frac{\sqrt{c_k(c_h - c_k) + c_l(c_l - c_h)}}{\sqrt{c_h(c_k - c_l)}}$$

$$= \sqrt{\frac{c_h - (c_k + c_l)}{c_k}}. \tag{8}$$

Theorem 4. The ratio of the sines of the kth parts of the distances from a point of a central conic to a focus and to the corresponding directrix is constant.

Theorem 4′. The ratio of the sines of the angles which a tangent to a central conic makes with a focal line and the absolute polar of the corresponding director point is constant.

$$\cos \frac{\overline{F_h F_h{}'}}{k} = \frac{c_l(c_h - c_k) - c_k(c_l - c_h)}{c_l(c_h - c_k) + c_k(c_l - c_h)}, \quad \tan^2 \tfrac{1}{2} \frac{\overline{F_h F_h{}'}}{k} = \frac{c_k(c_l - c_h)}{c_l(c_h - c_k)},$$

$$\tan^2 \tfrac{1}{2} \frac{\overline{F_h F_h{}'}}{k} \tan^2 \tfrac{1}{2} \frac{\overline{F_k F_k{}'}}{k} \tan^2 \tfrac{1}{2} \frac{\overline{F_l F_l{}'}}{k}$$
$$= \tan^2 \tfrac{1}{2}\measuredangle f_h f_h{}' \tan^2 \tfrac{1}{2}\measuredangle f_k f_k{}' \tan^2 \tfrac{1}{2}\measuredangle f_l f_l{}' = 1. \tag{9}$$

$$\sin \frac{\overline{PF_h}}{k} \sin \frac{\overline{PF_h{}'}}{k} = \frac{c_k(c_h - c_k)x_k{}^2 - c_l(c_l - c_h)x_l{}^2}{\left[(c_l - c_h)x_l{}^2 - (c_h - c_k)x_k{}^2\right](c_k - c_l)}$$

$$= \frac{\Sigma c_h{}^2 x_h{}^2}{c_h(c_k - c_l)(xx)},$$

$$\sin\frac{\overline{PF_h}}{k}\sin\frac{\overline{PF_h'}}{k} : \sin\frac{\overline{PF_k}}{k}\sin\frac{\overline{PF_k'}}{k} : \sin\frac{\overline{PF_l}}{k}\sin\frac{\overline{PF_l'}}{k}$$

$$= \frac{1}{c_h(c_k - c_l)} : \frac{1}{c_k(c_l - c_h)} : \frac{1}{c_l(c_h - c_k)}. \qquad (10)$$

$$\csc\frac{\overline{PF_h}}{k}\csc\frac{\overline{PF_h'}}{k} + \csc\frac{\overline{PF_k}}{k}\csc\frac{\overline{PF_k'}}{k} + \csc\frac{\overline{PF_l}}{k}\csc\frac{\overline{PF_l'}}{k} = 0. \qquad (11)$$

$$\cos\frac{\overline{PF_h}}{k}\cos\frac{\overline{PF_h'}}{k} = \frac{c_l(c_h - c_k)x_k{}^2 - c_k(c_l - c_h)x_l{}^2}{[(c_h - c_k)x_k{}^2 - (c_l - c_h)x_l{}^2](c_l - c_k)},$$

$$\cos\left[\frac{\overline{PF_h}}{k} \pm \frac{\overline{PF_h'}}{k}\right] = \frac{c_k + c_l}{c_k - c_l}. \qquad (12)$$

$$\tan\tfrac{1}{2}\left[\frac{\overline{PF_h}}{k} \pm \frac{\overline{PF_h'}}{k}\right]\tan\tfrac{1}{2}\left[\frac{\overline{PF_k}}{k} \pm \frac{\overline{PF_k'}}{k}\right]\tan\tfrac{1}{2}\left[\frac{\overline{PF_l}}{k} \pm \frac{\overline{PF_l'}}{k}\right] = \pm 1. \qquad (13)$$

With regard to the ambiguity of signs: the upper sign in (12) will go with the upper sign throughout in (13), and so for the lower sign. It is also geometrically evident that in the case of an ellipse we must take the upper, and in the case of a hyperbola the lower sign (when in the real domain).

Theorem 5. The sum of the distances from real points of an ellipse and the difference of the distances from real points of a hyperbola or semi-hyperbola to two real foci on the same axis is constant.

Theorem 5′. The sum of the angles which the real tangents to an ellipse or convex hyperbola, or the difference of the angles which the real tangents to a concave hyperbola or a semi-hyperbola make with two real focal lines through a centre is constant.

Reverting to our point (x) we see

$$\sin\frac{\overline{Pf_h}}{k} = \frac{\sqrt{c_h - c_k}\,x_k + \sqrt{c_l - c_h}\,x_l}{\sqrt{(c_l - c_h)x_l{}^2 - (c_h - c_k)x_k{}^2}\sqrt{\dfrac{-(c_k - c_l)}{c_h}}},$$

$$\sin\frac{\overline{Pf_h}}{k}\sin\frac{\overline{Pf_h'}}{k} = \pm\frac{c_h}{c_k - c_l}.$$

Theorem 6. The product of the sines of the kth parts of the distances from a point of a central conic to two focal lines through the same centre is constant.

Theorem 6′. The product of the sines of the kth parts of the distances to a tangent from two foci of a central conic on the same axis is constant.

Let us now recall Desargues' theorem, whereby a transversal meets the conics of a pencil in pairs of points of an involution. This will apply to a central conic, the Absolute, and the pairs of focal lines. A dual theorem will of course hold for a central conic, the Absolute, and the pairs of foci.

Theorem 7. The intersections of a line with a central conic, and with its pairs of corresponding focal lines, all have the same centres of gravity.

Theorem 7′. The tangents from a point to a central conic, and the pairs of lines thence to its pairs of corresponding foci, form angles with the same two bisectors.

Theorem 8. The polar of a point with regard to a central conic passes through one centre of gravity of the intersections of each focal line with the tangents from the point to the conic.

Theorem 8′. The pole of a line with regard to a central conic lies on one bisector of the angle determined at each focus by the lines thence to the intersections of the given line with the conic.

A variable point of a conic will determine projective pencils at any two fixed points thereof, and these will meet any line in projective ranges, hence

Theorem 9. If a variable point of a central conic be connected with two fixed points thereof, the distance which these lines cut on any focal line is constant.

Theorem 9′. If a variable tangent to a central conic be brought to intersect two fixed tangents thereof, the angle of the lines from a chosen focus to the two intersections is constant.

Recalling the properties of the eleven-point conic of two given conics and a line:

Theorem 10. If a line and a central conic be given, the two mutually conjugate and orthogonal points of the line, the points of the focal lines orthogonal to their intersections with the line, and the three centres lie on a conic.

Theorem 10′. If a point and a central conic be given, the two lines through the point which are mutually conjugate and perpendicular, the perpendiculars on the line from the foci, and the three axes all touch a conic.

It is a well-known theorem that the locus of points, whence tangents to two conics form a harmonic set, is a conic passing through the points of contact with the common tangents.

Theorem 11. The locus of points whence tangents to a central conic are mutually perpendicular is a conic meeting the given conic where it meets its directrices.

Theorem 11′. The envelope of lines which meet a central conic in pairs of mutually orthogonal points is a conic touching the tangents to the given circle from its director points.

It is clear that neither of these conics will, in general, be a circle, as in the euclidean case. If the mutually perpendicular tangents from the point (y) be

$$(ux) = 0, \quad (vx) = 0.$$

$$\sum_i^{0..2} \frac{{u_i}^2}{c_i} = \sum_i^{0..2} \frac{{v_i}^2}{c_i} = \sum_i^{0..2} u_i v_i = 0,$$

$$\sum_i^{0..2} \frac{{u_i}^2}{c_i}(vv) + \sum_i^{0..2} \frac{{v_i}^2}{c_i}(uu) - 2\sum_i^{0..2} \frac{u_i v_i}{c_i}(uv) = 0,$$

$$\sum_h^{0..2} c_h(c_k + c_l){y_i}^2 = 0. \tag{14}$$

Let the reader show that the equation of the other conic will be

$$\sum_h^{0..2} (c_k + c_l){u_i}^2 = 0.$$

We may extend the usual euclidean proof to the first of the following theorems—

Theorem 12. The locus of the reflection of a real focus of an ellipse in a variable tangent, is a circle whose centre is the corresponding focus.

Theorem 12′. The envelope of the reflection in a variable point of an ellipse, of a real focal line, is a circle whose axis is the corresponding focal line.

Let (y) be the coordinates of a point P of our conic. The equation of a line through the centre O_h conjugate to the line O_hP will be

$$c_k y_k x_k + c_l y_l x_l = 0.$$

This will meet the conic in two points P' having the coordinates

$$x_h : x_k : x_l = \pm\sqrt{c_k c_l}\, y_h : c_l y_l : -c_k y_k,$$

$$\tan^2 \frac{\overline{OP}}{k} + \tan^2 \frac{\overline{OP'}}{k} = \frac{-c_h(c_k + c_l)}{c_k c_l} \tag{15}$$

Theorem 13. The sum of the squares of the tangents of the kth parts of the distances from a centre of a central conic to any pair of intersections with two conjugate lines through this centre is constant.

Theorem 13′. The sum of the squares of the tangents of the angles which an axis of a central conic makes with a pair of tangents to the curve from two conjugate points of this axis is constant.

We shall call two such diameters as O_hP, O_hP' *conjugate diameters.*

$$\sin \measuredangle PO_hP' = \frac{(c_k{y_k}^2 + c_l{y_l}^2)}{\sqrt{{y_k}^2 + {y_l}^2}\,\sqrt{{c_k}^2{y_k}^2 + {c_l}^2{y_l}^2}}$$

$$= \frac{-c_h {y_h}^2}{\sqrt{{y_k}^2 + {y_l}^2}\,\sqrt{{c_k}^2{y_k}^2 + {c_l}^2{y_l}^2}};$$

$$\tan\frac{\overline{O_hP}}{k}\tan\frac{\overline{O_hP'}}{k}\sin\measuredangle PO_hP' = \pm\frac{c_h}{\sqrt{c_kc_l}}.$$

Theorem 14. The product of the tangents of the kth parts of the distances from a centre of a central conic to two intersections with a pair of conjugate diameters through that centre, multiplied by the sine of the angle of these diameters is constant.

Theorem 14′. The product of the tangents of the angles which an axis of a central conic makes with two tangents to it from a pair of conjugate points of this axis, multiplied by the sine of the kth part of the distance of these points is constant.

The equation of a line through the centre O_h perpendicular to O_hP will be

$$y_kx_k + y_lx_l = 0.$$

This will meet the conic in points P'' having coordinates

$$x_h : x_k : x_l = \pm\sqrt{\frac{-(c_l{y_k}^2 + c_k{y_l}^2)}{c_h}} : y_l : -y_k,$$

$$\cos\frac{\overline{OP''}}{k} = \frac{\sqrt{-(c_l{y_k}^2 + c_k{y_l}^2)}}{\sqrt{(c_h - c_l){y_k}^2 + (c_h - c_k){y_l}^2}},$$

$$\operatorname{ctn}^2\frac{\overline{OP''}}{k} = \frac{-(c_l{y_k}^2 + c_k{y_l}^2)}{c_h({y_k}^2 + {y_l}^2)},$$

$$\operatorname{ctn}^2\frac{\overline{OP}}{k} + \operatorname{ctn}^2\frac{\overline{OP''}}{k} = -\frac{c_k + c_l}{c_h}. \tag{16}$$

Theorem 15. The sum of the squares of the cotangents of the kth parts of the distances from a centre of a central conic to two intersections of the curve with mutually perpendicular diameters through this centre is constant.

Theorem 15′. The sum of the squares of the cotangents of the angles which an axis of a central conic makes with two tangents from a pair of orthogonal points of this axis is constant.

The equation of the tangent t' at the point P' is

$$c_hy_hx_h + \sqrt{c_kc_l}(x_ky_l - x_ly_k) = 0.$$

From this we get

$$\sin^2\frac{\overline{O_ht'}}{k} = \frac{{c_h}^2{y_h}^2}{(c_l - c_h)c_k{y_k}^2 + (c_k - c_h)c_l{y_l}^2},$$

$$\tan \frac{\overline{O_h P}}{k} \tan \frac{\overline{O_h t'}}{k} = \frac{c_h}{\sqrt{c_k c_l}}. \tag{17}$$

Theorem 16. The product of the tangents of the kth parts of the distances from a centre of a central conic to a point of the curve and to the tangent where the curve meets a diameter conjugate to that from the centre to the point of the curve, is constant.

Theorem 16′. The product of the tangents of the angles which an axis of a central conic makes with a tangent and with the absolute polar of a point of contact with a tangent from a point of this axis conjugate to the intersection with the given tangent, is constant.

The equations of two conjugate diameters through O_h have already been written

$$y_l x_k - y_k x_l = 0, \quad c_k y_k x_k + c_l y_l x_l = 0.$$

The product of the tangents of the angles which they make with the x_k axis is

$$\frac{y_k c_l y_l}{y_l c_k y_k} = \frac{c_l}{c_k}.$$

Theorem 17. The product of the tangents of the angles which two conjugate diameters through a centre make with either axis through this centre is constant.

Theorem 17′. The product of the tangents of the kth parts of the distances of two conjugate points of an axis from either centre on this axis is constant.

Let P_h, P_h' be the intersections of the x_h axis with the conic

$$\cos \frac{\overline{P_h P_h'}}{k} = \frac{c_h + c_l}{c_k - c_l},$$

$$\tan^2 \tfrac{1}{2} \frac{\overline{P_h P_h'}}{k} \cdot \tan^2 \tfrac{1}{2} \frac{\overline{P_k P_k'}}{k} \cdot \tan^2 \tfrac{1}{2} \frac{\overline{P_l P_l'}}{k} = -1. \tag{18}$$

Theorem 18. The product of the squares of the tangents of the $2k$th parts of the distances determined by a central conic on the axes is equal to -1.

Theorem 18′. The product of the squares of the tangents of the half-angles of the pairs of tangents to a central conic from its centres is constant.

If a circle have double contact with a conic, we have, with the Absolute, the figure of two conics having double contact with a third, already studied in the last chapter.

Theorem 19. If a circle have double contact with a conic, its axis and the lines connecting the points of contact are harmonically separated by a pair of focal lines.

Theorem 19′. If a circle have double contact with a conic, its centre and the intersections of the common tangents are harmonically separated by a pair of foci.

Of course we mean by foci and focal lines of any conic what we mean in the special case of the central conic.

A circle which has double contact with a central conic where the latter meets an axis is called an *auxiliary circle.* There will clearly be six such circles, their centres being the centres of the conic. Consider the circle having its centre at O_k while it has double contact with our central conic at the intersections with $x_h = 0$.

$$p\sum_{i}^{0..2} c_i {x_i}^2 + q{x_h}^2 \equiv r(xx) + s{x_k}^2 = 0,$$

$$\sum_{i}^{0..2} c_i {x_i}^2 + (c_l - c_h){x_h}^2 = c_h{x_h}^2 + c_k{x_k}^2 + c_l{x_l}^2 = 0.$$

This will meet the line (u) through O_h in points Q, Q', having coordinates

$$x_h : x_k : x_l = \sqrt{-\left(\frac{c_l{u_k}^2}{c_l} + \frac{c_k{u_l}^2}{c_l}\right)} : u_l : -u_k.$$

The same line will meet the conic in points P, P', having coordinates

$$x_h : x_k : x_l = \sqrt{-\frac{c_l{u_k}^2 + c_k{u_l}^2}{c_h}} : u_l : -u_k,$$

$$\tan^2 \frac{\overline{O_h Q}}{k} = \frac{-c_l({u_k}^2 + {u_l}^2)}{c_l{u_k}^2 + c_k{u_l}^2}, \quad \tan^2 \frac{\overline{O_h P}}{k} = \frac{-c_h({u_k}^2 + {u_l}^2)}{c_l{u_k}^2 + c_k{u_l}^2},$$

$$\tan \frac{\overline{O_h Q}}{k} : \tan \frac{\overline{O_h P}}{k} = \sqrt{c_l} : \sqrt{c_h}. \tag{19}$$

Let us remark, finally, that the tangent of the kth part of the distance from a point to a line, is the cotangent of the kth part of its distance to the pole of the line, and that if the tangents of two distances bear a constant ratio, so do their cotangents:

Theorem 20. If the tangents of the kth parts of the distances from the points of a circle to any diameter be altered in a constant ratio, the locus of the resulting points will be a conic having the given circle as an auxiliary.

Theorem 20′. If the tangents of the angles which the tangents to a circle make with a diameter be altered in a constant ratio, the envelope of the resulting lines will be a conic having the given circle as an auxiliary circle.

The normal at any point of a conic is the line connecting it with the absolute pole of its tangent. This line is also perpendicular to the absolute polar of the given point, so that the conic and its absolute polar conic are geodesically parallel curves. The equation of the normal to our conic (1) will be

$$\sum_{i}^{0..2} \frac{c_k - c_l}{y_h} x_h = 0. \tag{20}$$

The tangents to a central conic from a centre shall be called *asymptotes*. The equation of the pair of asymptotes through the centre (O_h) will evidently be

$$c_k x_k{}^2 + c_l x_l{}^2 = 0. \tag{21}$$

The tangent at the point P with coordinates (y) will meet them in two points R, R', whose coordinates are

$$x_h : x_k : x_l = \sqrt{-c_k c_l}(\sqrt{-c_l}y_l \pm \sqrt{c_k}y_k) : \mp c_h y_h \sqrt{-c_l} : -c_h y_h \sqrt{c_k},$$

$$\tan\frac{\overline{O_h R}}{k}\tan\frac{\overline{O_h R'}}{k} = \frac{(c_l - c_k)c_h{}^2 y_h{}^2}{c_k c_l (c_k y_k{}^2 + c_l y_l{}^2)} = \frac{c_h(c_k - c_l)}{c_k c_l}. \tag{22}$$

Theorem 21. The product of the tangents of the kth parts of the distances from a centre of a central conic to the intersection with the asymptotes through that centre of a tangent is constant.

Theorem 21′. The product of the tangents of the angles which an axis of a central conic makes with the lines from a point of the curve to the intersections of the curve with this axis is constant.

A set of conics which meet the Absolute in the same four points shall be said to be *homothetic*. If they have the same four absolute tangents they shall be called *confocal.* We get at once from Desargues' involution theorem:—

Theorem 22. One conic homothetic to a given conic will pass through every point of space, and two will touch every line, not through a point common to all the conics, in the centres of gravity of all pairs of intersections of the homothetic conics with this line.

Theorem 22′. One conic confocal with a given conic will touch every line, and two will pass through every point not on the common tangents to all. The tangents to these two will bisect the angles of the pairs of tangents from that point to all of the confocal conics.

Concentric circles are a special case both of homothetic and of confocal conics. The general form for the equations of conics homothetic and confocal respectively to our conic (1) will be

$$\sum_i^{0..2}(c_i + m)x_0{}^2 = 0. \quad (23); \qquad \sum_i^{0..2}\frac{c_i}{l + c_i}x_i = 0. \quad (24)$$

It is sometimes useful to modify the second of these equations, in order to introduce the elliptic coordinates of a point, i.e. the two parameters giving the conics of the confocal system which pass through it. Let us write $\frac{1}{c_i}$ in place of c_i.

$$\frac{x_i}{\sqrt{(xx)}} = X_i.$$

Our confocal conics have, then, the general equation

$$\sum_{i}^{0..2} \frac{X_i}{c_i - \lambda} = 0. \tag{25}$$

If λ_1 and λ_2 be the parameter values of the conic through (X) we have

$$X_h = \sqrt{\frac{(c_k - c_l)(c_h - \lambda_1)(c_h - \lambda_2)}{\sum\limits_{h}^{0..2} c_h{}^2(c_h - c_l)}}. \tag{26}$$

$$ds^2 = \sum_{i}^{0..2} dX_i{}^2 = \frac{1}{4}\left[\frac{(\lambda_1 - \lambda_2)d\lambda_1{}^2}{\prod\limits_{i}^{0..2}(c_i - \lambda_1)} + \frac{(\lambda_2 - \lambda_1)d\lambda_2{}^2}{\prod\limits_{i}^{0..2}(c_i - \lambda_2)}\right]. \tag{27}$$

With the aid of these coordinates, we may easily prove for the non-euclidean case Graves' theorem, namely, if a loop of thread be cast about an extremely thin elliptic disk, and pulled taut at a point, that point will trace a confocal ellipse. We shall not give the details here, however, for in the next chapter we shall work at length the more interesting corresponding problem in three dimensions, and the calculations are too fatiguing to make it advisable to carry them through twice.

CHAPTER XIII

QUADRIC SURFACES

The discussion of non-euclidean quadric surfaces may be carried on in the same spirit as that of conic sections in the preceding chapter. There is not, however, the same wealth of easy and interesting theorems, owing to the greater complication in the formation of the simultaneous covariants of two quadrics.

Let us begin by classifying non-euclidean quadrics under the group of real congruent transformations.[57] We begin in the actual domain of hyperbolic space, giving only those surfaces which have a real part in that domain and a non-vanishing discriminant. The names adopted are intended to give a certain idea of the shape of the surface. We shall mean by *curve*, the curve of intersection of the surface and Absolute, while *developable* is the developable of common tangent planes.

A. Central Quadrics.

(1) Ellipsoid. Imaginary quartic curve and developable.

(2) Concave, non-ruled hyperboloid. Real quartic curve and developable.

(3) Convex non-ruled hyperboloid. Real quartic curve, imaginary developable.

(4) Two-sheeted ruled hyperboloid. Real quartic curve and developable.

(5) One-sheeted ruled hyperboloid. Real quartic curve, imaginary developable.

(6) Non-ruled semi-hyperboloid. Real quartic curve and developable.

(7) Ruled semi-hyperboloid. Real quartic curve and developable.

The last two surfaces differ from the preceding ones in that here two vertices of the common self-conjugate tetrahedron (in the sense of projective geometry) of the surface and Absolute are conjugate imaginaries, while in the first five cases all four are real.

B.

(8) Elliptic paraboloid. Imaginary quartic curve with real acnode, imaginary developable.

(9) Tubular non-ruled hyperbolic paraboloid. Real quartic with acnode, real developable.

(10) Cup-shaped non-ruled hyperbolic paraboloid. Real quartic with acnode, imaginary developable.

(11) Open ruled hyperbolic paraboloid. Real acnodal quartic, real developable.

[57] The classification here given is that which appears in the author's article 'Quadric Surfaces in Hyperbolic Space', *Transactions of the American Mathematical Society*, vol. iv, 1903. This classification was simplified and put into better shape by Bromwich, 'The Classification of Quadratic Loci,' ibid., vol. vi, 1905. The latter, however, makes use of Weierstrassian Elementary Divisors, and it seemed wiser to avoid the introduction of these into the present work. Both Professor Bromwich and the author wrote in ignorance of the fact that they had been preceded by rather a crude article by Barbarin, 'Étude de géométrie non-euclidienne,' *Mémoires couronnés par l'Académie de Belgique*, vol. vi, 1900.

(12) Gathered ruled hyperbolic paraboloid. Real crunodal quartic, imaginary developable.

(13) Cuspidal non-ruled hyperbolic paraboloid. Real cuspidal quartic curve, real developable.

(14) Cuspidal ruled hyperbolic paraboloid. Real cuspidal quartic curve, real developable.

(15) Horocyclic non-ruled hyperbolic paraboloid. The curve is two mutually tangent conics, developable real.

(16) Horocyclic elliptic paraboloid. Curve is two mutually tangent imaginary conics, developable imaginary.

(17) Horocyclic ruled hyperbolic paraboloid. Curve is two real mutually tangent conics, developable imaginary.

(18) Non-ruled osculating semi-hyperbolic paraboloid. The curve is a real conic and two conjugate imaginary generators meeting on it. The developable is a real cone, and two imaginary lines.

C. Surfaces of Revolution.

(19) Prolate spheroid. Curve is two imaginary conics in real ultra-infinite planes, imaginary developable.

(20) Oblate spheroid. Curve is two imaginary conics in conjugate imaginary planes meeting in an ultra-infinite line, imaginary developable.

(21) Concave non-ruled hyperboloid of revolution. Curve is two real conics whose planes meet in an ideal line, real developable.

(22) Convex non-ruled hyperboloid of revolution. Absolute curve two real conics whose planes meet in an ideal line, imaginary developable.

(23) Ruled hyperboloid of revolution. Curve two real conics whose planes meet in an ideal line, imaginary developable.

(24) Semi-hyperboloid of revolution. The curve is a real conic, and an imaginary one in a real plane, the developable is a real cone and an imaginary one.

(25) Elliptic paraboloid of revolution. The absolute curve is an imaginary conic in an ultra-infinite plane, and two imaginary generators not intersecting on the conic. The developable is an imaginary cone, and the same two generators.

(26) Tubular semi-hyperbolic paraboloid of revolution. The curve is a real conic and two imaginary generators not intersecting on it; the developable is the same two lines and a real cone.

(27) Cup-shaped semi-hyperbolic paraboloid of revolution. Real conic and two imaginary lines not meeting on it. Developable same two lines and imaginary cone.

(28) Clifford surface. Curve and developable two generators of each set.

D. Canal Surfaces.[58]

(29) Elliptic canal surface. Curve is two imaginary conics whose planes meet in an actual line, developable imaginary.

(30) Non-ruled hyperbolic canal surface. Two real conics whose planes meet in an actual line, developable two real cones.

[58]Called *Surfaces of Translation* in the author's article 'Quadric Surfaces', loc. cit.

(31) Ruled hyperbolic canal surface. Curve two real conics whose planes meet in an actual line, imaginary developable.

E. Spheres.

(32) Proper sphere. Curve is two coincident imaginary conics, developable imaginary.

(33) Equidistant surface. Curve two real coincident conics, developable two real coincident cones.

(34) Horocyclic surface. Curve and developable two conjugate imaginary intersecting generators, each counted twice.

In elliptic or spherical space the number of real varieties will, of course, be much smaller. We have

(1) Non-ruled ellipsoid.

(2) Ruled ellipsoid.

(3) Prolate spheroid.

(4) Oblate spheroid.

(5) Ruled ellipsoid of revolution.

(6) Clifford surface.

(7) Sphere.

It is worth mentioning that the Clifford surface of elliptic space has real linear generators, while that in hyperbolic space has not.

Let us next turn our attention to that class of quadrics which we have termed central, and which are distinguished by the existence of a non-degenerate tetrahedron (in the projective sense) self-conjugate with regard both to the surface and the Absolute. The vertices of this tetrahedron shall be called the *centres* of the surface, and its planes the *axial planes.* When this tetrahedron is chosen as the basis of the coordinate system, the Absolute may be written in the typical form while the equation of the surface involves none but squared terms.

Theorem 1. A centre of a central quadric is equidistant from the intersections with the surface of every line through this centre.

Theorem 1′. An axial plane of a central quadric bisects a dihedral angle of every two tangent planes to the surface which meet in a line of this axial plane.

We obtain a good deal of information about our central quadrics by enumerating the Cayleyan characteristics of their curves of intersection with the Absolute, and the corresponding developables. The curve is a twisted quartic of deficiency one. Its osculating developable is of order eight and class twelve. It has sixteen stationary tangent planes, thirty-eight lines in every plane lie in two osculating planes, two secants, i.e. two lines meeting the curve twice, pass every point not on the curve, sixteen points in every plane are the intersection of two tangents, eight double tangent planes pass through every point. The developable will, of course, possess the dual characteristics.

Theorem 2. Through an arbitrary point in space will pass twelve planes cutting a central quadric in osculating parabolas, eight planes of parabolic section will pass through an arbitrary line. An arbitrary point will be the centre of one section. Sixteen planes cut the surface in horocycles, sixteen points in an arbitrary plane are the centres of circular sections, eight planes of circular section pass through an arbitrary point.

Theorem 2′. In an arbitrary plane there will be twelve points, vertices of cones circumscribed to a central quadric which have stationary contact with the cone of tangents to the Absolute, eight points on an arbitrary line are vertices of circumscribed cones which touch the Absolute. An arbitrary plane will be a plane of symmetry for one circumscribed cone. Sixteen points are vertices of circumscribed cones which have four-plane contact with the Absolute. Sixteen planes through an arbitrary point are perpendicular to the axes of revolution of circumscribed cones of revolution.

The planes of circular section are those which touch the cones whose vertices are the centres of the quadric, and which pass through the Absolute curve. It may be shown that not more than six real planes of circular section will pass through an actual point, and that only two of these will cut the surface in proper circles.[59]

Let us write as the equation of a typical quadric

$$\sum_{i}^{0..3} c_i {x_i}^2 = 0. \tag{1}$$

No two of the c's shall be equal, and none shall equal zero.

The cones whose vertices are the centres and which pass through the Absolute curves shall be called the *focal cones*. In like manner there will be four *focal conics* in the axial planes. The equation of the focal cone whose vertex is O_h will be

$$\sum_{i}^{0..3} (c_i - c_h) {x_i}^2 = 0. \tag{2}$$

The focal conic in the corresponding axial plane will be

$$x_h = 0, \quad \sum_{i}^{0..3} \frac{c_h - c_i}{c_h c_i} {w_i}^2 = 0. \tag{3}$$

Let the reader show that each of these conics passes through two foci of each other one.

We next seek the locus of points whence three mutually tangent planes may be drawn to the surface. Let these be the planes (v), (w), (ω), and let the

[59]See the author's 'Quadric Surfaces', loc. cit., p. 164.

equation of the surface and the Absolute in plane coordinates be, in the Clebsch-Aronhold notation

$$u_\gamma{}^2 = 0, \quad u_\alpha{}^2 \equiv u_\alpha{}'^2 = 0,$$
$$v_\gamma{}^2 = w_\gamma{}^2 = \omega_\gamma{}^2 = 0,$$
$$v_\alpha w_\alpha = w_\alpha \omega_\alpha = \omega_\alpha v_\alpha = 0,$$
$$\begin{vmatrix} v_\gamma & w_\gamma & \omega_\gamma \\ v_\alpha & w_\alpha & \omega_\alpha \\ v_\alpha{}' & w_\alpha{}' & \omega_\alpha{}' \end{vmatrix}^2 = |\gamma\alpha\alpha' x|^2 = 0,$$

where (x) is the point of concurrence of the planes (v), (w), (ω). Returning to actual coefficients, the coefficients of $x_i x_j$ will vanish, for they involve $\gamma_i \gamma_j$ or $\alpha_k \alpha_l$ which are zero. We shall find eventually

$$\sum_h^{0..3} c_h(c_k c_l + c_l c_m + c_m c_k) x_h{}^2 = 0. \tag{4}$$

This quadric is also the locus of points whence triads of tangents to the Absolute are conjugate with regard to the given quadric, hence interchanging γ and α, we get the locus of points whence triads of mutually perpendicular tangents may be drawn to the quadric (1)

$$\sum_h^{0..3} c_h(c_k + c_l + c_m) x_h{}^2 = 0. \tag{5}$$

If the quadric be ruled, the former of these loci will intersect it along a curve where generators of different sets intersect at right angles.

Theorem 3. A line will meet a central quadric and its focal cones in five pairs of points with the same centres of gravity.

Theorem 3′. The tangent planes to a central quadric and its focal conics through a line form five sets of dihedral angles with the same bisectors.

The proof of these two theorems is immediate.

If we mean by a diameter of a quadric, a line through a centre, we see that we may pass from any set of three concurrent conjugate diameters to any other such set through that same centre by changing two diameters at a time, and keeping the third one fixed. We may thus continually apply Theorem 14, of Chapter XII. In the same way we may pass from any set of three mutually perpendicular diameters to any other such set, and apply Theorem 15 of the same chapter.

Theorem 4. The sum of the squares of the tangents of the kth parts of the distances from a centre of a central quadric to three intersections of the surface with three conjugate diameters through that centre is constant.

Theorem 4′. The sum of the squares of the tangents of the angles which an axial plane of a central quadric makes with three tangent planes through three conjugate lines in that axial plane is constant.

Theorem 5. The sum of the squares of the cotangents of the kth parts of the distances from a centre of a central quadric to three intersections with the surface of three mutually perpendicular lines through that centre is constant.

Theorem 5′. The sum of the squares of the cotangents of the angles which an axial plane of a central quadric makes with three tangent planes through three mutually perpendicular lines in that axial plane is constant.

To find the values of the constants referred to in Theorems 4 and 5, we have but to choose a particular set of diameters, say the intersections of the axial planes through O_h. We thus get

$$\tan^2 \frac{\overline{O_h P}}{k} + \tan^2 \frac{\overline{O_h P'}}{k} + \tan^2 \frac{\overline{O_h P''}}{k} = -c_h \left(\frac{1}{c_k} + \frac{1}{c_l} + \frac{1}{c_m} \right). \tag{6}$$

$$\operatorname{ctn}^2 \frac{\overline{O_h Q}}{k} + \operatorname{ctn}^2 \frac{\overline{O_h Q'}}{k} + \operatorname{ctn}^2 \frac{\overline{O_h Q''}}{k} = -\frac{(c_k + c_l + c_m)}{c_h}. \tag{7}$$

A set of quadrics having the same absolute focal curve, and, hence, the same focal cones, shall be called *homothetic*. A set inscribed in the same absolute developable, and possessing, in consequence the same focal conics shall be called *confocal*.

Theorem 6. An arbitrary line will meet a set of confocal quadrics in pairs of points with the same centres of gravity.

Theorem 6′. The tangent planes to a set of confocal quadrics through an arbitrary line, form dihedral angles with the same bisectors.

Theorem 7. Three homothetic quadrics will touch an arbitrary plane in three mutually orthogonal points.

Theorem 7′. Three confocal quadrics will pass through an arbitrary point, and intersect orthogonally.

Let us now set up our system of elliptic coordinates as we did in the plane

$$X_i = \frac{x_i}{\sqrt{(xx)}}, \quad (XX) = 1. \tag{8}$$

These coordinates (X) are inapplicable to points of the Absolute; we imagine that all such points are excluded from consideration. The general equation for the system of quadrics confocal with that given by (1) will be,[60] if we replace

[60]The residue of the present chapter is closely analogous to the treatment of the corresponding euclidean problem given by Klein in his 'Einleitung in die höhere Geometrie', lithographed notes, Göttingen, 1893, pp. 38–73, and Staude, 'Fadenconstruktion des Ellipsoids,' *Mathematische Annalen*, vol. xx, 1882. Staude returns to the subject in his *Die Fokaleigenschaften der Flächen zweiter Ordnung*, Leipzig, 1896. This book is intended as a supplement to the usual textbooks on analytic geometry, and is somewhat prolix in its attempts at simplicity.

c_i by $\dfrac{1}{c_i}$,

$$\sum_i^{0..3} \frac{{X_i}^2}{c_i - \lambda} = 0. \tag{9}$$

If the roots be λ_1, λ_2, λ_3, we have

$$X_h = \sqrt{\frac{(c_h - \lambda_1)(c_h - \lambda_2)(c_h - \lambda_3)}{(c_h - c_k)(c_h - c_l)(c_h - c_m)}}. \tag{10}$$

For the differential of distance we have

$$\frac{ds^2}{k^2} = \frac{(xx)(dx\,dx) - (x\,dx)^2}{(xx)^2} = (dX\,dX). \tag{11}$$

We wish to express this in terms of our elliptic coordinates. It will be found that the coefficients of $d\lambda_p\, d\lambda_q$ will vanish, and, indeed, this is *a priori* evident if we have in mind that our coordinate system is a triply orthogonal one, and the general formulae for orthogonal curves, as will be shown in Chapter XV, are the same for euclidean as for non-euclidean We thus get

$$\frac{ds^2}{k^2} = \frac{1}{4} \sum_h^{0..3} \sum_p^{1..3} \frac{(c_h - \lambda_q)(c_h - \lambda_r){d\lambda_p}^2}{(c_h - c_k)(c_h - c_l)(c_h - c_m)(c_h - \lambda_p)}.$$

If we give to c_h each of its four values, divide the terms into partial fractions and recombine, we get

$$\frac{ds^2}{k^2} = \frac{1}{4} \sum_p^{1..3} \frac{(\lambda_p - \lambda_q)(\lambda_p - \lambda_r){d\lambda_p}^2}{\prod\limits_i^{0..3} (c_i - \lambda_p)}. \tag{12}$$

The analogy to the corresponding formula in euclidean space is striking.

The cones whose vertices are all at an arbitrary point, and which are circumscribed to a set of confocal quadrics, will themselves be confocal, i.e. they will have four common tangent planes which touch the Absolute. Any two of these cones will intersect orthogonally. This shows that the congruence of lines tangent to two confocal quadrics will be a normal one, the edges of regression of their developable surfaces being geodesics of the quadrics. These facts, well known in the euclidean case, will be proved for the noneuclidean one in Chapter XVI. Notice that we get the system of geodesics of a quadric by means of its ∞^3 common tangents with confocal quadrics. The difficulties which arise for special positions, as umbilical points, need not concern us here.

The equation of the cone whose vertex is (Y) and which circumscribes the quadric (1) will be

$$\sum_i^{0..3} \frac{{Y_i}^2}{c_i - \lambda} \sum_i^{0..3} \frac{{X_i}^2}{c_i - \lambda} - \Big[\sum_i^{0..3} \frac{Y_i X_i}{c_i - \lambda}\Big]^2 = 0.$$

$$\sum_{i}^{0..3}\sum_{j}^{0..3}\frac{(X_iY_j - X_jY_i)^2}{(c_i-\lambda)(c_j-\lambda)} = 0.$$

Putting $X = Y + dY$ we get the differential form

$$\sum_{i}^{0..3}\sum_{j}^{0..3}\frac{(Y_i dY_j - Y_j dY_i)^2}{(c_i-\lambda)(c_j-\lambda)} = 0.$$

Let us change this also to the elliptic form. We notice that the coefficients of the expressions $d\lambda_p\ d\lambda_q$ will be 0, for the axial planes of the cones will be given by tangents to

$$\lambda_p = 0, \quad \lambda_q = 0, \quad \lambda_r = 0.$$

The ∞^1 confocal cones form a one-parameter family all touching the same tangent planes to the cone $ds^2 = 0$. The equation of one cone of the family may be thrown into the form

$$\sum_{p}^{1..3}\frac{(\lambda_p-\lambda_q)(\lambda_p-\lambda_r)}{\left[\prod\limits_{i}^{0..3}(c_i-\lambda_p)\right]L_p}d{\lambda_p}^2 = 0,$$

where L_p is a function of λ. Hence the general form will be

$$\sum_{p}^{1..3}\frac{(\lambda_p-\lambda_q)(\lambda_p-\lambda_r)}{\left[\prod\limits_{i}^{0..3}(c_i-\lambda_p)\right](L_p-\mu)}d{\lambda_p}^2 = 0.$$

It remains to find the value of $L_p - \mu$. It is clearly a polynomial in powers of λ, which vanishes only when $\lambda = \lambda_p$, for then only shall we have $d{\lambda_p}^2 = 0$. We thus get

$$L_p - \mu = A_p(\lambda_p - \lambda)^m,$$

where A_p is a constant. Again, as two of these confocal quadrics contain every line through the vertex, we must have $m = 1$. Lastly, our expression is symmetrical in p, q, r, hence

$$A_p = A_q = A_r.$$

We finally get for our cone

$$\sum_{p}^{1..3}\frac{(\lambda_p-\lambda_q)(\lambda_p-\lambda_r)d{\lambda_p}^2}{\left[\prod\limits_{i}^{0..3}(c_i-\lambda_p)\right](\lambda_p-\lambda)} = 0. \tag{13}$$

For progress along an arc of a geodesic of $\lambda_r =$ const., we have

$$d\lambda_p\sqrt{\frac{\lambda_p-\lambda_r}{(\lambda_p-\lambda)\prod\limits_{i}^{0..3}(c_i-\lambda_p)}} \pm d\lambda_q\sqrt{\frac{\lambda_q-\lambda_r}{(\lambda_q-\lambda)\prod\limits_{i}^{0..3}(c_i-\lambda_q)}} = 0.$$

so that the problem of finding the geodesics of a quadric depends merely upon elliptic integrals. If we take $\lambda_r = \lambda$, we have double tangents to the surface, i.e. rectilinear generators,

$$\frac{d\lambda_p}{\sqrt{\prod_i^{0..3}(c_i - \lambda_p)}} \pm \frac{d\lambda_q}{\sqrt{\prod_i^{0..3}(c_i - \lambda_q)}} = 0.$$

The general differential of arc on a surface $\lambda_r =$ const. is

$$\frac{ds^2}{k^2} = \frac{1}{4}\left[\frac{(\lambda_p - \lambda_q)(\lambda_p - \lambda_r)}{\prod_i^{0..3}(c_i - \lambda_p)} d\lambda_p{}^2 + \frac{(\lambda_q - \lambda_p)(\lambda_q - \lambda_r)}{\prod_i^{0..3}(c_i - \lambda_q)} d\lambda_q{}^2\right],$$

we have, then, for a distance along a generator

$$s = \frac{k}{2}\int \frac{(\lambda_p - \lambda_q)d\lambda_p}{\sqrt{\prod_i^{0..3}(c_i - \lambda_p)}}.$$

This expression is independent of λ_r, whence

Theorem 8. If from a set of confocal central quadrics a one-parameter set of linear generators be so chosen that all intersect the same ∞^1 lines of curvature of ∞^1 confocal quadrics of the system, then any two of these lines of curvature will cut congruent distances on all of these linear generators.

Theorem 8′. If from a set of homothetic central quadrics a one-parameter set of linear generators be so chosen that all touch ∞^1 developables circumscribed to pairs of quadrics of the homothetic system, then the tangent planes to any two of these developables will determine congruent dihedral angles whose edges are the given linear generators.

Theorem 8 may also be easily proved by showing that the generators of a set of confocal quadrics form an isotropic congruence, whereof much more later.[61]

We now seek for the expression for the element of distance upon a common tangent to two confocal quadrics λ, λ'.

$$\sum_p^{1..3} \frac{(\lambda_q - \lambda_p)(\lambda_r - \lambda_p)d\lambda_p{}^2}{\left[\prod_i^{0..3}(c_i - \lambda_p)\right](\lambda - \lambda_p)} = 0,$$

[61]The general theorem concerning isotropic congruences upon which this depends will be proved in Chapter XVI, where also will be found a bibliography of the subject.

$$\sum_{p}^{1..3} \frac{(\lambda_q - \lambda_p)(\lambda_r - \lambda_p) d\lambda_p{}^2}{\left[\prod_i^{0..3} (c_i - \lambda_p)\right] [\lambda' - \lambda_p]} = 0.$$

$$\begin{aligned}
\frac{(\lambda_p - \lambda_q) d\lambda_q}{\sqrt{\left[\prod_i^{0..3} (c_i - \lambda_q)\right] (\lambda - \lambda_q)(\lambda' - \lambda_q)}} &= \pm \frac{(\lambda_p - \lambda_r) d\lambda_r}{\sqrt{\left[\prod_i^{0..3} (c_i - \lambda_r)\right] (\lambda - \lambda_r)(\lambda' - \lambda_r)}}. \\
\frac{(\lambda_q - \lambda_p) d\lambda_p}{\sqrt{\left[\prod_i^{0..3} (c_i - \lambda_p)\right] (\lambda - \lambda_p)(\lambda' - \lambda_p)}} &= \pm \frac{(\lambda_q - \lambda_r) d\lambda_r}{\sqrt{\left[\prod_i^{0..3} (c_i - \lambda_r)\right] (\lambda - \lambda_r)(\lambda' - \lambda_r)}}.
\end{aligned} \tag{14}$$

$$\frac{ds}{k} = \pm \frac{d\lambda_p}{2\sqrt{\left[\prod_i^{0..3} (c_i - \lambda_p)\right]}} \times \frac{\sqrt{(\lambda_q - \lambda_p)(\lambda_r - \lambda_p)}}{\sqrt{(\lambda - \lambda_p)(\lambda' - \lambda_p)}} \times \frac{\sqrt{\begin{vmatrix} \lambda_p{}^2 & \lambda_q{}^2 & \lambda_r{}^2 \\ \lambda_p & \lambda_q & \lambda_r \\ 1 & 1 & 1 \end{vmatrix}}}{\sqrt{\lambda_q - \lambda_r}}$$

$$(\lambda_q - \lambda_r) \frac{ds}{k} = \frac{d\lambda_p}{2\sqrt{\prod_i^{0..3} (c_i - \lambda_p)}} \times \frac{(\lambda_p - \lambda_q)(\lambda_q - \lambda_r)(\lambda_r - \lambda_p)}{\sqrt{(\lambda - \lambda_p)(\lambda' - \lambda_p)}}.$$

Multiplying through by $(\lambda - \lambda_p)$, $(\lambda' - \lambda_p)$, and summing for $p = 1, 2, 3$

$$\begin{aligned}
\frac{ds}{k} = \frac{1}{2} \sqrt{\frac{(\lambda - \lambda_1)(\lambda' - \lambda_1)}{\prod_i^{0..3} (c_i - \lambda_1)}} d\lambda_1 \\
+ \frac{1}{2} \sqrt{\frac{(\lambda - \lambda_2)(\lambda' - \lambda_2)}{\prod_i^{0..3} (c_i - \lambda_2)}} d\lambda_2 \\
+ \frac{1}{2} \sqrt{\frac{(\lambda - \lambda_3)(\lambda' - \lambda_3)}{\prod_i^{0..3} (c_i - \lambda_3)}} d\lambda_3.
\end{aligned} \tag{15}$$

For a geodesic on $\lambda = \lambda_1$ whose tangent touches λ' we have

$$\frac{ds}{k} = \frac{1}{2} \sqrt{\frac{(\lambda - \lambda_2)(\lambda' - \lambda_2)}{\prod_i^{0..3} (c_i - \lambda_2)}} d\lambda_2 + \frac{1}{2} \sqrt{\frac{(\lambda - \lambda_3)(\lambda' - \lambda_3)}{\prod_i^{0..3} (c_i - \lambda_3)}} d\lambda_3. \tag{16}$$

For a line of curvature common to $\lambda = \lambda_1$, $\lambda' = \lambda_2$

$$\frac{ds}{k} = \frac{1}{2}\sqrt{\frac{(\lambda_1 - \lambda_3)(\lambda_2 - \lambda_3)}{\prod\limits_{i}^{0..3}(c_i - \lambda_3)}}d\lambda_3. \tag{17}$$

It is now necessary to look more closely into the signs of the radicals in (15). We know that, at least in a restricted domain, three confocal quadrics will pass through each point. In elliptic space one of these will be ruled, and the other two not ruled; assuming, of course, that we are dealing with the case of central quadrics. In hyperbolic space, two possible cases can arise in the actual domain. If the developable be real, two ruled, and one non-ruled hyperboloid will pass through each point. If it be imaginary we shall have an ellipsoid, a ruled, and a not-ruled hyperboloid.[62] Let us confine ourselves to this case, taking λ_3 as the parameter of the non-ruled hyperboloid, λ_2 as that of the ruled one, while λ_1 gives the ellipsoid. The elliptic case will follow immediately if we suppress the word *hyperboloid* substituting *ellipsoid*. In (15) let us assume that λ refers to an ellipsoid, and λ' to a ruled hyperboloid. In two of the three actual axial planes we shall have real focal conics. There will be a real focal ellipse which, looked upon as an envelope, constitutes the transition between the ellipsoid and the ruled hyperboloid. It will be surrounded by all ellipsoids, and surround all ruled hyperboloids. If we take a point in this axial plane, without the focal ellipse, the ellipsoid and non-ruled hyperboloid will subsist, the ruled hyperboloid, looked upon as a point locus, will shrink into the plane counted doubly. The other real focal conic will be a hyperbola, and will serve as a transition between the two sorts of hyperboloids, looked upon as envelopes. It will surround the non-ruled hyperboloids, but be surrounded by the ruled ones. The plane counted doubly, will replace a non-ruled hyperboloid for each point without the hyperbola. If a point be taken in the remaining axial plane, this plane, counted doubly, will replace a non-ruled hyperboloid for each of its points. Similar considerations will hold in the elliptic case.

Once more, let us look at the signs of the terms in (15). $d\lambda_i$ will change sign as a point passes through an axial plane that counts doubly in the λ_i family, or when passing along a tangent to one of these surfaces, the point of contact is traversed. On the other hand we see from (14) that when $d\lambda_i$ changes sign, the radical associated with it in (15) changes sign also, and vice versa. The radical associated with $d\lambda_3$ will change sign as we pass through a point of the axial plane with an imaginary focal conic (which we shall call π_3), and for a point of the axial plane π_2 of the focal hyperbola, which is without this hyperbola. The radical with $d\lambda_2$ will change sign for points of π_1, the plane of the focal ellipse without this curve, or points of π_2 within the focal hyperbola. The radical with $d\lambda_1$ will change sign for points of π_1 within the focal ellipse.

We next suppose that a loop of inextensible thread is slung about an ellipsoid λ, and a confocal, ruled, one-sheeted hyperboloid λ', and pulled taut at a point P. The loop is supposed to surround the ellipsoid, so that it winds partly

[62]See the Author's 'Quadric Surfaces', p. 165.

on each of the portions of the hyperboloid, which, in a restricted domain, are separated by the ellipsoid. The form for the element of length throughout the whole string will be that given by (15). For when we pass from the ellipsoid to the hyperboloid we pass along a geodesic whose tangent touches both surfaces, and this will be true throughout the continuation of that geodesic, for a geodesic is traced by a line rolling on a quadric, and touching a confocal one. The same form of distance element will hold for the rectilinear parts of the loop. We see, moreover, that two, and only two surfaces, of a confocal system will touch any line; hence λ and λ' are the only two which will touch the rectilinear parts of the loop. Lastly, let us limit ourselves to those regions of the plane where the various portions of the loop may be named in order: straight, hyperboloidal, ellipsoidal, hyperboloidal, ellipsoidal, straight. The constant length of the thread may be written

$$C = \int_{\lambda_1}^{\lambda_1} F_1 d\lambda_1 + \int_{\lambda_2}^{\lambda_2} F_2 d\lambda_2 + \int_{\lambda_3}^{\lambda_3} F_3 d\lambda_3.$$

We see that F_3 can never vanish, for λ and λ' are the parameters of an ellipsoid and ruled hyperboloid respectively, while λ_3 refers to a non-ruled hyperboloid. It will become infinite four times, twice when the loop passes π_2 the plane of the focal hyperbola, and twice when it passes π_3. We may, however, integrate right up to these limits, and, as we have seen, $d\lambda_3$ changes sign with the radical. We thus have

$$\begin{aligned}\int_{\lambda_3}^{\lambda_3} F_3 d\lambda_3 &= \int_{\lambda_3}^{c_3} F_3 d\lambda_3 - \int_{c_3}^{c_2} F_3 d\lambda_3 + \int_{c_2}^{c_3} F_3 d\lambda_3 - \int_{c_3}^{c_2} F_3 d\lambda_3 + \int_{c_2}^{\lambda_3} F_3 d\lambda_3 \\ &= 4\int_{c_2}^{c_3} F_3 d\lambda_3 = \text{const.}\end{aligned}$$

We may approach the second integral in the same spirit. F_2 will become infinite twice when the loop passes the plane of the focal ellipse π_1. It will vanish throughout those two portions of the loop that lie on the ruled hyperboloid $\lambda_2 = \lambda'$, and these two are separated by an intersection with π_1 We have then

$$\begin{aligned}\int_{\lambda_2}^{\lambda_2} F_2 d\lambda_2 &= \int_{\lambda_2}^{\lambda'} F_2 d\lambda_2 - \int_{\lambda'}^{c_1} F_2 d\lambda_2 + \int_{c_1}^{\lambda'} F_2 d\lambda_2 - \int_{\lambda'}^{c_1} F_2 d\lambda_2 + \int_{c_1}^{\lambda_2} F_2 d\lambda_2 \\ &= 4\int_{c_1}^{\lambda'} F_2 d\lambda_2 = \text{const.}\end{aligned}$$

We must, in conclusion, consider the first integral. It will never become infinite, but will vanish along those two portions of the loop which lie on the ellipsoid $\lambda = \lambda_1$. We have therefore:

$$\int_{\lambda_1}^{\lambda_1} F_1 d\lambda_1 = \int_{\lambda_1}^{\lambda} F_1 d\lambda_1 - \int_{\lambda}^{\lambda_1} F_1 d\lambda_1 = 2\int_{\lambda_1}^{\lambda} F_1 d\lambda_1 = \phi(\lambda_1).$$

We have therefore, since the first two integrals and the sum are constant,

$$\phi(\lambda_1) = \text{const.},$$

and the locus of the moving point is an ellipsoid. Lastly, let the ellipsoid and hyperboloid shrink down to the focal ellipse and focal hyperbola respectively, we have in the limiting case:

Theorem 9. If an ellipse and hyperbola in mutually perpendicular planes pass each through two foci of the other, and if a loop of inextensible thread be slung around the ellipse and pulled taut at a point P in such a way that it meets the two curves alternately, then the locus of P will be an ellipsoid confocal with the given ellipse and hyperbola.

CHAPTER XIV

AREAS AND VOLUMES

The subjects *area* and *volume* offer some of the most striking points of disparity between euclidean and non-euclidean geometry.[63] A first notable difference arises from the fact that, in the non-euclidean cases, two different functions of a triangle appear to play the rôle of the euclidean area. The first is present in the analoga of those formulae which give the area in terms of the sides and angles; the second appears when the area is defined as the limit of a sum, i.e. as a definite integral. We shall reserve the name *area* for the second of these, giving to the first the name *amplitude*.[64]

Let us, as in elementary geometry, use the letters A, B, C to indicate, either the vertices of a triangle, or the measures of its angles. We assume that these points are real, and, in the hyperbolic case, situated in the actual domain. We shall define triangle as in Chapter II. We might carry through the same sort of work for any three points, but, as we saw in the closing pages of Chapter VII, we should thereby be compelled, in the hyperbolic case at least, to introduce certain very delicate considerations as to algebraic; sign, not only in our analytic expressions, but even in the trigonometric formulae first introduced in Chapter IV.

We begin by rewriting IV. 9

$$-\sin\frac{b}{k}\sin\frac{c}{k}\cos A = \cos\frac{b}{k}\cos\frac{c}{k} - \cos\frac{a}{k}.$$

This formula, established for one region, is seen at once to hold for all the others.

$$\begin{aligned}\sin\frac{b}{k}\sin\frac{c}{k}\sin A \\ &= \left[\sin^2\frac{b}{k}\sin^2\frac{c}{k} - \cos^2\frac{b}{k}\cos^2\frac{c}{k} + 2\cos\frac{a}{k}\cos\frac{b}{k}\cos\frac{c}{k} - \cos^2\frac{a}{k}\right]^{\frac{1}{2}} \\ &= \left[1 - \cos^2\frac{a}{k} - \cos^2\frac{b}{k} - \cos^2\frac{c}{k} + 2\cos\frac{a}{k}\cos\frac{b}{k}\cos\frac{c}{k}\right]^{\frac{1}{2}}.\end{aligned}$$

The right-hand side is symmetrical in the three letters a, b, c, so that we may write

$$\sin\frac{b}{k}\sin\frac{c}{k}\sin A = \sin\frac{c}{k}\sin\frac{a}{k}\sin B = \sin\frac{a}{k}\sin\frac{b}{k}\sin C$$

[63] For a bibliographical account of the subject-matter of the present chapter see the dissertation of Dannmeyer, *Die Oberflächen- und Volumenberechnung für Lobatschefskijsche Räume*, Göttingen, 1904.

[64] The concept *amplitude* of a triangle, and the various trigonometric identities connected with it, are taken directly from an admirable paper by D'Ovidio, 'Su varie questioni di metrica proiettiva,' *Atti della R. Accademia delle Scienze di Torino*, vol. xxviii, 1893. Unfortunately the author gives, p. 20, an incorrect formula for the volume of a tetrahedron.

$$= \begin{vmatrix} 1 & \cos\frac{c}{k} & \cos\frac{b}{k} \\ \cos\frac{c}{k} & 1 & \cos\frac{a}{k} \\ \cos\frac{b}{k} & \cos\frac{a}{k} & 1 \end{vmatrix}^{\frac{1}{2}} . \quad (1)$$

In the real domain, if the measures of sides and angles be taken positively, the left side is essentially negative in the hyperbolic case, and positive in the elliptic, so that the radical on the right must be chosen accordingly. It will vanish only when the three points are collinear (under the restrictions made at the outset of this chapter), and shall be called the *Sine Amplitude* of the triangle, written $\sin(ABC)$.

Let the reader show that if the coordinates of A, B, C be (x), (y), (z) respectively

$$\sin(ABC) = \frac{\begin{vmatrix} (xx) & (xy) & (xz) \\ (yx) & (yy) & (yz) \\ (zx) & (zy) & (zz) \end{vmatrix}^{\frac{1}{2}}}{\sqrt{(xx)}\sqrt{(yy)}\sqrt{(zz)}} = \frac{|xyz|}{\sqrt{(xx)}\sqrt{(yy)}\sqrt{(zz)}}. \quad (2)$$

We may rewrite (1) in the form

$$\frac{\sin A}{\sin\frac{a}{k}} = \frac{\sin B}{\sin\frac{b}{k}} = \frac{\sin C}{\sin\frac{c}{k}} \equiv \frac{\sin(ABC)}{\sin\frac{a}{k}\sin\frac{b}{k}\sin\frac{c}{k}}. \quad (3)$$

If A', B', C' be the points where the sides of the triangle meet the perpendiculars from the vertices, we have

$$\sin\frac{a}{k}\sin\frac{\overline{AA'}}{k} = \sin\frac{b}{k}\sin\frac{\overline{BB'}}{k} = \sin\frac{c}{k}\sin\frac{\overline{CC'}}{k} = \sin(ABC). \quad (4)$$

We see at once the close analogy of the sine amplitude of a non-euclidean triangle to double area of a euclidean triangle. Let the reader show that

$$\text{Lim.}\ \frac{1}{k^2} = 0, \quad k^2 \sin(ABC) = 2 \text{ Area } \triangle ABC.$$

A function correlative to the sine amplitude may be obtained from the correlative formula

$$\sin B \sin C \cos\frac{a}{k} = \cos B \cos C + \cos A.$$

$$\sin B \sin C \sin\frac{a}{k} = \sin C \sin A \sin\frac{b}{k} = \sin A \sin B \sin\frac{c}{k}$$

$$= \begin{vmatrix} 1 & \cos C & \cos B \\ \cos C & 1 & \cos A \\ \cos B & \cos A & 1 \end{vmatrix}^{\frac{1}{2}}$$

$$= \sin(abc). \tag{5}$$

This > 0 in the elliptic case, pure imaginary in the hyperbolic

$$\frac{\sin\frac{a}{k}}{\sin A} = \frac{\sin\frac{b}{k}}{\sin B} = \frac{\sin\frac{c}{k}}{\sin C} = \frac{\sin(abc)}{\sin A \sin B \sin C}. \tag{6}$$

$$\sin A \sin \frac{\overline{AA'}}{k} = \sin B \sin \frac{\overline{BB'}}{k} = \sin C \sin \frac{\overline{CC'}}{k} = \sin(abc). \tag{7}$$

$$\frac{\sin\frac{a}{k}}{\sin A} = \frac{\sin\frac{b}{k}}{\sin B} = \frac{\sin\frac{c}{k}}{\sin C} = \frac{\sin(ABC)}{\sin(abc)}. \tag{8}$$

$$\sin(abc) = \frac{\sin^2(ABC)}{\sin\frac{a}{k}\sin\frac{b}{k}\sin\frac{c}{k}}, \quad \sin(ABC) = \frac{\sin^2(abc)}{\sin A \sin B \sin C}. \tag{9}$$

If $$a + b + c = 2s,$$

$$\cos A = \frac{\cos\frac{a}{k} - \cos\frac{b}{k}\cos\frac{c}{k}}{\sin\frac{b}{k}\sin\frac{c}{k}},$$

$$\sin\tfrac{1}{2}A = \left[\frac{\sin\frac{s-b}{k}\sin\frac{s-c}{k}}{\sin\frac{b}{k}\sin\frac{c}{k}}\right]^{\frac{1}{2}},$$

$$\cos\tfrac{1}{2}A = \left[\frac{\sin\frac{s}{k}\sin\frac{s-a}{k}}{\sin\frac{b}{k}\sin\frac{c}{k}}\right]^{\frac{1}{2}},$$

$$\operatorname{ctn}\tfrac{1}{2}A = \left[\frac{\sin\frac{s}{k}\sin\frac{s-a}{k}}{\sin\frac{s-b}{k}\sin\frac{s-c}{k}}\right]^{\frac{1}{2}},$$

$$\sin(ABC) = 2\sqrt{\sin\frac{s}{k}\sin\frac{s-a}{k}\sin\frac{s-b}{k}\sin\frac{s-c}{k}}. \tag{10}$$

In like manner, let us put

$$A + B + C = 2\sigma.$$

$$\sin\tfrac{1}{2}\frac{a}{k} = \left[\frac{-\cos\sigma\cos(\sigma - A)}{\sin B \sin C}\right]^{\frac{1}{2}},$$

$$\cos\tfrac{1}{2}\frac{a}{k} = \left[\frac{\cos(\sigma - B)\cos(\sigma - C)}{\sin B \sin C}\right]^{\frac{1}{2}},$$

$$\operatorname{ctn}\tfrac{1}{2}\frac{a}{k} = \left[\frac{\cos(\sigma - B)\cos(\sigma - c)}{-\cos\sigma\cos(\sigma - a)}\right]^{\frac{1}{2}},$$

$$\sin(abc) = 2\sqrt{-\cos\sigma\cos(\sigma - A)\cos(\sigma - B)\cos(\sigma - C)}. \tag{11}$$

$$\sin\tfrac{1}{2}A\sin\tfrac{1}{2}B\sin\tfrac{1}{2}C = \frac{\left(\sin\frac{s-a}{k}\sin\frac{s-b}{k}\sin\frac{s-c}{k}\right)}{\sin\frac{a}{k}\sin\frac{b}{k}\sin\frac{c}{k}},$$

$$\sin\frac{s}{k} = \frac{\sin(abc)}{4\sin\tfrac{1}{2}A\sin\tfrac{1}{2}B\sin\tfrac{1}{2}C}. \tag{12}$$

$$-\cos\sigma = \frac{\sin(ABC)}{4\cos\tfrac{1}{2}\frac{a}{k}\cos\tfrac{1}{2}\frac{b}{k}\cos\tfrac{1}{2}\frac{c}{k}}. \tag{13}$$

It should be noticed that the denominator on the right of equation (13) is essentially positive. The numerator is negative in the hyperbolic case, as we have already seen, but here also $\sigma < \frac{\pi}{2}$ and $\cos\sigma > 0$. In the elliptic case the numerator is positive but $\sigma > \frac{\pi}{2}$, $\cos\sigma < 0$.

In Chapter III we defined as the *discrepancy* of a triangle, the absolute value of the difference between the sum of the measures of the angles and π. Let us now define as the *excess* of our triangle the expression

$$e = A + B + C - \pi.$$

This will have the same sign as $\frac{1}{k^2}$ the measure of curvature of space. We have

$$\sin\frac{e}{2} = -\cos\sigma = \frac{\sin(ABC)}{4\cos\tfrac{1}{2}\frac{a}{k}\cos\tfrac{1}{2}\frac{b}{k}\cos\tfrac{1}{2}\frac{c}{k}}. \tag{14}$$

Passing to the limiting case where the triangle becomes infinitesimal, we have

$$\begin{aligned}
\text{Lim.}\,\frac{\sin(ABC)}{\sin\frac{e}{2}} &= 4\,\text{lim.}\left(\cos\tfrac{1}{2}\frac{a}{k}\cos\tfrac{1}{2}\frac{b}{k}\cos\tfrac{1}{2}\frac{c}{k}\right)\\
&= 4\\
\text{lim.}\ e &= \tfrac{1}{2}\,\text{lim.}\,(ABC)\\
&= \frac{1}{2k^2}\,\text{lim.}\ bc\sin A\\
&= \frac{1}{2k^2}\,\text{lim.}\ a\,\overline{AA'}.
\end{aligned}$$

Theorem 1. In an infinitesimal triangle the limit of the ratio of the excess to the product of the euclidean area and the measure of curvature of space is unity.

Let us next examine the infinitesimal quadrilateral, whose vertices are A, B, C, D. AB and CD shall intersect in H (actual or ideal) while AC and BD intersect in K; the latter two points remaining at a finite distance from A, B, C, D.

$$\frac{\sin\dfrac{\overline{AB}}{k}}{\sin\dfrac{\overline{BK}}{k}} = \frac{\sin K}{\sin A}, \qquad \frac{\sin\dfrac{\overline{CD}}{k}}{\sin\dfrac{\overline{DK}}{k}} = \frac{\sin K}{\sin C},$$

$$\lim. \frac{\sin A}{\sin C} = 1, \quad \lim. \frac{\overline{AB}}{\overline{CD}} = 1. \qquad \text{(Ch. III. 2.)}$$

$$\begin{aligned}
\lim. \frac{\sin(CAB)}{\sin(DAB)} &= \lim. \frac{\sin\dfrac{\overline{AB}}{k}\sin\dfrac{\overline{AC}}{k}\sin A}{\sin\dfrac{\overline{DB}}{k}\sin\dfrac{\overline{DC}}{k}\sin D} \\
&= \lim. \frac{\overline{AB}\,.\,\overline{AC}\,.\,\sin A}{\overline{DB}\,.\,\overline{DC}\,.\,\sin D} \\
&= 1.
\end{aligned}$$

We shall define as the *area* of an infinitesimal triangle the common value of k^2 times its excess, its half-amplitude, and the euclidean expression for its area.

Theorem 2. If the opposite sides of an infinitesimal quadrilateral do not intersect in points infinitesimally near the vertices, the limit of the ratio of the areas of the triangles into which it is divided by a diagonal is unity.

The sum of these two infinitesimal areas shall be called the *area* of the infinitesimal quadrilateral; it will be equal (always neglecting infinitesimals of higher order) to the product of two adjacent sides multiplied into the sine of the included angle.

Suppose now that we have a region of the plane, connex right up to the boundary, which is limited by one or more closed curves, and let this be covered by a network of infinitesimal quadrilaterals of the sort just described. Let the area of each of these be multiplied by the value for a point therein of a continuous function of the coordinates of the point. The limit of this sum as the individual areas tend uniformly toward zero shall be called the *surface integral* of the given function for the given area. The proof of the existence of such a limit, and its independence of network employed will be identical with that used in the corresponding euclidean case, and need not detain us here.[65]

Definition. When the surface integral of the function 1 exists over a region of the plane, that integral shall be defined as the *area* of the region.

[65]Conf. e.g. Picard, *Traité d'Analyse*, first ed., Paris, 1891, vol. i, pp. 83–102.

Theorem 3. The area of a region of a plane is the sum of the areas of any two regions into which it may be divided provided that these two have no common area.

This follows immediately from the definition given above. As an application of these principles let us determine the area of a triangle. It is the limit of the sum of the areas of a network of infinitesimal triangles, or by (1) the limit of the sum of k^2 times their excesses. Now it is perfectly clear that if a triangle be divided in two by a segment whose extremities are a vertex and a point of the opposite side, the excess of the original triangle is the sum of the excesses of the parts, and we may establish our network by a repetition of this process of division, hence[66]

Theorem 4. The area of a triangle is the quotient of the excess divided by the measure of curvature of space.

Let us give a second demonstration of this fundamental theorem with the aid of integration. It will be sufficient to do so in the case of a right triangle, and we shall take a right triangle with one angle at C the intersection of $x_1 = 0$, $x_2 = 0$, the right angle being at B a point of the axis $x_2 = 0$. We may introduce polar coordinates

$$\frac{x_1}{x_0} = k \tan \frac{r}{k} \cos \phi, \qquad \frac{x_2}{x_0} = k \tan \frac{r}{k} \sin \phi,$$

the elements of arc along $\phi =$ const. and $r =$ const. will be dr and $k \sin \frac{r}{k} d\phi$ respectively. The element of area will be

$$df = k \sin \frac{r}{k} dr\, d\phi. \tag{15}$$

$$k \int_0^R \sin \frac{r}{k} dr = k^2 \left(1 - \cos \frac{R}{k}\right),$$

$$\tan \frac{R}{k} = \tan \frac{\overline{BC}}{k} \sec \phi. \qquad \text{(Ch. IV. (6).)}$$

$$\cos \frac{R}{k} = \frac{\cos \phi}{\sqrt{\cos^2 \phi + \tan^2 \frac{\overline{BC}}{k}}}.$$

Remembering that the limits for ϕ are 0 and C

$$\text{Area} = k^2 \int_0^C d\phi - k^2 \int_0^C \frac{\cos \phi\, d\phi}{\sqrt{\cos^2 \phi + \tan^2 \frac{\overline{BC}}{k}}}.$$

[66]It is surprising to see how unsatisfactory are the proofs usually given for this, the best-known theorem of non-euclidean geometry. In Frischauf, *Elemente der absoluten Geometrie*, Leipzig, 1876, will be found a geometrical proof applicable to the hyperbolic case but not, so far as I can see, to the elliptic, and the same remark will apply to the book of Liebmann, cit. Manning, loc. cit., makes an attempt at a general proof, but the use of intuition is scarcely disguised. In Clebsch-Lendemann, *Vorlesungen über Geometrie*, Leipzig, 1891, vol. ii, p. 49, is a proof by integration, but the analysis is unnecessarily complicated owing to the fact that, apparently, the author overlooked the consideration that it is sufficient to prove the theorem for a right triangle.

The first integral is k^2C. If, further, we put $\sin\phi = x$,

$$\int \frac{dx}{\sqrt{\sec^2 \frac{\overline{BC}}{k} - x^2}} = \sin^{-1}\left[x \cos \frac{\overline{BC}}{k}\right] + \text{const.}$$

Hence our second integral will be

$$-k^2 \left\{\sin^{-1}\left[\sin\phi \cos \frac{\overline{BC}}{k}\right]\right\}_0^C.$$

This vanishes at the lower limit. On the other hand by Chapter IV. (7)

$$\cos A = \sin C \cos \frac{\overline{BC}}{k},$$

our second integral becomes

$$-k^2\left[\frac{\pi}{2} - A\right] = k^2\left[A + B - \pi\right],$$

$$\text{Area} = k^2(A + B + C - \pi). \tag{16}$$

Two regions with the same area may, naturally, have very different shapes. There are, however, three simple cases where the equivalence of area is immediately evident. First, where the two figures are congruent; second, when they are composed of the same number of non-overlapping sub-regions (i.e. sub-regions no two of which have in common a region which has an area) congruent in pairs; third, where by the adjunction of pairs of mutually congruent non-overlapping sub-regions to them, they may be transformed into congruent regions. In this latter case they may be said to be *equivalent by completion.*[67]

Definition. Given n successive coplanar segments (A_1A_2), (A_kA_{k+1}), $(A_{n-1}A_1)$ so situated that no line other than one through a point A_i can contain points of more than two of the segments; the assemblage of all points of all segments whose extremities are points of the given segments shall be called a *convex polygon* or, more simply, a polygon. The definition of sides, vertices, and angles is immediate. If one vertex, say A_1 be connected with all the others, the polygon will be divided into $n-2$ triangles, no two of which have in common any area. The area of the polygon will thus be the sum of the areas of these triangles. We may convince ourselves of the compatibility of these statements as follows. A triangle is certainly a polygon, and if a polygon of $n-1$ sides exist, we may easily enlarge it to have n sides by taking an additional vertex near one side. On the other hand, if a polygon of $n-1$ sides may be divided up in the manner suggested, it is immediately evident that one of n sides may be so divided also.

[67]The term *equivalent by completion* is borrowed from Halsted, loc. cit., p. 109. The distinction between *equivalent* and *equivalent by completion* is, I believe, due to Hilbert, loc. cit., p. 40. For an admirable discussion of the question of area see Amaldi, in the fifth article in Enriques, *Questioni riguardanti la geometria elementare*, Bologna, 1900.

Theorem 5. The area of a convex polygon is the quotient of the excess of the sum of its angles over $(n-2)\pi$ divided by the measure of curvature of Space.

Let the reader show that the area of a proper circle is

$$2\pi k^2\left(1-\cos\frac{r}{k}\right). \tag{17}$$

The total areas of the elliptic and the spherical planes will be respectively

$$2\pi k^2, \quad 4\pi k^2.$$

In the hyperbolic plane regions may be found having any desired area.

Our next undertaking shall be to see how far the methods which we have established for studying areas are applicable in three dimensions. We shall begin, as before, with amplitudes, following, however, an analytical rather than a trigonometric method.

Let the vertices of a tetrahedron, as defined in Chapter II, be A, B, C, D with the coordinates (x), (y), (z), (t) respectively. The opposite faces shall be α, β, γ, δ with coordinates (u), (v), (w), (ω), so that, e.g.

$$r(\omega X) \equiv (X\,xyz).$$

We shall define as sine amplitude of the tetrahedron

$$\begin{aligned}\sin(ABCD) &= \left|\cos\frac{\overline{AA}}{k}\cos\frac{\overline{BB}}{k}\cos\frac{\overline{CC}}{k}\cos\frac{\overline{DD}}{k}\right|^{\frac{1}{2}}\\ &= \frac{|(xx)(yy)(zz)(tt)|^{\frac{1}{2}}}{\sqrt{(xx)}\sqrt{(yy)}\sqrt{(zz)}\sqrt{(tt)}}\\ &= \frac{|xyzt|}{\sqrt{(xx)}\sqrt{(yy)}\sqrt{(zz)}\sqrt{(tt)}}.\end{aligned} \tag{18}$$

We shall give to the radicals involved such signs that k sine amplitude shall have the sign of k^2. Recalling the concept of the moment of two lines introduced in Chapter IX, we get

$$\sin\frac{\overline{AB}}{k}\sin\frac{\overline{CD}}{k}(\text{Moment}\,AB, CD) = \sin(ABCD). \tag{19}$$

$$\sin(ABC) = \frac{|(xx)(yy)(zz)|^{\frac{1}{2}}}{\sqrt{(xx)}\sqrt{(yy)}\sqrt{(zz)}}.$$

Let A', B', C', D' be the points where perpendiculars from the vertices of a tetrahedron meet the opposite faces. Then

$$\sin\frac{\overline{DD'}}{k} = \frac{|xyzt|}{\sqrt{(tt)}\,|(xx)(yy)(zz)|^{\frac{1}{2}}},$$

$$\sin(BCD)\sin\frac{\overline{AA'}}{k} = \sin(CDA)\sin\frac{\overline{BB'}}{k} = \sin(DBA)\sin\frac{\overline{CC'}}{k}$$

$$= \sin(ABC) \sin \frac{\overline{DD'}}{k} = \sin(ABCD). \tag{20}$$

If we mean by $\measuredangle\alpha\beta$ the dihedral angle of these two faces

$$\cos \measuredangle\alpha\beta = \frac{(uv)}{\sqrt{(uu)}\sqrt{(vv)}}$$

$$= \frac{\begin{vmatrix} (xy) & (xz) & (xt) \\ (zy) & (zz) & (zt) \\ (ty) & (tz) & (tt) \end{vmatrix}}{\sqrt{\dfrac{\partial|(xx)(yy)(zz)(tt)|}{\partial(xx)}}\sqrt{\dfrac{\partial|(xx)(yy)(zz)(tt)|}{\partial(yy)}}},$$

$$\sin \measuredangle\alpha\beta = \frac{\sin(ABCD)\sin\dfrac{\overline{AB}}{k}}{\sin(BCD)\sin(ACD)},$$

$$\sin(BCD)\sin(ACD)\frac{\sin\measuredangle\alpha\beta}{\sin\dfrac{\overline{AB}}{k}} = \sin(ABCD). \tag{21}$$

The geometry of lines through a point is an example of the geometry of the elliptic plane, where $k^2 = 1$. We may thus speak of the sine amplitude of a trihedral angle

$$\sin(AB, AC, AD) = \frac{\begin{Vmatrix} \begin{vmatrix} (tt) & (tx) \\ (xt) & (xx) \end{vmatrix} & \begin{vmatrix} (tt) & (ty) \\ (xt) & (xy) \end{vmatrix} & \begin{vmatrix} (tt) & (tz) \\ (xt) & (xz) \end{vmatrix} \\ \begin{vmatrix} (tt) & (ty) \\ (xt) & (xy) \end{vmatrix} & \begin{vmatrix} (tt) & (ty) \\ (yt) & (yy) \end{vmatrix} & \begin{vmatrix} (tt) & (tz) \\ (yt) & (yz) \end{vmatrix} \\ \begin{vmatrix} (tt) & (tx) \\ (zt) & (zx) \end{vmatrix} & \begin{vmatrix} (tt) & (ty) \\ (zt) & (zy) \end{vmatrix} & \begin{vmatrix} (tt) & (tz) \\ (zt) & (zz) \end{vmatrix} \end{Vmatrix}^{\frac{1}{2}}}{\sqrt{\begin{vmatrix} (tt) & (tx) \\ (xt) & (xx) \end{vmatrix}}\sqrt{\begin{vmatrix} (tt) & (ty) \\ (yt) & (yy) \end{vmatrix}}\sqrt{\begin{vmatrix} (tt) & (tz) \\ (zt) & (zz) \end{vmatrix}}}$$

$$= \frac{(tt)\,|xyzt|}{\sqrt{\begin{vmatrix} (tt) & (tx) \\ (xt) & (xx) \end{vmatrix}}\sqrt{\begin{vmatrix} (tt) & (ty) \\ (yt) & (yy) \end{vmatrix}}\sqrt{\begin{vmatrix} (tt) & (tz) \\ (zt) & (zz) \end{vmatrix}}}.$$

$$\sin\frac{\overline{DA}}{k}\sin\frac{\overline{DB}}{k}\sin\frac{\overline{DC}}{k}\sin(AB, AC, AD) = \sin(ABCD). \tag{22}$$

The reader will not fail to notice in formulae (19), (20), and (22) the striking analogy between the sine amplitude and six times the euclidean volume. There will be a function correlative to $\sin(ABCD)$ which we shall call $\sin(\alpha\beta\gamma\delta)$.

$$\sin\measuredangle\alpha\beta\sin\measuredangle(\gamma\delta)(\text{Moment } AB, CD) = \sin(\alpha\beta\gamma\delta). \tag{23}$$

$$\sin(\alpha\beta\gamma)\sin\frac{\overline{DD'}}{k}=\sin(\alpha\beta\gamma\delta). \tag{24}$$

$$\sin(\alpha\gamma\delta)\sin(\beta\gamma\delta)\frac{\sin\dfrac{\overline{AB}}{k}}{\sin\measuredangle\alpha\beta}=\sin(\alpha\beta\gamma\delta). \tag{25}$$

$$\sin\measuredangle\alpha\delta\sin\measuredangle\beta\delta\sin\measuredangle\gamma\delta\sin(\alpha\delta,\beta\delta,\gamma\delta)=\sin(\alpha\beta\gamma\delta). \tag{26}$$

$$\frac{\sin(BCD)}{\sin(\beta\gamma\delta)}=\frac{\sin(CDA)}{\sin(\gamma\delta\alpha)}=\frac{\sin(DBA)}{\sin(\delta\beta\alpha)}=\frac{\sin(ABC)}{\sin(\alpha\beta\gamma)}=\frac{\sin(ABCD)}{\sin(\alpha\beta\gamma\delta)}. \tag{27}$$

Our two tetrahedral functions are connected by the relations

$$\sin(\alpha\beta\gamma\delta)=\frac{\sin^3(ABCD)}{\sin(BCD)\sin(CDA)\sin(DBA)\sin(ABC)},$$
$$\sin(ABCD)=\frac{\sin^3(\alpha\beta\gamma\delta)}{\sin(\beta\gamma\delta)\sin(\gamma\delta\alpha)\sin(\delta\beta\alpha)\sin(\alpha\beta\gamma)}.$$

The analogy between the sine amplitude and the sextuple of the euclidean expression for the volume appears even more distinctly in the infinitesimal domain.

$$\begin{aligned}\text{Lim.}\sin(ABC)&=\frac{1}{k^2}\overline{AB}\,.\,\overline{AC}\,.\,\sin\measuredangle BAC\\&=\frac{2}{k^2}\,\text{Area}\,\triangle ABC.\\\text{Lim.}\sin(ABCD)&=\text{lim.}\,(ABCD)\\&=\frac{6}{k^3}\,\text{Vol. tetrahedron}\,ABCD.\end{aligned} \tag{28}$$

Following our previous analogy, suppose that we have six planes, no three coaxal, passing by fours through four actual or ideal, but not collinear points. Let the remaining intersections be at a finite distance from the three chosen points, but infinitesimally near one another. An infinitesimal region will thus be formed, on the analogy of a euclidean parallelepiped, which may be divided into six tetrahedra of such sort that the limit of the ratio of the sine amplitudes, or of the euclidean volumes, of any two is unity. Six times the euclidean volume of any one of these tetrahedra may be defined as the euclidean volume of the region.

So far the analogy between two and three dimensions has been sufficiently good. Each time we have had a function called *sine amplitude* corresponding in many particulars to a simple multiple of the euclidean area or volume, and approaching a multiple of the area or volume as a limit, when the figure becomes infinitesimal. In the plane there appeared, besides half the sine amplitude and the euclidean area, a third expression, namely, the discrepancy or excess. In three dimensions this function is, sad to relate, entirely lacking; that is to say, there is no simple function of the measures of a tetrahedron which possesses the property that when one tetrahedron is the logical sum of two others, the function of the sum is the sum of the functions. It is the lack of this function that renders the problem of non-euclidean volumes difficult.[68]

Suppose, in general, that we have a three dimensional region connex up to the boundary, and that we divide it into a number of extremely tiny tetrahedra. The limit of the sum of the euclidean volume of each, multiplied by the value for a point therein of a continuous function of the coordinates of that point, as all the volumes approach zero uniformly, shall be called the *volume integral* for that region of that function. The proofs for the existence of that volume integral, and its independence of the method of subdivision, are analogous to those already referred to for the surface integral. In particular, the volume integral of the function unity shall be called the *volume* of the region. Two regions will have the same volume if they be congruent, made up of the same number of parts, mutually congruent in pairs, or if by the adjunction of such pairs they may be completed to be congruent.

If the limiting surface of a region be made up of a series of plane surfaces, and if no line, not lying in a plane of the surface, can contain more than two points of the surface, then it is easy to show that the region may be divided up into a number of tetrahedra, and the problem of finding the volume of any such region reduces to the problem of finding the volume of a tetrahedron. This problem may, in turn, be reduced to that of finding the volume of a tetrahedron of particularly simple structure. To begin with, we may assume that there is one face which makes with the three others dihedral angles whose measures are less than $\frac{\pi}{2}$, for the bisectors of the dihedral angles of the original tetrahedron will always divide it into smaller tetrahedra possessing this property. The perpendicular on the plane of this face, from the opposite vertex, will, then, pass through a point within the face, and, with the help of this perpendicular, we may subdivide into three smaller tetrahedra, for each of which the line of one edge is perpendicular to the plane of one face.

Consider, next, a tetrahedron where the line of one edge is indeed perpendicular to the plane of a face. There are two possibilities. First, in the plane of this face neither of the face angles whose vertex is not at the foot of the perpendicular is obtuse; secondly, one of these angles is obtuse. (The case where both were obtuse could not occur in a small region.) In the first case we might draw a line from the foot of the perpendicular to a point of the opposite edge in this particular face, perpendicular to the line of that edge, and thus, by a familiar theorem in elementary geometry, which holds equally in the non-euclidean case, divide the tetrahedron into two others, each of which possesses the property that the lines of two opposite edges are perpendicular to two of the faces. These we shall for the moment call *simplest type*. In the second case, from the vertex of the obtuse angle mentioned, draw a line perpendicular to the line of the opposite edge in this particular face (and passing through a point within this edge), and connect the intersection with the vertex opposite this face. The

[68]It is highly interesting that in four dimensions a function playing the role of the discrepancy appears once more. See Dehn, 'Die eulersche Formel in Zusammenhang mit dem Inhalt in der nicht-euklidischen Geometrie,' *Mathematische Annalen*, vol. lxi, 1906.

tetrahedron will be divided up into a tetrahedron of the simplest type, and one of the sort considered in case 1. We have, then, merely to consider the volume of a tetrahedron of the simplest type.

Let the vertices of the tetrahedron be A, B, C, D, where AB is perpendicular to BCD and DC perpendicular to ABC. Let a plane perpendicular to AB contain a point B_1 of (AB) whose distance from A shall have the measure x; while this plane meets (AC) and (AD) in C_1 and D_1 respectively. The volume of the region bounded by this plane, and an adjacent one of the same type and the three faces through A, will be dx, multiplied by the surface integral over the $\triangle B_1C_1D_1$ of the cosine of the kth part of the distance of a point from B_1 (Cf. Ch. IV. (2).) This integral takes a striking form.[69]

Let the distance from B_1 to a variable point P of the triangle be r, while ϕ is the measure of $\measuredangle C_1B_1P$. We wish to find

$$k\iint \sin\frac{r}{k}\cos\frac{r}{k}dr\,d\phi.$$

Let B_1P meet (C_1D_1) in E_1. The limits of integration for r are 0 and $\overline{B_1E_1}$; hence we have merely to find

$$\frac{k^2}{2}\int_0^{\measuredangle C_1B_1D_1}\sin^2\frac{\overline{B_1E_1}}{k}d\phi.$$

Now C_1D_1 is perpendicular to B_1C_1, hence

$$\tan\phi\sin\frac{\overline{B_1C_1}}{k}=\tan\frac{\overline{E_1C_1}}{k},$$

$$\cos\frac{\overline{B_1E_1}}{k}=\cos\frac{\overline{B_1C_1}}{k}\cos\frac{\overline{E_1C_1}}{k}\tan\frac{\overline{B_1E_1}}{k}=\tan\frac{\overline{B_1C_1}}{k}\sec\phi.$$

(Ch. IV. (5), (6).)

$$\sin^2\frac{\overline{B_1E_1}}{k}d\phi=\frac{1}{k}\sin\frac{\overline{B_1C_1}}{k}d\overline{E_1C_1}.$$

Our required integral is then

$$\frac{k}{2}\int\sin\frac{\overline{B_1C_1}}{k}d\overline{E_1C_1}=\frac{k}{2}\sin\frac{\overline{B_1C_1}}{k}\cdot\overline{C_1D_1}$$

Let the reader note the astonishing feature of this result, namely, that it involves one side of a triangle directly, and another trigonometrically.

[69]The integration which follows is a very special case of a much more general one for n dimensions given by Schläfli, *Theorie der vielfachen Kontinuität*, Zurich, 1901, p. 646. This paper of Schläfli's is posthumous; it was originally written in 1855, when the science of non-euclidean geometry had not reached its present recognition. It is very general, extremely difficult reading, and hampered by a fearful and wonderful terminology, e.g. our tetrahedron of the simplest type is a special case of an *Artiothoscheme*. It is, however, a striking piece of geometrical work. Schläfli gives a shorter account of his work in his 'Réduction d'une intégrale multiple qui comprend l'arc d'un cercle et l'aire d'un triangle sphérique comme cas partieuliers', *Lionville's Journal*, vol. xxii, 1855.

Let the measure of the dihedral angle whose edge is (C_1D_1) be θ, this will also be the measure of $\measuredangle AC_1B_1$ which is the plane angle of the dihedral one.

$$\cos\theta = \cos\frac{\overline{AB_1}}{k}\sin\measuredangle BAC,$$

$$\sin\theta d\theta = \frac{1}{k}\sin\frac{\overline{AB_1}}{k}\sin\measuredangle BAC dx$$

$$= \frac{1}{k}\sin\frac{\overline{AB_1}}{k}\cdot\frac{\sin\frac{\overline{B_1C_1}}{k}}{\sin\frac{\overline{AC_1}}{k}}dx$$

$$= \frac{1}{k}\sin\theta\sin\frac{\overline{B_1C_1}}{k}dx.$$

We thus get for our volume the strange formula[70]

$$\text{Vol.} = \frac{k^2}{2}\int\overline{C_1D_1}d\theta. \tag{29}$$

We can easily express this integral in terms of θ,

$$\tan\frac{\overline{C_1D_1}}{k} = \sin\frac{\overline{AC_1}}{k}\tan\measuredangle DAC = a\sin\frac{\overline{AC_1}}{k},$$

$$\cos\frac{\overline{AC_1}}{k} = \operatorname{ctn}\measuredangle BAC\operatorname{ctn}\theta = b\operatorname{ctn}\theta.$$

$$\text{Vol.} = \frac{k^3}{2}\int\tan^{-1}[a\sqrt{1-b^2\operatorname{ctn}^2\theta}]d\theta. \tag{30}$$

This formula apparently represents about as close an approach as can be made towards *finding the volume* of this tetrahedron, for, in the general case,[71] it does not seem possible to effect the quadrature in terms of elementary functions.

If a right triangle be rotated completely about one of the sides adjacent to the right angle, the figure so generated shall be called a *cone of revolution*. The volume within the surface may be found as follows. Let the vertex of the cone be A and the centre of the base O, while P is a point within the cone. Let Q be the intersection of (AO) with a perpendicular from P, while the base circle meets the plane AOP in B. (AB) shall meet PQ in R. Let us also write

$$\overline{AB} = s, \quad \overline{AR} = r, \quad \overline{AO} = h, \quad \measuredangle OAB = \theta.$$

$$\text{Vol.} = k\int_0^{\overline{QR}}\int_0^h\int_0^{2\pi}\sin\frac{\overline{QP}}{k}\cos\frac{\overline{QP}}{k}d\overline{AQ}\,d\overline{QP}\,d\theta$$

[70] See Schläfli, *Réduction*, p. 381, where it is stated that this integral cannot be evaluated by integration by parts. This same integral was discovered, apparently independently, by Richmond, 'The Volume of a Tetrahedron in Elliptic Space,' *Quarterly Journal of Mathematics*, vol. xxxiv, 1902, p. 175.

[71] Schläfli, *Vielfache Kontinuität*, p. 95, gives a formula for the special case where the sum of the squares of the cosines of the dihedral angles is equal to unity. The proof is highly intricate, and not suitable to reproduce here.

$$= 2\pi k \int_0^h \int_0^{\overline{QR}} \sin\frac{\overline{QP}}{k} \cos\frac{\overline{QP}}{k} d\overline{AQ}.\, d\overline{QP}$$

$$= \pi k^2 \int_0^h \sin^2 \frac{\overline{QR}}{k} d\overline{AQ}.$$

$$\tan\frac{\overline{AQ}}{k} = \tan\frac{r}{k}\cos\theta. \qquad \text{(Ch. V. (6).)}$$

$$d\overline{AQ} = \frac{\cos\theta\sec^2\frac{r}{k}dr}{1+\cos^2\theta\tan^2\frac{r}{k}}.$$

$$\sin\frac{\overline{QR}}{k} = \sin\frac{r}{k}\sin\theta.$$

$$\text{Vol.} = \pi k^2 \sin^2\theta\cos\theta \int_0^h \frac{\tan^2\frac{r}{k}}{1+\cos^2\theta\tan^2\frac{r}{k}} dr.$$

$$\text{Put} \quad \tan\frac{r}{k} = x.$$

$$\begin{aligned}
\text{Vol.} &= \pi k^3 \cos\theta\sin^2\theta \int_0^{\tan\frac{h}{k}} \frac{x^2 dx}{(1+x^2)(1+x^2\cos^2\theta)} \\
&= \pi k^3\cos\theta\left[\int_0^{\tan\frac{h}{k}} \frac{dx}{1+x^2\cos\theta} - \int_0^{\tan\frac{h}{k}} \frac{dx}{1+x^2}\right] \\
&= \pi k^3 \cos\theta\left[\frac{1}{\cos\theta}\tan^{-1}(x\cos\theta) - \tan^{-1}x\right]_0^{\tan\frac{h}{k}} \\
&= \pi k^2[h - s\cos\theta].^{72} \qquad (31)
\end{aligned}$$

To find the volume within a proper sphere, where the distance from the centre to every point of the surface has the constant value R,

$$\begin{aligned}
\text{Vol.} &= k^2 \int_0^R \int_0^\pi \int_0^{2\pi} \sin^2\frac{2}{k}\sin\theta\, dr\, d\theta\, d\phi \\
&= 4\pi k^2 \int_0^R \sin^2\frac{r}{k} dr \\
&= \pi k^3\left(\frac{2R}{k} - \sin\frac{2R}{k}\right). \qquad (32)
\end{aligned}$$

Let the reader show that the total volumes of elliptic and of spherical space, where $k = 1$ will be, respectively,

$$\pi^2, \quad 2\pi^2.$$

---

[72]This formula is given without sufficiently detailed proof by Frischauf, loc. cit., p. 99. A tedious demonstration was subsequently worked out by Von Frank, 'Der Körperinhalt des senkrechten Cylinders und Kegels in der absoluten Geometrie,' *Grunerts Archiven*, vol. lix, 1876.

CHAPTER XV

INTRODUCTION TO DIFFERENTIAL GEOMETRY

The task which we shall undertake in the present chapter is to develop the differential geometry of curves and surfaces in non-euclidean space.[73] We shall introduce a notable simplification in our work by abandoning homogeneous coordinates, and assuming that

$$(xx) = k^2. \tag{1}$$

In the elliptic case we shall take $x_0 \geqq 0$; in the hyperbolic, $\dot{x}_0 = \frac{1}{k}x_0 \geqq 0$ for all real points.

Of course in exceptional cases, where we wish to include points of the Absolute or beyond, this proceeding is not legitimate; we shall therefore assume, unless we specifically state the contrary, that we are limiting ourselves to a real region, where no absolute or ultra infinite points are included in the hyperbolic case. We shall, further, have for the distance of two points (x), (x').

$$\cos\frac{d}{k} = \frac{(xx')}{k^2}, \quad \sin^2\frac{d}{k} = \frac{\begin{Vmatrix} x_0 & x_1 & x_2 & x_3 \\ x_0{}' & x_1{}' & x_2{}' & x_3{}' \end{Vmatrix}^2}{k^4}. \tag{2}$$

When $x_i{}' = x_i + dx_i$ we have for the square of the differential of distance

$$k^2\frac{ds^2}{k^2} = ds^2 = \frac{(xx)(dx\,dx) - (x\,dx)^2}{k^2}.$$

$$(x + dx,\ x + dx) = k^2, \quad (x\,dx) = -\tfrac{1}{2}(dx\,dx),$$

$$ds^2 = (dx\,dx). \tag{3}$$

We shall mean by an analytic curve, such a curve that the coordinates of its points are analytic functions of a single variable. The formulae developed in this chapter will hold equally well under the supposition that the functions and their first three partial derivatives exist and are finite in our region, but the gain in generality is of little interest to the geometer, and we shall assume from here on that when we speak of curve we mean analytic curve.

Let us imagine that at a chosen point of a curve, say P, a tangent is drawn. We shall take two near points P' and P'' on the curve and tangent respectively, so situated near P and on the same side of the normal plane that $\overline{PP'} = \overline{PP''}$. Then we shall define[74]

$$\lim.\ \frac{2\overline{P'P''}}{\overline{PP'^2}},$$

[73]The developments of this chapter follow the general scheme worked out for the euclidean case in Bianchi-Lukat, *Vorlesungen über Differentialgeometrie*, Leipzig, 1899, Chapters I, III, IV, and VI. In Chapters XXI and XXII of the same work will be found a different development of the non-euclidean case. It is, however, so general, yet so concise, as to be scarcely suitable to serve as an introduction to the subject.

[74]This definition is taken from Bianchi, loc. cit., p. 603. It is there ascribed to Voss.

as the curvature of the given curve at that point. If we compare with Chapter XI. (2), and define as the osculating circle to a curve at a point, the limit of the circle through that and two adjacent points, we shall have

Theorem 1. The curvature of a curve at any point is equal to that of its osculating circle, and is equal to the absolute value of the product of the square root of the curvature of space and the cotangent of the kth part of the distance of each point of the circle from its centre.

Let us now suppose that the equations of our curve are written in the form

$$x_i = x_i(t_0) + (t - t_0)x_i'(t_0) + \frac{(t-t_0)^2}{2}x_i''(t_0) + \dots$$

$$x_i^{(n)} = \frac{d^n}{dt^n}x_i(t).$$

Then for a point on the tangent we shall have coordinates

$$X_i = \lambda[x_i(t_0) + (t - t_0)x_i'(t_0)].$$

To get the value of λ.

$$(XX) = xx = k^2, \quad (xx') = 0,$$

$$X_i = \frac{x_i(t_0) + (t - t_0)x_i'(t_0)}{\sqrt{1 + \frac{(t-t_0)^2}{k^2}(x_i'x_i')}}.$$

Developing by the binomial theorem, and rejecting powers of $(t - t_0)$ above the second

$$X_i = x_i(t_0) + (t - t_0)x_i'(t_0) - \frac{(t-t_0)^2}{2k^2}(x'x')x_i(t_0).$$

Subtracting from the series development of x_i we get for our curvature $\frac{1}{\rho}$.

$$\frac{1}{\rho^2} = \frac{\left[(x''x'') + \frac{2}{k^2}(xx'')(x'x') + \frac{1}{k^4}(x'x')^2(xx)\right]}{(x'x')^2},$$

$$\frac{1}{\rho^2} = \frac{(x''x'')}{(x'x')^2} - \frac{1}{k^2}. \tag{4}$$

Theorem 2. The square of the curvature of a curve is the square of its curvature treated as a curve in a four-dimensional euclidean space, minus the measure of curvature of the non-euclidean space.

It will be convenient to consider, besides our point (x), three other points allied to it. (t) shall be orthogonal to (x) and on the tangent, (z) orthogonal to (x) on the principal normal, and (ξ) orthogonal to (x) on the binormal. These three will replace the direction cosines of tangent, principal normal, and binormal, which figure so prominently in the euclidean theory. In hyperbolic space these points lie without the actual domain to which we suppose (x) confined.

$$(xt) = (xz) = (x\xi) = (tz) = (t\xi) = (z\xi) = 0.$$

If a point trace an infinitesimal arc ds, the angle of the corresponding absolute polar planes is $\left|\sqrt{\dfrac{ds^2}{k^2}}\right|$.

We shall, hereafter, take as our parameter on the given curve s, the length of arc, so that

$$x_i{}' = \frac{dx_i}{ds}, \quad (x'x') = 1.$$

As (t) lies on the tangent, its coordinates will be of the form

$$t_i = lx_i + mx_i{}',$$

$$(tt) = (xx) = k^2, \quad (tx) = 0, \quad (xx') = 0,$$

$$t_i = kx_i{}'. \tag{5}$$

For the point (z) we shall have

$$z_i = \lambda x_i + \mu x_i{}' + \nu x_i{}'',$$

$$(zx) = (zx') = (xx') = (x'x') + (xx'') = 0,$$

$$(zz) = (xx) = k^2, \quad (x'x') = 1.$$

$$z_i = \frac{x_i + k^2 x_i{}''}{\sqrt{k^2(x''x'') - 1}},$$

$$z_i = \frac{\rho}{k}(x_i + k^2 x_i{}''). \tag{6}$$

To determine ξ we shall have the conditions

$$(\xi x) = (\xi z) = (\xi t) = 0, \quad (\xi\xi) = k^2,$$

$$\xi_i = \rho \frac{\partial}{\partial y_i}|yxx'x''|. \tag{7}$$

We shall define the *torsion* of our curve as the limit of the ratio of the angle of two successive osculating planes to the differential of arc. We thus get

$$\frac{1}{T} = \frac{1}{k}\frac{\sqrt{(d\xi\, d\xi)}}{ds}. \tag{8}$$

Reverting to our formulae (5) and (6)

$$\frac{dt_i}{ds} = \frac{z_i}{\rho} - \frac{x_i}{k}. \tag{9}$$

$$(x\xi) = (x'\xi) = (x''\xi) = (x\xi') = (x'\xi') = (\xi\xi') = 0.$$

Hence
$$\frac{d\xi_i}{ds} = lz_i,$$

or, more specifically
$$\frac{d\xi_i}{ds} = \frac{z_i}{T}. \tag{10}$$

We have also
$$(xz) = (xz') = (x'z) = (zz') = 0,$$
$$z_i' = \lambda t_i + \mu \xi_i,$$
$$\frac{dz_i}{ds} = -\frac{t_i}{\rho} - \frac{\xi_i}{T}. \tag{11}$$

The reader will see at once that (9), (10), (11) are the analoga of Frenet's formulae for euclidean curves.

We have, so far, overlooked the question of the sign of the torsion, but that is well determined from the above formulae, and it is important now to find the geometric difference between the case where the torsion is negative, and that where it is positive. We shall carry through the work for the elliptic case only, the hyperbolic may be treated in the same way, but it is wiser there to replace the coordinates (x) by $(\dot{x})$.

As before we shall choose s as the independent variable, so that

$$(xx) = k^2, \quad (xx') = (x'x'') = 0, \quad (x'x') = -(xx'') = 1.$$

The sign of t_i (which may be ideal) will be found from (5), that of z_i from (6), and that of ξ_i from (7), while the sign of T will be given by (10).

The equation of the plane of the tangent and binormal will be

$$|Xxt\xi| = (Xx) + k^2(Xx'') = 0.$$

Putting in the coordinates of a near-by point of the curve,

$$x_i + x_i'\Delta s + x_i''\frac{(\Delta s)^2}{2},$$

$$k^2 - \frac{(\Delta s)^2}{2} - k^2 + k^2(x''x'')\frac{\Delta s^2}{2} = \frac{k^2}{\rho^2}\frac{(\Delta s)^2}{2},$$

and this is essentially positive, so that, in general, the curve will not cross this plane here. Again, we see by (6) that we may give to a point on the principal normal close to (x) the coordinates

$$x_i + \epsilon x_i''.$$

Substituting in the equation of the plane we get

$$\frac{k^2}{\rho^2}\epsilon,$$

so that this will lie on the same side as the curve if $\epsilon > 0$.

Let us call *positive* that part of the curve near our point for which $\Delta s > 0$. The positive part of the tangent shall be that which lies on the same side of the normal plane as the positive part of the curve, while that part of the principal normal shall be called positive which lies on the same side of the plane of tangent and binormal as does the curve. Let us find the Plueckerian coordinates of a ray from $x_i + x_i'\Delta s$ on the positive part of the tangent to $x_i + \epsilon x_i''$ on the positive part of the principal normal. We get

$$p_{ij} = \epsilon \begin{vmatrix} x_i & x_j \\ x_i'' & x_j'' \end{vmatrix} + \Delta s \begin{vmatrix} x_i' & x_j' \\ x_i & x_j \end{vmatrix} + \epsilon\Delta s \begin{vmatrix} x_i' & x_j' \\ x_i'' & x_j'' \end{vmatrix}.$$

In like manner for a ray from (x) to a point on the positive part of the curve

$$x_i + x_i'\Delta_1 s + x_i''\frac{(\Delta_1 s)^2}{2} + x_i'''\frac{(\Delta_1 s)^3}{3!},$$

we get

$$q_{kl} = \Delta_1 s \begin{vmatrix} x_k & x_l \\ x_k' & x_l' \end{vmatrix} + \frac{(\Delta_1 s)^2}{2} \begin{vmatrix} x_k & x_l \\ x_k'' & x_l'' \end{vmatrix} + \frac{(\Delta_1 s)^3}{3!} \begin{vmatrix} x_k & x_l \\ x_k''' & x_l''' \end{vmatrix}.$$

The relative moment of these two rays, as defined at the close of Chapter IX, will be

$$\Sigma\, p_{ij}q_{kl} \equiv \epsilon\frac{\Delta s(\Delta_1 s)^3}{6}|xx'x''x'''|.$$

The factors outside of the determinant are all, by hypothesis, positive, so that the sign depends merely upon that of the determinant, and this by (7) is equal to $\dfrac{\rho(\xi x''')}{k}$.

Now

$$(\xi x'') = 0, \quad (\xi x''') = -(\xi' x'').$$

Hence the relative moment will have the sign of

$$\frac{-\rho}{kT}(zx'') = \frac{-\rho^2}{k^2T}[(xx'') + k^2(x''x'')] = -\frac{1}{T}.$$

Theorem 3. The torsion at a general point of a curve is positive when the relative moment of a ray thence to a point on the positive part of the curve, and a ray from a point on the positive part of the tangent to one on the positive part of the principal normal is negative; when the latter product is positive, the torsion is negative.

Intuitively stated this means that the torsion is positive when the curve resembles a left-hand screw, otherwise negative.

We shall next take up the evolutes of a curve. Let $(\overline{x})$ be a point of an evolute. Then

$$x_i = \cos\frac{\overline{s}}{k}\overline{x_i} - \sin\frac{\overline{s}}{k}\overline{t_i},$$

$$\frac{dx_i}{d\overline{s}} = -\sin\frac{\overline{s}}{k}\frac{\overline{z_i}}{\overline{\rho}}.$$

Remembering that $\frac{dx_i}{d\overline{s}} = kt_i$, while $\overline{z_i}$ is on the principal normal of the evolute.

Theorem 4. A tangent to an analytic curve at a general point will be in the osculating plane at the corresponding point of any evolute.

Since $(\overline{x})$ lies in the normal plane at (x), we may write

$$w\overline{x_i} = x_i + u\xi_i + vz_i,$$

$$w\frac{d\overline{x_i}}{ds} = -\frac{1}{w}(x_i + u\xi_i + vz_i)\frac{dw}{ds} + \frac{t_i}{k} + u\frac{z_i}{T} - v\left(\frac{t_i}{\rho} + \frac{\xi_i}{T}\right) + \xi_i\frac{du}{ds} + z_i\frac{dx}{ds}.$$

Now $\frac{d\overline{x_i}}{ds}$ is linearly dependent on (x) and $(\overline{x})$,

$$\left(t\frac{d\overline{x}}{ds}\right) = 0, \quad v = \frac{\rho}{k},$$

and, for the same reason, the assemblage of all terms in (ξ) and (z) must be a linear combination of (x) and $(\overline{x})$, and so proportional to $w\overline{x_i} - x_i = u\xi_i + vz_i$

$$\left[\frac{du}{ds} - \frac{\rho}{kT}\right]\xi_i + \left[\frac{u}{T} + \frac{d\rho}{kds}\right]z_i = \lambda\left[u\xi_i + \frac{\rho}{k}z_i\right],$$

$$\frac{\frac{du}{ds} - \frac{\rho}{kT}}{\frac{u}{T} + \frac{1}{k}\frac{d\rho}{ds}} = \frac{u}{\frac{\rho}{k}},$$

$$\tan^{-1}\left(\frac{u}{\frac{\rho}{k}}\right) = \int\frac{ds}{T} + C = (\sigma + C).$$

To get (w) we have

$$(\overline{x}\,\overline{x}) = k^2,$$

$$w = \sqrt{1 + u^2 + v^2} = \sqrt{1 + \frac{\rho^2}{k^2}\sec^2(\sigma + C)}.$$

$$\overline{x_i} = \frac{\left(x_i + z_i\frac{\rho}{k}\right)\cos(\sigma + C) + \frac{\rho}{k}\xi_i\sin(\sigma + C)}{\sqrt{\frac{\rho^2}{k^2} + \cos^2(\sigma + C)}}. \qquad (12)$$

The coordinates of the point of the line $(x)(\overline{x})$ orthogonal to (x) will be

$$\lambda x_i + \mu\overline{x_i},$$

$$\lambda k^2 + \frac{\mu k^2\cos(\sigma + C)}{\sqrt{\frac{\rho^2}{k^2} + \cos^2(\sigma + C)}} = 0,$$

$$(\lambda^2+\mu^2)k^2+\frac{2\lambda\mu k^2\cos(\sigma+C)}{\sqrt{\frac{\rho^2}{k^2}+\cos(\sigma+C)}}=k^2,$$

$$\mu=\frac{-\sqrt{\frac{\rho^2}{k^2}+\cos(\sigma+C)}}{\frac{\rho}{k}},\quad \lambda=\frac{\cos(\sigma+C)}{\frac{\rho}{k}}.$$

The point in question will therefore have the coordinates

$$\xi_i\sin(\sigma+C)+z_i\cos(\sigma+C).$$

This gives us the significance of σ, namely $(\sigma+C)$ is the kth part of the distance from this point to (z), i.e. $(\sigma+C)$ represents the angle which this normal makes with the principal normal. If, then, we take two evolutes of our curve the angle between their corresponding tangents, i.e. those which meet on the involute, is

$$(\sigma+C_1)-(\sigma+C_2)=C_1-C_2.$$

Theorem 5. Corresponding tangents to two evolutes of a curve meet at a constant angle.

Theorem 6. If the generators of a developable surface be turned through a constant angle about the tangents to one of their orthogonal trajectories, the resulting surface is developable.

Theorem 7. The tangents to an evolute of a plane curve make a constant angle with the plane of the curve.

The foregoing theorems and formulae exhibit sufficiently the close analogy between the differential theory of curves in euclidean and in non-euclidean space. It is our next task to take up the theory of surfaces, and we shall find a no less striking analogy there. We shall mean by an *analytic surface* the locus of a point whose coordinates are analytic functions of two independent parameters. We shall exclude from consideration all singular points of such surfaces. If the parameters be (u) and (v), we shall have for the squared distance element

$$ds^2=E\,du^2+2F\,du\,dv+G\,dv^2,$$

$$E=\left(\frac{\partial x}{\partial u}\frac{\partial x}{\partial u}\right),\quad F=\left(\frac{\partial x}{\partial u}\frac{\partial x}{\partial v}\right),\quad G=\left(\frac{\partial x}{\partial v}\frac{\partial x}{\partial v}\right),$$

$$EG-F^2=\left\|\begin{matrix}\frac{\partial x_0}{\partial u} & \frac{\partial x_1}{\partial u} & \frac{\partial x_2}{\partial u} & \frac{\partial x_3}{\partial u}\\ \frac{\partial x_0}{\partial v} & \frac{\partial x_1}{\partial v} & \frac{\partial x_2}{\partial v} & \frac{\partial x_3}{\partial v}\end{matrix}\right\|^2. \tag{13}$$

This is a positive definite form in the elliptic case, and in the actual domain of hyperbolic space, to which we shall restrict ourselves. The discriminant, under this same restriction, will always be greater than zero, for it will vanish only when the tangent plane to the surface is also tangent to the Absolute.

The equation of the tangent plane at (x) will be

$$\left| Xx \frac{\partial x}{\partial u} \frac{\partial x}{\partial v} \right| = 0.$$

The Absolute pole of this plane will be

$$y_i = \frac{\dfrac{\partial}{r_i} \left| rx \dfrac{\partial x}{\partial u} \dfrac{\partial x}{\partial v} \right|}{\sqrt{EG - F^2}}. \tag{14}$$

We shall consistently use the letter (y) throughout the present chapter to indicate this point. The equation of the plane through the normal, and the point $(x + dx)$, will be

$$\begin{vmatrix} (Xx) & (xx) & \left(x\dfrac{\partial x}{\partial u}\right) \\ \left(X\dfrac{\partial x}{\partial u}\right) & \left(x\dfrac{\partial x}{\partial u}\right) & E \\ \left(X\dfrac{\partial x}{\partial v}\right) & \left(x\dfrac{\partial x}{\partial v}\right) & F \end{vmatrix} du + \begin{vmatrix} (Xx) & (xx) & \left(x\dfrac{\partial x}{\partial u}\right) \\ \left(X\dfrac{\partial x}{\partial u}\right) & \left(x\dfrac{\partial x}{\partial u}\right) & F \\ \left(X\dfrac{\partial x}{\partial v}\right) & \left(x\dfrac{\partial x}{\partial v}\right) & G \end{vmatrix} dv = 0.$$

$$\sum_i^{0..3} \left[\left(F\frac{\partial x_i}{\partial u} - E\frac{\partial x_i}{\partial v} \right) du + \left(G\frac{\partial x_i}{\partial u} - F\frac{\partial x_i}{\partial v} \right) dv \right] X_i = 0.$$

The cosine of the angle which this plane makes with that through the normal and the point $(x + \delta x)$, or the cosine of the angle of the two arcs from (x) to $(x + dx)$ and $(x + \delta x)$, will be

$$\frac{E\,du\,\delta u + F(du\,\delta v + \delta u\,dv) + G\,dv\,\delta v}{ds\,\delta s}. \tag{15}$$

The two will be mutually perpendicular if

$$E\,du\,\delta u + F(du\,\delta v + \delta u\,dv) + G\,dv\,\delta v = 0.$$

The condition for perpendicularity between the parameter curves will be

$$F = 0. \tag{16}$$

The equation of the tangent plane at $(x + dx)$ is

$$\left| X\left(x + \frac{\partial x}{\partial u}du + \frac{\partial x}{\partial v}dv\right)\left(\frac{\partial x}{\partial u} + \frac{\partial^2 x}{\partial u^2}du + \frac{\partial^2 x}{\partial u\,\partial v}dv\right) \right.$$
$$\left. \left(\frac{\partial x}{\partial v} + \frac{\partial^2 x}{\partial u\,\partial v}du + \frac{\partial^2 x}{\partial v^2}dv\right) \right| = 0.$$

Neglecting differentials of higher order than the first, we have

$$\left|Xx\frac{\partial x}{\partial u}\frac{\partial x}{\partial v}\right| + \left[\left|Xx\frac{\partial^2 x}{\partial u^2}\frac{\partial x}{\partial v}\right| + \left|Xx\frac{\partial x}{\partial u}\frac{\partial^2 x}{\partial u\,\partial v}\right|\right] du$$
$$+ \left[\left|Xx\frac{\partial^2 x}{\partial u\,\partial v}\frac{\partial x}{\partial v}\right| + \left|Xx\frac{\partial x}{\partial u}\frac{\partial^2 x}{\partial v^2}\right|\right] dv = 0.$$

The line of intersection with the tangent plane at (x) will be found by equating to zero separately the first and the last four terms. This line will contain the point $(x+\delta x)$ if

$$D\,du\,\delta u + D'(du\,\delta v + dv\,\delta u) + D''dv\,\delta v = 0.$$

$$D = \frac{\left|x\frac{\partial x}{\partial u}\frac{\partial x}{\partial v}\frac{\partial^2 x}{\partial u^2}\right|}{\sqrt{EG-F^2}},\quad D' = \frac{\left|x\frac{\partial x}{\partial u}\frac{\partial x}{\partial v}\frac{\partial^2 x}{\partial u\,\partial v}\right|}{\sqrt{EG-F^2}},\quad D'' = \frac{\left|x\frac{\partial x}{\partial u}\frac{\partial x}{\partial v}\frac{\partial^2 x}{\partial v^2}\right|}{\sqrt{EG-F^2}}. \tag{17}$$

The signs of D, D', D'' to be determined presently.

These are the equations for tangents to conjugate systems of curves, or, briefly put, the equations determining differentials in conjugate directions. The parameter curves will be mutually conjugate if

$$D' = 0. \tag{18}$$

The differential equation for self-conjugate, or asymptotic lines, will be

$$D\,du^2 + 2D'\,du\,dv + D''\,dv^2 = 0. \tag{19}$$

Returning to the point (y), the pole of the tangent plane, we have

$$\left(y\frac{\partial^2 x}{\partial u^2}\right) = D,\quad \left(y\frac{\partial^2 x}{\partial u\,\partial v}\right) = D',\quad \left(y\frac{\partial^2 x}{\partial v^2}\right) = D'';$$
$$(xy) = (y\,dx) = (x\,dy) = 0,$$
$$\left(\frac{\partial x}{\partial u}\frac{\partial y}{\partial u}\right) = -\left(y\frac{\partial^2 x}{\partial u^2}\right)\quad \left(\frac{\partial x}{\partial u}\frac{\partial y}{\partial v}\right) = \left(\frac{\partial x}{\partial v}\frac{\partial y}{\partial u}\right) = -\left(y\frac{\partial^2 x}{\partial u\,\partial v}\right)$$
$$\left(\frac{\partial x}{\partial v}\frac{\partial y}{\partial v}\right) = -\left(y\frac{\partial^2 x}{\partial v^2}\right),$$
$$-(dy\,dx) = D\,du^2 + 2D'\,du\,dv + D''\,dv^2. \tag{20}$$

These equations will determine the signs of D, D', D''.

Under what circumstances will the normals at two adjacent points intersect, i.e. when will their minimum distance be an infinitesimal of higher order than the element of arc? Geometrically we see that the characteristic of the two adjacent tangent planes must be perpendicular to its conjugate. Conversely, when we do progress along such an infinitesimal arc, the tangent plane may be said to rotate about a line perpendicular to the element of progression, and adjacent normals are coplanar. At any general point of the surface, except at an umbilical point where the involution of conjugate tangents is made up of mutually perpendicular tangents, there will be just two tangents which are mutually conjugate and mutually perpendicular, and these give the elements desired.

This fairly plausible geometrical reasoning may easily be put on a sound analytical basis. The necessary and sufficient condition that the four points (x), (y), $(x+dx)$, $(y+dy)$ should be coplanar is

$$|yx\,dx\,dy| = 0,$$

$$\begin{vmatrix} (xx) & (x\,dx) & (x\,dy) \\ \left(x\dfrac{\partial x}{\partial u}\right) & \left(\dfrac{\partial x}{\partial u}dx\right) & \left(\dfrac{\partial x}{\partial u}dy\right) \\ \left(x\dfrac{\partial x}{\partial v}\right) & \left(\dfrac{\partial x}{\partial v}dx\right) & \left(\dfrac{\partial x}{\partial v}dy\right) \end{vmatrix} = 0. \qquad \text{by (14)}$$

$$\begin{vmatrix} Edu + Fdv & Ddu + D'dv \\ Fdu + Gdv & D'du + D''dv \end{vmatrix} = 0. \tag{21}$$

This is the Jacobian of the binary homogeneous forms (13) and (20), and gives the two tangents which are both mutually perpendicular and mutually conjugate; the indetermination mentioned above occurs in the case where

$$E : F : G = D : D' : D''.$$

Theorem 8. The normals to a surface may be assembled into two families of developable surfaces. Each normal, with the exception of those at umbilical points, lies in one surface of each family.

The integral curves of the differential equation (20) are called *lines of curvature.* We see at once that

Theorem 9. If two surfaces intersect along a line which is a line of curvature for each, they intersect at a constant angle, and if two surfaces intersect at a constant angle along a curve which is a line of curvature for one it is a line of curvature for the other.

This is the theorem of Joachimsthal, well known in the euclidean case. No less celebrated is the beautiful theorem of Dupin.

Theorem 10. In any triply orthogonal system of surfaces, the curves of intersection are lines of curvature.

Let the three families of surfaces be given by the equations

$$x_i = f_i(uv), \quad x_i = \phi_i(vw), \quad x_i = \psi_i(wu),$$

$$(xx) = k^2, \quad \left(x\frac{\partial x}{\partial u}\right) = \left(x\frac{\partial x}{\partial v}\right) = \left(x\frac{\partial x}{\partial w}\right) = 0.$$

As the parameter lines are, in every case, mutually perpendicular

$$\left(\frac{\partial x}{\partial v}\frac{\partial x}{\partial w}\right) = \left(\frac{\partial x}{\partial w}\frac{\partial x}{\partial u}\right) = \left(\frac{\partial x}{\partial u}\frac{\partial x}{\partial v}\right) = 0,$$

$$\left(\frac{\partial x}{\partial u}\frac{\partial^2 x}{\partial v\,\partial w}\right)+\left(\frac{\partial x}{\partial w}\frac{\partial^2 x}{\partial u\,\partial v}\right)=\left(\frac{\partial x}{\partial u}\frac{\partial^2 x}{\partial v\,\partial w}\right)+\left(\frac{\partial x}{\partial v}\frac{\partial^2 x}{\partial w\,\partial u}\right)$$
$$=\left(\frac{\partial x}{\partial v}\frac{\partial^2 x}{\partial w\,\partial u}\right)+\left(\frac{\partial x}{\partial w}\frac{\partial^2 x}{\partial u\,\partial v}\right)=0,$$

$$\left(x\frac{\partial x}{\partial w}\right)=\left(\frac{\partial x}{\partial u}\frac{\partial x}{\partial w}\right)=\left(\frac{\partial x}{\partial v}\frac{\partial x}{\partial w}\right)=\left(\frac{\partial^2 x}{\partial u\,\partial v}\frac{\partial x}{\partial w}\right)=0,$$
$$\left|x\frac{\partial x}{\partial u}\frac{\partial x}{\partial v}\frac{\partial^2 x}{\partial u\,\partial v}\right|=D'\sqrt{EG-F^2}=0,$$
$$D'=0.$$

The vanishing of D' and F proves our theorem. Our statement in Chapter XIII that confocal quadrics intersect in lines of curvature is hereby justified.

A surface all of whose curves are lines of curvature must be a sphere. The normal at any point P will determine, with any other point Q of the surface, a plane. The normals to the surface along this curve, will, by hypothesis, generate an evolute, and hence, by (7) make a fixed angle with the plane; and this angle must be null, since, by hypothesis, one normal lies in the plane. Hence the normals at P and Q intersect, or all normals must pass through one point. Evidently the orthogonal surface to a bundle of concurrent lines is a sphere.

Let us suppose that we have a conformal transformation of space. It will carry a triply orthogonal system of surfaces into another such system, hence a line of curvature into a line of curvature. It will, therefore, carry any surface all of whose curves are lines of curvature into another such surface, hence

Theorem 11. Every conformal transformation of space carries a sphere into a sphere.

Of course a plane is here regarded as a special case of a sphere.

Let us now examine the normals along a line of curvature. Let r be the distance from the point (x) to the intersection of the normal there with the adjacent normal, a point whose coordinates shall be called $(\bar{x})$.

$$\bar{x}_i=x_i\cos\frac{r}{k}-y_i\sin\frac{r}{k},$$

$$\frac{d\bar{x}_i}{ds}=\frac{dx_i}{ds}\cos\frac{r}{k}-\frac{dy_i}{ds}\sin\frac{r}{k}-\left[x_i\sin\frac{r}{k}-y_i\cos\frac{r}{k}\right]\frac{dr}{ds}.$$

Now, by hypothesis, $\left(\dfrac{d\bar{x}}{ds}\right)$ is linearly dependent on (x) and (y).

$$dx_i\cos\frac{r}{k}-dy_i\sin\frac{r}{k}=\lambda(x_i+\mu y_i).$$

But $$(x\,dx)=(x\,dy)=(y\,dx)=(y\,dy)=(xy)=0,$$

$$\lambda=\mu=0,$$
$$dx_i\equiv dy_i\tan\frac{r}{k},$$

$$\frac{\partial x_i}{\partial u}du + \frac{\partial x_i}{\partial v}dv = \tan\frac{r}{k}\Big[\frac{\partial y_i}{\partial u}du + \frac{\partial y_i}{\partial v}dv\Big].$$

In particular, let us take as parameter lines the lines of curvature

$$\frac{\partial x_i}{\partial u} = \tan\frac{r_1}{k}\frac{\partial y_i}{\partial u}, \quad \frac{\partial x_i}{\partial v} = \tan\frac{r_2}{k}\frac{\partial y_i}{\partial v},$$

$$(dx\,dy) = \frac{E}{\tan\frac{r_1}{k}}du^2 + \frac{G}{\tan\frac{r_2}{k}}dv^2,$$

$$(dy\,dy) = \frac{E}{\tan^2\frac{r_1}{k}}du^2 + \frac{G}{\tan^2\frac{r_2}{k}}dv^2. \tag{22}$$

In the general case,

$$Edu + Fdv = -\tan\frac{r}{k}[Ddu + D'dv],$$

$$Fdu + Gdv = -\tan\frac{r}{k}[D'du + D''dv].$$

Eliminating $\tan\frac{r}{k}$ we get our previous differential equation for the lines of curvature. On the other hand, if we eliminate du, dv we get

$$(DD'' - D'^2)\tan^2\frac{r}{k} + [ED'' + GD - 2FD']\tan\frac{r}{k} + (EG - F^2) = 0. \tag{23}$$

$$\frac{1}{k\tan\frac{r_1}{k}} + \frac{1}{k\tan\frac{r_2}{k}} = -\frac{ED'' + GD - 2FD'}{k[EG - F^2]};$$

$$\frac{1}{k^2\tan\frac{r_1}{k}\tan\frac{r_2}{k}} = \frac{DD'' - D'^2}{k^2(EG - F^2)}. \tag{24}$$

These last two expressions shall be called the *mean relative curvature* and the *total relative curvature*, respectively. They are, by XI. (2), the sum and the product of the curvatures of normal sections through the tangents to the lines of curvature. Notice that they are absolute simultaneous invariants of the two binary forms (13), (20).

Let us now look at the more general question of the curvature of a curve on our surface. As, by (4), this does not involve derivatives of higher order than the second, the curvature at any point of a curve of the surface is identical with that of the curve of intersection of the osculating plane with the surface. Along our curve u and v will be functions of s the parameter of length of arc, so that, using our previous notation,

$$t_i = k\Big[\frac{\partial x_i}{\partial u}\frac{du}{ds} + \frac{\partial x_i}{\partial v}\frac{dv}{ds}\Big].$$

The cosine of the angle which the principal normal to this curve makes with the normal to the surface may be written

$$\cos\sigma = \pm\frac{(yz)}{k^2},$$

$$\frac{z_i}{\rho} = \frac{dt_i}{ds} + \frac{x_i}{k}, \qquad \frac{\cos\sigma}{\rho} = \pm\left(\frac{y\dfrac{dt}{ds}}{k^2}\right),$$

$$\frac{dt_i}{ds} = k\left[\frac{\partial^2 x_i}{\partial u^2}\left(\frac{du}{ds}\right)^2 + 2\frac{\partial^2 x_i}{\partial u\,\partial v}\frac{du}{ds}\frac{dv}{ds} + \frac{\partial^2 x_i}{\partial v^2}\left(\frac{dv}{ds}\right)^2\right] + k\left[\frac{\partial x_i}{\partial u}\frac{d^2u}{ds^2} + \frac{\partial x_i}{\partial v}\frac{d^2v}{ds^2}\right],$$

$$\frac{\cos\sigma}{\rho} = \pm\frac{Ddu^2 + 2D'du\,dv + D''dv^2}{k[Edu^2 + 2Fdu\,dv + Gdv^2]}.$$

The indetermination of sign may be used to make the curvature essentially positive.

Theorem 12. Meunier's. The curvature of a curve on a surface at any point is equal to the curvature of the normal section with the same tangent divided by the cosine of the angle which the principal normal makes with the normal to the surface.

Reverting to our previous expressions r_1, r_2 and taking the lines of curvature as parameter lines, the curvature of the normal sections through the tangents to the lines of curvature are

$$\frac{1}{k\tan\dfrac{r_1}{k}}, \qquad \frac{1}{k\tan\dfrac{r_2}{k}},$$

$$dx_i = \tan\frac{r_1}{k}dy_i, \qquad \delta x_i = \tan\frac{r_2}{k}\delta y_i,$$

$$E = \tan\frac{r_1}{k}D, \quad G = \tan\frac{r_2}{k}D'',$$

$$\frac{1}{\rho} = \pm\left[\frac{E}{k\tan\dfrac{r_1}{k}}\left(\frac{du}{ds}\right)^2 + \frac{G}{k\tan\dfrac{r_2}{k}}\left(\frac{dv}{ds}\right)^2\right];$$

or, if θ be the angle which the chosen tangent makes with that to $v =$ cons.

$$\frac{1}{\rho} = \frac{\cos^2\theta}{k\tan\dfrac{r_1}{k}} + \frac{\sin^2\theta}{k\tan\dfrac{r_2}{k}}.$$

Theorem 13. The normal sections of a surface at any point having the greatest and the least curvature are those determined by the tangents to the lines of curvature.

Theorem 14. If on each tangent to a surface at a point a distance be laid off equal to the square root of the reciprocal of the measure of curvature of the normal section with that tangent, the locus of the points so formed will be a central conic.

We leave to the reader the task of filling in the details of the proof of the last theorem, they will come very easily from considering the equation of a central conic as given in Chapter XII. Of course the theorem is untrue at a point where the tangents to the two lines of curvature coincide. This central conic is called *Dupin's Indicatrix* in the euclidean case, and we may well use the same name in the non-euclidean case also.

The curvature of a surface bears a close relation to the element of arc of the point (y).

$$-(dx\,dy) = Ddu^2 + 2D'du\,dv + D''dv^2,$$

$$(dy\,dy) = e\,du^2 + 2f\,du\,dv + g\,dv^2,$$

$$\left(y\frac{\partial y}{\partial u}\right) = \left(x\frac{\partial y}{\partial u}\right) = D'\left(\frac{\partial x}{\partial u}\frac{\partial y}{\partial u}\right) - D\left(\frac{\partial x}{\partial v}\frac{\partial y}{\partial u}\right) = 0,$$

$$\lambda\frac{\partial y_i}{\partial u} = D'\frac{\partial}{\partial s_i}\left|sxy\frac{\partial x}{\partial u}\right| - D\frac{\partial}{\partial s_i}\left|sxy\frac{\partial x}{\partial v}\right|,$$

$$\lambda\left(\frac{\partial x}{\partial u}\frac{\partial y}{\partial u}\right) = -\lambda D = -D\sqrt{EG-F^2},$$

$$\left(\frac{\partial y}{\partial u}\frac{\partial y}{\partial u}\right) = \frac{D'^2E + D^2G - 2DD'F}{EG-F^2},$$

$$\left(\frac{\partial y}{\partial u}\frac{\partial y}{\partial v}\right) = \frac{D'D''E - (DD'' + D'^2)F + DD'G}{EG-F^2},$$

$$\left(\frac{\partial y}{\partial v}\frac{\partial y}{\partial v}\right) = \frac{D''^2E - 2D'D''F + D'^2G}{EG-F^2},$$

$$\begin{aligned}-(e\,du^2 + 2f\,du\,dv + g\,dv^2)&\\ &= \frac{1}{\tan\frac{r_1}{k}\tan\frac{r_2}{k}}(Edu^2 + 2Fdu\,dv + Gdv^2) +\\ &+ \left(\frac{1}{\tan\frac{r_1}{k}} + \frac{1}{\tan\frac{r_2}{k}}\right)(Ddu^2 + 2D'du\,dv + D''dv^2). \quad (25)\end{aligned}$$

An asymptotic curve has the property that as a point moves along it, the tangent plane to the surface tends to rotate about the tangent to this curve, i.e. the tangent plane to the surface is the osculating plane to the curve, and the normal to the surface is the binormal to the curve. In dealing with such a curve the point (y) on the normal will replace the point we previously called (ξ). The torsion of any asymptotic line will be, by (8),

$$\frac{1}{T} = \frac{\sqrt{(dy\,dy)}}{kds}.$$

But, in the case of an asymptotic curve, the second part of the right-hand side of (25) will be zero, while the parenthesis in the first part is equal to ds^2, hence, for an asymptotic line

$$\frac{(dy\,dy)}{k^2 ds^2} = \frac{1}{T^2} = \frac{-1}{k^2 \tan\frac{r_1}{k}\tan\frac{r_2}{k}}.$$

It is not difficult to see that the two asymptotic lines at a point, when real, have torsion with opposite signs, we have but to look at the special case of a ruled quadric, hence:

Theorem 15. The two asymptotic lines at a point, when real, have torsions equal to the two square roots of the negative of the total relative curvature of the surface.

Theorem 16. In any surface of constant total relative curvature, the torsion of every asymptotic line is constant and equal to a square root of the total relative curvature, and the necessary and sufficient condition that a surface should have constant total relative curvature is that the asymptotic lines of one set should have constant torsion. Under these circumstances the asymptotic lines of the other set will have a constant torsion equal to the negative of that already given, and the square of either torsion will be the total relative curvature.

In speaking of the total curvature of a surface we have used the word *relative*. It is now time to explain why that adjective is chosen. Let us try to express our total relative curvature in terms of E, F, G and their derivatives. We have

$$\frac{1}{k^2 \tan\frac{r_1}{k}\tan\frac{r_2}{k}} = \frac{DD'' - D'^2}{k^2(EG - F^2)}. \qquad (24)$$

For the sake of simplicity we shall take as parameter lines u, v the isotropic curves of the surface, i.e. those whose tangents also touch the Absolute. We assume that our surface is not a developable circumscribed to the Absolute, and that in the region considered no tangent plane to the surface touches the Absolute. The isotropic curves at every point will therefore be distinct. We shall have

$$E = G = 0, \quad (xx) = k^2,$$

$$\left(x\frac{\partial x}{\partial u}\right) = \left(x\frac{\partial x}{\partial v}\right) = \left(x\frac{\partial^2 x}{\partial u^2}\right) = \left(x\frac{\partial^2 x}{\partial v^2}\right) = 0,$$

$$2F du\,dv = ds^2,$$

$$\left(\frac{\partial^2 x}{\partial u^2}\frac{\partial x}{\partial v}\right) = \frac{\partial F}{\partial u},$$

$$\left(\frac{\partial x}{\partial u}\frac{\partial^2 x}{\partial v^2}\right) = \frac{\partial F}{\partial v},$$

$$\left(\frac{\partial^2 x}{\partial u^2}\frac{\partial^2 x}{\partial v^2}\right) - \left(\frac{\partial^2 x}{\partial u\,\partial v}\frac{\partial^2 x}{\partial u\,\partial v}\right) = \frac{\partial^2 F}{\partial u\,\partial v};$$

$$D'^2 = \frac{-1}{F^2}\begin{vmatrix} k^2 & 0 & 0 & -F \\ 0 & 0 & F & 0 \\ 0 & F & 0 & 0 \\ -F & 0 & 0 & \left(\frac{\partial^2 x}{\partial u\,\partial v}\frac{\partial^2 x}{\partial u\,\partial v}\right) \end{vmatrix},$$

$$DD'' = \frac{-1}{F^2}\begin{vmatrix} k^2 & 0 & 0 & 0 \\ 0 & 0 & F & \frac{\partial F}{\partial v} \\ 0 & F & 0 & 0 \\ 0 & 0 & \frac{\partial F}{\partial u} & \left(\frac{\partial^2 x}{\partial u^2}\frac{\partial^2 x}{\partial v^2}\right) \end{vmatrix},$$

$$\frac{DD'' - D'^2}{k^2(EG - F^2)} = \frac{1}{F^2}\left[\frac{1}{F}\frac{\partial F}{\partial u}\frac{\partial F}{\partial v} - \frac{\partial^2 F}{\partial u\,\partial v}\right] - \frac{1}{k^2}. \tag{26}$$

The first expression on the right is the Gaussian curvature of a two-dimensional manifold whose squared distance element is $2F du\, dv$[75].

Theorem 17[76]. The total relative curvature of a surface is equal to the difference between its total Gaussian curvature and the measure of curvature of space.

The Gaussian curvature may also be called the *total absolute curvature.* Notice that this theorem remains true in euclidean space where the measure of curvature is 0.

The problem of finding all surfaces of total relative curvature zero is quickly solved. Let us assume that

$$\tan\frac{r_2}{k} = \infty.$$

Then, by an equation just preceding (22), as

$$\frac{\partial x_i}{\partial v} \neq 0, \quad \frac{\partial y_i}{\partial v} = 0,$$

and there will be the same tangent plane all along $u = \text{const}$.

Theorem 18. A surface of total relative curvature zero is a developable.

Clearly every developable has total relative curvature zero.

Much more interest attaches to the surfaces of total Gaussian curvature zero, i.e. those which are developable upon the euclidean plane. The total relative

[75]Cf. Bianchi, loc. cit., p. 68.

[76]Cf. Bianchi, loc. cit., p. 609.

curvature will be $-\frac{1}{k^2}$. There is an advantage in considering the hyperbolic and elliptic cases separately.

In the hyperbolic case let (y) be the centre of a sphere, the constant distance thence to points of the surface being r

$$\cos\frac{r}{k} = \frac{(xy)}{k^2}, \quad k^2\tan^2\frac{r}{k} = k^2\left[\frac{(xx)(yy)-(xy)^2}{(xy)^2}\right].$$

If the surface is to be actual $(xx) = k^2$. If the sphere be a proper one $(yy) = k^2$, the total relative curvature will be $> \frac{-1}{k^2}$. In the case of a horocyclic surface we may not assume $(yy) = k^2$, but must treat (y) as homogeneous coordinates where $(yy) = 0$. We get then

$$\frac{1}{k^2\tan^2\frac{r}{k}} = -\frac{1}{k^2}.$$

Theorem 19.[77] The horocyclic surface of hyperbolic space is developable on the euclidean plane.

In elliptic space there is a peculiarly notable class of surfaces of Gaussian curvature zero, ruled surfaces. We have already seen one example, the Clifford Surface of Chapter X. This quadric, be it remembered, cuts the Absolute in two generators of each set, and its own generators form an orthogonal system. Now Dupin's indicatrix shows that the normal sections of greatest and of least curvature will be determined by tangents bisecting the angles of the two generators, and the planes of these normal sections will cut the surface in two circles whose axes are the axes of revolution of the surface, and whose centres lie on these axes. The centres are thus mutually orthogonal points, hence the total relative curvature is $-\frac{1}{k^2}$, and the Gaussian curvature is zero. This statement was given without proof in Chapter X. We notice also that the generators of either set are paratactic, and the question arises, will not this fact alone constitute a sufficient condition that a surface should have Gaussian curvature zero?

Let us imagine that we have a surface generated by ∞^1 paratactic lines.[78] The parameter v shall give the actual distance measured on each line from an orthogonal trajectory $v =$ const. We have for our distance element

$$ds^2 = Edu^2 + dv^2.$$

We know, moreover, by Chapter IX that if two lines be paratactic they have an infinite number of common perpendiculars on which they determine congruent distances. Hence E is a function of u alone, and we may choose u so

[77] Cf. Manning, loc. cit., p. 52; Killing, *Die Grundlagen der Geometrie*, Paderborn, 1898, p. 33.

[78] For an interesting treatment of these surfaces see Bianchi, 'Le superficie a curvatura nulla nella geometria ellitica,' *Annali di Matematica*, Serie 2, Tomo 24, 1896.

that it shall be equal to unity

$$ds^2 = du^2 + dv^2, \tag{27}$$

and the Gaussian curvature is zero.

Conversely, suppose that we have a ruled surface of Gaussian curvature zero. The square of the element of arc may be written

$$ds^2 = Edu^2 + dv^2.$$

Since the Gaussian curvature is zero

$$\frac{\partial^2 \sqrt{E}}{\partial v^2} = 0, \quad \sqrt{E} = \theta(u)v + \psi(u).$$

On the other hand we may write our surface parametrically in the form

$$x_i = f_i(u) \cos \frac{v_i}{k} + \phi_i(u) \sin \frac{v}{k},$$

with the additional conditions

$$(ff) = (\phi\phi) = k^2, \quad (ff') = (\phi\phi') = (f\phi) = (f\phi') + (\phi f') = 0;$$

$$E = (f'f') \cos^2 \frac{v}{k} + (\phi'\phi') \sin^2 \frac{v}{k} + 2(f'\phi') \sin \frac{v}{k} \cos \frac{v}{k},$$

$$kF = (\phi f') \cos^2 \frac{v}{k} - (f\phi') \sin^2 \frac{v}{k} = 0, \quad (f\phi') = (\phi f') = 0.$$

These are identical with previous

$$E = [\theta(u)]^2 v^2 + 2\theta(u)\psi(u)v + [\psi(u)]^2,$$

only when

$$\theta(u) \equiv 0.$$

We may, then, take

$$E = 1, \quad ds^2 = du^2 + dv^2;$$

and this shows that two adjacent generators determine equal distances on all their orthogonal trajectories, and so are paratactic.

Theorem 20. The necessary and sufficient condition that a ruled surface in elliptic space should have Gaussian curvature zero is that its generators should be paratactic.

Another highly interesting criterion for a surface of constant Gaussian curvature zero is obtained as follows:

$$E = G = 1, \quad F = 0;$$

$$\left(\frac{\partial x}{\partial u}\frac{\partial^2 x}{\partial u\,\partial v}\right) = \left(\frac{\partial^2 x}{\partial u^2}\frac{\partial x}{\partial v}\right) = \left(\frac{\partial x}{\partial u}\frac{\partial^2 x}{\partial v^2}\right) = 0, \quad \left(x\frac{\partial^2 x}{\partial u^2}\right) = -1.$$

The coordinates of the absolute pole of the tangent plane are

$$y_i = \frac{\partial}{\partial s_i}\left| sx \frac{\partial x}{\partial u} \frac{\partial x}{\partial v} \right|.$$

The coordinates of the absolute pole of the osculating plane to the orthogonal trajectory of the generators, i.e. to a curve $v = \text{const}$, are

$$\lambda \xi_i = \frac{\partial}{\partial r_i}\left| rx \frac{\partial x}{\partial u} \frac{\partial^2 x}{\partial u^2} \right|,$$

$$(y\xi) = 0.$$

This shows that the generators are binormals to their orthogonal trajectories. Our given surface may be written in the form

$$x_i = x_i(u)\cos\frac{v}{k} + \xi_i(u)\sin\frac{v}{k},$$

$$ds^2 = dv^2 + \left[\cos^2\frac{v}{k} + \frac{k^2}{T^2}\sin^2\frac{v}{k}\right]du^2.$$

This reduces to

$$du^2 + dv^2,$$

when, and only when

$$\frac{1}{T^2} = \frac{1}{k^2}.$$

Theorem 21. The necessary and sufficient condition that a ruled surface should have Gaussian curvature zero is that it should be generated by the binormals to a curve whose squared torsion is equal to the measure of curvature of space.

The proof given holds equally in hyperbolic space; the surface is, however, in that case imaginary. If we compare theorems 16 and 21, we get

Theorem 22. The necessary and sufficient condition that it should be possible to assemble the normals to a surface into one parameter families of left (right) paratactics, is that the given surface should have Gaussian curvature zero. It will, then, be possible to assemble the normals into families of right (left) paratactics also. The intersections of the given surface with the various families of paratactics will be the asymptotic lines of the former.

We shall, as in euclidean space, define as the geodesic curvature at any point of a curve on our surface, the curvature of its orthogonal projection on the tangent plane at that point. Let us denote this by $\frac{1}{\rho_g}$, while σ is the angle which the osculating plane makes with the tangent plane to the surface. Then, applying Meunier's theorem to the projecting cone

$$\frac{1}{\rho_g} = \frac{\cos\sigma}{\rho}. \tag{28}$$

As a first exercise, assuming $F=0$, let us find the geodesic curvature of one of our parameter lines

$$ds_v = \sqrt{G}\,dv,$$
$$t_i = \frac{k}{\sqrt{G}}\frac{\partial x_i}{\partial v},$$
$$\frac{z_i}{\rho} = \frac{dt_i}{ds} + \frac{x_i}{k} = \frac{k}{\sqrt{G}}\left[\frac{\partial}{\partial v}\left(\frac{1}{\sqrt{G}}\frac{\partial x_i}{\partial v}\right)\right] + \frac{x_i}{k}.$$

To find $\cos\sigma$ must determine the distance of (z) from the point orthogonal to (x) on the curve $v=$ const., i.e. to the point $\frac{k}{\sqrt{E}}\left(\frac{\partial x}{\partial u}\right)$.

$$\cos\frac{\sigma}{\rho} = \frac{1}{\sqrt{EG}}\left(\frac{\partial x}{\partial u}\frac{\partial}{\partial v}\left(\frac{1}{\sqrt{G}}\frac{\partial x}{\partial v}\right)\right),$$

$$\frac{1}{\rho_g} = \frac{-1}{\sqrt{EG}}\frac{\partial\sqrt{G}}{\partial u}. \tag{29}$$

For the other parameter line

$$\frac{1}{\rho_g} = \frac{-1}{\sqrt{EG}}\frac{\partial\sqrt{E}}{\partial v}.$$

Let us now, more generally, find the geodesic curvature of the curve

$$v\cdot = v\cdot(u).$$

Once more we shall make use of the isotropic parameters, so that

$$E=G=0,$$

$$ds = \sqrt{2Fv'}du, \quad v' = \frac{dv}{du},$$

$$t_i = \frac{k}{\sqrt{2Fv'}}\left[\frac{\partial x_i}{\partial u} + v'\frac{\partial x_i}{\partial v}\right],$$
$$\frac{z_i}{\rho} = \frac{k}{2Fv'}\left[\frac{\partial^2 x_i}{\partial u^2} + 2\frac{\partial^2 x_i}{\partial u\,\partial v}v' + \frac{\partial^2 x_i}{\partial v^2}v'^2 + \frac{\partial x_i}{\partial v}v''\right] +$$
$$+\frac{k}{\sqrt{2Fv'}}\left[\frac{\partial x_i}{\partial u} + \frac{\partial x_i}{\partial v}v'\right]\frac{d}{du}\frac{1}{\sqrt{2Fv'}} + \frac{x_i}{k}.$$

For an orthogonal trajectory to this curve

$$\frac{\delta v}{\delta u} = -\frac{dv}{du} = -v',$$
$$\delta s = \delta u\sqrt{-2Fv'},$$

$$\bar{t}_i = \frac{-k}{\sqrt{-2Fv'}}\left[\frac{\partial x_i}{\partial u} - v'\frac{\partial x_i}{\partial v}\right],$$

$$\cos\frac{\sigma}{\rho} = \frac{1}{\rho k^2}(z\bar{t}),$$

$$\frac{1}{\rho_g} = \frac{-1}{\sqrt{-2Fv'}}\left[\frac{\dfrac{\partial F}{\partial v}v' - \dfrac{\partial F}{\partial u}}{2F} + \frac{v''}{2v'}\right]$$

$$= \frac{1}{\sqrt{-F^2}}\left[\frac{d}{du}\frac{\sqrt{F}}{\sqrt{2v'}} - \frac{\partial}{\partial v}\sqrt{2Fv'}\right]. \tag{30}$$

What will be the nature of those curves whose geodesic curvature vanishes, i.e. those curves whose osculating planes pass through the normal? These shall be called geodesic lines, and, evidently, we shall have

$$\frac{dv}{du}\frac{\sqrt{F}}{\sqrt{2v'}} = \frac{\partial}{\partial v}\sqrt{2Fv'}.$$

This merely tells us that our given curve is an extremal, i.e. the first variation of the length between two fixed points is zero. If we assume that two sufficiently near points can always be connected by a curve of minimum length[79] we shall get

Theorem 23. The curve of shortest length between two points of a surface is a geodesic line.

Remembering 21, we have further

Theorem 24. The orthogonal trajectories of a family of paratactic lines are geodesics of the surface generated by these lines.

If we consider the two planes through the normal to a surface and the two tangents to the lines of curvature, we see that they are mutually perpendicular, and that each touches the focal surface of the congruence of normals at the point of intersection of the two adjacent normals in the other plane.[80]

Theorem 25. In any congruence of normals, the edges of regression of the developable surfaces are geodesics of the focal surfaces of the congruence.

The osculating plane to any straight line is indeterminate; the line is, therefore, a geodesic for all space; a result also evident from Chapter II. 30. It is also clear that as the expressions for the geodesic curvature of a parameter line in terms of E, F, G and their derivatives are the same in euclidean and in non-euclidean space, and the formula for the distance element is written in the same shape, so will the formula for the geodesic curvature of any curve be the same. We might, for instance, have given this formula in terms of the Beltrami invariants. We have, however, purposely avoided the introduction of these into the

[79]For a proof of the existence of this curve, see Bolza, *Lectures on the Calculus of Variations*, Chicago, 1904, Ch. VIII.

[80]For a simple proof of this general theorem see Picard, loc. cit., vol. i, pp 307, 308.

present work, and will therefore merely refer the reader to the current textbooks in differential geometry,[81]

As a last problem in the differential geometry of surfaces let us take up that of minimal surfaces. To begin with, what will be the element of area? It is perfectly clear that the expression for this will be the same as that in the euclidean case. The sine of the angle formed by the parameter lines will be, by (15)

$$\frac{\sqrt{EG-F^2}}{\sqrt{EG}},$$

and the area of the elementary quadrilateral

$$\sqrt{EG-F^2}du\,dv.$$

Let us, in particular, take the lines of curvature as parameter lines. The formula for the area enclosed by a given curve will be

$$\iint \sqrt{EG}du\,dv.$$

Let us compare this with the area enclosed by this curve upon a surface reached by laying off on each normal an extremely small distance $w(uv)$.

$$\overline{x_i} = x_i \cos\frac{w}{k} + y_i \sin\frac{w}{k},$$
$$d\overline{x_i} = dx_i \cos\frac{w}{k} + dy_i \sin\frac{w}{k} - \frac{1}{k}\left[x_i \cos\frac{w}{k} - y_i \sin\frac{w}{k}\right] dw.$$

The squared element of arc for this surface will be by (22)

$$d\overline{s}^2 = E\left[\cos\frac{w}{k} + \frac{\sin\frac{w}{k}}{\tan\frac{r_1}{k}}\right]^2 du^2 + G\left[\cos\frac{w}{k} + \frac{\sin\frac{w}{k}}{\tan\frac{r_2}{k}}\right] dv^2 + \frac{dw^2}{k^2}.$$

This becomes, when we neglect powers of w above the first,

$$d\overline{s}^2 = E\left[1 + \frac{2\frac{w}{k}}{\tan\frac{r_1}{k}}\right] du^2 + G\left[1 + \frac{2\frac{w}{k}}{\tan\frac{r_2}{k}}\right] dv^2.$$

For the surface element we have

$$\sqrt{EG}\left[1 + 2\frac{w}{k}\left(\frac{\tan\frac{r_1}{k} + \tan\frac{r_2}{k}}{\tan\frac{r_1}{k}\tan\frac{r_2}{k}}\right) + 4\frac{\frac{w^2}{k^2}}{\tan\frac{r_1}{k}\tan\frac{r_2}{k}}\right]^{\frac{1}{2}} du\,dv.$$

[81]e.g. Bianchi, *Differentialgeometrie*, cit. p. 258.

Developing by the binomial theorem, and neglecting higher powers of w we have

$$\iint \sqrt{EG}\left[1+\frac{w}{k}\left(\frac{\tan\dfrac{r_1}{k}+\tan\dfrac{r_2}{k}}{\tan\dfrac{r_1}{k}\tan\dfrac{r_2}{k}}\right)\right] du\, dv.$$

If we define as a minimal surface one where the first variation of the area is zero, certainly a necessary condition, we have

Theorem 26. The necessary and sufficient condition that a surface should be minimal is that the mean relative curvature should be zero.

We see from (23) that the numerator of the expression for the relative mean curvature is the simultaneous invariant of (13) and (20), and vanishes when, and only when, the tangents to the asymptotic lines are harmonically separated by those to the isotropic ones, hence

Theorem 27. The necessary and sufficient condition that a surface should be minimal is that the asymptotic lines should form an orthogonal system.

This theorem justifies our statement in Chapter X that a Clifford surface is a minimal surface. It is very interesting that in non-euclidean space we should have an algebraic minimal surface (other than the plane) whose order is as low as two.

We may go one long step further towards the solution of the problem of minimal surfaces, namely, exhibit the differential equations on which they depend.[82]

We shall once more take as parameter lines the isotropic ones. These will form a conjugate system, since they are harmonically separated by the asymptotic lines, hence

$$E = G = D' = 0,$$

$$\frac{\partial^2 x_i}{\partial u\, \partial v} = Ax_i + B\frac{\partial x_i}{\partial u} + C\frac{\partial x_i}{\partial v},$$

$$BF = \frac{1}{2}\frac{\partial G}{\partial u} = 0, \quad CF = \frac{1}{2}\frac{\partial E}{\partial u} = 0, \quad F = -Ak^2,$$

$$\frac{\partial^2 x_i}{\partial u\, \partial v} + \frac{1}{k^2}Fx_i = 0. \tag{31}$$

It is merely necessary to find F and take for (x) four solutions of (3) subject to the restriction $(xx) = k^2$. Let us put

$$\frac{\partial^2 x_i}{\partial u^2} = P\frac{\partial x_i}{\partial u} + Q\frac{\partial x_i}{\partial v} + Rx_i + Sy_i,$$

which is certainly possible, since

$$\left| xy\frac{\partial x_i}{\partial u}\frac{\partial x}{\partial v}\right| \not\equiv 0.$$

[82]Cf. Darboux, *Leçons sur la théorie générale des surfaces*, vol. iii, ch. xiv, Paris, 1894. The reader is strongly urged to read this interesting chapter in connection with the present work.

We easily find

$$R = Q = 0, \quad FP = \frac{\partial F}{\partial u},$$

$$\frac{\partial^2 x_i}{\partial u^2} = \frac{1}{F}\frac{\partial F}{\partial w}\frac{\partial x_i}{\partial u} + Sy_i.$$

Now

$$\frac{\partial}{\partial v}\Big(\frac{\partial^2 x}{\partial u^2}\frac{\partial^2 x}{\partial u^2}\Big) = 2\Big(\frac{\partial^2 x}{\partial u^2}\frac{\partial^3 x}{\partial u^2\,\partial v}\Big) = -2\Big(\frac{\partial^2 x}{\partial u^2}\frac{\partial}{\partial u}(Fx)\Big) = 0, \text{ by (31).}$$

Hence $$\Big(\frac{\partial^2 x}{\partial u^2}\frac{\partial^2 x}{\partial u^2}\Big) = \phi(u).$$

If $$\phi(u) \equiv 0, \quad D = 0.$$

The total relative curvature is zero, and the surface is developable. In a developable surface the asymptotic lines fall together, by (24); hence a minimal developable must be circumscribed to the Absolute, and cannot be real in the actual domain. Conversely it is clear that every developable circumscribed to the Absolute is a minimal surface in that its asymptotic lines are mutually perpendicular, even though it lie in a region of our space where the concept area has not been defined.

In the second case let us suppose $\phi(u) \not\equiv 0$.

Let us replace u by $\bar{u}(u)$ so that $\Big(\frac{\partial^2 x}{\partial \bar{u}}\frac{\partial^2 x}{\partial \bar{u}}\Big) = \frac{1}{k^2}$. Then replace the letter $\bar{u}$ by the letter u once more.

Then $$S = \frac{1}{k^2}, \quad \frac{\partial^2 x_i}{\partial u^2} = \frac{1}{F}\frac{\partial F}{\partial u}\frac{\partial x_i}{\partial u} + \frac{y_i}{k^2}.$$

In like manner $$\frac{\partial^2 x_i}{\partial v^2} = \frac{1}{F}\frac{\partial F}{\partial v}\frac{\partial x_i}{\partial v} + \frac{y_i}{k^2}.$$

Multiplying through by $\frac{\partial^2 x_i}{\partial u^2}$ and adding

$$\Big(\frac{\partial^2 x}{\partial u^2}\frac{\partial^2 x}{\partial v^2}\Big) = \frac{1}{k^2} + \frac{1}{F}\frac{\partial F}{\partial u}\frac{\partial F}{\partial v}.$$

On the other hand

$$\begin{aligned}\frac{\partial^2 F}{\partial u\,\partial v} &= \Big(\frac{\partial^2 x}{\partial u^2}\frac{\partial^2 x}{\partial v^2}\Big) + \Big(\frac{\partial x}{\partial u}\frac{\partial^3 x}{\partial u\,\partial v^2}\Big), \\ &= \Big(\frac{\partial^2 x}{\partial u^2}\frac{\partial^2 x}{\partial v^2}\Big) - \frac{1}{k^2}\Big(\frac{\partial x}{\partial u}\frac{\partial}{\partial v}(xF)\Big),\end{aligned}$$

$$= \left(\frac{\partial^2 x}{\partial u^2}\frac{\partial^2 x}{\partial v^2}\right) - \frac{1}{k^2}F^2,$$

$$\frac{\partial^2 F}{\partial u\,\partial v} = \frac{1-F^2}{k^2} + \frac{1}{F}\frac{\partial F}{\partial u}\frac{\partial F}{\partial v},$$

$$k^2\frac{\partial^2 \log F}{\partial u\,\partial v} = \frac{1}{F} - F. \tag{32}$$

Lastly, let us put $$F = e^{2iw},$$

$$k^2\frac{\partial^2 w}{\partial u\,\partial v} + \sin 2w = 0. \tag{33}$$

When F has been found we may, as already noted, find (x) from (31).

CHAPTER XVI

DIFFERENTIAL LINE-GEOMETRY

In Chapter IX we gave the foundations of the Plückerian line-geometry, and the fundamental invariants of a metrical character; in Chapter X we saw what advantages arose from taking the cross instead of the line as element, and introducing suitable coordinates. Chapter XV was given to the differential geometry of curves and surfaces. It is the object of the present chapter to draw all of these threads together into a theory of differential line-geometry, and, in particular, a theory of two-parameter line systems or congruences.[83]

We shall define as an analytic line-congruence a system whose Plückerian coordinates are analytic functions of two independent parameters, say u and v. This is equivalent to supposing that our lines are determined by two points, which we may assume mutually orthogonal, whose coordinates are analytic functions of the two independent parameters in question.

$$x_i = x_i(uv), \quad y_i = y_i(uv), \quad (xx) = (yy) = k^2, \quad (xy) = 0. \tag{1}$$

Following Kummer's classical method, we shall write the following fundamental quadratic expression:

$$k^2(dx\,dx) - (y\,dx)^2 = \begin{Vmatrix} y_0 & y_1 & y_2 & y_3 \\ dx_0 & dx_1 & dx_2 & dx_3 \end{Vmatrix}^2 = Edu^2 + 2Fdu\,dv + Gdv^2,$$

$$k^2(dy\,dy) - (x\,dy)^2 = \begin{Vmatrix} x_0 & x_1 & x_2 & x_3 \\ dy_0 & dy_1 & dy_2 & dy_3 \end{Vmatrix}^2 = E'du^2 + 2F'du\,dv + G'dv^2. \tag{2}$$

$$k^2(dx\,dy) = e\,du^2 + (f + f')du\,dv + g\,dv^2,$$

$$k^2\left(\frac{\partial x}{\partial u}\frac{\partial x}{\partial u}\right) - \left(y\frac{\partial x}{\partial u}\right)^2 = E,$$
$$k^2\left(\frac{\partial x}{\partial u}\frac{\partial x}{\partial v}\right) - \left(y\frac{\partial x}{\partial u}\right)\left(y\frac{\partial x}{\partial v}\right) = F,$$
$$k^2\left(\frac{\partial x}{\partial v}\frac{\partial x}{\partial v}\right) - \left(y\frac{\partial x}{\partial v}\right)^2 = G. \tag{3}$$

$$k^2\left(\frac{\partial y}{\partial u}\frac{\partial y}{\partial u}\right) - \left(x\frac{\partial y}{\partial u}\right)^2 = E',$$
$$k^2\left(\frac{\partial y}{\partial u}\frac{\partial y}{\partial v}\right) - \left(x\frac{\partial y}{\partial u}\right)\left(x\frac{\partial y}{\partial v}\right) = F',$$
$$k^2\left(\frac{\partial y}{\partial v}\frac{\partial y}{\partial v}\right) - \left(x\frac{\partial y}{\partial v}\right)^2 = G'. \tag{4}$$

[83]The first part of the present chapter follows, with slight modifications, a rather inaccessible memoir by Fibbi, 'I sistemi doppiamente infiniti di raggi negli spazii di curvatura costante,' *Annali della R. Scuola Normale Superiore*, Pisa, 1891.

$$k^2\left(\frac{\partial x}{\partial u}\frac{\partial y}{\partial u}\right) = e, \qquad k^2\left(\frac{\partial x}{\partial v}\frac{\partial y}{\partial u}\right) = f,$$

$$k^2\left(\frac{\partial x}{\partial u}\frac{\partial y}{\partial v}\right) = f', \qquad k^2\left(\frac{\partial y}{\partial v}\frac{\partial y}{\partial v}\right) = g. \tag{5}$$

$$EG - F^2 = \left|yx\frac{\partial x}{\partial u}\frac{\partial x}{\partial v}\right|^2 \equiv \Delta^2, \quad E'G' - F'^2 = \left|xy\frac{\partial y}{\partial u}\frac{\partial y}{\partial v}\right|^2 \equiv \Delta'^2. \tag{6}$$

The following relations will subsist between these various expressions:

$$\Delta x_i = k^2\frac{\partial \Delta}{\partial x_i}, \quad \Delta' y_i = k^2\frac{\partial \Delta'}{\partial y_i},$$

since $$(xy) = \left(x\frac{\partial x}{\partial u}\right) = \left(x\frac{\partial x}{\partial v}\right) = \left(y\frac{\partial y}{\partial u}\right) = \left(y\frac{\partial y}{\partial v}\right) = 0,$$

$$E' = k^2\left(\frac{\partial y}{\partial u}\frac{\partial y}{\partial u}\right) - \frac{k^4}{\Delta^2}\left|y\frac{\partial y}{\partial u}\frac{\partial x}{\partial u}\frac{\partial x}{\partial v}\right|^2,$$

$$E' = \frac{1}{\Delta^2}[Ge^2 - 2Fef + Ef^2],$$

$$F' = \frac{1}{\Delta^2}[Gef' - F(eg + ff') + Efg]. \tag{7}$$

$$G' = \frac{1}{\Delta^2}[Gf'^2 - 2F(f'g) + Eg^2],$$

$$E = \frac{1}{\Delta'^2}[G'e^2 - 2F'ef' + E'f'^2]. \tag{8}$$

$$F = \frac{1}{\Delta'^2}[G'ef - F'(eg + ff') + E'f'g],$$

$$G = \frac{1}{\Delta'^2}[G'f^2 - 2F'(fg) + E'g^2],$$

$$\Delta\Delta' = (eg - ff'). \tag{9}$$

Notice that Δ and Δ' being square roots of positive definite forms cannot vanish in the real domain.

We remember from Chapter IX, that two lines which are not paratactic have two common perpendiculars meeting them in pairs of mutually orthogonal points. Let us, as a first problem, find where the common perpendicular to a line of our congruence and an adjacent line meets the given line. The coordinates of an arbitrary point of our line may be written $\left(x\cos\frac{r}{k} + y\sin\frac{r}{k}\right)$ while an arbitrary point of an adjacent line will be $\lambda(x+dx) + \mu(y+dy)$.

Let us begin by writing that the second of these points is orthogonal to $\left(x\sin\frac{r}{k} - y\cos\frac{r}{k}\right)$ the point of the first line orthogonal to the first point, while, on the other hand, the first point lies in the absolute polar plane of $\mu(x+dx) - \lambda(y+dy)$. There will result two linear homogeneous equations in λ and μ whose determinant must be equated to zero. When this is simplified in view of the identities

$$(x\,dx) = -\tfrac{1}{2}(dx\,dx), \quad (y\,dy) = -\tfrac{1}{2}(dy\,dy),$$
$$(x\,dy) + (y\,dx) = -(dx\,dy),$$

we shall have

$$\begin{vmatrix} [k^2 - \frac{1}{2}(dx\,dx)]\sin\frac{r}{k} - (y\,dx)\cos\frac{r}{k} & (x\,dy)\sin\frac{r}{k} - [k^2 - \frac{1}{2}(dy\,dy)]\cos\frac{r}{k} \\ -[k^2 - \frac{1}{2}(dy\,dy)]\sin\frac{r}{k} - (x\,dy)\cos\frac{r}{k} & (y\,dx)\sin\frac{r}{k} + [k^2 - \frac{1}{2}(dx\,dx)]\cos\frac{r}{k} \end{vmatrix} = 0. \qquad (10)$$

Casting aside infinitesimals above the second order

$$k^2(dx\,dy)\left(\cos^2\frac{r}{k} - \sin^2\frac{r}{k}\right)$$
$$- \left[k^2(dx\,dx) - (y\,dx)^2 - k^2(dy\,dy) + (x\,dy)^2\right]\sin\frac{r}{k}\cos\frac{r}{k} = 0,$$
$$(e\,du^2 + (f+f')du\,dv + g\,dv^2)\left(\cos^2\frac{r}{k} - \sin^2\frac{r}{k}\right)$$
$$+ \left[(E-E')du^2 + 2(F-F')du\,dv + (G-G')dv^2\right]\sin\frac{r}{k}\cos\frac{r}{k} = 0. \qquad (11)$$

This will give ∞^1 determinations for r in the general case where

$$e : \left(\frac{f+f'}{2}\right) : g \not\equiv (E-E') : (F-F') : (G-G'), \qquad (12)$$

and, as we saw in Chapter X, Theorem 5, with the corresponding elliptic case, these common perpendiculars will generate a surface of the fourth order, analogous to the euclidean cylindroid. We shall call a congruence where inequality (12) holds a 'general' congruence.

Let us now ask what are the maximum and minimum values for r in (11). Equating to zero the partial derivatives to du and dv we get

$$\left[e\,du + \frac{f+f'}{2}dv\right]\left(\tan^2\frac{r}{k} - 1\right) + [(E-E')du + (F-F')dv]\tan\frac{r}{k} = 0,$$

$$\left[\frac{(f+f')}{2}du + g\,dv\right]\left(\tan^2\frac{r}{k} - 1\right) + [(F-F')du + (G-G')dv]\tan\frac{r}{k} = 0.$$

Eliminating r we have

$$\left[e(F-F') - \frac{(f+f')}{2}(E-E')\right]du^2$$
$$+ [e(G-G') - g(E-E')]du\,dv$$

$$+\left[\frac{(f+f')}{2}(G-G')-g(E-E')\right]dv^2=0. \quad (13)$$

Each root of this will give two values to $\tan\frac{r}{k}$ corresponding to two mutually orthogonal points. On the other hand, if we eliminate $du : dv$ we get

$$\left(eg-\tfrac{1}{4}(f+f')^2\right)\left(\tan^2\frac{r}{k}-1\right)^2+[e(G-G') \\ -(F-F')(f+f')+g(E-E')]\left(\tan^2\frac{r}{k}-1\right)\tan\frac{r}{k} \\ +[(E-E')(G-G')-(F-F')^2]\tan^2\frac{r}{k}=0. \quad (14)$$

The left-hand side of this equation is the discriminant of (11) looked upon as an equation in $du : dv$. It gives, therefore, those points of the given line where the two perpendiculars coalesce. Such points shall be called 'limiting points'. They will determine two regions (when real) point by point mutually orthogonal, which contain the intersections of the line with the real common perpendiculars. In the same way we might find limiting planes through the line determining two dihedral angles whose faces are, in pairs, mutually perpendicular, and which when real, with their verticals, determine all planes wherein lie all real common perpendiculars to the given line and its immediate neighbours.

Theorem 1. A line of a general analytic congruence contains four limiting points, mutually orthogonal in pairs, and these, when real, determine two real regions of the line where it meets the real common perpendiculars with adjacent lines of the congruence. They are also the points where the two perpendiculars coincide.

Theorem 1′. Through a line of a general analytic congruence will pass four limiting planes, mutually perpendicular in pairs, and these, when real, determine two real regions of the axial pencil through the line which contain all planes wherein are real common perpendiculars to the line and adjacent lines of the congruence. They are also the planes in which the two perpendiculars coincide.

We shall now look more closely into the question of the reality of limiting points and places. We may so choose our coordinate system that the equations of the line in question shall be $x_1 = x_2 = 0$. Reverting to equation (8) of Chapter X the equation of the ruled quartic surface will be, in the hyperbolic case

$$a(-\dot{x}_0{}^2+\dot{x}_3{}^2)\dot{x}_1\dot{x}_2+b(\dot{x}_1{}^2+\dot{x}_2{}^2)x_0x_3=0. \quad (15)$$

Let the reader show[84] that in the elliptic case we shall have

$$(a_1-a_2)(x_0{}^2+x_3{}^2)x_1x_2+(a_1+a_2)(x_1{}^2+x_2{}^2)x_0x_3=0. \quad (15')$$

[84] See the author's *Dual Projective Geometry*, cit., p. 26.

To find the limiting points on the line $x_1 = x_2 = 0$, equate to zero the discriminant of this looked upon as an equation in

$$\dot{x}_1 : \dot{x}_2 \quad \text{or} \quad x_1 : x_2.$$

$$a^2(-\dot{x}_0{}^2 + \dot{x}_3{}^2) - 4b^2\dot{x}_0{}^2\dot{x}_3{}^2 = 0. \tag{16}$$

$$(a_1 - a_2)^2(x_0{}^2 + x_3{}^2)^2 - 4(a_1 + a_2)^2 x_0{}^2 x_3{}^2 = 0. \tag{16'}$$

In like manner for the limiting planes we shall have

$$b^2(\dot{x}_1{}^2 + \dot{x}_2{}^2)^2 + 4a^2\dot{x}_1{}^2\dot{x}_2{}^2 = 0. \tag{17}$$

$$(a_1 + a_2)^2(x_1{}^2 + x_2{}^2) - 4(a_1 - a_2)^2 x_1{}^2 x_2{}^2 = 0. \tag{17'}$$

Notice that the centres of gravity of the limiting points are $(1, 0, 0, 0)$ $(0, 0, 0, 1)$; while the bisectors of the dihedral angles of the limiting planes are $(0, 1, 0, 0)$ $(0, 0, 1, 0)$.

If we look more closely into the roots of the last four equations we see that the roots of (16) are all real, those of (17) all imaginary. As for the two equations (16′) and (17′) the one will have real roots, the other imaginary ones, whence

Theorem 2. In hyperbolic space the limiting points of an actual line are real, and the limiting planes imaginary. In elliptic space this may occur, or the planes may be all real and the points all imaginary.

Giving to $x_0 : x_3$ one of the values from (16′) we see that

$$\frac{x_0{}^2 + x_3{}^2}{x_0 x_3} = \pm\frac{2(a_1 + a_2)}{a_1 - a_2}.$$

Substituting in (15′) we have

$$x_1 + x_2 = 0 \quad \text{or} \quad x_1 - x_2 = 0$$

The four limiting points will yield but these two planes, hence

Theorem 3. The perpendiculars at the limiting points line in two planes called 'principal planes' whose dihedral angles have the same bisectors as pairs of limiting planes.

Theorem 3′. The perpendiculars in the limiting planes meet the line in two points called 'principal points' whose centres of gravity are those of two pairs of limiting points.

Reverting to (16′) we see that we may also write

$$x_0 : x_3 = \pm(\sqrt{a_1} \pm \sqrt{a_2}) : (\sqrt{a_1} \mp \sqrt{a_2}).$$

Let us pick out a pair of limiting points which are not mutually orthogonal, say

$$(\sqrt{a_1} + \sqrt{a_2}, 0, 0, \sqrt{a_1} - \sqrt{a_2})\ (-(\sqrt{a_1} + \sqrt{a_2}), 0, 0, \sqrt{a_1} - \sqrt{a_2}).$$

The perpendicular from the point (x) to the line $x_1 = x_2 = 0$ meets it in the point $(x_0, 0, 0, x_3)$. Calling d_1, d_2 the distances thence to the limiting points just chosen we have

$$\tan\frac{d_1}{k} = \frac{(\sqrt{a_1}-\sqrt{a_2})x_0 - (\sqrt{a_1}+\sqrt{a_2})x_3}{(\sqrt{a_1}+\sqrt{a_2})x_0 + (\sqrt{a_1}-\sqrt{a_2})x_3},$$
$$\tan\frac{d_2}{k} = \frac{(\sqrt{a_1}-\sqrt{a_2})x_0 + (\sqrt{a_1}+\sqrt{a_2})x_3}{-(\sqrt{a_1}+\sqrt{a_2})x_0 + (\sqrt{a_1}-\sqrt{a_2})x_3}.$$

Further, let (ω) be the angle which the plane through $x_1 = x_2 = 0$ and (x) makes with the principal plane

$$x_1 + x_2 = 0.$$

$$\cos^2\omega = \frac{(x_1 - x_2)^2}{2({x_1}^2 + {x_2}^2)}, \qquad \sin^2\omega = \frac{(x_1 + x_2)^2}{2({x_1}^2 + {x_2}^2)},$$
$$\tan\frac{d_1}{k}\cos^2\omega + \tan\frac{d_2}{k}\sin^2\omega = 0. \tag{18}$$

This is, of course, the direct analog of Hamilton's well-known formula for the cylindroid.[85]

Returning to the notations wherewith we opened the present chapter, let us find the focal points of our line, i.e. the points where it intersects adjacent lines of the congruence, or rather, the points where the distance becomes infinitesimal to a higher order. Here, if the focal point be

$$\left(x\cos\frac{r}{k} + y\sin\frac{r}{k}\right),$$

we shall have

$$x_i\cos\frac{r}{k} + y_i\sin\frac{r}{k} = (x_i + dx_i)\cos\frac{r+dr}{k} + (y_i + dy_i)\sin\frac{r+dr}{k}$$
$$dx_i\cos\frac{r}{k} + dy_i\sin\frac{r}{k} - \frac{1}{k}\left(x_i\cos\frac{r}{k} - y_i\sin\frac{r}{k}\right)dr = 0.$$
$$k\,dr = (x\,dy),$$

$$\left[k^2\left(\frac{\partial x_i}{\partial u}\cos\frac{r}{k} + \frac{\partial y_i}{\partial u}\sin\frac{r}{k}\right) - \left(x_i\cos\frac{r}{k} - y_i\sin\frac{r}{k}\right)\left(x\frac{\partial y}{\partial u}\right)\right]du +$$
$$+\left[k^2\left(\frac{\partial x_i}{\partial v}\cos\frac{r}{k} + \frac{\partial y_i}{\partial v}\sin\frac{r}{k}\right) - \left(x_i\cos\frac{r}{k} - y_i\sin\frac{r}{k}\right)\left(x\frac{\partial y}{\partial v}\right)\right]dv = 0.$$

[85]For the Hamiltonian equation see Bianchi, *Differentialgeometrie*, cit., p. 261. For the non-euclidean form here given, cf. Fibbi, loc. cit., p. 57. Fibbi's work is burdened with many long formulae; one cannot help admiring his skill in handling such cumbersome expressions at all.

Multiplying through by $\frac{\partial y_i}{\partial u}$ and adding, then multiplying through by $\frac{\partial y_i}{\partial v}$ and adding again

$$[e\,du + f\,dv]\cos\frac{r}{k} + [E'du + F'dv]\sin\frac{r}{k} = 0,$$
$$[f'du + g\,dv]\cos\frac{r}{k} + [F'du + G'dv]\sin\frac{r}{k} = 0.$$

Replacing $(y\,dx)$ by $(-x\,dy)$ we have, similarly

$$\begin{aligned}[e\,du + f'dv]\sin\frac{r}{k} + [Edu + Fdv]\cos\frac{r}{k} &= 0,\\ [f\,du + g\,dv]\sin\frac{r}{k} + [Fdu + Gdv]\cos\frac{r}{k} &= 0.\end{aligned} \tag{19}$$

Eliminating r

$$\begin{aligned}(E'f' - F'e)du^2 + [E'g - F'(f - f') - G'e]du\,dv + (F'g - G'f)dv^2 &= 0,\\ (Ef - Fe)du^2 + [Eg - F(f' - f) - Ge]du\,dv + (Fg - Gf)dv^2 &= 0.\end{aligned} \tag{20}$$

Eliminating $du : dv$

$$\begin{aligned}(E'G' - F')^2\tan^2\frac{r}{k} + [E'g - F'(f + f') + G'e]\tan\frac{r}{k} + (eg - ff') &= 0,\\ (eg - ff')\tan^2\frac{r}{k} + [Eg - F(f + f') + Ge]\tan\frac{r}{k} + (EG - F^2) &= 0.\end{aligned} \tag{21}$$

Subtracting one of these equations from the other

$$\begin{aligned}[(eg - ff') - (E'G' - F'^2)]\tan^2\frac{r}{k} + [(E - E')g - (F - F')(f + f')&\\ + (G - G')e]\tan\frac{r}{k} + [(EG - F^2) - (eg - ff')] &= 0.\end{aligned} \tag{22}$$

We see at once that the middle coefficients are identical in (14) and (22), and these will vanish when, and only when, we are measuring from a centre of gravity of the roots.

Theorem 4. The centres of gravity of the focal points are identical with those of two pairs of limiting points.

Theorem 4′. The bisectors of the dihedral angles of two focal planes are identical with those of two pairs of limiting planes.

The focal properties of a congruence of normals are especially interesting. Here we may suppose that (y) is the Absolute pole of the tangent plane to the surface described by (x). We have then

$$\left(y\frac{\partial x}{\partial u}\right) = \left(y\frac{\partial x}{\partial v}\right) = \left(x\frac{\partial y}{\partial u}\right) = \left(x\frac{\partial y}{\partial v}\right) = 0,$$

$$-\left(x\frac{\partial^2 y}{\partial u\,\partial v}\right) = f = f'.$$

Suppose, conversely, that

$$f = f'.$$

Let us put $\bar{x}_i = x_i \cos\frac{r}{k} + y_i \sin\frac{r}{k}$ and show that we may find r so that our line is normal to the surface traced by $(\bar{x})$. For this it is necessary and sufficient that the point of the line orthogonal to $(\bar{x})$ should be orthogonal to every displacement of $(\bar{x})$. This point being $\left(x \sin\frac{r}{k} - y \cos\frac{r}{k}\right)$, we must have

$$\sin\frac{r}{k}(x\,d\bar{x}) - \cos\frac{r}{k}(y\,d\bar{x}) = 0,$$

$$(y\,dx) = -k\,dr,$$

and $(y\,dx)$ must be an exact differential, i.e.

$$\frac{\partial}{\partial u}\left(y\frac{\partial x}{\partial v}\right) = \frac{\partial}{\partial v}\left(y\frac{\partial x}{\partial u}\right), \quad f = f'. \tag{23}$$

This condition can be put into a more geometrical form. Let us, in fact, find the necessary and sufficient condition that the focal planes should be mutually perpendicular. Writing their equations in the form

$$|Xxy\,dx| = 0, \quad |Xxy\,\delta x| = 0,$$

the numerator of the expression for the cosine of their angle will be

$$\begin{vmatrix} k^2 & 0 & (y\,\delta x) \\ 0 & k^2 & -\frac{1}{2}(\delta x\,\delta x) \\ (y\,dx) & -\frac{1}{2}(dx\,dx) & (dx\,\delta x) \end{vmatrix} = k^2[k^2(dx\,\delta x) - (y\,dx)(y\,\delta x)].$$

For perpendicularity,

$$E du\,\delta u + F(du\,\delta v + \delta u\,dv) + G dv\,\delta v = 0.$$

Now, by (20),

$$\frac{du\,\delta u}{dv\,\delta v} = \frac{Fg - Gf'}{Ef - Fe}, \quad \left[\frac{du}{dv} + \frac{\delta u}{\delta v}\right] = \frac{Ge + F(f' - f) - Eg}{Ef - Fe}.$$

Hence

$$(EG - F^2)(f - f') = 0.$$

Let us give the name *pseudo-normal* to the absolute polar of a normal congruence. We thus get

Theorem 5. The necessary and sufficient condition that a congruence should be normal is that the focal planes through each line should be mutually perpendicular.

Theorem 5$'$. The necessary and sufficient condition that a congruence should be pseudo-normal is that the focal points on each line should be mutually orthogonal.

If we subtract one of the equivalent equations (20) from the other, we get an equation which reduces to (13) when, and only when

$$f = f'.$$

Theorem 6. The necessary and sufficient condition that a general congruence should be composed of normals is that the focal points should coincide with a pair of limiting points.

In a normal congruence let us suppose that (x) traces a surface to which the given lines are normal so that

$$(y\,dx) = -(x\,dy) = 0.$$

Let us then put

$$\overline{x_i} = x_i \cos\frac{r}{k} + y_i \sin\frac{r}{k}, \quad \overline{y_i} = x_i \cos\frac{r}{k} - y_i \sin\frac{r}{k},$$

where y is constant. We see at once that

$$(\overline{y}\,d\overline{x}) = -(\overline{x}\,d\overline{y}) = 0.$$

Theorem 7. If a constant distance be laid off on each normal to a surface from the foot, in such a way that the points on adjacent normals are on the same side of the tangent plane corresponding to either, the locus of the points so found is a surface with the same normals as the original one.

Let us suppose that we have a normal congruence determined by mutually orthogonal points (x) and (y), where $x_i = x_i(uv)$ traces a surface, not one of the orthogonal trajectories of the congruence. We shall choose as parameter lines in this surface the isotropic curves, so that

$$\left(\frac{\partial x}{\partial u}\frac{\partial x}{\partial u}\right) = \left(\frac{\partial x}{\partial v}\frac{\partial x}{\partial v}\right) = 0.$$

The sine of the angle which our given line makes with the normal to this surface is

$$\sin\theta = \sqrt{\frac{2\left(y\frac{\partial x}{\partial u}\right)\left(y\frac{\partial x}{\partial v}\right)}{k^2\left(\frac{\partial x}{\partial u}\frac{\partial x}{\partial v}\right)}}$$

Let all the lines of our congruence be reflected or refracted in this surface in such a way that

$$\sin\overline{\theta} = n\sin\theta.$$

We must replace y by $\overline{y}$ where

$$\overline{y_i} = ny_i + \lambda\frac{\partial}{\partial t_i}\left|tx\frac{\partial x}{\partial u}\frac{\partial x}{\partial v}\right|.$$

It is easily seen that for the new congruence also

$$f = f'.$$

Theorem 8. If a normal congruence be subjected to any finite number of reflections or refractions, the resulting congruence is normal.

We shall now abandon the general congruence and assume that, contrary to (12)

$$e : \frac{f+f'}{2} : g \equiv (E - E') : (F - F') : (G - G'). \tag{24}$$

There are two sharply distinct sub-cases which must not be confused:

$$\text{(a) } f \equiv f', \quad \text{(b) } f \not\equiv f'.$$

In either case, as we readily see, (11) is illusory, and there is no ruled quartic determined by the common perpendiculars to a line and its neighbours; these perpendiculars will either all meet the given line at one of two mutually orthogonal points, or two adjacent lines will be paratactic, and have ∞^1 common perpendiculars.

Our condition for focal points expressed in (23) was independent of (12), and this shows that our two sub-cases just mentioned differ in this, that the first is a normal congruence, while the second is not. Let (x) be a point where our line meets a set of perpendiculars, (y) being thus the other such point. Then under our first hypothesis, we shall have

$$e = f = f' = g = 0.$$

We see that the focal points will fall into (x) and (y) likewise. These are mutually orthogonal, and so by equation (26) of the last Chapter, that the total relative curvature of the surface will be $-\frac{1}{k^2}$ or the Gaussian curvature zero. We see also by theorem (22) of that chapter that it is possible to assemble the lines of our congruence into families of left or right paratactics according as we assemble them by means of the one or the other set of asymptotic lines of the given surface. Conversely, if we have given a congruence of normals to a surface of Gaussian curvature zero, two normals adjacent to a given one are paratactic thereunto. There must be, then, two values of $du : dv$ for which (11), looked upon as an equation in r, becomes entirely illusory. Hence (24) must hold, and as we have normal congruence (23) is also true.

We now make the second assumption

$$f \not\equiv f'.$$

We shall still take (x) as a point where the line meets the various common perpendiculars, so that we may put

$$e = \frac{f+f'}{2} = g = 0.$$

We may take as coordinates of a focal plane

$$u_i = \frac{\partial}{\partial t_i} |t\, xy\, dx|,$$

$$(uu) = k^2[Edu^2 + 2F du\, dv + Gdv^2].$$

But by (20) this expression vanishes. Hence the focal planes all touch the Absolute, and the focal surface must be a developable circumscribed thereunto. It is clear that the lines of such a congruence cannot be assembled into paratactic families.

This type of congruence shall be called 'isotropic'.[86]

Let us take an isotropic congruence, or congruence of normals to a surface of Gaussian curvature zero, and choose (x) and (y) so that

$$e = \tfrac{1}{2}(f + f') = g = 0,$$

$$\overline{x_i} = x \cos \frac{r}{k} + y \sin \frac{r}{k},$$

$$(d\overline{x}\, d\overline{x}) = \cos^2 \frac{r}{k} (dx\, dx) + \sin^2 \frac{r}{k} (dy\, dy).$$

This expression will be unaltered if we change r into $-r$. Conversely, when such is the case, we must have $(dx\, dy) = 0$, and the congruence will be either isotropic, or composed of normals to a surface of Gaussian curvature zero.

Theorem 9. The necessary and sufficient condition that a congruence should be either isotropic, or composed of normals to a surface of Gaussian curvature zero, is that it should consist of lines connecting corresponding points of two mutually applicable surfaces, which pairs of points determine always the same distance. The centres of gravity of these pairs of points will be the points where the various lines meet the common perpendiculars to themselves and the adjacent lines.

In elliptic (or spherical) space, there is advantage in studying our last two types of congruence from a different point of view, suggested by the developments of Chapter X.

Let us rewrite the equations (11) there given.

$$\begin{aligned}(x_0 y_i - x_i y_0) + (x_j y_k - x_k y_j) &= {}_l X_i,\\ (x_0 y_i - x_i y_0) - (x_j y_k - x_k y_j) &= {}_r X_i.\end{aligned} \tag{25}$$

[86]The earliest discussion of these interesting congruences in non-euclidean space will be found in the author's article 'Les congruences isotropes qui servent à représenter les fonctions d'une variable complexe', *Atti della R. Accademia delle Scienze di Torino*, xxxix, 1903, and xl, 1904. In the same number of the same journal as the first of these will be found an article by Bianchi, 'Sulla rappresentazione di Clifford delle congruenze rettilinee nello spazio ellitico.' Professor Bianchi uses the word 'isotropic' to cover both what we have here defined as isotropic congruences, and also congruences of normals to surfaces of Gaussian curvature zero, distinguishing the latter by the name of 'normal'. The author, on the other hand, included in his definition of isotropic congruences those which, later, we shall define as 'pseudo-isotropic'. A discussion of these definitions will be found in a note at the beginning of the second of the author's articles.

These equations were originally written under the supposition that (x) and (y) were homogeneous. At present if we so choose the unit of measure that $k = 1$ we have

$$({}_lX\,{}_lX) = ({}_rX\,{}_rX) = 1. \tag{26}$$

These coordinates $({}_lX)$, $({}_rX)$ were formerly looked upon as giving the lines through the origin $(1,0,0,0)$ respectively left and right paratactic to the given line. They may now be looked upon as coordinates of two points of two unit spheres of euclidean space, called, respectively, the left and right *representing spheres*[87] The representation is not, however, unique. On the one hand the two lines of a cross will be represented by the same points, on the other, we get the same line if we replace either representing point by its diametrical opposite. We shall avoid ambiguity by assuming that each line is doubly overlaid with two opposite 'rays', meaning thereby a line with a sense or sequence attached to its points, as indicated in the beginning of Chapter V or end of Chapter IX. We shall assume that by reversing the signs in one triad of coordinates we replace our ray by a ray on the absolute polar of its line, while by reversing both sets of signs, we replace the ray by its opposite.

Theorem 10. There is a perfect one to one correspondence between the assemblage of all real rays of elliptic or spherical space, and that of pairs of real points of two euclidean spheres. Opposite rays of the same line will be represented by diametrically opposite pairs of points, rays on mutually absolute polar lines by identical points on one sphere and opposite points of the other. Rays on left (right) paratactic lines will be represented by identical or opposite points of the left (right) sphere.

Two rays shall be said to be paratactic when their lines are. Reverting to Theorem 12 of Chapter X.

Theorem 11. The perpendicular distances of the lines of two rays or the angles of these rays are half the difference and half the sum of the pairs of spherical distances of their representing points.

Theorem 12. The necessary and sufficient condition that the lines of two rays should intersect is that the spherical distances of the pairs of representing points should be equal; each will intersect the absolute polar of the other if these spherical distances be supplementary.

Theorem 13. Each ray of a common perpendicular to the lines of two rays will be represented by a pair of poles of two great circles which connect the pairs of representing points.

It is clear that an analytic congruence may be represented in the form

$${}_lX_i = {}_lX_i(uv), \quad {}_rX_i = {}_rX_i(uv),$$

or else, in general,

$${}_lX_i = {}_lX_i({}_rX_1\,{}_rX_2\,{}_rX_3).$$

[87]This representation was first published independently by Study, 'Zur nichteuklidischen etc.,' and Fubini, 'Il parallelismo di Clifford negli spazii ellitici,' *Annali della R. Scuola Normale di Pisa*, Vol. ix, 1900. The latter writer does not, however, distinguish with sufficient clearness between rays and lines.

Two adjacent rays will intersect, or intersect one another's polars if

$$(d_l X\, d_l X) = (d_r X\, d_r X).$$

The common perpendicular to two adjacent rays will have coordinates

$$\lambda_l Y_i = \frac{\partial}{\partial_l Z_i}\left|{}_l Z\, {}_l X\, d_l X\right|, \quad \mu_r X_i = \frac{\partial}{\partial_r Z_i}\left|{}_r Z\, {}_r X\, d_r X\right|.$$

The condition that a congruence should be either normal or pseudo-normal is

$$(d_l X d_l X) = (d_r X d_r X),$$

$$(\delta_l X \delta_l X) = (\delta_r X \delta_r X),$$

$$\begin{vmatrix} ({}_l X\, {}_l X)({}_l X\, \delta\, {}_l X) \\ ({}_l X\, d\, {}_l X)(d\, {}_l X\, \delta\, {}_l X) \end{vmatrix} = \pm \begin{vmatrix} ({}_r X\, {}_r X)({}_r X\, \delta\, {}_r X) \\ ({}_r X\, d\, {}_r X)(d\, {}_r X\, \delta\, {}_r X) \end{vmatrix},$$

from these

$$(d\, {}_l X\, \delta\, {}_l X) = \pm(d\, {}_r X\, \delta\, {}_r X). \tag{27}$$

Let us determine the significance of the double sign. If, in particular, we take the congruence of normals to a sphere whose centre is $(1, 0, 0, 0)$ we shall get the equations

$${}_l X_i = {}_r X_i,$$

and this transformation keeps areas invariant in value and sign. On the other hand, the congruence of rays in the absolute polar of this plane will be

$${}_l X_i = -{}_r X_i,$$

a transformation which changes the signs of all areas. Lastly, we may pass from one normal congruence to another by a continuous change, wherein the sign in equation (27) will not be changed, hence[88]

Theorem 14. A normal congruence will be represented by a relation between the two spheres which keeps areas invariant in actual value and sign, and every such relation will give a normal congruence.

Theorem 14′. A pseudo-normal congruence will be represented by a relation between the two spheres where the sum of corresponding areas on the two is zero, and every such relation will give a pseudo-normal congruence.

Let us next take an isotropic congruence. Here two common perpendiculars to two adjacent lines necessarily intersect, or each intersects the absolute polar of the other. The same will hold for the absolute polar of an isotropic congruence, a 'pseudo-isotropic' congruence, let us say. Such a congruence will not have a focal surface at all, but a focal curve, which lies on the Absolute. On the representing spheres, in the case of either of these congruences, two intersecting

[88] Cf. Study, loc. cit., p. 321; Fubini, p. 46.

arcs of one will make the same angle, in absolute value, as the corresponding arcs on the other. In the particular case of the isotropic congruence of all lines through the point $(1, 0, 0, 0)$ the relation between the two representing spheres is a directly conformal one, while in the case of the pseudo-isotropic congruence of all lines in the plane $(1, 0, 0, 0)$ we have an inversely conformal relation. We may now repeat the reasoning by continuity used in the case of the normal congruence, and get[89]

Theorem 15. The necessary and sufficient condition that a congruence should be isotropic is that the corresponding relation between the representing spheres should be directly conformal.

Theorem 15′. The necessary and sufficient condition that a congruence should be pseudo-isotropic is that the corresponding relation between the representing spheres should be inversely conformal.

Let us take up the isotropic case more fully. Any directly conformal relation between the real domains of two euclidean spheres of radius unity may be represented by an analytic function of the complex variable. Let us give the coordinates of points of our representing spheres in the following parametric form:

$$
\begin{aligned}
{}_lX_1 &= \frac{u_1u_2 - 1}{u_1u_2 + 1}, & {}_rX_1 &= \frac{z_1z_2 - 1}{z_1z_2 + 1}, \\
{}_lX_2 &= \frac{i(u_1 - u_2)}{u_1u_2 + 1}, & {}_rX_2 &= \frac{i(z_1 - z_2)}{z_1z_2 + 1}, \\
{}_lX_3 &= \frac{u_1 + u_2}{u_1u_2 + 1}, & {}_rX_3 &= \frac{z_1 + z_2}{z_1z_2 + 1}.
\end{aligned}
\tag{28}
$$

We shall get a real ray when

$$u_2 = \bar{u}_1, \quad z_2 = \bar{z}_1.$$

In order to have a real directly conformal relation between the two spheres, our transformation must be such as to carry a rectilinear generator into another generator, i.e.

$$u_1 = u_1(z_1), \quad u_2 = \bar{u}_1(z_2). \tag{29}$$

For an inversely conformal transformation

$$u_1 = u_1(z_2), \quad u_2 = \bar{u}_1(z_1). \tag{30}$$

All will thus depend on the single analytic function $u_1(z)$.

The opposite of the ray (u) (z) will be

$$
\begin{aligned}
u_1{}' &= -\frac{1}{u_2}, & z_1{}' &= -\frac{1}{z_2}, \\
u_2{}' &= -\frac{1}{u_1}, & z_2{}' &= -\frac{1}{z_1}.
\end{aligned}
$$

[89]First given in the Author's first article on isotropic congruences, recently cited.

Let us now inquire under what circumstances the following equation will hold:

$$\bar{u}_1\left(-\frac{1}{z_1}\right) = \frac{-1}{u_1(z_1)}. \tag{31}$$

If this hold identically, the opposite of every ray of the congruence will belong thereto. If not, there will still be certain rays of the congruence for which it is true. To begin with it will be satisfied by all rays of the congruence for which

$$u_1 u_2 + 1 = 0, \quad z_1 z_2 + 1 = 0.$$

This amounts to putting

$$({}_lX\,{}_lX) = ({}_rX\,{}_rX) = 0.$$

We saw in Chapter X that, interpreted in cross coordinates, these are the equations which characterize an improper cross of the second sort, which is made up of a pencil of tangents to the Absolute. Such a pencil we may also call an improper ray of the second sort. Let us see under what circumstances such a ray (uz) will intersect a proper ray $(u'z')$ orthogonally. Geometrically, we see that either the proper ray must pass through the vertex of the pencil, or lie in the plane thereof, and analytically we shall have

$$(u_1 - u_1')(u_2 - u_2') = (z_1 - z_1')(z_2 - z_2') = 0,$$

$$u_1 u_2 + 1 = z_1 z_2 + 1 = 0.$$

There are four solutions to these equations. By considering a special case we are able to pick out those two where the ray lies in the plane of the pencil

$$u_1 = u_1', \qquad z_1 = z_1',$$
$$u_2 = -\frac{1}{u_1'}, \qquad z_2 = -\frac{1}{z_1'},$$

or else

$$u_1 = -\frac{1}{u_2'}, \qquad z_1 = -\frac{1}{z_2'},$$
$$u_2 = u_2', \qquad z_2 = z_2',$$

The proper ray $(u')(z')$ was supposed to belong to our congruence. The condition that the improper one $(u)(z)$ shall also belong thereto will be

$$\bar{u}_1\left(-\frac{1}{z_1'}\right) = -\frac{1}{u_1(z_1')}.$$

Theorem 16.[90] The necessary and sufficient condition that the opposite of a real ray of an isotropic congruence should also belong thereunto is that the ray should be coplanar with an improper ray of the second sort belonging to the

[90]See the Author's second note on isotropic congruences, p. 13.

congruence. When the latter are present in infinite number in an irreducible congruence, the congruence contains the opposite of each of its rays.

The two cases here given may be still more sharply distinguished by geometrical considerations. The focal surface of an isotropic congruence is a developable circumscribed to the Absolute, and will have a real equation when the congruence is real. There are two distinct possibilities; first, the equation of this surface is reducible in the rational domain; second, it is not. In the first case the surface is made up of two conjugate imaginary portions; in the second there is one portion which is its own conjugate imaginary. In the first case there will be a finite number of planes which touch the Absolute and also each of the two portions of the focal surface at the same point, namely, those which touch the Absolute at the points of intersection of the two curves of contact with the two portions of the focal surface. In these planes only shall we have improper rays of the second sort belonging to the congruence. If, on the other hand, the focal surface be irreducible, every point of the curve of contact may be looked upon as being in the intersection of two adjacent planes tangent to the Absolute, and the focal surface which is its own conjugate imaginary. The tangents at each of these points will be improper rays of the second sort of the congruence. Theorem 17 may now be given in a better form.

Theorem 17. The necessary and sufficient condition that an isotropic congruence should contain the opposite of each of its rays is that the focal surface should be irreducible.

It is very easy to observe the distinction between the two cases in the case of the linear function

$$u_1 = \frac{\alpha z_1 + \beta}{\gamma z_1 + \delta}.$$

If $\beta = -\bar{\gamma}$, $\delta = \bar{\alpha}$, (29) is identically satisfied. But here it will be seen that if we write

$$\alpha = a + bi, \quad \gamma = -c + di,$$

our congruence is nought else than the assemblage of all rays through the point (a, b, c, d). The focal surface is the cone of tangents thence to the Absolute, clearly its own conjugate imaginary. On the other hand, when α, β, γ, δ are not connected by these relations, we shall have a line congruence of the fourth order, and second class, as is easily verified. It is well known[91] that a congruence of the second order and fourth class has no focal surface, but a focal curve composed of two conics, so our present congruence has as focal surface two conjugate imaginary quadric cones which are circumscribed to the Absolute. When their conjugate imaginary centres fall together in a real point, we revert to the previous case.

When (u) and (z) are connected by the vanishing of a polynomial of order m in u_1 and order n in z_1, in the general case where (31) does not hold identically, we shall have a line-congruence of order $(m+n)^2$. When, however, (31) does hold, we must subtract from this the order of the curve of contact of the focal

[91]Cf. Sturm, *Gebilde erster und zweiter Ordnung der Liniengeometrie*, Leipzig, 1892-96, Vol. ii, p. 320.

surface and Absolute, and then divide by 2 to allow for the fact that there are two opposite rays on each line.

If u_1 be a function of z_1 that possesses an essential singularity corresponding to a certain value of z_1 we see that as u_1 takes all possible values (except at most two) in the immediate neighbourhood, there will be a whole bundle of right paratactic lines in the congruence. If u_1 be periodic, there will be an infinite number of lines of the congruence left paratactic to each line thereof. If u_1 be one of the functions of the regular bodies, we have a congruence which is transformed into itself by a group of orthogonal substitutions in $({}_rX)$, i.e. by a group of left translations.

We have still to consider the congruence of normals to a surface of Gaussian curvature zero in ray coordinates. Here there will be ∞^1 paratactics of each sort to each line. We may therefore express $({}_lX)$ and $({}_rX)$ each as functions of one independent variable, or merely write

$$\phi({}_lX_1\,{}_lX_2\,{}_lX_3) = \psi({}_rX_1\,{}_rX_2\,{}_rX_3) = 0. \tag{32}$$

All our work here developed for the elliptic case may be brought into immediate relation with the hyperbolic case, and in so doing we shall get to the inmost kernel of the whole matter. The parameters u_1u_2 will determine generators of the left representing sphere. They have, however, a more direct significance. For if u_2 remain constant while u_1 varies, the left paratactics to the ray in question passing through the point $(1, 0, 0, 0)$ will trace a pencil, and this pencil will lie in a plane tangent to the Absolute, for there is only one value for u_1, namely, $-\frac{1}{u_2}$, which will make the moving ray tangent to the Absolute. When, therefore, u_2 is fixed, one of the left generators of the Absolute met by the ray in question is fixed, and this shows that u_1u_2 are the parameters determining the left generators which the ray intersects, while z_1z_2 in like manner determine the right generators.

If two rays meet the same two generators of one set they are paratactic, i.e. their lines are. If they meet the same two generators of different sets, they are either parallel or pseudoparallel. The conditions for parallelism or pseudoparallelism will be that two rays shall have the same value for one (u) and for one (z). Let us, in fact, assume that the subscripts are assigned to the letters u_1u_2, z_1z_2 in such a way that a direct conformal transformation, or isotropic congruence, is given by equations (29). Such a congruence will contain ∞^1 rays pseudo-parallel to a given ray, but only a finite number parallel to it. The conditions for pseudo-parallelism will thus be

$$u_1' = u_1,\ z_1' = z_1,\ \text{or}\ u_2' = u_2,\ z_2' = z_2. \tag{33}$$

On the other hand a pseudo-isotropic congruence will be given by (30), and the conditions for parallelism will be

$$u_1' = u_1,\ z_2' = z_2,\ \text{or}\ u_2' = u_2,\ z_1' = z_1. \tag{34}$$

To pass to the hyperbolic case, let us now assume that $({}_lX)({}_rX)$ are two points of the hyperbolic Absolute, and that, taken in order, they give a ray from $({}_lX)$ to $({}_rX)$. Two rays will be parallel if

$$({}_lX) = ({}_lX') \text{ or } ({}_rX) = ({}_rX').$$

Equations (33) will give the conditions for parataxy, while (34) give those for pseudo-parallelism. We might push the matter still further by distinguishing between syntaxy and anti-taxy, synparallelism and anti-parallelism, but we shall not enter into such questions here. Equations (29) will give a congruence whose rays can be assembled into surfaces with paratactic generators, i.e. a congruence of normals to a surface of Gaussian curvature zero; (30) will give an isotropic congruence, while (32) will give a pseudo-isotropic congruence. We may tabulate our results as follows.[92]

Hyperbolic Space.	*Elliptic Space.*
Ray.	Ray.
Real ray in actual domain or pencil of tangents to Absolute.	Real Ray
Real parallelism.	Real parataxy.
Imaginary pseudo-parallelism.	Imaginary parallelism.
Imaginary parataxy.	Imaginary pseudo-parallelism.
Real congruence of normals to surface of Gaussian curvature zero.	Real isotropic congruence.
Real isotropic congruence.	Real pseudo-isotropic congruence.
Real pseudo-isotropic congruence.	Real congruence of normals to a surface of Gaussian curvature zero.

[92]The Author's attention was first called to this remarkable correspondence by Professor Study in a letter in the summer of 1905. It is developed, without proof, but in detail, in his second memoir, 'Ueber nichteuklidische und Liniengeometrie,' *Jahresbericht der deutschen Mathematikervereinigung*, xv, 1906.

CHAPTER XVII

MULTIPLY CONNECTED SPACES

In Chapters I and II we laid down a system of axioms for our fundamental objects *points* and *distances*, and showed how, thereby, we might build up the geometry of a restricted region. We also saw that with the addition of an assumption concerning the sum of the angles of a single triangle, we were in a position to develop fully the elliptic, hyperbolic, or euclidean geometry of the restricted region in question. Our spaces so defined were not, however, perfect analytic continua, even in the real domain. To reach such continua it was necessary to assume that any chosen segment might be extended beyond either extremity by a chosen amount. We saw in the beginning of Chapter VII that this assumption, though allowable in the euclidean and hyperbolic cases, will involve a contradiction when added to the assumptions already made for elliptic space. The difficulty was overcome by assuming the existence of a space which contained as sub-regions (called *consistent regions*) spaces where our previous axioms held good. For this new type of space we set up our Axioms I′–VI′.

Our next task was to show that under Axioms I′–V′ each point will surely have one set of homogeneous coordinates (x), and conversely, to each set of real coordinates subject to the restriction that in hyperbolic space

$$k^2\dot{x}_0{}^2 + \dot{x}_1{}^2+\dot{x}_2{}^2 + \dot{x}_3{}^2 < 0,$$

in elliptic space $\qquad (xx) > 0,$

and in euclidean space $\qquad x_0 \neq 0,$

there will surely correspond one real point. Under the euclidean or hyperbolic hypotheses each set of real coordinates can correspond to one real point, at most; under the elliptic hypothesis, on the contrary, we found it necessary to distinguish between elliptic space where but one point goes with each coordinate set, and the spherical case where two equivalent points necessarily have the same coordinates.

One further point was established in connexion with these developments; to each point there will correspond but a single set of homogeneous coordinates (x). The proof of this depended upon Axiom VI′, which required that a congruent transformation of one consistent region should produce one definite transformation of space as a whole. Of course such an assumption, when applied to our space of experience, can neither be proved nor disproved empirically. In the present chapter we shall set ourselves the task of examining whether, under Axioms I′–V′ of Chapter VII, it be possible to have a space where each point shall correspond to several sets of coordinate values.[93] For simplicity we shall assume that no two different points can have the same coordinates.

[93]The present chapter is in close accord with Killing, *Die Grundlagen der Geometrie*, Paderborn, 1893, Part iv. Another account will be found in Woods' 'Forms of Non-Euclidean-Space', published in *Lectures on Mathematics*, Woods, Van Vleck, and White, New York, 1905.

What will be the meaning of the statement that under our set of axioms two sets of coordinate values (x), (x') belong to the same point? Let a coordinate system be set up, as in Chapter V, in some consistent region; let this region be connected with the given point by two different sets of overlapping consistent regions; then (x) and (x') shall be two different sets of coordinate values for this point, obtained by two different sets of analytic extension of the original coordinate system.

Let us first assume that there is a consistent region which is reached by each chain of overlapping consistent regions, a statement which will always hold true when there is a single point so reached. We may set up a coordinate system in this region, and then make successive analytic extensions for the change of axes from one to another of the overlapping consistent regions, until we have run through the whole circuit, and come back to the region in which we started. If, then, one point of the region have different values for its coordinates from what it had at the start, the same will be true of all, or all but a finite number of points of the region, and the new coordinate values will be obtained from the old ones (in the non-euclidean cases) by means of an orthogonal substitution. If (x) and (x') be two sets of coordinates for one point we shall have

$$x_i' = \sum_{j}^{0..3} a_{ij} x_j, \quad |a_{ij}| \neq 0. \tag{1}$$

Conversely, if these equations hold for any point, they will represent an identical transformation of the region, and give two sets of coordinate values for every point of the region. We see also by analytic extension that these equations will give two sets of coordinate values for every point in space.

There is one possible variation in our axioms which should be mentioned at this point. It is entirely possible to build up a geometrical system where IV′ holds *in general* only, and there are special points, called *singular points*, which can lie in two consistent regions which have no sub-region in common. In two dimensions we have a simple example in the case of the geometry of the euclidean cone with a singular line. We shall, however, exclude this possibility by sticking closely to our axioms.

Let us suppose that we have two overlapping systems of consistent regions going from the one wherein our coordinate axes were set up to a chosen point P. We may connect P with a chosen point A of the original region by two continuous curves, thus making, in all, a continuous loop. If now, P_1 be a point which will have two different sets of coordinate values, according as we arrive at it by the one or the other set of extensions, we see that our loop is of a sort which cannot be reduced in size beyond a definite amount without losing its characteristic property. This shows that, in the sense of analysis situs, our space is multiply connected. In speaking of spaces which obey Axioms I′–V′, but where each point can have several sets of coordinate values, we shall use the term *multiply connected spaces.*

Suppose that we have a third set of coordinate values for a point of our consistent region. These will be connected with the second set by a relation

$$x_i'' = \sum_j^{0..3} b_{ij} x_j', \quad |b_{ij}| \neq 0.$$

We see that (x'') and (x) are also connected by a relation of this type, hence

Theorem 1. The assemblage of all coordinate transformations which represent the identical transformation of a multiply connected space form a group.

If (x) and (x') be two sets of coordinates for the same point the expression

$$\left| \cos^{-1} \frac{(xx')}{\sqrt{(xx)}\sqrt{(x'x')}} \right|$$

cannot sink below a definite minimum value greater than zero, for then we should have two different points of the same consistent region with the same coordinate values, which we have seen is impossible (Chapter VII).

For the sake of clearness in our subsequent work let us introduce, besides our multiply connected space S, a space Σ, having the same value for the constant k as our space S. and giving to each point one set of coordinate values only. The group of identical transformations of S will appear in Σ as a group of congruent transformations, a group which has the property that none of its transformations can leave a real point of the actual domain invariant, nor produce an infinitesimal transformation of that domain. We lay stress upon the actual domain of Σ, for in S we are interested in actual points only. Let us further define as *fundamental* such a region of Σ, that every point of Σ has an equivalent in this region under the congruent sub-group which we are now considering, yet no two points of a fundamental region are equivalent to one another. The points of S may be put into one to one correspondence with those of a fundamental region of this sort or of a portion thereof, and, conversely, such a fundamental region will furnish an example of a multiply connected space obeying Axioms I′–V′.

Theorem 2. Every real group of congruent transformations of euclidean, hyperbolic, or elliptic space, which carries the actual domain into itself, and none of whose members leave an actual point invariant, nor transport such a point an infinitesimal amount, may be taken as the group of identical transformations of a multiply connected space whose points may be put into one to one correspondence with the points of a portion of any fundamental domain of the given space for that group.

Our interest will, from now on, centre in the space Σ. We shall also find it advisable to treat the euclidean and the two non-euclidean cases separately.

We shall begin by asking what groups of congruent transformations of the euclidean plane fulfil the requirements of Theorem 2. Every congruent transformation of the euclidean plane is either a translation or a rotation, but the latter type is inadmissible for our present purpose. What then are the groups of translations of the euclidean plane? The simplest is evidently composed of the repetitions of a single translation. If the amplitude of the translation be l, while n is an integer, positive or negative, this group may be expressed in the form

$$x' = x + nl, \quad y' = y.$$

The fundamental regions will be strips bounded by lines parallel to the y axis, each strip including one of the bounding lines. A corresponding space S will be furnished by a euclidean cylinder of circumference l.

What translation groups can be compounded from two given translations? It is clear that the lines of motion of the two should not be parallel. For if, in that case, their amplitudes were commensurable, we should fall back upon the preceding system; but if the amplitudes were incommensurable, the group would contain infinitesimal transformations; and these we must exclude. On the other hand, the group compounded from repetitions of two non-parallel translations will suit our purpose very well. If the amplitudes of the two be l and λ, while m and n are integers, we may write our group in the form

$$x' = x + nl, \quad y' = y + m\lambda.$$

The fundamental regions are parallelograms, each including two adjacent sides, excepting two extremities. The Clifford surface discussed in Chapters X and XV offers an excellent example of a multiply connected surface of this type.

It is interesting to notice that with these two examples we exhaust the possibilities of the euclidean plane. Suppose, in fact, that P is any point of this plane, that is to say, any point in the finite domain. The points equivalent to it under the congruent group in question may not cluster anywhere, hence there is one equivalent, or a finite number of such, nearer to it than any other. If these nearest equivalents do not all lie on a line with P, we may pick out two of them, non-collinear with P, thus determining one-half of a fundamental parallelogram. If the nearest equivalents are collinear with P (and, hence, two only in number), we may pick out one of them and one of the next nearest (which will be off that line, unless we are under our previous first case), and thus construct a parallelogram within which there is no equivalent to P, for every point within such a parallelogram is nearer to one vertex than any two vertices are to one another. This parallelogram, including two adjacent sides, except the vertices which are not common, will constitute a fundamental region, and we are back on the second previous case. Let the reader notice an exactly similar line of reasoning will show that there cannot exist any single valued continuous function of the complex variable which possesses more than two independent periods.

In a three-dimensional euclidean space we shall find suitable groups compounded of one, two, or three independent translations. The fundamental regions will be respectively layers between parallel planes, four-faced prismatic spaces, and parallelepipeds. It is easy to determine how much of the bounding surface should be included in each case. It is also evident that there can be no other groups composed of translations only, which fulfil the requirements.

Let us glance for a moment at the various forms of straight line which will exist in a multiply connected euclidean space S, which corresponds to a euclidean parallelepiped in Σ. The corresponding lines in Σ shall all pass through one vertex of the fundamental parallelepiped. If the line in Σ be one edge of the parallelepiped, the line in S will be a simple loop of length equal to one period. If the line in Σ connect the vertex with any other equivalent point, the line in S will still be a loop, but of greater length. If, lastly, the line in Σ do not contain any other point equivalent to the vertex, the line in S will be open, but, if followed sufficiently far, will pass again as close as desired to the chosen point.

There are other groups of motions of euclidean space, besides translations which give rise to multiply connected spaces. An obvious example is furnished by the repetitions of a single screw motion. This may be expressed, n being an integer, in the form

$$x' = x\cos n\theta - y\sin n\theta, \quad y' = x\sin n\theta + y\cos n\theta, \quad z' = z + nd.$$

The fundamental regions in Σ will be layers bounded by parallel planes. In S we shall have various types of straight lines. The Z axis will be a simple closed loop of length d. Will there be any other closed lines in S? The corresponding lines in Σ must be parallel to the axis, there being an infinite number of points of each at the same distance from that axis. When θ and 2π are commensurable, we see that every parallel to the Z axis will go into a closed line of the type required, when θ and 2π are incommensurable, the Z axis is the only closed line.

Let us now take two points of Σ separated by a distance r

$$\begin{aligned} \xi &= x + r\cos\alpha, \\ \eta &= y + r\cos\beta, \\ \zeta &= z + r\cos\gamma. \end{aligned}$$

The necessary and sufficient condition that they should be equivalent is

$$\begin{aligned} x\cos n\theta - y\sin n\theta &= x + r\cos\alpha, \\ x\sin n\theta + y\cos n\theta &= y + r\cos\beta, \\ nd &= r\cos\gamma. \end{aligned}$$

The last of these equations shows that a line in Σ perpendicular to the Z axis (i.e. parallel to a line meeting it perpendicularly) cannot return to itself. On the other hand, if

$$\cos\alpha = \cos\beta = 0: \quad n\theta = 2m\pi,$$

and we have a closed loop of the type just discussed. If α, β, γ, n be given, r may be determined by the last equation, and x, y from the two preceding, since the determinant of the coefficients will not, in general, vanish. We thus see that in S the lines with direction angles α, β, γ, and possessing double points, will form an infinite discontinuous assemblage. If, on the other hand, x, y, z, n be given, α, β, γ, r may be determined from the given equations, coupled with the fact that the sum of the squares of the direction cosines is unity; through each point in S, not on the Z axis, will pass an infinite number of straight lines, having this as a double point.

The planes in S will be of three sorts. Those which are perpendicular to the Z axis will contain open lines only, those whose equations lack the Z term will contain all sorts of lines. Other planes will contain no lines which are simple loops.

Another type of multiply connected space will be determined by

$$\begin{aligned} x' &= (-1)^l x + ma, \\ y' &= (-1)^l y + nb, \\ z' &= z + lc. \end{aligned}$$

l, m, n being integers.

The fundamental regions in Σ will be triangular right prisms. Lines in Σ parallel to the Z axis will appear in S as simple closed loops of length $2c$. To find lines which cross themselves, let us write

$$\begin{aligned} x + r\cos\alpha &= (-1)^l x + ma, \\ y + r\cos\beta &= (-1)^l y + nb, \\ z + r\cos\gamma &= z + lc. \end{aligned}$$

For each even integral value of l, and each integral value of m and n, we get a bundle of loop lines in S with direction cosines

$$\cos\alpha = \frac{ma}{\sqrt{m^2a^2 + n^2b^2 + l^2c^2}}, \text{ \&c.}$$

When l is odd, we shall have through each point an infinite number of lines which have a double point there, the direction cosines being

$$\cos\alpha = \frac{-2x + ma}{\sqrt{(-2x + ma)^2 + (-2y + nb)^2 + l^2c^2}}, \text{ \&c.}$$

Such lines will, in general, be open. We see, however, that whereas the length of a loop perpendicular to the x, y plane is $2c$, if the point $\frac{ma}{2}, \frac{nb}{2}$ happen to be on such a loop, this point is reached again after a distance C. This loop has therefore, the general form of a lemniscate.[94]

When we turn from the euclidean to the hyperbolic hypothesis, we find a less satisfactory state of affairs. The real congruent group of the hyperbolic plane was shown in Chapter VIII to depend upon the real binary group

$$\begin{aligned} \sigma t_1' &= \alpha_{11}t_1 + \alpha_{12}t_2, \\ \sigma t_2' &= \alpha_{21}t_1 + \alpha_{12}t_2, \end{aligned}$$

[94] These and the preceding example are taken from Killing, *Grundlagen*, loc. cit. The last is not, however, worked out.

the homogeneous coordinates (t) being supposed to define a point of the absolute conic. The two fixed points must be real, in order that the line joining them shall be actual, and its pole, the fixed point, ideal. In other words, we wish for groups of binary linear substitutions which contain members of the hyperbolic type exclusively. Apparently such groups have not, as yet, been found. It might seem, at first, that parabolic transformations where the two fixed points of the conic fall together, would also answer, but such is not the case. We may show, in fact, that in such a substitution there will be points of the plane which are transformed by as small a distance as we please. The path curves are horocycles touching the absolute conic at the fixed point: having in fact, four-point contact with it. It is merely necessary to show that a horocycle of the family may be found which cuts two lines through the fixed point in two points as near together as we please. Let this fixed point be $(0, 0, 1)$ while the absolute conic has an equation of the form

$$x_0{}^2 + x_1 x_2 = 0.$$

The general type for the equation of a horocycle tangent at $(0, 0, 1)$ will be

$$(x_0{}^2 + x_1 x_2) + p x_1{}^2 = 0.$$

This will intersect the two lines

$$x_0 - l x_1 = 0, \quad x_0 - m x_1 = 0,$$

in the points $(l, 1, -(l^2 + p))$ $(m, 1, -(m^2 + p))$. The cosine of the kth part of their distance will be

$$\frac{(l-m)^2 + 2p}{2p},$$

an expression which will approach unity as a limit, as $\dfrac{1}{p}$ approaches zero.

The group of hyperbolic motions in three dimensions will, as we saw in Chapter VIII, depend upon the linear function of the complex variable

$$z' = \frac{\alpha z + \beta}{\gamma z + \delta}.$$

The group which we require must not contain rotations about a line tangent to the Absolute, for the reason which we have just seen, hence the complex substitution must not be parabolic. Again, we may not have rotations about actual lines, hence the path curves on the Absolute may not be conics in planes through an ideal line (the absolute polar of the axis of rotation); the substitutions may not be elliptic. The only allowable motions of hyperbolic space are rotations about ideal lines, which give hyperbolic substitutions, and screw motions, which give loxodromic ones. There does not seem to be any general theory of groups of linear transformations of the complex variable, which include merely hyperbolic and loxodromic members only.[95]

[95] For the general theory of discontinuous groups of linear substitutions, see Fricke-Klein, *Vorlesungen über die Theorie der automorphen Funktionen*, vol. i, Leipzig, 1897.

The group of repetitions of a single rotation about an ideal line may be put into the form $(k^2 = -1)$,

$$\begin{aligned}
\dot{x}_0{}' &= \dot{x}_0 \cosh n\theta - \dot{x}_3 \sin n\theta,\\
\dot{x}_1{}' &= \dot{x}_1,\\
\dot{x}_2{}' &= \dot{x}_2,\\
\dot{x}_3{}' &= \dot{x}_0 \sinh \theta + \dot{x}_3 \cosh \theta.
\end{aligned}$$

The fundamental regions in Σ will be bounded by pairs of planes through the line

$$x_0 = x_3 = 0.$$

The orthogonal trajectories of planes through this line will be equidistant curves whose centres lie thereon. A line in Σ connecting two points which are equivalent under the group will appear in S as a line crossing itself once.

We may, in like manner, write the group of repetitions of a single screw motion

$$\begin{aligned}
\dot{x}_0{}' &= \dot{x}_0 \cosh n\theta - \dot{x}_3 \sinh n\theta,\\
\dot{x}_1{}' &= \dot{x}_1 \cos n\phi - \dot{x}_2 \sin n\phi,\\
\dot{x}_2{}' &= \dot{x}_1 \sin n\phi + \dot{x}_2 \cos n\phi,\\
\dot{x}_3{}' &= \dot{x}_0 \sinh n\theta + \dot{x}_3 \cosh n\theta.
\end{aligned}$$

In elliptic space we obtain rather more satisfactory results. Every congruent transformation of the real elliptic plane is a rotation about an actual point, there being no ideal points. Hence, there are no two-dimensional multiply connected elliptic spaces. In three dimensions the case is different. Let us assume that $k = 1$, and consider the group of repetitions of a single screw motion. The angle of rotation about one axis is equal to the distance of translation along the other, and the two distances or angles of rotation must be of the form $\frac{\lambda\pi}{\nu}$, $\frac{\mu\pi}{\nu'}$ in order that there shall be no infinitesimal transformations in the group. Moreover, these two fractions must have the same denominator, for otherwise the group would contain rotations. We may therefore write the general equations

$$\begin{aligned}
x_0{}' &= x_0 \cos n\frac{\lambda\pi}{\nu} - x_1 \sin n\frac{\lambda\pi}{\nu},\\
x_1{}' &= x_0 \sin n\frac{\lambda\pi}{\nu} + x_1 \cos n\frac{\lambda\pi}{\nu},\\
x_2{}' &= x_2 \cos n\frac{\mu\pi}{\nu} - x_3 \sin n\frac{\mu\pi}{\nu},\\
x_3{}' &= x_2 \sin n\frac{\mu\pi}{\nu} + x_3 \cos n\frac{\mu\pi}{\nu},
\end{aligned}$$

where λ, μ, ν are constant integers, and n a variable integer. It will be found that the cosine of the distance of the points (x), (x') will be equal to unity only when n is divisible by ν, i.e. we have the identical transformation, so that there are no real fixed points nor points moved an infinitesimal distance. If $\lambda = \mu$ we have a translation (cf. Chapter VIII), for our transformation may be written in the quaternion form:[96]

$$(x_0' + x_1'i + x_2'j + x_3'k) = (\cos n\frac{\lambda\pi}{\nu} + \sin n\frac{\lambda\pi}{\nu}i)(x_0 + x_1 i + x_2 j + x_3 k).$$

The path-curves in Σ will be lines paratactic to either axis of rotation, and they will appear in S as simple closed loops of length $\frac{\pi}{\nu}$. Notice the close analogy of this case to the simplest case in euclidean space.

There is another translation group of elliptic space giving rise to a multiply connected space of a simple and interesting description. Let $\lambda_1 : \lambda_2$ be homogeneous parameters, locating the generators of one set on the Absolute. Each linear transformation of these will determine a translation. In particular, if we put

$$x_0 + ix_1 = \lambda_1, \quad x_2 - ix_3 = \lambda_2,$$

then the translation

$$(x_0' + x_1'i + x_2'j + x_3'k) = (a + bi + cj + dk)(x_0 + x_1 i + x_2 j + x_3 k),$$

may also be written

$$\lambda_1' = (a + bi)\lambda_1 - (c + di)\lambda_2,$$
$$\lambda_2' = (c - di)\lambda_1 + (a - bi)\lambda_2.$$

Now this is precisely the formula for the rotation of the euclidean sphere. The cosine of the distance traversed by the point (x) will be

$$\frac{a}{\sqrt{a^2 + b^2 + c^2 + d^2}},$$

which becomes equal to unity only when $b = c = d = 0$, i.e. when we have the identical transformation. The groups of elliptic translations which contain no infinitesimal transformations, are therefore identical with those of euclidean rotations about a fixed point which contain no infinitesimal members, whence

Theorem 3.[97] If a multiply connected elliptic space be transformed identically by a group of translations, that group is isomorphic with one of the groups of the regular solids. Conversely each group of the regular solids gives rise to a group of right or left elliptic translations, suitable to define a multiply connected space of elliptic type.

Of course the inner reason for this identity is that a real line meets the elliptic Absolute in conjugate imaginary points, corresponding to diametral imaginary

[96]Killing, *Grundlagen*, cit. p. 342, erroneously states that these translations are the only motions along one fixed line yielding a group of the desired type. The mistake is corrected by Woods, loc. cit., p. 68.

[97]Cf. Woods, loc. cit., p. 68.

values of the parameter for either set of generators, and a real point of a euclidean sphere is given by the value of its coordinate as a point of the Gauss sphere, while diametrically opposite points will be given by diametral values of the complex variable. The problem of finding elliptic translations, or euclidean rotations, depend therefore, merely on the problem of finding linear transformations of the complex variable which transport diametral values into diametral values.

CHAPTER XVIII

THE PROJECTIVE BASIS OF NON-EUCLIDEAN GEOMETRY

Our non-euclidean system of metrics, as developed in Chapter VII and subsequently, rests in the last analysis, upon a projective concept, namely, the cross ratio. The group of congruent transformations appeared in Chapter VII as a six-parameter collineation group, which left invariant a certain quadric called the Absolute. An exception must be made in the euclidean case where the congruent group was a six-parameter sub-group of the seven-parameter group which left a conic in place. We thus come naturally to the idea that a basis for our whole edifice may be found in projective geometry, and that non-euclidean metrical geometry may be built up by positing the Absolute, and defining distance as in Chapter VII. It is the object of the present chapter to show precisely how this may be done, starting once more at the very beginning.[98]

Axiom I. **There exists a class of objects, containing at least two distinct members, called points.**

Axiom II. **Each pair of distinct points belongs to a single sub-class called a line.**

The points shall also be said to be on the line, the line to pass through the points. A point common to two lines shall be called their intersection. It is evident from Axiom II that two lines with two common points are identical. We have thus ruled out the possibility of building up spherical geometry upon the present basis.

Axiom III. **Two distinct points determine among the remaining points of their line two mutually exclusive sub-classes, neither of which is empty.**

If the given points be A and B, two points belonging to different classes according to Axiom III shall be said to be *separated* by them, two belonging to the same class *not separated*.[99] We shall call such classes *separation classes*.

Axiom IV. **If P and Q be separated by A and B, then Q and P are separated by A and B.**

Axiom V. **If P and Q be separated by A and B, then A and B are separated by P and Q.**

We shall write this relation $PQ \int AB$ or $AB \int PQ$. If PQ be not separated by A and B, though on a line, or collinear, with them, we shall write $PQ \not\int AB$.

[98] The first writer to set up a suitable set of axioms for projective geometry was Pieri, in his *Principii della geometria di posizione*, cit. He has had many successors, as Enriques, *Lezioni di geometria proiettiva*, Bologna, 1898, or Vahlen, *Abstrakte Geometric*, cit., Parts II and III. Veblen and Young, 'A system of axioms for projective geometry,' *American Journal of Mathematics*, Vol. xxx, 1908.

[99] The axioms of separation were first given by Vailati, 'Sulle proprietà caratteristiche delle varietà a una dimensione,' *Rivista di Matematica*, v, 1895.

Axiom VI. **If four distinct collinear points be given there is a single way in which they may be divided into two mutually separating pairs.**

Theorem 1. $AB \int CD$ and $AE \int CD$, then $EB \not\int CD$.

For C and D determine but two separation classes on the line, and both B and E belong to that class which does not include A.

Theorem 2. If five collinear points be given, a chosen pair of them will either separate two of the pairs formed by the other three or none of them.

Let the five points be A, B, C, D, E. Let $AC \int DE$. Then, if $BC \int DE$, $AB \not\int DE$, and if $AB \int DE$, $BC \not\int DE$. But if we had $BC \not\int DE$ and $AB \not\int DE$, ABC would belong to the same separation class with regard to DE, and hence $AC \not\int DE$.

Theorem 3. If $AC \int BD$ and $AE \int CD$, then $AE \int BD$.

To begin with $BC \not\int AD$, $EC \not\int AD$; hence $BE \not\int AD$. Again, if we had $AB \int ED$, we should have $AB \int EC$, i.e. $AE \not\int BC$. But we have $AE \int CD$, hence $AE \int BD$ a contradiction with $AB \int ED$. As a result, since $BE \not\int AD$ and $AB \not\int ED$, we must have $AE \int BD$.

It will be clear that this theorem includes as a special case Theorem 3 of Chapter I. We have but to take A at a great distance.

Theorem 4. If $PA \int CD$, $PB \int CD$, $PQ \int AB$, then $PQ \int CD$. The proof is left to the reader.

It will follow from the fact that neither of our separation classes is empty that the assemblage of all points of a line is infinite and dense. We have but to choose one point of the line, and say that a point is between two others when it be separated thereby from the chosen point.

Axiom VII. **If all points of either separation class determined by two points A, B, be so divided into two sub-classes that no point of the first is separated from A by B and a point of the second, there will exist a single point C of this separation class of such a nature that no point of the first sub-class is separated from A by B and C, and none of the second is separated from B by A and C.**

It is clear that C may be reckoned as belonging to either sub-class, but that no other point enjoys this property. This axiom is one of continuity, let the reader make a careful comparison with XVIII of Chapter II.

Axiom VIII. **All points do not belong to one line.**

Definition. The assemblage of all points of all lines determined by a given point and all points of a line not containing the first shall be called a *plane*. Points or lines in the same plane shall be called *coplanar*.

Axiom IX. **A line intersecting in distinct points two of the three lines determined by three non-collinear points, intersects the third line.**

Let the reader compare this with the weaker Axiom XVI of Chapter I.

Theorem 5. A plane will contain completely every line whereof it contains two points.

Let the plane be determined by the point A and the line BC. If the two given points of the given line belong to BC or be A and a point of BC, the theorem is immediate. If not, let the line contain the points B' and C' of AB and AC respectively. Let P be any other point of the given line. Then BP will intersect AC, hence AP will intersect BC or will lie in the given plane.

Theorem 6. If A, B, C be three non-collinear points, then the planes determined by A and BC, by B and CA, and by C and AB are identical.

We have but to notice that the lines generating each plane lie wholly in each of the others.

Theorem 7. If A', B', C' be three non-collinear points of the plane determined by ABC, then the planes determined by $A'B'C'$ and ABC are identical.

This will come immediately from the two preceding.

Theorem 8. Two lines in the same plane always intersect.

Let B and C be two points of the one line, and A a point of the other, If A be also a point of BC the theorem is proved. If not, we may use the point A and the line BC to determine the plane, and our second line must be identical with a line through A meeting BC.

AXIOM X. **All points do not lie in one plane.**

Definition. The assemblage of all points of all lines which arc determined by a chosen point, and all points of a plane not containing the first point shall be called a *space*.

We leave to the reader the proofs of the following very simple theorems.

Theorem 9. A space contains completely every line whereof it contains two points.

Theorem 10. A space contains completely every plane whereof it contains three non-collinear points.

Theorem 11. The space determined by a point A and the plane BCD is identical with that determined by B and the plane CDA.

Theorem 12. If A', B', C', D' be four non-coplanar points of the space determined by A, B, C, D, then the two spaces determined by the two sets of four points are identical.

With regard to the last theorem it is clear that all points of the space determined by A', B', C', D' lie in that determined by A, B, C, D. Let us assume that B', C', D' are points of AB, AC, AD respectively. The planes BCD and $B'C'D'$ have a common line l, which naturally belongs to both spaces. Let us first assume that AA' does not intersect this line. Let A'' be the intersection of AA' with BCD. Then $A''B$ meets both $A'B'$ and l, hence, has two points in each space, or lies in each. Then the plane BCD lies in both spaces, as do the line $A'A''$ and the point A; the two spaces are identical. If, on the other hand, AA' meet l in A'', then A lies in both spaces. Furthermore $A'B$ will meet $A''B'$

in a point of both spaces, so that B will lie in both, and, by similar reasoning, C and D lie in both.

Theorem 13. Two planes in the same space have a common line.

Theorem 14. Three planes in the same space have a common line or a common point.

Practical limitation. All points, lines, and planes hereinafter considered are supposed to belong to one space.

Theorem 15. If three lines AA', BB', CC' be concurrent, then the intersections of AB and $A'B'$, of BC and $B'C'$, of CA and $C'A'$ are collinear, and conversely.

This is Desargues' theorem of two triangles. The following is the usual proof. To begin with, let us suppose that the planes ABC and $A'B'C$ are distinct. The lines AA', BB', and CC' will be concurrent in O outside of both planes. Then as AB and $A'B'$ are coplanar, they intersect in a point which must lie on the line l of intersection of the two planes ABC and $A'B'C'$, and a similar remark applies to the intersections of BC and $B'C'$, of CA and $C'A'$. Conversely, when these last-named three pairs of lines intersect, the intersections must be on l. Considering the lines AA', BB', and CC', we see that each two are coplanar, and must intersect, but all three are not coplanar. Hence the three are concurrent. The second case occurs where $A'B'C'$ are three non-collinear points of the plane determined by ABC. Let V and V' be two points without this plane collinear with O the point of concurrence of AA', BB', CC'. Then VA will meet $V'A'$ in A'', VB will meet $V'B'$ in B'', and VC will meet $V'C'$ in C''. The planes ABC and $A''B''C''$ will meet in a line l, and $B''C''$ will meet both BC and $B'C'$ in a point of l. In the same way CA will meet $C'A'$ on l, and AB will meet $A'B'$ on l. Conversely, if the last-named three pairs of lines meet in points of a line l in their plane, we may find $A''B''C''$ non-collinear points in another plane through l, so that $B''C''$ meets BC and $B'C'$ in a point of l, and similarly for $C''A''$, CA, $C'A'$ and for $A''B''$, AB, $A'B'$. Then by the converse of the first part of our theorem AA'', BB'', CC'' will be concurrent in V, and $A'A''$, $B'B''$, $C'C''$ concurrent in V'. Lastly, the three coaxal planes $VV'A''$, $VV'B''$, $VV'C''$ will meet the plane ABC in three concurrent lines AA', BB', CC'.

We have already remarked in Chapter VI on the dependence of this theorem for the plane either on the assumption of the existence of a third dimension, or of a congruent group.

Definition. If four coplanar points, no three of which are collinear, be given, the figure formed by the three pairs of lines determined by them is called a *complete quadrangle*. The original points are called the *vertices*, the pairs of lines the *sides*. Two sides which do not contain a common vertex shall be said to be *opposite*. The intersections of pairs of opposite sides shall be called *diagonal points*.

Theorem 16. If two complete quadrangles be so situated that five sides of one meet five sides of the other in points of a line, the sixth side of the first meets the sixth side of the second in a point of that line.

The figure formed by four coplanar lines, no three of which are concurrent, shall be called a *complete quadrilateral*. Their six intersections shall be called the *vertices*; two vertices being said to be opposite when they are not on the same side. The three lines which connect opposite pairs of vertices shall be called *diagonals*.

Definition. If A and C be two opposite vertices of a complete quadrilateral, while the diagonal which connects them meets the other two in B and D, then A and B shall be said to be *harmonically separated* by C and D.

Theorem 17. If A and C be harmonically separated by B and D, then B and D are harmonically separated by A and C.

The proof will come immediately from 15, after drawing two or three lines; we leave the details to the reader.

Definition. If A and C be harmonically separated by B and D, each is said to be the *harmonic conjugate* of the other with regard to these two points; the four points may also be said to form a *harmonic set*.

Theorem 18. A given point has a unique harmonic conjugate with regard to any two points collinear with it.

This is an immediate result of 16.

Theorem 19. If a point O be connected with four points A, B, C, D not collinear with it by lines OA, OB, OC, OD, and if these lines meet another line in A', B'. C', D' respectively, and, lastly, if A and C be harmonic conjugates with regard to B and D, then A' and C' are harmonic conjugates with regard to B' and D'.

We may legitimately assume that the quadrilateral construction which yielded A, B, C, D was in a plane which did not contain O, for this construction may be effected in any plane which contains AD. Then radiating lines through O will transfer this quadrilateral construction into another giving A', B', C', D'.

Definition. If a, b, c, d be four concurrent lines which pass through A, B, C, D respectively, and if A and C be harmonically separated by B and D, then a and c may properly be said to be harmonically separated by b and d, and b and d harmonically separated by a and c. We may also speak of a and c as harmonic conjugates with regard to b and d, or say that the four lines form a harmonic set.

Theorem 20. If four planes α, β, γ, δ determined by a line l and four points A, B, C, D meet another line in four points A', B', C', D' respectively, and if A and C be harmonically separated by B and D, then A' and C' are harmonically separated by B' and D'.

It is sufficient to draw the line AD' and apply 19.

Definition. If four coaxal planes α, β, γ, δ pass respectively through four points A, B, C, D where A and C are harmonically separated by B and D; then we may speak of α and γ as harmonically separated by β and δ, or β and δ as harmonically separated by α and γ. We shall also say that α and γ are harmonic conjugates with regard to β and δ, or that the four planes form a harmonic set.

We shall understand by *projection* the transformation (recently used) whereby coplanar points and lines are carried, by means of concurrent lines, into other coplanar points and lines. With this in mind, we have the theorem.

Theorem 21. Any finite number of projections and intersections will carry a harmonic set into a harmonic set.

Axiom XI. **If four coaxal planes meet two lines respectively in A, B, C, D and A', B', C', D' distinct points, and if $AC \int BD$ then $A'C' \int B'D'$.**

Definition. If $AC \int BD$ and l be any line not intersecting AD, we shall say that the planes lA and lC separate the planes lB and lD.

Definition. If the planes α and γ separate the planes β and δ, and if a fifth plane meet the four in a, b, c, d respectively, then we shall say that a and c separate b and d. A complete justification for this terminology will be found in Axiom XI and in the two theorems which now follow.

Theorem 22. The laws of separation laid down for points in Axioms III–VII hold equally for coplanar concurrent lines, and coaxal planes.

We have merely to bring the four lines or planes to intersect another line in distinct points, and apply XI.

Theorem 23. The relation of separation is unaltered by any finite number of projections and intersections.

Theorem 24. If A, B, C, D be four collinear points, and A and C be harmonically separated by B and D, then $AC \int BD$.

We have merely to observe that our quadrilateral construction for harmonic separation permits us to pass by two projections from A, B, C, D to C, B, A, D respectively, so that if we had $AB \int CD$ we should also have $CB \int AD$, and vice versa. Hence our theorem.

Before proceeding further, let us glance for a moment at the question of the independence of our axioms.

The author is not familiar with any system of projective geometry where XI is lacking. X naturally fails in plane geometry. Here IX must be suitably modified, and Desargues' theorem, our 15, must be assumed as an axiom. IX is lacking in the projective euclidean geometry where the ideal plane is excluded. VIII fails in the geometry of the single line, while VII is untrue in the system of all points with rational Cartesian coordinates. III, IV, V, VI may be shown to be serially independent.[100] II is lacking in the geometry of four points.

Besides being independent, our axioms possess the far more important characteristic of being consistent. They will be satisfied by any class of objects in one to one correspondence with all sets of real homogeneous coordinate values $x_0 : x_1 : x_2 : x_3$ not all simultaneously zero. A line may be defined as the assemblage of all objects whose coordinates are linearly dependent on those of

[100] Vailati, loc. cit., note quoting Padoa.

two. If A and C have the coordinates (x) and (y) respectively, while B and D have the coordinates $\lambda(x) + \mu(y)$ and $\lambda'(x) + \mu'(y)$, then A and C shall be said to be separated by B and D if

$$\frac{\lambda\mu'}{\lambda'\mu} < 0.$$

When this is not the case, they shall be said to be not separated by B and D.

As a next step in our development of the science of projective geometry, let us take up the concept of cross ratio. Suppose that we have three distinct collinear points P_∞, P_0, P_1. Construct the harmonic conjugate of P_0 with regard to P_1 and P_∞, and call it P_2, that of P_1 with regard to P_2 and P_∞, and call it P_3, that of P_1 with regard to P_0 and P_∞, and call it P_{-1}, and so, in general, construct P_{n+1} and P_{n-1} harmonic conjugates with regard to P_n and P_∞. The construction is very rapidly performed as follows. Take O and V collinear with P_∞, while our given points lie on the line l_0. Let l_1 be the line from the intersection of OP_1 and VP_0 to P_∞. Then OP_{n+1} and VP_n will always intersect on l_1, the generic name for such a point being Q_{n+1}.[101]

Theorem 25. $\qquad P_0P_{n+1} \int P_nP_\infty$ if $n > 0$.

The theorem certainly holds when $n = 1$. Suppose that $P_0P_n \int P_{n-1}P_\infty$. We also know that $P_{n-1}P_{n+1} \int P_nP_\infty$. Hence, clearly $P_0P_{n+1} \int P_nP_\infty$. We notice also that $P_0P_{n+2} \int P_nP_\infty$, and, in general $P_0P_{n+k} \int P_nP_\infty$. A similar proof may be found for the case where negative subscripts are involved.

Theorem 26. If P be any point which satisfies the condition $P_0P \int P_1P_\infty$, then such a positive integer n may be found that $P_0P \int P_nP_\infty$, $P_0P_{n+1} \int PP_\infty$.

Let us divide all points of the separation class determined by P_0P_∞ which include P_1 and P the positive separation class let us say, into two sub-classes as follows. A point A shall be assigned to the first class if we may find such a positive integer n that $P_0P_{n+1} \int AP_\infty$, otherwise it shall be assigned to the second class, i.e. for every point of the second class and every positive integral value of n, $P_0B \int P_{n+1}P_\infty$. Then, by 3, as long as A and B are distinct we shall have $P_0B \int AP_\infty$, giving a dichotomy of the sort demanded by Axiom VII, and a point of division D. Let us further assume that OD meets l_1 in $\overline{D}$, and $V\overline{D}$ meets l_0 in C. We know that $\overline{D}Q_1 \not\int Q_0Q_\infty$. Hence lines from P_0 to V and $\overline{D}$ are not separated by those to O and P_∞. Hence lines from $\overline{D}$ to P_0 and V, are not separated by those to O and P_∞, so that $P_0C \not\int DP_\infty$ or C is a point of the first sub-class. We may, then, find n so great that $P_0P_n \int CP_\infty$, hence $Q_1Q_{n+1} \int DP_\infty$ and $P_1P_{n+1} \int DP_\infty$. But $P_0P_1 \not\int DP_\infty$; hence $P_0P_{n+1} \int DP_\infty$.

---

[101]See Fig. 4 on page following.

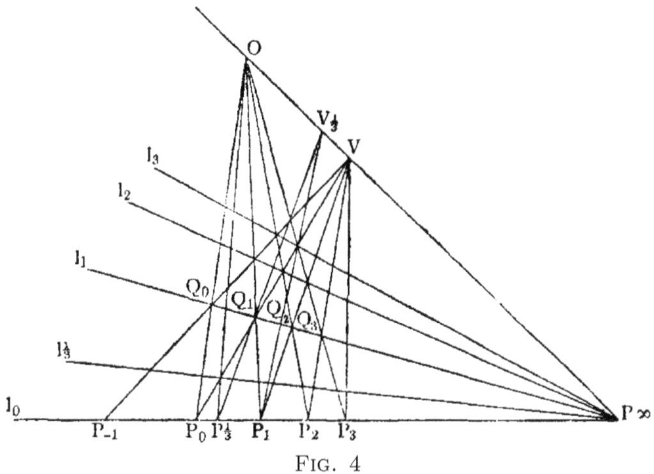

FIG. 4

This, however, is absurd, for a point separated from P_0 by D and P_{n+1} would have to belong to both classes. Our theorem results from this contradiction.

We might treat the case where $P_0P \int P_{-1}P_\infty$ in exactly the same way. Our net result is that if P be any point of the line l_0, it is either a point of the system we have constructed, or else we may find two such successive integers (calling $_0$ an integer) n, $n+1$ that $P_nP_{n+1} \int PP_\infty$.

Our next care shall be to find points of the line to which we may properly assign fractional subscripts. Let l_k be the line from P_∞, to the intersection of OP_k with VP_0. Then I say that VP_m and OP_{m+k} meet on l_k. This is certainly true when $k = 1$ Let us assume it to be true in the case of l_{k-1} so that VP_1 and OP_k meet on l_{k-1}. Then l_k is constructed with regard to l_{k-1} as was l_1 with regard to l_0, for we take a point of l_{k-1}, connect it with O and find where that line meets VP_0. In like manner VP_2 meets OP_{k+1} on l_{k-1} and OP_{k+2} on l_k and so on; VP_m meets OP_{m+k} on l_k, which was to be proved.

As an application of this we observe that l_n meets VP_n on the line OP_{2n}, hence we easily see that P_n and P_∞ are harmonically separated by P_0 and P_{2n}. Secondly, find the points into which the points P_h, P_k, P_l are projected from O on the line VP_m. These points lie on the lines l_{h-m}, l_{k-m}, l_{l-m}. Find the intersections of the latter with VP_n and project back from O on l_0; we get the points P_{n+h-m}, P_{n+k-m}, P_{n+l-m}. A particular result of this will be that $P_kP_{k+n}P_{k+2n}P_\infty$ form a harmonic set.

Let us now draw a line from P_1 to the intersection of VP_0 and l_n, and let this meet $P_\infty V$ in $V_{\frac{1}{n}}$ Then if P_0, P_k, P_l, P_∞ be projected from O upon P_0V and then projected back from $V_{\frac{1}{n}}$ upon l_0, we get points which we may call P_0, $P_{\frac{k}{n}}$, $P_{\frac{l}{n}}$, P_∞ where $P_{\frac{n}{n}} = P_1$. Connect P_∞ with the intersection of VP_0 and $OP_{\frac{1}{n}}$

by a line $l_{\frac{1}{n}}$. We may use this line to find $P_{\frac{k}{n}}$ as formerly we used l_1 to find P_k. We shall thus find that P_0 and $P_{\frac{2n}{n}}$ are harmonically separated by $P_{\frac{n}{n}}$ and P_∞, or $P_{\frac{2n}{n}}$ is identical with P_2, and similarly $P_{\frac{rn}{n}}$ is identical with P_r. Subdividing still further we shall find that $P_{\frac{r}{rn}}$ is identical with $P_{\frac{1}{n}}$ or $P_{\frac{rm}{rn}}$ identical with $P_{\frac{m}{n}}$. We have thus found a single definite point to correspond to each positive rational subscript. Negative rational subscripts might be treated in the same way, and eventually we shall find a single point whose subscript is any chosen rational number. We shall also find by reducing to a common denominator, that if

$$q > p > 0, \quad P_0P_q \int P_pP_\infty,$$

with a similar rule for negative numbers.

It remains to take up the irrational case. Let P be any point of the positive separation class determined by P_0 and P_∞. Then either it is a point with a rational subscript, according to our scheme, or else, however great soever n may be, we may find m so that $P_0P \int P_{\frac{m}{n}}P_\infty$, $P_0P_{\frac{m+1}{n}} \int PP_\infty$. We thus have a dichotomy of the positive rational number system of such a nature that a number of the lower class will correspond to a point separated from P_∞ by P_0 and P while one of the upper class will correspond to a point separated from P_0 by P and P_∞. There will be no largest number in the lower class. We know, in fact, that wherever R may be in the positive separation class of P_0P_∞ we may find n' so great that $P_0P_{n'} \int RP_\infty$. We may express this by saying that $P_{n'}$ approaches P_∞ as a limit as n' increases. Hence, as separation is invariant under projection, $l_{n'}$ approaches $P_\infty O$ as a limit and $P_{\frac{1}{n'}}$ approaches P_0 as a limit, or $P_{\frac{m}{n}+\frac{1}{n'}}$ approaches $P_{\frac{m}{n}}$ as a limit. We can thus find n' so large that $P_{\frac{m}{n}+\frac{1}{n'}}$ is also a number of the first class, and surely $\dfrac{m}{n} + \dfrac{1}{n'} > \dfrac{m}{n}$. In the same way we show that there can be no smallest number in the upper class. Finally each number of the upper is greater than each of the lower. Hence a perfect dichotomy is effected in the system of positive rationals defining a precise irrational number, and this may be assigned as a subscript to P. A similar proceeding will assign a definite subscript to each point of the other negative separation class of P_0P_∞.

Conversely, suppose that we have given a positive irrational number. This will be given by a dichotomy in the system of positive rationals, and corresponding thereto we may establish a classification among the points of the positive separation class of P_0P_∞ according to the requirement of Axiom VII. We shall, in fact, assign a point A of this separation class to the lower sub-class if we may find such a number in the lower number class that the point with the corresponding subscript is separated from P_0 by P_∞ and A; otherwise a point shall be assigned to the upper sub-class. If thus A and B be any two points of the lower and upper sub-classes respectively, we can find $\dfrac{m}{n}$ in the lower number class so that $P_0P_{\frac{m}{n}} \int AP_\infty$ whereas $P_0B \int P_{\frac{m}{n}}P_\infty$, and, hence, by 3, $P_0B \int AP_\infty$.

This shows that all of the requirements of Axiom VII are fulfilled, we may assign as subscript to the resulting point of division the irrational in question. In the same way we may assign a definite point to any negative irrational. The one to one correspondence between points of a line and the real number system including ∞ is thus complete.

Definition. If A, B, C, D be four collinear points, whereof the first three are necessarily distinct, the subscript which should be attached to D, when A, B, C are made to play respectively the rôles of P_∞, P_0, P_1 in the preceding discussion, shall be called a *cross ratio* of the four given points, and indicated by the symbol (AB, CD). Four points which are distinct would thus seem to have twenty-four different cross ratios, as a matter of fact they have but six.

We know that the harmonic relation is unaltered by any finite number of projections and intersections. We may therefore define the cross ratios of four concurrent coplanar lines, or four coaxal planes, by the corresponding cross ratios of the points where they meet any other line.

Theorem 27. Cross ratios are unaltered by any finite number of projections and intersections.

Definition. The range of all collinear points, the pencil of all concurrent coplanar lines, and the pencil of coaxal planes shall be called *fundamental one-dimensional forms*.

Definition. Two fundamental one-dimensional forms shall be said to be *projective* if they may be put into such a one to one correspondence that corresponding cross ratios are equal.

Theorem 28. If in two projective one-dimensional forms three elements of one lie in the corresponding elements of the other, then every element of the first lies in the corresponding element of the second.

For we may use these three elements in each case as ∞, 0, 1, and then, remembering the definition of cross ratio, make use of the fact that the construction of the harmonic conjugate of a point with regard to two others is unique. This theorem is known as the fundamental one of projective geometry.[102]

Theorem 29. If two fundamental one-dimensional forms be connected by a finite number of projections and intersections they are projective.

This comes immediately from 27.

Theorem 30. If two fundamental one-dimensional forms be projective, they may be connected by a finite number of projections and intersections.

It is, in fact, easy to connect them with two other projective forms whereof one contains three, and hence all corresponding members of the other.

Let us now turn back for a moment to our cross ratio scale. We have already seen that in the case of integers, and, hence, by reducing to least common denominator, in the case of all rational numbers k, l, m, n.

$$(P_\infty P_m, P_l P_n) = (P_\infty P_{m+k}, P_{l+k} P_{n+k}).$$

By letting k, l, m, n become irrational, one at a time, and applying a limiting process, we see that this equation is always true.

[102]For an interesting historical note concerning this theorem, see Vahlen, loc. cit., p. 161.

In like manner we see that P_0, P_q, P_{2q}, P_∞ form a harmonic set, as do P_k, P_{q+k}, P_{2q+k}, P_∞. In general, therefore,

$$\begin{aligned}(P_\infty P_0, P_1 P_\nu) &= (P_\infty P_0, P_n P_{n\nu}) \\ &= (P_\infty P_\alpha, P_{n+\alpha} P_{n\nu+\alpha}) \\ &= \nu.\end{aligned}$$

Putting $\quad n + \alpha = \beta, \quad n\nu + \alpha = \gamma,$

$$(P_\infty P_\alpha,\ P_\beta P_\gamma) = \frac{\gamma - \alpha}{\beta - \alpha}.$$

We next remark that the cross ratio of four points is that of their harmonic conjugates with regard to two fixed points. Reverting to our previous construction for $P_{\frac{1}{n}}$ we see that it is collinear with $V_{\frac{1}{n}}$ and Q_1. VQ_0P_{-1} are also on a line. If, then, we compare the triads of points VP_0Q_0, $V_{\frac{1}{n}}P_1Q_1$, since lines connecting corresponding points are concurrent in P_∞, the intersections of corresponding lines are collinear. But the line from O to the intersection of $V_{\frac{1}{n}}P_1$ with VP_0 (or VQ_1) is, by construction, the line OP_n. Hence VP_{-1}, which is identical with VQ_0, meets $V_{\frac{1}{n}}P_{\frac{1}{n}}$ on OP_n. Furthermore O and Q_1 are harmonically separated by the intersections of their line with VP_{-1} and $V_{\frac{1}{n}}P_1$; i.e. by P_1 and the intersection with VQ_0. Project these four upon l_0 from the intersection of OP_n and VP_{-1}. We shall find P_n and $P_{\frac{1}{n}}$ are harmonic conjugates with regard to P_1 and P_{-1}. Let the reader show that this last relation holds equally when n is a rational fraction, and, hence, when it takes any real value.

The preceding considerations will enable us to find the cross ratio of four points which do not include P_∞ in their number. To begin with

$$\begin{aligned}(P_0P_\beta, P_\gamma P_\delta) &= (P_\infty P_{\frac{1}{\beta}}, P_{\frac{1}{\gamma}} P_{\frac{1}{\delta}}) \\ &= \frac{\gamma}{\beta} \times \frac{\beta - \delta}{\beta - \gamma}.\end{aligned}$$

Let us project our four points from V upon l_α, then back upon l_0 from O. This will add α to each subscript. Then replace $\gamma + \alpha$ by γ, &c.

$$(P_\alpha B_\beta, P_\gamma P_\delta) = \frac{\alpha - \gamma}{\alpha - \delta} \times \frac{\beta - \delta}{\beta - \gamma}. \tag{1}$$

Theorem 31. Four elements of a fundamental one-dimensional form determine six cross ratios which bear to one another the relations of the six numbers

$$\lambda, \quad \frac{1}{\lambda}, \quad 1 - \lambda, \quad \frac{1}{1-\lambda}, \quad \frac{\lambda - 1}{\lambda}, \quad \frac{\lambda}{\lambda - 1}.$$

The proof is perfectly straightforward, and is left to the reader.

If three points be taken as fundamental upon a straight line, any other point thereon may be located by a pair of homogeneous coordinates whose ratio is a definite cross ratio of the four points. We shall assign to the fundamental points the coordinates $(1,0)$, $(0,1)$, $(1,1)$. A cross ratio of four points (x), (y), (z), (t) will then be

$$\frac{\begin{vmatrix} x_0 & z_0 \\ x_1 & z_1 \end{vmatrix} \cdot \begin{vmatrix} y_0 & t_0 \\ y_1 & t_1 \end{vmatrix}}{\begin{vmatrix} y_0 & z_0 \\ y_1 & z_1 \end{vmatrix} \cdot \begin{vmatrix} x_0 & t_0 \\ x_1 & t_1 \end{vmatrix}}. \tag{2}$$

Any projective transformation of the line into itself, i.e. any point to point transformation which leaves cross ratios unaltered, will thus take the form

$$\begin{aligned} P{x_0}' &= a_{00}x_0 + a_{01}x_1, \\ P{x_2}' &= a_{10}x_0 + a_{11}x_1, \end{aligned} \qquad |a_{ij}| \neq 0. \tag{3}$$

To demonstrate this we have merely to point out that surely this transformation is a projective one, and that we may so dispose of our arbitrary constants as to carry any three distinct points into any other three, the maximum amount of freedom for any projective transformation of a fundamental one-dimensional form. Let the reader show that the necessary and sufficient condition that there should be two real self-corresponding points which separate each pair of corresponding points is

$$|a_{ij}| < 0.$$

Two projective sets on the same fundamental one-dimensional form whose elements correspond interchangeably, are said to form an *involution.* By this is meant that each element of the form has the same corresponding element whether it be assigned to the first or to the second set. It will be found that the necessary and sufficient condition for an involution in the case of equation (3) will be

$$a_{01} = a_{10}. \tag{4}$$

When the determinant $|a_{ij}| > 0$, there will be no self-corresponding points, and the involution is said to be *elliptic.* Let the reader show that under these circumstances each pair of the involution separates each other pair.

Our next task shall be to set up a suitable coordinate system for the plane and for space. Let us take in the plane four points A, B, C, D, no three being collinear. We shall assign to these respectively the coordinates $(1,0,0)$, $(0,1,0)$, $(0,0,1)$, $(1,1,1)$. Let AD meet BC in A_1, BD meet CA in B_1, and CD meet AB in C_1. The intersections of AB, A_1B_1, of BC, B_1C_1, and of CA, C_1A_1, are, by 15, on a line d. Now let P be any other point in the plane

$$\begin{aligned} &(AB\,AC, AD\,AP) = (PC_1PC, PD\,PA) = (PC\,PC_1, PA\,PD) \\ &(BC\,BA, BD\,BP) = (PC\,PC_1, PD\,PB) \\ &(CA\,CB, CD\,CP) = (PC_1PC, PA\,PB) = \frac{1}{(PC\,PC_1, PA\,PB)}. \end{aligned}$$

From this it is clear that the product of the three is equal to unity, and we may represent them by three numbers of the type $\frac{x_1}{x_0}$, $\frac{x_2}{x_1}$, $\frac{x_0}{x_2}$. We may therefore take $x_0 : x_1 : x_2$ as three homogeneous coordinates for the point P. One coordinate will vanish for a point lying on one of the lines AB, BC, CA. Let the reader convince himself that the usual cartesian system is but a special case of this homogeneous coordinate system where two of the four given points are ideal, and

$$\frac{x_1}{x_0} = x, \quad \frac{x_2}{x_0} = y.$$

The equations of the lines connecting two of the points A, B, C are of the form

$$x_i = 0.$$

Those which connect each of these with the point D are similarly

$$x_i - x_j = 0.$$

If (y) and (z) be two points, not collinear with A, B, or C, while P is a variable point with coordinates $\lambda(y) + \mu(z)$, the lines connecting it with A and B will meet BC and (CA) respectively in the points

$$(0,\ \lambda y_1 + \mu z_1,\ \lambda y_2 + \mu z_2) \quad (\lambda y_0 + \mu z_0,\ 0,\ \lambda y_2 + \mu z_2).$$

It is easy to see that the expressions for corresponding cross ratios in these two ranges are identical, hence the ranges are projective. The pencils which they determine at A and B are therefore projective, and have the line AB self-corresponding, for this will correspond to the parameter value

$$\lambda : \mu = z_2 : -y_2.$$

But it will follow immediately from 28, that if two pencils be coplanar and projective, with a self-corresponding line, the locus of the intersection of their corresponding members is also a line. Hence the locus of the point P with the coordinates $\lambda(y) + \mu(z)$ is the line connecting (y) and (z). Conversely, it is evident that every point of the line from (y) to (z) will have coordinates linearly dependent on those of (y) and (z). If, then, we put

$$x_i = \lambda y_i + \mu z_i,$$

and eliminate $\lambda : \mu$, we have as equation of the line

$$|xyz| = (ux) = 0.$$

Conversely, it is evident that such an equation will always represent a line, except, of course, in the trivial case where the u's are all zero. Let the reader show that the coefficients u_i have a geometrical interpretation dual to that of the coordinates x_i; for this purpose the line which we have above called d will be found useful.

Our system of homogeneous coordinates may be extended with great ease to space. Suppose that we have given five points A, B, C, D, O no four being coplanar. Let P be any other point in space. We may write

$$(ABC\,ABD, ABO\,ABP) = \frac{x_3}{x_2}, \quad (ACD\,ACB, ACO\,ACP) = \frac{x_1}{x_3},$$

$$(ADB\,ADC, ADO\,ADP) = \frac{x_2}{x_1}.$$

We shall then be able to write also

$$(CDA\,CDB, CDO\,CDP) = \frac{x_1}{x_0}, \quad (DBA\,DBC, DBO\,DBP) = \frac{x_2}{x_0},$$

$$(BCD\,BCA, BCO\,BCP) = \frac{x_0}{x_3}.$$

In other words, we may give to a point four homogeneous coordinates $x_0 : x_1 : x_2 : x_3$. Two points collinear with A, B, C, or D will differ (or may be made to differ) in one coordinate only. An equation of the first degree in three coordinates will represent a plane through one of these four points. Every line will be the intersection of two such planes, and will be represented by the combination of two linear equations one of which lacks x_i while the other lacks x_j. The coordinates of all points of a line may therefore be expressed as a linear combination of the coordinates of any two points thereof. A plane may be represented as the assemblage of all points whose coordinates are linearly dependent on those of three non-collinear points. Eliminating the variable parameters from the four equations for the coordinates of a point in a plane, we see that a plane may also be given by an equation of the type

$$(ux) = 0. \tag{5}$$

Conversely, the assemblage of all points whose coordinates satisfy an equation such as (5) will be of such a nature that it will contain all points of a line whereof it contains two distinct points, yet will meet a chosen line, not in it, but once. Let the reader show that such an assemblage must be a plane. The homogeneous parameters (u) which, naturally, may not all vanish together, may be called the coordinates of the plane. They will have a significance dual to that of the coordinates of a point.[103]

If we have four collinear points

$$(y), \quad (z), \quad \lambda(y) + \mu(z), \quad \lambda'(y) + \mu'(z),$$

one cross ratio will be $$\frac{\lambda\mu'}{\lambda'\mu}.$$

[103]The treatment of cross ratios in the present chapter is based on that of Pasch, loc. cit. The development of the coordinate system is also taken from the same source, though it has been possible to introduce notable simplification, especially in three dimensions. This method of procedure seemed to the author more direct and natural than the more modern method of 'Streckenrechnung' of Hilbert or Vahlen, loc. cit.

The proof will consist in finding the points where four coaxal planes through these four points meet the line

$$x_2 = x_3 = 0$$

and then applying (2).

Suppose that we have a transformation of the type

$$\rho x_i{}' = \sum_{j}^{0..3} a_{ij} x_j. \tag{6}$$

This shall be called a *collineation.* We shall restrict ourselves to those collineations for which

$$|a_{ij}| \neq 0.$$

The transformation is, clearly, one to one, with no exceptional points. It will carry a plane into a plane, a line into a line, a complete quadrilateral into a complete quadrilateral, and a harmonic set into a harmonic set. It will therefore leave cross ratios invariant. Moreover, every point to point and plane to plane transformation will be a collineation. For every such transformation will enjoy all of the properties which we have mentioned with regard to a collineation, and will, therefore, be completely determined when once we know the fate of five points, no four of which are coplanar. But we easily see that we may dispose of the arbitrary constants in (6), to carry any such five points into any other five.

It is worth while to pause for a moment at this point in order to see what geometrical meaning may be attached to coordinate sets which have imaginary values. This question has already been discussed in Chapter VII. Every set of complex coordinates

$$(y) + i(z),$$

may be taken to define the elliptic involution

$$(x) = \lambda(y) + \mu(z), \quad x' = \lambda'(y) + \mu'(z), \quad \lambda\lambda' + \mu\mu' = 0. \tag{7}$$

To verify this statement we have merely to notice that an involution will, by definition, be carried into an involution by any number of projections and intersections, and that equations such as (7) will go into other such equations. But in the case of the line

$$x_2 = x_3 = 0,$$

these equations will give an involution, for the relation between (x) and (x') may readily be reduced to the type of (3) and (4). Did we seek the analytic expression for the coordinates of a self-corresponding point in (7) we should get the values

$$(y) + i(z).$$

Conversely, it is easy to show that any elliptic involution may be reduced to the type of (7). There is, therefore, a one to one correspondence between the assemblage of all elliptic point involutions, and all sets of pairs of conjugate imaginary coordinate values.

The correspondence between coordinate sets and elliptic involutions may be made more precise in the following fashion. Two triads of collinear points ABC, $A'B'C'$ shall be said to have the *same sense* when the projective transformation which carries the one set, taken in order, into the other, has a positive determinant; when the determinant is negative they shall be said to have *opposite senses*. In this latter case alone, as we have already seen, will there be two real self-corresponding points which separate each distinct pair of corresponding points. Two triads which have like or opposite senses to a third, have like senses to one another, for the determinant of the product of two projective transformations of the line into itself is the product of the determinants. We shall also find that the triads ABC, BCA, CAB have like senses, while each has the sense opposite to that of either of the triads ACB, CBA, BAC. We may thus say that three points given in order will determine a sense of description for the whole range of points on the line, in that the cyclic order of any other three points which are to have the same sense as the first three is completely determined. It is immediately evident that any triad of points and their mates in an elliptic involution have the same sense. We may therefore attach to such an elliptic involution either the one or the other sense of description for the whole range of points.

Definition. An elliptic involution of points to which is attached a particular sense of description of the line on which they are situated shall be defined as an *imaginary point*. The same involution considered in connexion with the other sense shall be called the *conjugate imaginary point.*

Starting with this, we may define an imaginary plane as an elliptic involution in an axial pencil, in connexion with a sense of description for the pencil; when the other sense is taken in connexion with this involution we shall say that we have the conjugate imaginary plane. An imaginary point shall be said to be in an imaginary plane if the pairs of the involution which determine the point lie in pairs of planes of the involution determining the plane, and if the sense of description of the line associated with the point engenders among the planes the same sense as is associated with the imaginary plane. Analytically let us assume that besides the involution of points given by (7) we have the following involution of planes.

$$(u) = l(v) + m(w), \quad (u') = l'(v) + m'(w), \quad ll' + mm' = 0,$$

$$(vy) = (wz) = 0. \tag{8}$$

The plane (u) will contain the point $l(vz)(y) - m(wy)(z)$ while its mate in the involution contains the point

$$m(vz)(y) + l(wy)(z).$$

These points will be mates in the point involution, if

$$[(vz) + (wy)]\,[(vz) - (wy)] = 0,$$

and these equations tell us that the imaginary plane $(v) + i(w)$ will contain either the point $(y) + i(z)$, or the point $(y) - i(z)$. An imaginary line may be defined as the assemblage of all points common to two imaginary planes. Imaginary points, lines, and planes obey the same laws of connexion as do real ones. A geometric proof may be found based upon the definitions given, but it is immediately evident analytically.[104]

Theorem 32. If a fundamental one-dimensional form be projectively transformed into itself there will be two distinct or coincident self-corresponding elements.

We have merely to put (ρx) for (x') in (3), and solve the quadratic equation in ρ obtained by equating to zero the determinant of the two linear homogeneous equations in x_0, x_1.

The assemblage of all points whose coordinates satisfy an equation of the type

$$\Sigma\, a_{ij}x_ix_j = 0, \quad |a_{ij}| \neq 0,$$

shall be called a *quadric*. We should find no difficulty in proving all of the well-known theorems of a descriptive sort connected with quadrics in terms of our present coordinates.

We have now, at length, reached the point where we may profitably introduce metrical concepts. Let us recall that the group of congruent transformations which we considered in Chapter II, and, more fully, in Chapter VIII, is a group of collineations which leaves invariant either a quadric or a conic, and depends upon six parameters. We also saw in Chapter II, that the congruent group may be characterized as follows (cf. p. 38):—

(*a*) Any real point of a certain domain may be carried into any other such point.

(*b*) Any chosen real point may be left invariant, and any chosen real line through it carried into any other such line.

(*c*) Any real point and line through it may be left invariant, and any real plane through this line may be carried into any other such plane.

(*d*) If a real point, a line through it, and a plane through the line be invariant, no further infinitesimal congruent transformations are possible.

It shall be our present task to show that these assumptions, or rather the last three, joined to the ones already made in the present chapter, will serve to define hyperbolic elliptic and euclidean geometry.

It is assumed that there exists an assemblage of transformations, called congruent transformations, obeying the following laws:—

Axiom XII. **The assemblage of all congruent transformations is a group of collineations, including the inverse of each member.**[105]

[104]See von Staudt, loc. cit., and Lüroth, loc. cit. It is to be noted that in these works the idea of sense of description is taken intuitively, and not given by precise definitions.

[105]It is highly remarkable that this axiom is superfluous. Cf. Lie-Engel, *Theorie der Transformationsgruppen*, Leipzig, 1888–93, vol. iii, Ch. XXII, § 98. The assumption that our congruent transformations are collineations, does, however, save an incredible amount of labour, and, for that reason, is included here.

Axiom XIII. **The group of congruent transformations may be expressed by means of analytic relations among the parameters of the general collineation group.**

Definition. The assemblage of all real points whose coordinates satisfy three inequalities of the type

$$\xi_i < \frac{x_i}{x_0} < X_i, \quad i = 1, 2, 3,$$

shall be called a *restricted region.*

Axiom XIV. **A congruent transformation may be found leaving invariant any point of a restricted region, and transforming any real line through that point into any other such line.**

Axiom XV. **A congruent transformation may be found leaving invariant any point of a restricted region, and any real line through that point; yet carrying any real plane through that line into any other such plane.**

Axiom XVI. **There exists no continuous assemblage of congruent transformations which leave invariant a point of a restricted region, a real line through that point, and a real plane through that line.**

Theorem 33. The congruent group is transitive for a sufficiently small restricted region.

This comes at once by *reductio ad absurdum.* For the tangents to all possible paths which a chosen point might follow would, if 33 were untrue, generate a surface or set of surfaces, or a line or set of lines, and this assemblage of surfaces or lines would be carried into itself by every congruent transformation which left this point invariant. The tangent planes to the surfaces, or the lines in question, could not, then, be freely interchanged with other planes or lines through the point.

Theorem 34. The congruent group depends on six essential parameters.

The number of parameters is certainly finite since the congruent group arises from analytic relations among the fifteen essential parameters of the general collineation group. The transference from a point to a point imposes three restrictions, necessarily distinct, as three independent parameters are needed to determine a point. A fixed point being chosen, two more independent restrictions are imposed by determining the fate of any chosen real line through it. When a point and line through it are chosen, one more restriction is imposed by determining what shall become of any assigned plane through the line. When, however, a real plane, a real line therein, and a real point in the line are fixed, there can be no independent parameter remaining, as no further infinitesimal transformations are possible.

Let us now look more closely at the one-parameter family of projective transformations of the axial pencil through a fixed line of the chosen restricted region.[106] Let us determine any plane through this line by two homogeneous

[106]Cf. Lie-Scheffers, *Vorlesungen über continuierliche Gruppen.* Leipzig, 1893, p. 125.

parameters $\lambda_1 : \lambda_2$, and take an infinitesimal transformation of the group

$$\Delta\begin{pmatrix} \lambda_1 \\ \lambda_2 \end{pmatrix} = f\begin{pmatrix} \lambda_1 \\ \lambda_2 \end{pmatrix} dt.$$

The product of two such infinitesimal transformations will belong to our group, hence also, as none but analytic functions are involved, the limit of the product of an infinite number of such transformations as dt approaches zero; that is to say, the transformation obtained by integrating this equation belongs to the group. Now this integral will involve one arbitrary constant, which may be used to make the transformation transitive, and for all transformations obtained by this integration, that pair of planes will be invariant which was invariant for the infinitesimal transformation. Our one-parameter group has thus a transitive one-parameter sub-group with a single pair of planes invariant. These planes are surely conjugate imaginary, for otherwise there would be infinitesimal congruent transformations which left a point, line, and real plane invariant; contrary to our last axiom. The question of whether our whole one-parameter group is generated by this integration or not, need not detain us here. What is essential is that this pair of planes will be invariant for the whole group. For suppose that S_i indicate a generic transformation of the sub-group which leaves invariant the two planes α, α', and the transformation T carries the two planes α, α' into two planes β, β'. Then all transformations of the type

$$TS_iT^{-1}$$

will belong to our group, and leave the planes β, β' invariant, and combining these with the transformations S_i we have a two-parameter sub-group of our one-parameter group; an absurd result.

Let us next consider the three-parameter congruent group composed of all transformations which have a fixed point. If a real line l be carried into a real line l', then the two planes which were invariant with l will go into those which are invariant with l'. To prove this we have but to repeat the reasoning which lately showed that the two planes which were invariant for a sub-group, are invariant for the total one-parameter group. The envelope of all these invariant planes which pass through a point will thus depend upon one parameter, for if it depended on two it would include real planes, and this is not the case. It is well known that this system of planes must envelope lines or a quadric cone.[107] The first case is surely excluded for such lines would have to appear in conjugate imaginary pairs, giving rise to invariant real planes through this point, and there are no such in the three-parameter group. The envelope is therefore a cone with no real tangent planes. Each pair of conjugate imaginary tangent planes must touch it along two conjugate imaginary lines; the plane connecting these is real, and invariant for the one-parameter congruent group associated with the line of intersection of the two imaginary planes. Let us fix our attention upon one such one-parameter group and choose our coordinate system in such a way that the

[107]Cf. Lie-Scheffers, loc. cit., p. 289.

non-homogeneous coordinates $u, v, 1$ of our three fixed planes are proportional respectively to

$$(0,\ 0,\ 1), \quad (1,\ i,\ 0), \quad (1,\ -i,\ 0).$$

The general linear transformation keeping these three invariant is

$$u' = r\cos\theta u - r\sin\theta v, \quad v' = r\sin\theta u + r\cos\theta v.$$

Here r must be a constant, as otherwise we should have congruent transformations of the type

$$u' = ru, \quad v' = rv,$$

which kept a point, a line, and all planes through that line invariant, yet depended on an arbitrary parameter. In order to see what sort of cones are carried into themselves by this group, the cone we are seeking for being necessarily of the number, let us take an infinitesimal transformation

$$\Delta u = -\,vd\theta, \quad \Delta v = ud\theta.$$

Integrating $$u^2 + v^2 = C.$$

The cone we seek is therefore a quadric cone.

We see by a repetition of the sort of reasoning given above that if we take a congruent transformation that carries a point P into a point P', it will carry the invariant quadric cone whose vertex is P into that whose vertex is P'. The envelope of these quadric cones is, thus, invariant under the whole congruent group. The envelope of these cones must be a quadric or conic. This theorem is simpler when put into the dual form, i.e. a surface which meets every plane in a conic is a quadric or quadric cone. For it has just the same points in every plane as the quadric or cone through two of its conics and one other of its points. In our present case our quadric must have a real equation, since it touches the conjugate to each imaginary plane tangent thereto. There are, hence, three possibilities:

(a) The quadric is real, but the restricted region in question is within it.

(b) The quadric is imaginary.

(c) The quadric is an imaginary conic in a real plane.

Theorem 35. The congruent group is a six-parameter collineation group which leaves invariant a quadric or a conic.

It remains for us to find the expression for distance. We make the following assumptions.

Axiom XVII. **The distance of two points of a restricted region is a real value of an analytic function of their coordinates.**

Axiom XVIII. **If ABC be three collinear real points, and if B be separated by A and C from a point of their line not belonging to this restricted region; then the distance from A to C is the sum of the distance from A to B and the distance from B to C.**

Let the reader show that this definition is legitimate as all points separated from A by B and C, or from C by A and B will belong to the restricted region.

Let us first take cases (a) and (b) together. The distance must be a continuous function of each cross ratio determined by the two points and the intersections of their line with the quadric. If we call a distance d, and the corresponding cross ratio of this type c, we must have

$$c = f(d).$$

Moreover, from equation (1) and Axiom XIII,

$$f(d) \times f(d') = f(d + d').$$

Now this functional equation is well known, and the only continuous solution is[108]

$$\begin{aligned} c &= e^{2i\frac{d}{k}}. \\ \frac{d}{k} &= \frac{1}{2i} \log_e c. \end{aligned}$$

If, in particular, the two points be P_1P_2 while their line meets the quadric in Q_1Q_2, we shall have for our distance, equation (5) of Chapter VII

$$\frac{d}{k} = \frac{1}{2i} \log_e (P_1P_2, Q_1Q_2).$$

From this we may easily work back to the familiar expressions for the cosine of the kth part of the distance.

The case of an invariant conic is handled somewhat differently. Let the equations of the invariant conic be

$$x_0 = 0, \quad {x_1}^2 + {x_2}^2 + {x_3}^2 = 0.$$

These are unaltered by a seven-parameter group

$$\begin{aligned} x_0' &= a_{00}x_0, \\ x_1' &= a_{10}x_0 + a_{11}x_1 + a_{12}x_2 + a_{13}x_3, \\ x_2' &= a_{20}x_0 + a_{21}x_1 + a_{22}x_2 + a_{23}x_3, \\ x_3' &= a_{30}x_0 + a_{31}x_1 + a_{32}x_2 + a_{33}x_3, \end{aligned}$$

where $\| a_{11}\, a_{22}\, a_{33} \|$ is the matrix of a ternary orthogonal substitution. For our congruent group we must have the six-parameter sub-group where the determinant of this orthogonal substitution has the value ${a_{00}}^3$, for then only will there be no further infinitesimal transformations possible when a point, a line through it, and a plane through the line are fixed. We shall find that, under the present circumstances the expression

$$D = \left| \sqrt{\left(\frac{x_1}{x_0} - \frac{y_1}{y_0}\right)^2 + \left(\frac{x_2}{x_0} - \frac{y_2}{y_0}\right)^2 + \left(\frac{x_3}{x_0} - \frac{y_3}{y_0}\right)^2} \right|$$

[108]Cf. e.g. Tannery, *Théorie des fonctions d'une variable*, second edition, Paris, 1904, p. 275.

is an absolute invariant. If the distance of two points (x), (y) be d, we shall have

$$d = f(D).$$

This function is continuous and real, and satisfies the functional equation

$$f(D) + f(D') = f(D + D').$$

The solution of this equation is easily thrown back upon the preceding one. Let us put

$$\begin{aligned} f(x) &= \log \phi(x), \\ \phi(x)\phi(y) &= \phi(x + y), \\ \phi(x) &= e^{rx}. \end{aligned}$$

We thus get finally

$$d = r \left| \sqrt{\left(\frac{x_1}{x_0} - \frac{y_1}{y_0}\right)^2 + \left(\frac{x_2}{x_0} - \frac{y_2}{y_0}\right)^2 + \left(\frac{x_3}{x_0} - \frac{y_3}{y_0}\right)^2} \right|.$$

Theorem 36. Axioms I–XVIII are compatible with the hyperbolic, elliptic, or euclidean hypotheses, and with these only.

CHAPTER XIX

THE DIFFERENTIAL BASIS FOR EUCLIDEAN AND NON-EUCLIDEAN GEOMETRY

We saw in Chapter XV, Theorem 17, that the Gaussian curvature of a surface is equal to the sum of the total relative curvature, and the measure of curvature of space. A noneuclidean plane is thus a surface of Gaussian curvature equal to $\frac{1}{k^2}$. This fact was also brought out in Chapter V, Theorem 3, and we there promised to return in the present chapter to a more extensive examination of this aspect of our noneuclidean geometry.

In Chapter II, Theorem 30, we saw that the sum of the distances from a point to any other two, not collinear with it, when such a sum exists, is greater than the distance of these latter. We thus come naturally to look upon a straight line as a geodesic, or curve of minimum length between two points. A plane may be generated by a pencil of geodesics through a point; the geometrical simplicity of the plane may be said to arise from the fact that it is capable of ∞^2 such generations. The task which we now undertake is as follows:—to determine the nature of a three-dimensional point-manifold which possesses the property that every surface generated by a pencil of geodesics has constant Gaussian curvature. We must begin, as in previous chapters, with a sufficient set of axioms.[109]

Definition. Any set of objects which may be put into one to one correspondence with sets of real values of three independent coordinates z_1, z_2, z_3 shall be called *points*.

Definition. An assemblage of points shall be said to form a *restricted region*, when their coordinates are limited merely by inequalities of the type

$$\zeta_i < z_i < Z_i, \quad i = 1, 2, 3.$$

AXIOM I. **There exists a restricted region.**

AXIOM II. **There exist nine functions a_{ij}, $i, j = 1, 2, 3$ of z_1, z_2, z_3 real and analytic throughout the restricted region, and possessing the following properties**

$$a_{ij} = a_{ji}, \quad |a_{ij}| \not\equiv 0.$$

$$\sum_{ij}^{1,2,3} a_{ij} dz_i dz_j$$

is a positive definite form for all real values of dz_1, dz_2, dz_3 and all values of z_1, z_2, z_3 corresponding to points of the given restricted region.

[109]The first writer to approach the subject from this point of view was Riemann, loc. cit. The best presentation of the problem in its general form, and in a space of n-dimensions, will be found in Schur, 'Ueber den Zusammenhang der Räume constanten Riemannschen Krümmungsmasses mit den projectiven Räumen,' *Mathematische Annalen*, vol. 27, 1886.

Limitation. We shall restrict ourselves to such a portion of the original restricted region that for no point thereof shall the discriminant of our quadratic form be zero. This amounts to confining ourselves to the original region, or to a smaller restricted region within the original one.

Definition. The expression

$$ds = +\sqrt{\sum_{i,j}^{1,2,3} a_{ij} dz_i dz_j}$$

shall be called the *distance element.*

Definition. The assemblage of all points whose coordinates are analytic functions of a single parameter shall be called an *analytic curve*, or, more simply, a curve. As we have defined only those points whose coordinates are real, it is evident that the functions involved in the definition of a curve must be real also. The definite integral of the distance element between two chosen points along a curve shall be called the *length* of the corresponding portion or *arc* of the curve. If the curve pass many times through the chosen points, the expression *length* must be applied to that portion along which the integration was performed.

Definition. An arc of a curve between two fixed points which possesses the property that the first variation of its length is zero, shall be called *geodesic arc.* The curve whereon this arc lies shall be called a *geodesic* connecting the two points.

Let us begin by setting up the differential equations for a geodesic. Let us write

$$ds = \sqrt{\sum_{ij}^{1,2,3} a_{ij} \frac{dz_i}{dt} \frac{dz_j}{dt}} dt.$$

It is clear that s is an analytic function of t with no singularities in our region, hence t is an analytic function of s. We may, then, by taking our restricted region sufficiently small, express a_{ij} as functions of s, and write

$$\sum_{i,j}^{1,2,3} a_{ij} \frac{dz_i}{ds} \frac{dz_j}{ds} = 1. \tag{1}$$

Replacing $\frac{dz_i}{ds}$ temporarily by $z_i{}'$, we have

$$s = \int_0^s \sqrt{\sum_{i,j}^{1,2,3} a_{ij} z_i{}' z_j{}' ds}.$$

We have now a simple problem in the calculus of variations.

$$2\delta s = \int_0^s \sum_{i,j}^{1,2,3} \sum_{k}^{1,2,3} \left(\frac{\partial a_{ij}}{\partial z_k} z_i{}' z_j{}' \delta z_k + 2 a_{ij} z_i{}' \delta z_j{}' \right) ds.$$

$$\frac{d}{ds}\sum_{i,j}^{1,2,3} a_{ij}z_i{}'\delta z_j = \sum_{ij}^{1,2,3}\frac{d(a_{ij}z_i{}')}{ds}\delta z_j + \sum_{ij}^{1,2,3} a_{ij}z_i{}'\delta z_j{}',$$

hence, since δz_j vanishes at the extremities of the interval

$$2\delta s = \int_0^s \sum_j^{1,2,3}\left[\sum_{ik}^{1,2,3}\frac{\partial a_{ik}}{\partial z_j}z_i{}'z_k{}' - 2\sum_i \frac{d}{ds}(a_{ij}z_i{}')\right]\delta z_j ds,$$

the increments δz_j are arbitrary, hence the coefficients of each must vanish, or

$$\frac{d}{ds}\sum_i^{1,2,3} a_{ij}\frac{dz_i}{ds} = \frac{1}{2}\sum_{ik}^{1,2,3}\frac{\partial a_{ik}}{\partial z_j}\frac{\partial z_i}{\partial s}\frac{\partial z_k}{\partial s}. \tag{2}$$

These three equations are of the second order. There will exist a single set of solutions corresponding to a single set of initial values for (z) and (z').[110] Let these be (z^0) and (ζ) respectively. Any point of such a geodesic will be determined by $\zeta_1\zeta_2\zeta_3$ and r the length of the arc connecting it with (z^0). We have thus

$$z_i = z_i{}^0 + r\zeta_i + r^2\sum_{j,k}^{1,2,3}\alpha_{jk}\zeta_j\zeta_k. \tag{3}$$

Now the expression $\dfrac{D(z_1z_2z_3)}{D(r\zeta_1\, r\zeta_2\, r\zeta_3)}$ has the value unity when $r = 0$. We may therefore revert our series, and write

$$r\zeta_i = z_i - z_i{}^0 + \sum_{jk}^{1,2,3}\beta_{jk}(z_j - z_j{}^0)(z_k - z_k{}^0) + \ldots. \tag{4}$$

We shall take our restricted region so small that (4) shall be uniformly convergent therein, for all values for (z) and (z^0) in the region. Hence two points of the region may be connected by a single geodesic arc lying entirely therein.[111]

Theorem 1. Two points of a restricted region whose coordinates differ by a sufficiently small amount may be connected by a single geodesic arc lying wholly in a sufficiently small restricted region which includes the two points.

We shall from now on, suppose that we have limited ourselves to such a small restricted region that any two points may be so connected by a single geodesic arc.

Definition. A real analytic transformation of a restricted region which leaves the distance element absolutely invariant shall be called a congruent transformation.

[110] Cf. e.g. Jordan, *Cours d'Analyse*, Paris, 1893-6, vol. iii, p. 88.
[111] Cf. Darboux, loc. cit., vol. ii, p. 408.

Definition. Given a geodesic through a point (z^0). The three expressions

$$\left.\frac{dz_i}{ds}\right|_{z_i=z_i^0} = \zeta_i, \quad i = 1, 2, 3$$

shall be called the *direction cosines* of the geodesic at that point. Notice that

$$1 - \sum_{i,j}^{1,2,3} a_{ij}\zeta_i\dot{\zeta}_j = \sum_{i,j}^{1,2,3} a_{ij}\zeta_i\zeta_j \sum_{ij}^{1,2,3} a_{ij}\dot{\zeta}_i\dot{\zeta}_j - \left(\sum_{i,j}^{1,2,3} a_{ij}\zeta_i\dot{\zeta}_j\right)^2$$
$$= \sum_{ij}^{1,2,3} (a_{ii}a_{jj} - a_{ij}^2)(\zeta_i\dot{\zeta}_j - \zeta_j\dot{\zeta}_i)^2.$$

This is a positive definite form, for the coefficients are the minors of a positive definite form. Hence

$$\sum_{i,j}^{1,2,3} a_{ij}\zeta_i\dot{\zeta}_j \leqq 1.$$

This expression shall be defined as the *cosine of the angle* formed by the two geodesics. When it vanishes, the geodesics shall be said to be *mutually perpendicular* or to cut at right angles.

Theorem 2. The angle of two intersecting geodesics is an absolute invariant for all congruent transformations.

This comes at once from the fact that

$$\frac{\sum_{ij}^{1,2,3} a_{ij}dz_i\delta z_j}{ds\delta s}$$

is obviously an absolute invariant for all congruent transformations.

Definition. A set of geodesics through a chosen point whose direction cosines there, are linearly dependent upon those of two of their number, shall be said to form a *pencil.* The surface which they trace shall be called a *geodesic surface*. We shall later show that the choice of the name *geodesic surface* is entirely justified, for each surface of this sort may be generated in ∞^2 ways by means of pencils of geodesics.

Axiom III. **There exists a congruent transformation which carries two sufficiently small arcs of two intersecting geodesics whose lengths are measured from the common point, into two arcs of equal length on any two intersecting geodesics whose angle is equal to the angle of the original two.**[112]

[112]Our Axioms I–III, are, with slight verbal alterations, those used by Woods, loc. cit. His article, though vitiated by a certain haziness of definition, leaves nothing to be desired from the point of view of simplicity. In the present chapter we shall use a different coordinate system from his, in order to avoid too close plagiarism. It is also noteworthy that he uses k where we conformably to our previous practice use $\frac{1}{k}$.

It is clear that a congruent transformation will carry an arc whose variation is zero into another such, hence a geodesic into a geodesic. It will also transform a geodesic surface into a geodesic surface, for it is immediately evident that we might have defined a geodesic surface as generated by those geodesics through a point which are perpendicular to a chosen geodesic through that point.

It is now necessary to choose a particular coordinate system, and we shall make use of one which will turn out to be identical with the polar coordinate system of elementary geometry. Let us choose a fixed point (z^0), and a fixed geodesic through it with direction cosines (ζ^0). Finally, we choose a geodesic surface determined by our given geodesic, and another through (z^0). Let ϕ be the angle which a geodesic through (z^0) makes with the geodesic (ζ^0), while θ is the angle which a geodesic perpendicular to the last chosen geodesic and to (ζ^0) makes with a geodesic perpendicular to the given geodesic surface, i.e. perpendicular to the geodesics of the generating pencil. Let r be the length of the geodesic arc of (ζ) from (z^0) to a chosen point. We may take ϕ, θ, r as coordinates of this point. The square of the distance element will take the form

$$ds^2 = dr^2 + Ed\theta^2 + 2F d\theta\, d\phi + G d\phi^2. \tag{5}$$

We see, in fact, that there will be no term in $dr\, d\phi$ or $dr\, d\theta$. For if we take $\theta =$ const. we have a geodesic surface, and the geodesic lines of space radiating from (z^0) and lying in this surface will be geodesics of the surface. The curves $r =$ const. will be orthogonal to these radiating geodesics.[113] The surfaces $\phi =$ const. are not geodesic surfaces, but the curves $\theta =$ const. and $r =$ const. form an orthogonal system for the same reason as before. The coefficients E, F, G are independent of θ, for, by Axiom III, we may transform congruently from one surface $\theta =$ const. into another such. The coefficient G is independent of ϕ also, for in any surface $\theta =$ const. we may transform congruently from any two geodesics through (z^0) into any other two making the same angle. We may, in fact, write

$$E = G(r)E'(\phi), \quad F = G(r)F'(\phi),$$

for the square of any distance element can be put into the form

$$ds^2 = dr^2 + Gd\phi_1{}^2,$$

where ϕ_1 is a function of ϕ and θ.

Let us at this point rewrite our differential equations (2) in terms of our present coordinates

$$\begin{aligned}
&\frac{d}{ds}\left[\frac{dr}{ds}\right] = \frac{1}{2}\left[\frac{\partial E}{\partial r}\left(\frac{d\theta}{ds}\right)^2 + 2\frac{\partial F}{\partial r}\left(\frac{d\theta}{ds}\right)\left(\frac{d\phi}{ds}\right) + \frac{\partial G}{\partial r}\left(\frac{d\phi}{ds}\right)^2\right],\\
&\frac{d}{ds}\left[E\frac{d\theta}{ds} + F\frac{d\phi}{ds}\right] = 0,\\
&\frac{d}{ds}\left[F\frac{d\theta}{ds} + G\frac{d\phi}{ds}\right] = \frac{1}{2}\left[\frac{\partial E}{\partial \phi}\left(\frac{d\theta}{ds}\right)^2 + 2\frac{\partial F}{\partial \phi}\left(\frac{d\theta}{ds}\right)\left(\frac{d\phi}{ds}\right)\right].
\end{aligned} \tag{6}$$

[113] Bianchi, *Differentialgeometrie*, cit., p. 160.

Consider the geodesic surface $\phi = \frac{\pi}{2}$ which may, indeed, be taken to stand for any geodesic surface. Here we must have

$$E = cG,$$

where c is constant. The differential equations for a geodesic curve on this surface will be[114]

$$\frac{d}{ds}\left[\frac{dr}{ds}\right] = \frac{1}{2}\left[\frac{\partial E}{\partial r}\left(\frac{d\theta}{ds}\right)^2\right],$$
$$\frac{d}{ds}\left[G\frac{d\theta}{ds}\right] = 0.$$

These are exactly equivalent to the combination of (6) and ϕ =const. Lastly, if we remember that two near points of a surface can be connected by a single geodesic arc lying therein.

Theorem 2. The geodesic connecting two near points of a geodesic surface lies wholly in that surface, and is identical with the geodesic of the surface which connects those two points.

Theorem 3. There is a group of ∞^3 congruent transformations which carry a geodesic surface transitively into itself.

Theorem 4. All geodesic surfaces have the same constant Gaussian curvature.

These theorems enable us to solve completely our differential equations (6). The Gaussian curvature of each geodesic surface is an invariant of space which we may call its *measure of curvature*. We shall denote this constant by $\frac{1}{k^2}$, and distinguish with care the two following cases

$$\frac{1}{k^2} \neq 0, \quad \frac{1}{k^2} = 0.$$

The determination of our coefficients E, F, G is now an easy task. The square of the distance element for a geodesic surface θ = const., will be

$$ds^2 = dr^2 + G(r)d\phi^2.$$

Writing that this shall have Gaussian curvature $\frac{1}{k^2}$, we get

$$\frac{-1}{\sqrt{G}}\frac{\partial^2\sqrt{G}}{\partial r^2} = \frac{1}{k^2},$$
$$\sqrt{G} = A\sin\frac{r}{k} + B\cos\frac{r}{k}.$$

The determination of the constants A, B requires a little care. It is clear to begin with that when

$$r = 0, \quad G = 0.$$

---

[114]Bianchi, ibid., p. 153.

Hence $$B = 0.$$

Again $$G = \sum_{i,j}^{1,2,3} a_{ij} \frac{\partial z_i}{\partial \phi} \frac{\partial z_j}{\partial \phi} = r^2 \sum_{ij}^{1,2,3} a_{ij} \frac{\partial \zeta_i}{\partial \phi} \frac{\partial \zeta_j}{\partial \phi} + r^3 R(r\phi),$$

$$\left(\frac{\partial \sqrt{G}}{\partial r}\right)_{r=0} = \sqrt{\sum_{i,j}^{1,2,3} a_{ij} \frac{\partial \zeta_i}{\partial \phi} \frac{\partial \zeta_j}{\partial \phi}}.$$

But, from (1)

$$1 = \sum_{i,j}^{1,2,3} a_{ij} \zeta_i \zeta_j = \sum_{i,j}^{1,2,3} a_{ij} \left(\zeta_i + \frac{\partial \zeta_i}{\partial \phi} d\phi\right)\left(\zeta_j + \frac{\partial \zeta_j}{\partial \phi} d\phi\right),$$

$$\cos d\phi = \sum_{i,j}^{1,2,3} a_{ij} \zeta_i \left(\zeta_j + \frac{\partial \zeta_i}{\partial \phi} d\phi\right),$$

$$\cos \frac{d\phi}{2} = 1 - \frac{1}{2} \sum_{i,j}^{1,2,3} a_{ij} \frac{\partial \zeta_i}{\partial \phi} \frac{\partial \zeta_j}{\partial \phi} d\phi,$$

$$\sin \frac{d\phi}{2} = \frac{d\phi}{2} = \frac{d\phi}{2} \sqrt{\sum_{i,j}^{1,2,3} a_{ij} \frac{\partial \zeta_i}{\partial \phi} \frac{\partial \zeta_j}{\partial \phi}},$$

giving eventually

$$\left(\frac{\partial \sqrt{G}}{\partial r}\right)_{r=0} = 1; \quad A = k.$$

Hence, by the equations preceding (6)

$$ds^2 = dr^2 + k^2 \sin^2 \frac{r}{k} [E' d\theta^2 + 2F' d\theta \, d\phi + d\phi^2].$$

We proceed to calculate F'. The differential equations for a geodesic curve of the surface $\theta =$ const., will be

$$\frac{d}{ds}\left(\frac{dr}{ds}\right) = \frac{1}{2} \frac{\partial \theta}{\partial r} \left(\frac{d\phi}{ds}\right)^2,$$

$$\frac{d}{ds}\left(G \frac{d\phi}{ds}\right) = 0.$$

These must be equivalent to those obtained from (6), when $\theta =$ const., i.e. we must have

$$\frac{d}{ds}\left(F' G \frac{d\phi}{ds}\right) = 0,$$

$$F' = \text{const.},$$

and as F' is not a function of θ it is a constant everywhere. Now when $\phi = 0$, there is no $d\theta$ term in ds^2, so that $E = 0$; but $\dfrac{E}{\sqrt{FG}}$, which is the cosine of the angle which curves $\theta = \text{const.}$ and $\phi = \text{const.}$, make on the surface $r = \text{const.}$, is surely less than unity. Hence

$$F' = 0.$$

Lastly, we must find E'. The surfaces $r = \text{const.}$ have constant Gaussian curvature, for each is capable of ∞^3 congruent transformations into itself. Hence

$$ds^2 = k^2 \sin^2 \frac{r}{k}[E' d\theta^2 + d\phi^2],$$

$$\frac{1}{\sqrt{E'}} \frac{d^2\sqrt{E'}}{d\phi^2} = \text{const.},$$

$$\sqrt{E} = A \sin l\phi + B \cos l\phi.$$

As we saw a moment ago $B = 0$, for E vanishes with ϕ. On the other hand, when

$$\phi = \frac{\pi}{2}, \quad \sqrt{E'} = 1, \quad A \sin \frac{l\pi}{2} = 1.$$

But also
$$A \sin l\pi = 0.$$

Hence l is an odd integer, and

$$A^2 = 1.$$

$$ds^2 = dr^2 + k^2 \sin^2 \frac{r}{k}[\sin^2 \phi \, d\theta^2 + d\phi^2]. \tag{7}$$

This is our ultimate form for the square of the distance element. Let the reader show that under the second case $\dfrac{1}{k^2} = 0$, we have

$$ds^2 = dr^2 + r^2 \left[\sin^2 \phi \, d\theta^2 + d\phi^2\right]. \tag{7'}$$

It is now time to return to coordinates of a more familiar sort. Let us write

$$\begin{aligned} x_0 &= k \cos \frac{r}{k}, \\ x_1 &= k \sin \frac{r}{k} \cos \theta \cos \phi, \\ x_2 &= k \sin \frac{r}{k} \sin \theta \cos \phi, \\ x_3 &= k \sin \frac{r}{k} \sin \phi, \end{aligned} \tag{8}$$

$$(xx) = k^2,$$

$$(dx\, dx) = ds^2.$$

To find the differential equation of a geodesic, we have a problem in relative minima

$$\int_0^s \left(\sqrt{\left(\frac{dx}{ds}\frac{dx}{ds}\right)} + \lambda[(xx) - k^2]\right) ds = 0,$$

$$\frac{d}{ds}\left(\frac{dx_i}{ds}\right) = 2\lambda x_i, \quad i = 0, 1, 2, 3.$$

To determine λ

$$(xx) = k^2, \quad (x\,dx) = -\tfrac{1}{2}ds^2,$$

$$(x\,d^2x) + ds^2 = d(-\tfrac{1}{2}ds^2) = 0.$$

But from our equations

$$(x\,d^2x) + ds^2 = 2\lambda k^2 ds^2,$$

$$2\lambda = -\frac{1}{k^2}.$$

We thus get for the final form for our differential equation

$$\frac{d^2x_i}{ds^2} + \frac{x_i}{k^2} = 0. \tag{9}$$

Let the reader show that in the other case we have

$$\frac{d^2x}{ds^2} = \frac{d^2y}{ds^2} = \frac{d^2z}{ds^2} = 0. \tag{9'}$$

Integrating

$$x_i = y_i \cos\frac{s}{k} + z_i \sin\frac{s}{k},$$

$$k^2 = (xx) = (yy) = (zz),$$

$$(yz) = 0.$$

We have then for the length of the geodesic arc from (y) to (x)

$$k^2 \cos\frac{d}{k} = (xy),$$

or, if we replace our coordinates by homogeneous ones proportional to them

$$\cos\frac{d}{k} = \frac{(xy)}{\sqrt{(xx)}\,\sqrt{(yy)}}. \tag{10}$$

Let the reader show that when $\frac{1}{k^2} = 0$,

$$d = \sqrt{(x - x_0)^2 + (y - y_0)^2 + (z - z_0)^2}.$$

Theorem 5. Axioms I, II, III are compatible with the euclidean hyperbolic and elliptic hypotheses, and with these alone.

Our task is now completed. At bottom, the essential feature of a geometrical system where the elements are points is the expression for distance, for the projective theory is the same for a limited domain in all restricted regions. We have established our distance formulae three several times, each time approaching the subject from a new point of view. In Chapters I–IV we took as fundamental the concepts point, distance, and sum of distances. We reached our analytic formulae by proceeding from elementary geometry to trigonometry, and then introducing a simple coordinate system, such as we do when we first take up the study of elementary analytic geometry. The Chapters VI–XVII were devoted to erecting a superstructure upon the foundation which we had established. In Chapter XVIII we took a fresh start, laid down point line and separation as fundamental, constructed the common projective geometry for all of our systems (except the spherical, which would involve slight modifications), and established the system of projective coordinates. We then introduced certain collineations called *congruent transformations*, and worked around to our previous distance formulae through group-theory. In the present chapter we took as fundamental the concepts point and correspondence of point and coordinate set. The essentials in our development were the distance element, the geodesic curve, and the space constant, or measure of curvature. We reached our familiar formulae by means of surface theory, integration, and the calculus of variations.

Which of the three methods of approach is the best? To this question no definite answer may be given, for that method which is best for one purpose is not, necessarily, best for another. The first method depended upon the simplest and most natural fundamental conceptions, and presupposed a minimum of mathematical knowledge. It also corresponded most closely to the line of historical development. On the other hand it is the longest, even after cutting out a number of theorems, interesting in themselves, but not essential as steps towards the ultimate goal. The second method possessed the advantage of beginning with the assumptions which serve as a basis for the important subject of projective geometry; metrical ideas were grafted upon this stem as a natural development. Moreover, the fundamental importance of the six-parameter collineation group which keeps a conic or quadric invariant was brought into the clearest light. On the other hand, we were obliged to develop a coordinate system, which to some readers might seem a trifle unnatural or forced, and exposed ourselves to being put down among those whom the late Professor Tait has stigmatized as 'That section of mathematicians for whom transversals and anharmonic pencils have a, to us, incomprehensible charm'.[115] third and last method is, beyond a peradventure, the quickest and most direct; and has the advantage of bringing out the full significance of the space constant. It may, however, be urged with some justice, that too high a price has been paid for this directness, by assuming at the outset that space is something whose elements depend in a definite manner on three independent parameters. The modern tendency is to take a more abstract view, to look upon space, in the last analysis, as a set of objects

[115]Tait, *An Elementary Treatise on Quaternions*, third edition, Cambridge, 1890, p. 309.

which can be arranged in multiple series.[116] The battle is more than half over when the coordinate system has been set up.

No, there is no answer to the question which method of approach is the best. The determining choice among the three, will, in the end, be a matter of personal aesthetic preference. And this is well. Let us not forget that, in large measure, we study pure mathematics to satisfy an aesthetic need. We are fortunate when, as in the present case, we are free at the outset to choose our line of approach.

[116]Cf. Russell, loc. cit., p. 372.

INDEX

www.ingramcontent.com/pod-product-compliance
Ingram Content Group UK Ltd.
Pitfield, Milton Keynes, MK11 3LW, UK
UKHW041827200726
13854UKWH00002BA/648